I0605836

Building with Nature

Frei Otto

1925–2015

Edited by Joaquín Medina Warmburg and Anna-Maria Meister
with Mechthild Ebert and Martin Kunz

PRESTEL Munich · London · New York

Project study for 'Schatten in der Wüste' (Shadows in the Desert; 1972)

Concept for the cultural and recreational centre Monarto Hub, Australia (1974)

Airship study for *Airfish 1* (1978)

The Tanzbrunnen tent structure at the German National Garden Show in Cologne (1957)

Four-point sail (c. 1956)

Pointed tent for the German National Garden Show in Cologne (1957)

Adjustable umbrellas for Pink Floyd's concert tour in the USA (1977)

Project study for an exhibition hall in Cologne (1956/57)

Aviary at Hellabrunn Zoo in Munich (1978–1980)

Roofing of the principal sports stadium at Munich's Olympic Park (1968–1972)

Concept for the roofing of an ice rink in Dortmund (1963)

Entrance arch for the German National Garden Show in Cologne (1957), model

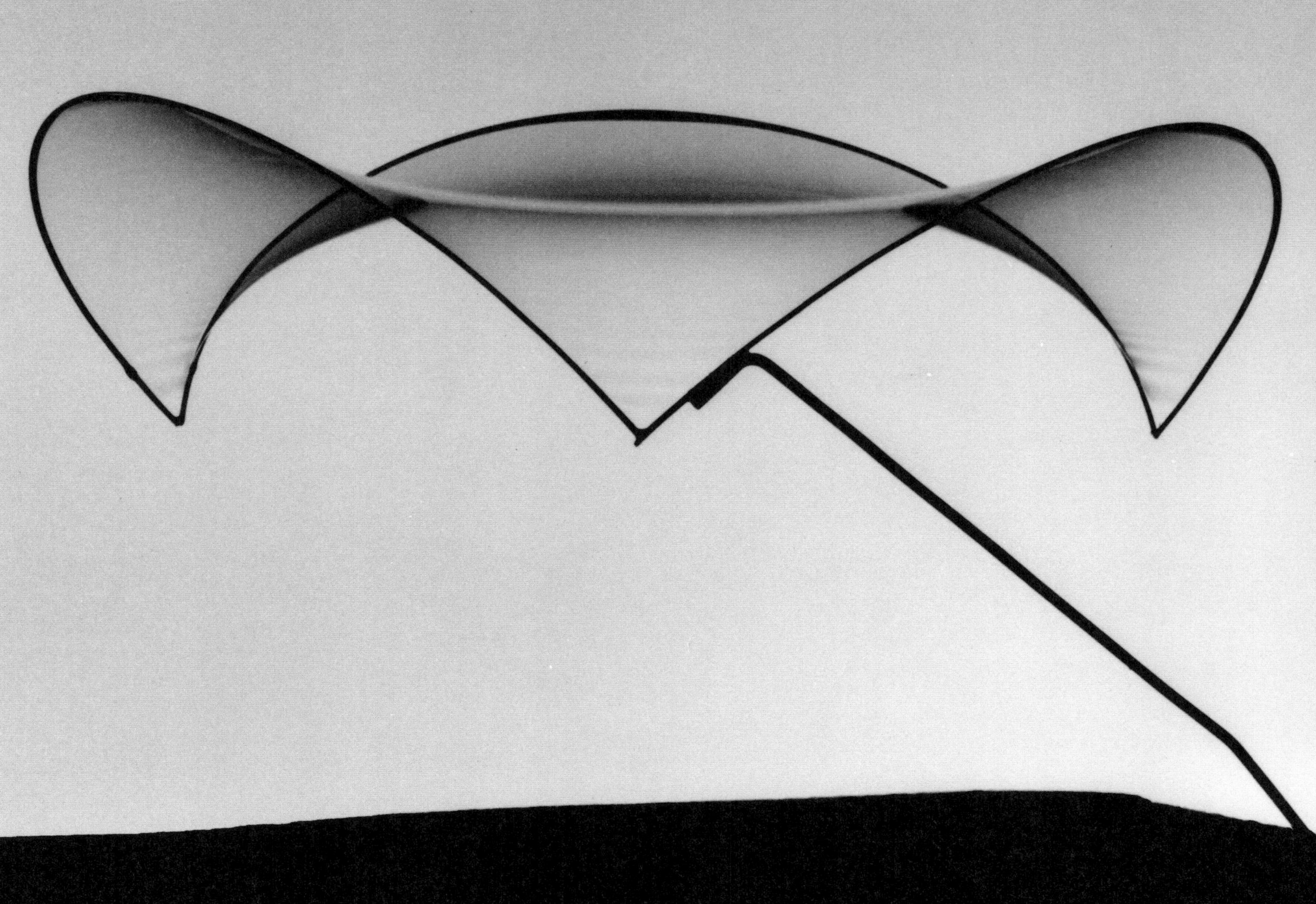

Sand pour test (1984)

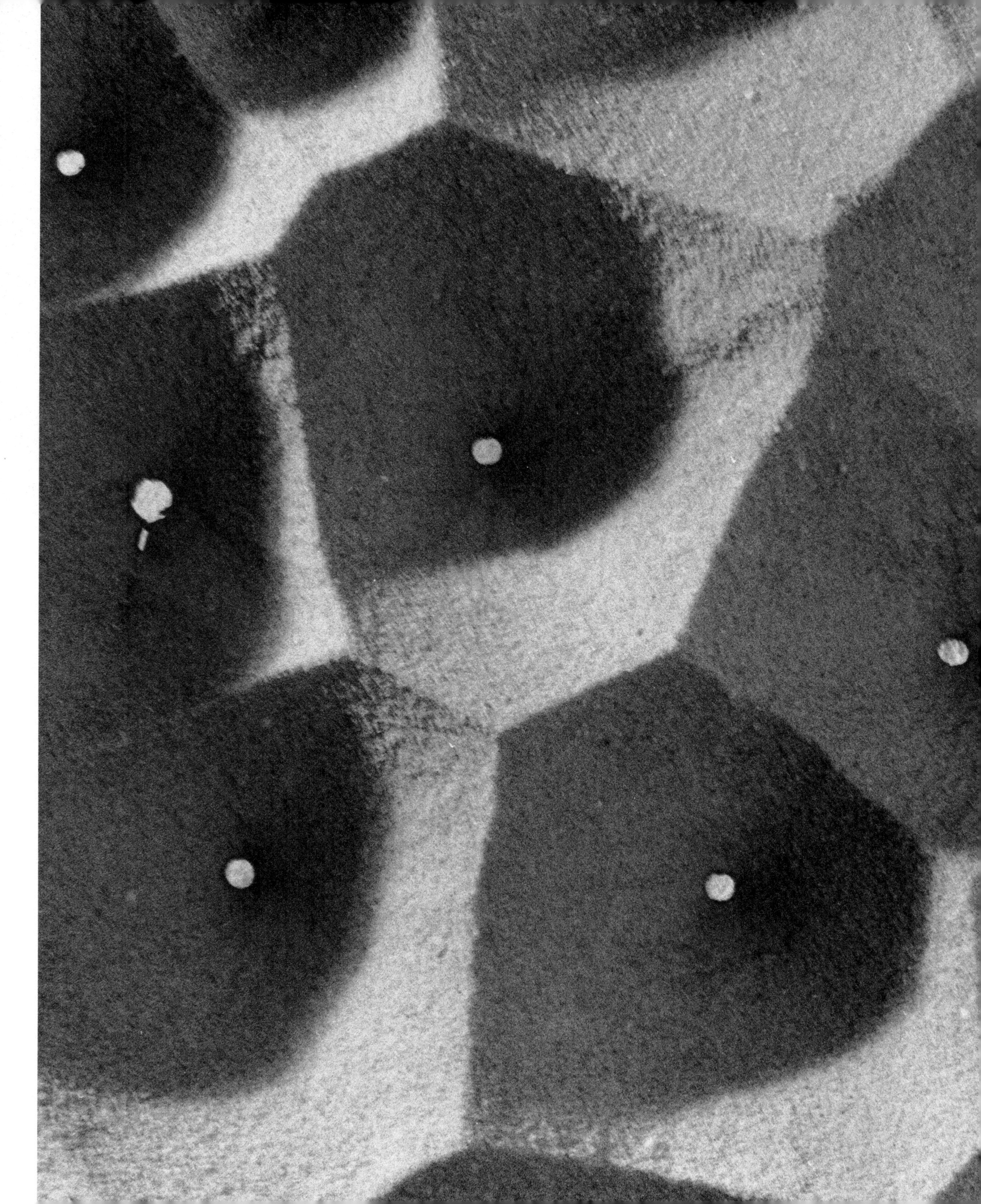

Nature studies, close-up of a seashell (1978)

Nature studies, close-up of a spider's web (1978)

Preface

The year 2025 marks the centenary of the birth, and the tenth anniversary of the death, of the architect, design engineer and researcher Frei Otto (born in Chemnitz-Siegmar in 1925; died in Leonberg near Stuttgart in 2015). Since Otto posthumously received the prestigious Pritzker Architecture Prize ten years ago, his lifework has again become the focus of intense public interest. For the saai | Archiv für Architektur und Ingenieurbau, the Southwest German Archive for Architecture and Civil Engineering, at the Karlsruhe Institute of Technology (KIT), where the extensive archive from Frei Otto's atelier in Warmbronn – containing, among other things, more than four hundred architectural models, plans, sketches, photographs, studio diaries, manuscripts and correspondence – has been preserved and studied since 2010, and is accessible to scholars from around the world, the period following the prize award has been characterized by intense research investigation and publication activity. This culminated in a series of internationally recognized exhibitions and books, in particular the exhibition *Frei Otto: Thinking by Modeling*, curated by the saai under the direction of Georg Vrachliotis, and on view at ZKM | Center for Art and Media Karlsruhe in 2016. The collection of models, which were on public display for the first time in that exhibition on an extensive scale, elicited international interest, and served as a stimulus to subsequent exhibitions as part of the Venice Biennale of Architecture (*Sleeping Beauty: Reinventing Frei Otto's Multihalle*, 2018), at the Yale School of Architecture in New Haven, Connecticut (*Models, Media, and Methods: Frei Otto's Architectural Research*, 2020), and at Jeddah Arts in Saudi Arabia (*Architecture of Tomorrow: Frei Otto's Legacy in Saudi Arabia*, 2020). In addition to the corresponding catalogues and accompanying publications, the saai published two volumes during this same time devoted to Otto's two key works, his main contributions to German post-war architecture: *Frei Otto, Carlfried Mutschler: Multihalle* (2017), edited by Georg Vrachliotis, and Joachim Kleinmanns's *Der deutsche Pavillon der Expo 67 in Montreal* (2020) on the German Pavilion at the 1967 International and Universal Exposition.

International researchers have long shown noticeably greater interest in Frei Otto than have their German-language counterparts, but the current spike in enthusiasm has led to an increasing number of research requests from both Germany and abroad in recent years. Indeed, a decade after his death, it would seem that Frei Otto is more relevant than ever – which may be attributable to the currency and urgency of the issues he addressed. It is probably the ecological exigencies of the present moment, and the new demands on contemporary architecture emerging from them, that have given renewed impetus to Otto's long-standing search for an appropriate relationship between nature and architecture. Frei Otto's outlook, his attempt to create liveable and humane spaces not through elaborate, highly technological solutions, but instead by using minimal resources, was perhaps not always successful, but was pursued tirelessly – not least of all in order to hone his thinking on the questions that mattered to him. The relevance of these topics is also confirmed by the research requests we receive, which – very much like the many historical and theoretical approaches pursued at the saai and at the KIT Department of Architecture – repeatedly take up his concerns. It therefore seems appropriate to devote a book to Frei Otto's understanding of nature – in an attempt to define his ideas with greater precision. As our authors, we gathered together a group of researchers who have recently sought to shed light on the relationship between nature, technology and culture in Otto's oeuvre from a range of perspectives.

Today, definitions of 'nature' are highly varied and to some extent contradictory. The boundary separating technological production and cultivated growth have now become remarkably fluid. The long-dominant aesthetic experience of the sublime forces of nature by a humanity that stands before it in powerlessness has lost its hegemony. Currently, such experiences of nature coexist, for example, with the recognition of a self-aware and – in conjunction with further biotic and abiotic agents – self-shaping nature, which resides in the human spirit and in human artefacts. Such ideas were proposed already in the German-speaking world as early as the late eighteenth, early nineteenth centuries, for example in Goethe's morphology, in Herder's interpretation of the interdependencies between culture and climate, and – most notably – in the organic, process-based *Naturphilosophie* of Schelling, a native of Leonberg. In his writings on art theory, Schelling had already rejected the external imitation of nature, calling instead for the translation and recasting of its inner laws, effects and productivity. And already at that time, reflections on the foundations of nature signalled a fundamental critique of the aberrations of civilizational development in connection with the hope for a reconciliation between nature, technology and culture. Otto reflected explicitly on the proximity between such ideas and his holistic conception of nature, as documented in many of his publications. Among his contributions as a researcher-architect was to have investigated and initiated a debate about the historico-philosophical background of his own understanding of nature, which oscillated between the objective lawfulness of a nature that was amenable to modelling, quantification and calculability, on the one hand, and subjective perceptions of nature, on the other hand. In Otto's work, the relationship between nature, technology and culture was continually reconfigured, analysed, thought through, rejected and reconstructed anew. Leafing through the issues of his legendary *IL* publication (the organ of the Institut für leichte Flächentragwerke, the Institute for Lightweight Structures, which was headed by Otto at the University of Stuttgart), the *Mitteilungen* published in association with Otto's Institute for the Development of Lightweight Construction (Entwicklungsstätte für den Leichtbau, EL) in Berlin and the series *Konzepte des SFB 230* in conjunction with the associated Collaborative Research Centre, the reader can only respond with astonishment to the breadth of the topics addressed. Nor did these publications shy away from observations concerning the changing relationship between nature and architecture, and between technology and culture, at the same time consistently historicizing the approaches employed by the authors.

As early as the 1950s, Otto initiated a path towards building with nature, thereby developing approaches and concepts that, to some extent, still shape environmentally conscious construction today. He supplied vital impulses for the holistic thinking of the 1960s and 1970s in the areas of architecture, structural engineering and urban planning – not least of all through the influence exercised by his students, with their international backgrounds. The full implications of his trailblazing contributions in the areas of bionics, ecological building and self-building or participatory architecture – themes that have once again become highly charged today – can only by truly appreciated when seen in the historical context of post-war society and post-war architectural modernism. From a historical perspective, the degree to which nature and society were conceived at that time as shapeable realities becomes clear, a realization that serves as a stimulus to an investigation of natural-historical relationships and positions, as well as reflections on Otto's understanding of nature as a historically conditioned socio-cultural construct.

With this present publication, we seek to do justice to the pluralism of Otto's conceptualizations and visualizations of nature, and in a way that is reflected in the heterogeneity and, to some extent, the contradictory character of the assembled contributions: with approaches ranging from the empiricist history of technology all the way to critical discourse analysis, we seek to trigger a deeper discussion rather than providing a unified interpretation. Together with the invited authors, we strive to illuminate the central concepts developed by Frei Otto, including lightweight construction, natural structures, form-finding and adaptability, always from at least two different perspectives and influenced by diverse intellectual premises. The topics, grouped in three chapters on Nature, Technics and Society are addressed in nine essays, which are introduced by individual presentations also of nine selected works by Frei Otto. It is our hope that this will contribute to opening up a historiographic and theoretical discussion on Frei Otto and his achievements. These expanded interpretive approaches are designed to stimulate an intensification of international research on Otto's visions, principles and methods of building with nature.

Finally, we hope that this monograph will also be of interest to readers not yet familiar with Frei Otto's achievements, as well as to interested laypeople, and that it will serve to make his work and his conceptual universe accessible to the broadest possible public. For the questions he investigated and posed with such intellectual rigor to himself, his students, his colleagues and to society at large are not only consistently fascinating but urgent. We are indebted to all of our contributors and collaborators for taking part in this joint effort.

Joaquín Medina Warmburg, Anna-Maria Meister,
Mechthild Ebert, Martin Kunz

Frei Otto with the model for the roofing of the Olympic Park's swimming hall, Munich (c. 1970)

On the Unity of the World: Frei Otto and the Biotechnical Traditions of Modernism

Joaquín Medina Warmburg

'So for me there is no such thing as "non-nature". For me, the unnatural, anti-natural and artificial also make up a part of nature just as shadows are a form of light.' – Frei Otto, 'Meine drei Bilder von Natur'[1]

In interviews and articles towards the end of his career, Frei Otto emphasized the decisive influence that the heritage of Modernism had exerted over his development. He highlighted, for example, the importance of his early encounters in the United States with a number of representatives of modern architecture, such as Ludwig Mies van der Rohe, Erich Mendelsohn and Richard Neutra, who had emigrated from Europe. It was none other than another emigrant, the Bauhaus founder Walter Gropius, who had arranged these meetings in 1950/51 when Frei Otto was studying on a scholarship at the University of Virginia in Charlottesville. Indeed, even before this, Frei Otto had had contacts in the circle of the Deutscher Werkbund, to which his father belonged, the sculptor and stonecutter Paul Otto. The younger Otto's architectural studies and doctoral work at the Technische Hochschule (technical college) in Berlin-Charlottenburg, where such diverse Berlin architects as Hans Poelzig, Hermann Jansen, Bruno Taut and Heinrich Tessenow had taught before the war, also brought him into close contact with Modernism and its luminaries. In a 2008 interview, he noted that he had developed a nuanced view of Modernism also thanks to Poelzig's son Peter, for whom Frei Otto served as an assistant at the Berlin school in 1961. He named, for instance, the brothers Hans and Wassili Luckhardt, Poelzig and Mendelsohn as precursors of a first 'green' Modernism, which has long been forgotten owing to the incomparably greater influence of Le Corbusier.[2] What he actually meant with this 'green' alternative to 'classical' Modernism shall serve as the subject of this introduction to Frei Otto's understanding of nature – including his concepts and images of nature – which can be thought of as a further development of Modernism's central biotechnical and biocentric traditions.

Analogies of an Organic Technology

Significantly, Frei Otto would serve on the first board of the association for Friends of the Weissenhofsiedlung, the housing estate built in Stuttgart under the direction of Mies van der Rohe fifty years before for the Deutscher Werkbund exhibition *Die Wohnung* (The Dwelling; 1927). In a 1978 publication, Otto joined his comrades-in-arms Bodo Rasch and Berthold Burkhardt in pointing to the sorry state of the houses and calling that they be restored to their original condition with a professionalism reflecting their monumental significance.[3] A new international building exhibition was to be held in Stuttgart to consider, among other things, the following questions: 'Does the primal house still exist, the natural dwelling? Is there such a thing as a self-growing dwelling made of plants?

What does the energy-independent, self-sufficient, crisis-proof house look like? Where have the true kitchen gardens gone, the vegetables, the herbs, the bees and flowers, the pets and songbirds?'[4]

These questions, by no means meant to be merely rhetorical, may seem surprising in relation to the Weissenhofsiedlung and its architecture designed for practicality and rationality, especially when one considers that the traditionalist Stuttgart School had criticized the estate's disregard for respecting the surrounding landscape and regional building traditions – as epitomized in the *Heimatschutz* movement. Stuttgart's professor of urban planning Heinz Wetzel noted the architecture's sharp contrast with the 'soft and supple lines of the Stuttgart landscape' and felt that in its 'hotchpotch collection of austere cubes' everything was improvised, 'nothing is connected to the climate or the soil, everything seems still borrowed, haphazard and alien.'[5] The polarity between an organic relationship with the landscape and the technological forms of a mechanical world set down by Wetzel and other Stuttgart critics stood in opposition to debates held in Deutscher Werkbund circles about a new, enlarged concept of nature. This is apparent from issues of the journal *Die Form*, the Werkbund's official organ, contemporaneous to the creation of the Weissenhofsiedlung. Its publication on the houses of the Stuttgart estate in the August 1927 issue was thus preceded by an editorial by Walter Riezler titled 'Einheit der Welt' (Unity of the World).[6] It was cast in the form of a Platonic dialogue, a conversation between the editor and a fictitious reader. In it, the editor tries to convince his sceptical interlocuter of the naturalness of forms in art and technology, not in the sense of a merely mimetic translation of natural shapes into human artefacts but as formal analogies resulting from the effects of natural forces and principles: for example, common laws of growth or material economy. A selection of juxtaposed images supported the theory of analogy by showing corresponding formal similarities between plants, machines, architectural forms and works of art. Most of the illustrations, with commentary by Wilhelm Lotz, had been taken by the photographer Albert Renger-Patzsch, one of the pioneers of the New Objectivity (*Neue Sachlichkeit*). Two years later, his work would be used with similar intentions to illustrate Rudolf Schwarz's book *Wegweisung der Technik* (Technology's Directive; 1929).[7] Like Riezler, Schwarz also maintained that a new phase of 'high technology' had been reached in which technology, nature and art were coming together, whereby the old enmity between technology and nature (which was still stoked by the folkloric *Heimatschutz* movement) now seemed obsolete.[8] Riezler's arguments culminated in 1927 in his exegesis 'Technik als kulturelles Problem' (Technology as a Cultural Problem) and its thesis 'that "technology" meant a new phase of natural development, not some rupture between man and nature, that out of this technology a whole new world of forms, the "rigid form" will arise, which has its analogies in nature but whose full development is still reserved for the future.'[9] As a natural being, humankind was no longer to be positioned outside the 'circle of nature', which explains the commonalities between creations of nature and those of humanity.

In Riezler's dialogue, it becomes clear that the debate is by no means new. Friedrich Schiller's aesthetics and Johann Wolfgang von Goethe's morphology are unsurprisingly incorporated as arguments. A yearning for the unity of the world was obviously rooted in the speculative traditions of Romantic idealism and in various vitalist philosophies of the nineteenth century, but above all in the scientific contributions of the century to biology and the ongoing controversy over morphogenesis. Riezler did not hesitate, for example, to criticize the positions of Ernst Haeckel – not his *Generelle Morphologie der Organismen* (General Morphology of Organisms; 1866) in which he coined the term 'Ökologie' (ecology), but rather his series of illustrative plates titled, *Kunstformen der Natur* (*Art Forms in Nature*; 1899–1904), which Riezler disqualified as a merely superficial comparison of forms in nature and art. Riezler claimed that the mimetic adoption of microorganisms as formal patterns for ornaments, for example, had proved to be disastrous.

WERKBUND-AUSSTELLUNG
DIE WOHNUNG

Exhibition *Die Wohnung* (The Dwelling) on the Weissenhof, Stuttgart, in the Werkbund magazine, *Die Form* (August 1927)

Walter Riezler, 'Einheit der Welt' (Unity of the World), a double page showing analogies between technology, art and nature, in *Die Form* (August 1927), photographs by Albert Renger-Patzsch

Image series from the book *Wegweisung der Technik* (Technology's Directive; 1929) by Rudolf Schwarz and Albert Renger-Patzsch

He did not discuss the unified worldview of Haeckel's naturalistic monism with any more detail. Thanks to his popular publications, Haeckel's conviction that the laws of nature represent the world's fundamental principle and constitute its unity was well known. In his attack, Riezler took the position of Raoul Heinrich Francé's no less popular book *Die Pflanze als Erfinder* (*Plants as Innovator*; 1920) which discussed the neologism 'Biotechnik' (biotechnic) as the technique of the organic, using the example of the wealth of inventiveness in plants and their potential value for humankind. Moreover, Riezler posited that contemporary technology was nothing less than a new phase in the evolution of nature. He thereby positioned himself in the proximity of 'biocentrism', in which both traditionalists like Wetzel and avant-gardists like Mies van der Rohe were interested.[10] The latter owned several works by Francé, as Fritz Neumeyer already noted years ago in his analyses of Mies van der Rohe's writings.[11] Detlef Mertins has taken up this line of investigation in his monumental monograph on Mies and embedded the years-long interest in this theme more broadly within the context of contemporary debates about *Lebensphilosophie* (philosophy of life) and biocentrism.[12] As indicated by Riezler, its genealogy can be traced well back into the nineteenth century – the century of biology.[13] From today's point of view, it is rather astonishing that Louis Sullivan's motto 'form follows function', which he adopted under the influence of German-language *Lebensphilosophie,* as well as from the works of biologists like Herbert Spencer, was long held to be an all too reductionist slogan of Modernism, and it was accordingly criticized – ignoring, to be sure, its original derivation as a law of nature and as an analogy.[14]

In relation to the Weissenhofsiedlung, there are other interpretations regarding the analogies between nature and architecture, some of whose lines of tradition extend still farther back, as shown by the example of Le Corbusier. In his compilation of articles from the journal *L'Esprit Nouveau*, which appeared in book form in Paris in 1922 as *Vers une Architecture* (*Toward an Architecture*) and was published four years later in a German translation as *Kommende Baukunst* (1926), Le Corbusier repeatedly referred to natural laws as the foundation of the new architecture, spoke of leaving behind preconceived forms in favour of form as the result of a winnowing process and claimed that the functional 'shape of nature's creatures' had been taken over by the modern technology of aeroplanes and race cars. He even postulated an analogy between nature and morality: 'A sovereign determinism clarifies natural creation for our eyes and gives us the certainty of something balanced and reasonably made, of something infinitely modulated, evolving, varied, and unitary. The primordial physical laws are simple and few. The laws of morality are simple and few.'[15]

Yet despite his statements to the contrary, Le Corbusier found a geometric concept for his Stuttgart houses, as an example, for which he was accused of preconceived abstract formalism. To distinguish himself from Le Corbusier, Hugo Häring wrote in *Die Form* of two opposing paths. In his own case, the path to form led from a prior exploration of the human being to an 'organ-like' architecture, which was akin to finding form with nature and, as a result, bore definite natural, biomorphic features.[16] At that time, Le Corbusier still rejected such biomorphic features, which would be of central importance for him a few years later.[17] Thus, he explicitly rejected the long tradition that postulated the origin of the column as a mimetic derivation from a tree trunk – with the straightforward argument that trees with straight trunks were unknown in Greece.[18] He did not consider the possibility of historical change to the landscape and the environment as a result of human activities, even though an environmental-historical approach had long been a factor in human geography and the related settlement history.

Raoul Heinrich Francé, *Die Pflanze als Erfinder* (*Plants as Innovator;* 1920), book cover

A spider's web and hammock as examples of the principle of a suspension system, from the book *Wie Bauen?* (How to Build?; 1927), published by Heinz and Bodo Rasch in connection with the Weissenhofsiedlung housing estate

Linking the concept of 'environment' with the context of 1920s Modernism may at first seem anachronistic. Yet the environment was in fact already a consideration in architectural discourse at the time, as a fresh look at Stuttgart's Weissenhofsiedlung illustrates. As part of the opening event, the Breslau-based architect Adolf Rading, himself a contributor to the exhibition with a house opened to the landscape and sun, spoke on the basic principles of the Neues Bauen (New Building). In his speech, he explained that the new houses attested to an act of overcoming fear of the uncontrolled 'environment' – 'The environment penetrates the houses completely and, ideally, absorbs them into itself.'[19] This is a remarkable statement to the extent that fear becomes an acceptable explanation for the rise of modern architecture: fear of diseases like tuberculosis, for example, or as an escapist withdrawal into abstraction. Rading's interpretation, however, makes the vitalism or even hedonism associated with the *Lebensreform* (life-reform) movements seem a credible driving force. As early as 1923, the Stuttgart native Richard Döcker, a central figure in the Weissenhofsiedlung, had spoken of the interrelationships between house, humans, sun and landscape, as well as of the housing estate as an organic unity needing to fulfil various demands of the 'environment'.[20] In the mid-1920s, even Walter Gropius began to speak of the new international architecture's approach as a 'design of life processes'.[21] Adolf Behne went further and spoke of the 'objective inventory of elementary life values' by way of which modern architecture enters into a more intimate bond with the 'given soil' than do the representatives of *Heimatschutz*.[22] That the concept of the environment came into increasing use is equally remarkable, for it had only been coined – or reinterpreted – in the term's modern sense a few years before by biologist Jakob Johann von Uexküll.[23] The new interpretation was soon taken up in Berlin art circles and was also a debated issue immediately after the First World War in connection, for example, to the founding of the Bauhaus and in the Arbeitsrat für Kunst (workers' council for art). Thus, in his book *Die Wiederkehr der Kunst* (The Return of Art; 1919), Behne expressly referred to Uexküll, whose theories served as arguments both for moving beyond technological, positivist determinism and for an integral design approach in the modern arts.[24] Crucial to this was Uexküll's neo-Kantian distinction between multiple environments depending on the perceptive and transformational abilities of various species with their respective 'instruments of perception and tools'. The human environment was thus one of many, something the anthropocentric worldview tended to relativize. Even so, this reinterpretation implied that the human environment was characterized by an extraordinary push for expansion, since the use of technological means (*Werkzeuge* or 'tools') enabled it to penetrate environments that would have otherwise remained unknown as experiential worlds to those instruments of perception (*Merkzeuge*).

This conceptual expansion of the environment also extended to its scale, from the microscopically small to the immeasurably vast. In 1929, in a lecture also delivered on the occasion of a Deutscher Werkbund exhibition, this time in Breslau and under the title *Wohnung und Werkraum* (Dwelling and Workplace), the physicist Friedrich Dessauer spoke of the new experience of seeing the earth's surface from an aeroplane. To his thinking, the admittedly increasing artificiality visible from the bird's eye perspective should not give rise to any feelings of fear or helplessness in the face of technology. To be sure, he felt that it was appropriate to adapt the artefacts of humanity to nature, especially human nature. Dessauer also called for abandoning the dichotomy of nature and technology and instead proposed a common 'culture' in its fundamental sense: a cautious cultivation of the natural by technological means.[25]

In view of such demands, the dividing lines in Germany between the innovative and conservative forces in architecture and urban planning of the 1920s and 1930s become somewhat fluid. This was especially true in connection

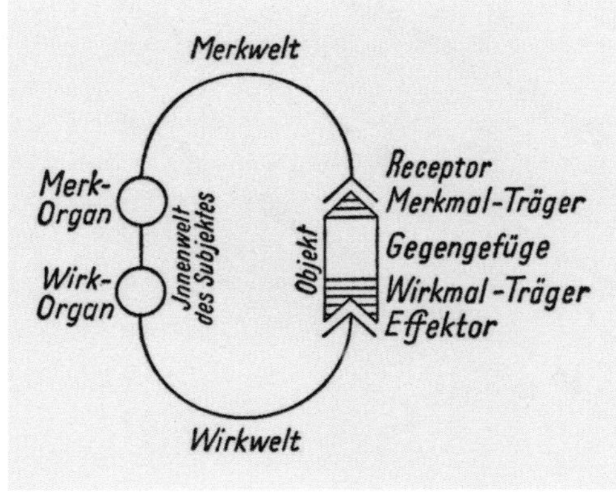

Jakob Johann von Uexküll's functional circle showing the world of perception and action, the 'Merk- und Wirkungswelt' in *Umwelt und Innenwelt der Tiere* (Environment and Inner World of Animals; 1921)

with the various social *Lebensreform* reform movements, such as in connection with the urban building and settlement planning approaches of the garden city movement or the *Heimatschutz* movement. As a rediscovery of the homeland (*Heimat*, as opposed to *Vaterland*: i.e., the fatherland) along with a simultaneous return to nature, Bruno Taut explained his tentlike Volkshaus (people's house) design in *Die Auflösung der Städte* (The Dissolution of Cities; 1920). On the page following his biomorphic design 'Die Große Blume' (The Large Flower), he wrote that technology was now altogether different from what it had been back in the 'factory smokestack era'.[26] And already in his first pages, Taut introduced his idea of houses capable of growth and change that would populate the new urban-country continuum following the demise of cities of stone.

Elke Sohn and David Haney have traced multiple sources and in part contradictory lines of tradition for the 'topoi of the city close to nature' from these years. Many were also related to Francé's biotechnic or Haeckel's monism.[27] The garden architect Leberecht Migge played a special role in this. Despite their primary orientation towards financial returns, his organic settlement gardens designed for self-sufficiency in particular already presented 'proto-ecological' approaches: for example, the operation of urban gardens and systems of green spaces designed in productive cycles. Such approaches were particularly desirable in times of crisis, specifically in the post-war period and during the inflation of the early 1920s or as a result of the world economic crisis after 1929. The latter led to a rediscovery of urban agriculture and its natural principles. Migge's book *Die wachsende Siedlung nach biologischen Gesetzen* (The Growing Settlement According to Biological Laws; 1932) can be seen as both a guidebook and a manifesto. It outlined the historical background into which Martin Wagner's book from the same year, *Das wachsende Haus. Ein Beitrag zur Lösung der städtischen*

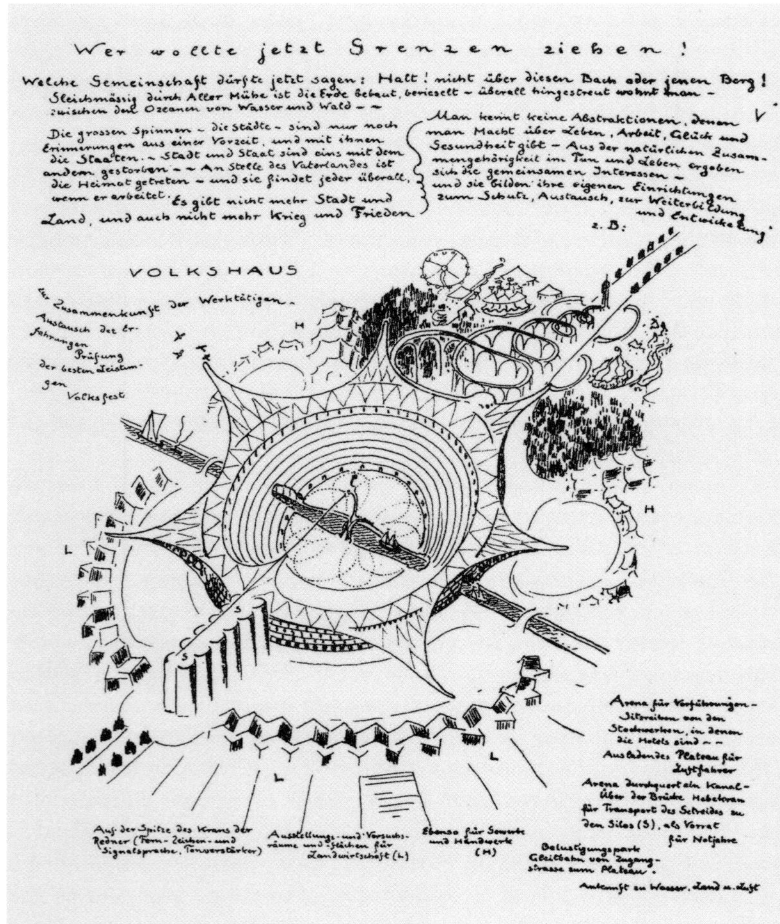

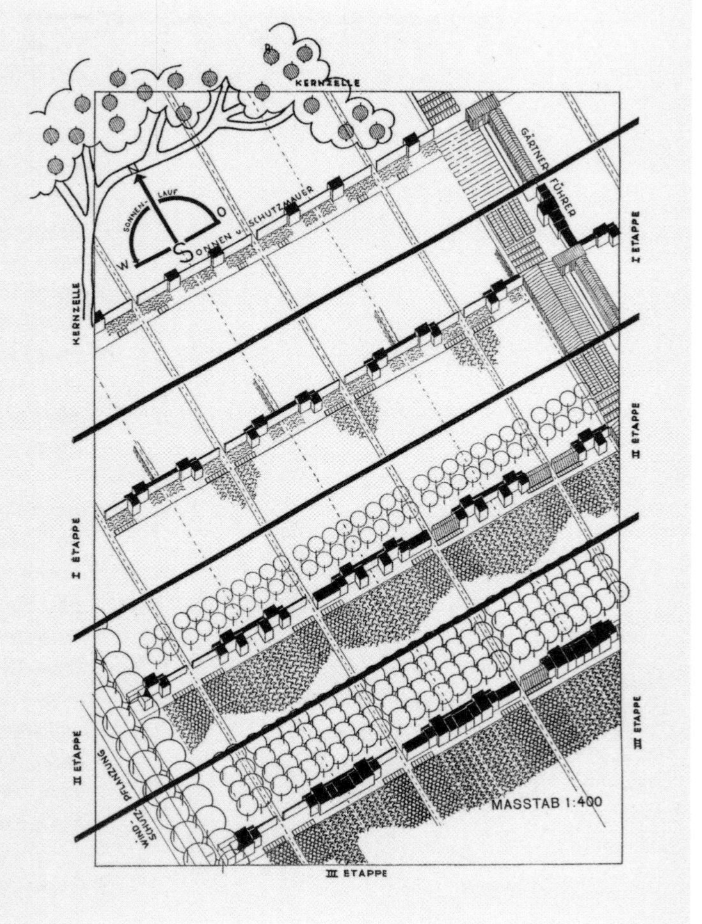

Design for a Volkshaus (people's house) by Bruno Taut, in *Die Auflösung der Städte* (The Dissolution of Cities; 1920)

'Das an der Schutzmauer wachsende Haus in der wachsenden Siedlung' (The house growing on the protective wall in the growing settlement) by Leberecht Migge, in *Die wachsende Siedlung nach biologischen Gesetzen* (The Growing Settlement According to Biological Laws; 1932)

Wohnungsfrage (*The Growing House: A Contribution to Resolving the Urban Housing Question*; 1932), may be placed. Wagner described potential future inhabitants as follows: 'Sick and tired of the big city, uprooted and disappointed, they seek a new and more natural lifestyle for themselves. The holy spirit of Mother Earth and Nature has taken hold of them. Not only recently, but for decades now!'[28]

With his concept of the growing house, Wagner devised an alternative to the subsidized housing of the Weimar Republic and the modern housing developments of the Golden Twenties. In view of the profound economic and social crisis after 1929, he saw industrially prefabricated, expandable dwellings as a possible solution, which people could assemble themselves and that he situated in ribbon developments close to nature. A group of well-respected colleagues like Hugo Häring, Otto Bartning, Egon Eiermann, Ludwig Hilberseimer, Walter Gropius, Erich Mendelsohn, Hans Poelzig and Hans Scharoun participated together in the working group with this goal established by Wagner and produced preliminary prototypes that were shown in 1932 at the Berlin exhibition *Sonne, Luft und Haus für Alle* (Sun, Air and Housing for All).[29] Growth was primarily to be understood in a figurative sense as expandability, unlike Arthur Wiechula's earlier concept of 'growing houses made from living trees.'[30] To be sure, a few of the houses had a provision for added greenhouses so that growth beyond the expansion or shrinking of the family was interpreted literally as a biological process of production.

The growing house was rediscovered by Frei Otto more than two decades later. From it, he developed a recurring motif in his own architecture and expanded it into the general principle of 'adaptable building'.[31] Here too organic growth, bioclimate equipment, industrial prefabrication and social self-help combined to foster a lifestyle close to nature yet urban. After the Second World War, however, conditions had fundamentally changed so that it was impossible to adopt Wagner's concept without adapting its original formal ideas. The personal implications, as well as historical consequences, of this process can be deduced from Otto's critical review of his years-long engagement with 'natural constructions', which he traced back to his time as a young man just returned from the war: one of the 'soldiers deceived by an ideology', who as architecture students around 1950 no longer believed in the 'disciplining of specialties' and who developed visions of the future appearance of their destroyed homeland of their own volition.[32] But even beyond this very personal perspective it is apparent that in planning the rebuilding of German cities there was often a return to their natural substructure. In Berlin, it was Hans Scharoun who saw this as an opportunity to return to nature, after the 'mechanical tilling' caused by the bombing war.[33] It was necessary to restore city dwellers' relationship with a previously estranged nature: a new relationship with 'Mother Earth', with the climate, the seasons, with day and night and all this upon the geo-physical foundation provided by the primeval glacial valley of the Spree.[34] In planning the rebuilding of Cologne, Rudolf Schwarz considered the city's natural setting, the lowlands of the Lower Rhine. In line with his notion of an organic cityscape as postulated in his book *Von der Bebauung der Erde* (On the Development of the Earth; 1949), he assumed a fluid transition from geological to constructed tectonics.[35] Martin Wagner, whom Otto admired and who was by now teaching in the United States, also spoke at the time of the 'geophysics of living space' as being the natural prerequisite in the novel planning of organic cityscapes.[36]

In 1956, Frei Otto criticized the process of rebuilding in the journal *Baukunst und Werkform*, arguing for the construction of single-storey, single-family houses, which he held to be the form for settlement in the future. He hoped that they would produce a residential landscape more culturally valuable than reconstruction had unfortunately done up to that point. To his thinking, such rebuilding had produced a 'destruction of the European cultural landscape with state-owned barracks-like apartment blocks'. He held that growing, adaptable houses were the solution: 'The dwelling of tomorrow will not be static and

Martin Wagner, *Das wachsende Haus. Ein Beitrag zur Lösung der städtischen Wohnungsfrage* (*The Growing House: A Contribution to Resolving the Urban Housing Question*; 1932), book cover inflexible but rather adaptable. It grows and dies with its inhabitants and never goes out of date. It is therefore more tent than castle.'[37]

It is perhaps fitting that also in 1956 the American cultural theorist and philosopher of technology Lewis Mumford – a contributor to *Die Form* in the 1920s – called for work on a 'natural history of urbanization', about which until then, even in the realm of urban ecology, only the first rudimentary steps had been taken.[38] A few years before, with his book *Technics and Civilization* (1934), Mumford had undertaken to describe the interplay between technology, society and nature in a comprehensive historical outline. In doing so, he adopted the periodization of history proposed by the biologist and urban planner Patrick Geddes in *Cities in Evolution* (1915) and, like him, spoke of a 'neotechnic' in which the mechanical and organic had converged into a more harmonious environment.[39] He therefore heralded a new, integrative organic ideology of ecological relationships that could already be seen in the field of modern physics, as well as in modern architecture and urban planning.[40]

Historicizations of Nature, Environment and Architecture

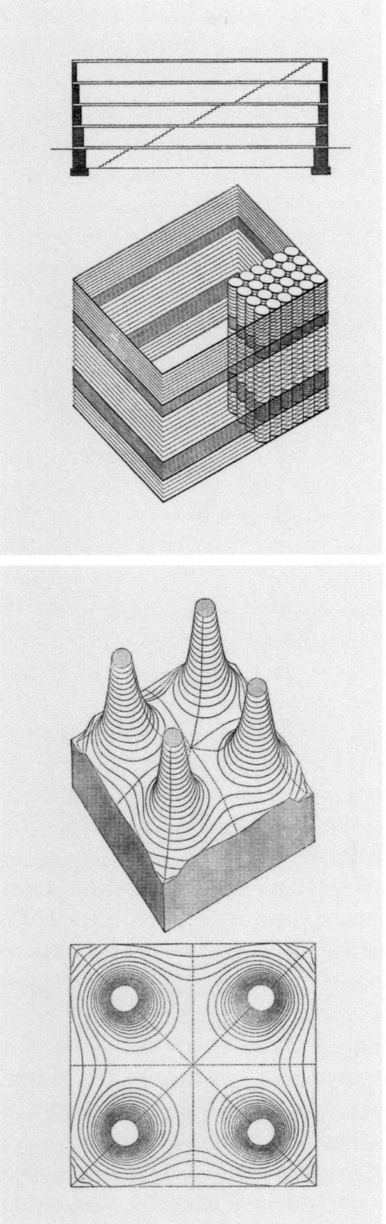

Analogies between the tectonic structures of architecture and geology according to Rudolf Schwarz in *Von der Bebauung der Erde* (On the Development of the Earth; 1949)

In his multifaceted work, Frei Otto took into consideration relationships that extend indeed from the microscopically small to the cosmically large. In doing so, like Uexküll, he opened up new environments for architecture – or else he envisioned an expanded human environment of technological artefacts from an architect's perspective. Nevertheless, this expansion of the field of architecture also came about owing to the temporal context, which was sought in the present and future along with the past. Remarkably, this historicization encompassed the continuum of natural and cultural history. Thus, human existence and human artefacts were embedded in the larger contexts of the developmental stages of animate and inanimate nature. For example, in a single synoptic drawing under the rubric 'Vom Pneu zur Technik' (From the Pneu to Technics) in his book *Natürliche Konstruktionen* (Natural Structures; 1982), Otto summarized the developmental stages from the tiniest structural element of the primal cell to human art and technology. A few pages later, moreover, he placed these on a level with the technology of animals – together in a series with additional 'elements of the whole', namely of animate, inanimate and dead nature.[41] The publication's lengthy subtitle, *Formen und Konstruktionen in Natur und Technik und Prozesse ihrer Entstehung* (Forms and Structures in Nature and Technology and Processes in Their Development), is also noteworthy. For origin and developmental process are basic themes in the historical consciousness relevant to both dating in natural history and the modern descriptions of the change in architecture. For example, the concepts of an architectural structure's expandability and adaptability that run as constants through Otto's entire life's work may be seen as analogous to the biological temporality of the life processes it shelters. Even now one speaks of the individual biography of a residential or urban organism in analogy to biological temporalities in the ontogenetic sense: speaking, for example, of its growth. And phylogenesis is also occasionally used to illustrate, for example, the changes in structural types over time as analogous to the evolutionary process of a species. The latter, logically enough, is often supplemented by the distinction between structural genotypes and phenotypes.[42] As early as the late 1970s, Philip Steadman had already criticized the overuse of the biological analogy as a way to explain the causal and necessary appearance or adaptation of cultural artefacts in the sense of historical determinism as a 'biological fallacy'.[43] In doing so, he echoed the criticism Peter Collins had previously levelled at the evolutionary biological analogy as one of the functionalist architectural ideals of Modernism.[44]

Within the framework of the DFG – German Research Foundation's interdisciplinary institution Collaborative Research Centre, SFB 230 'Natürliche Konstruktionen'/CRC 230 'Natural Structures' (Universities of Stuttgart and Tübingen,

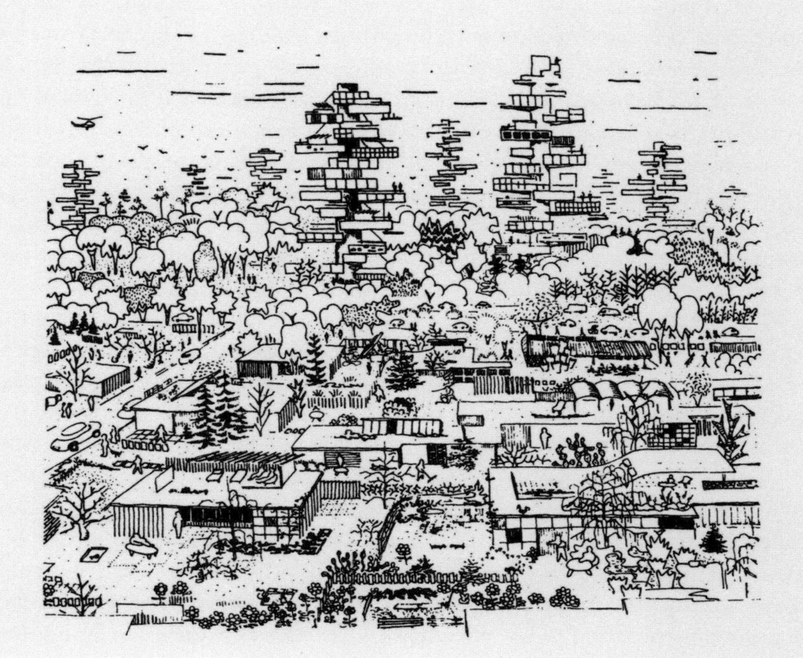

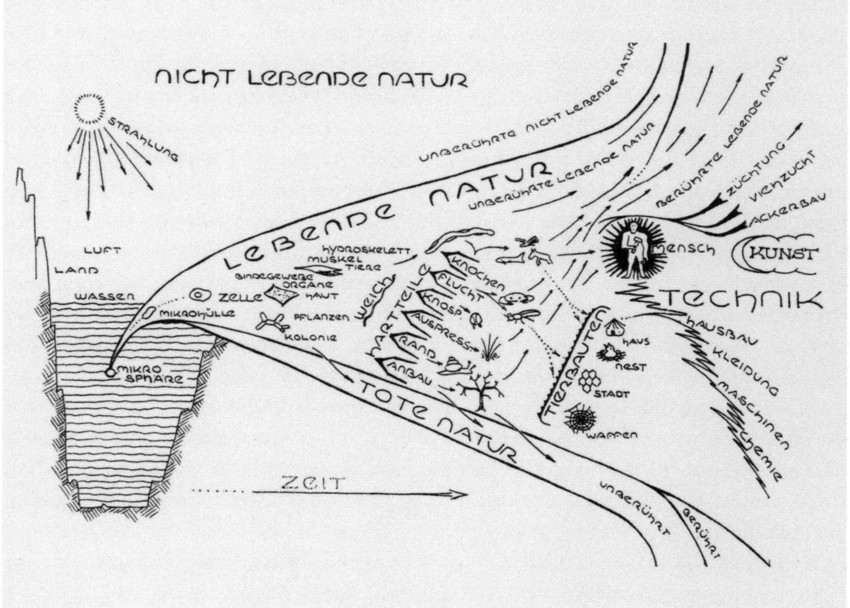

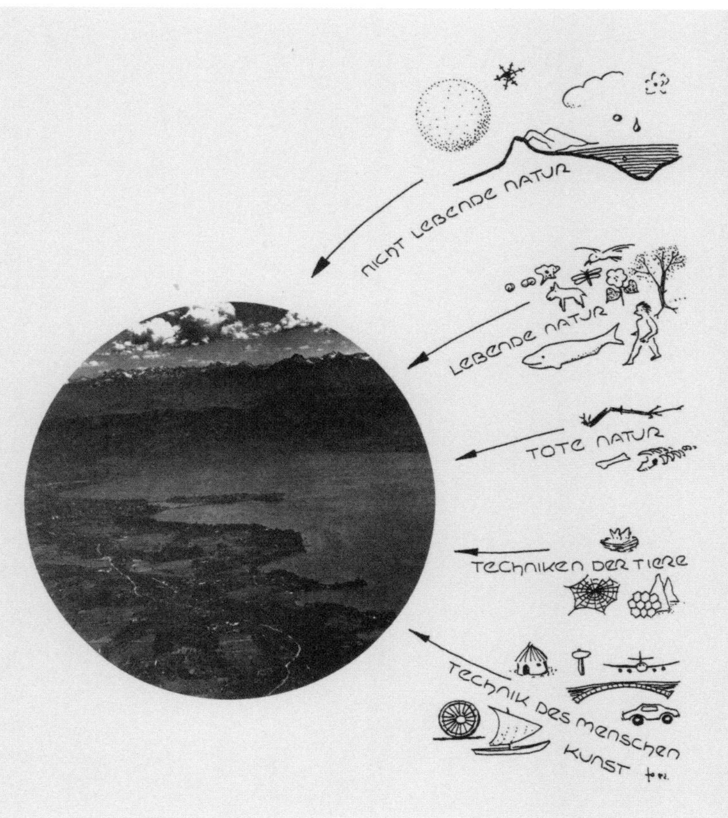

1984–1995), which had been largely initiated and shaped by Otto, a number of publications were produced in which the temporal relationships between architecture and biology were highlighted. At the very beginning, in October 1984, a colloquium was held in Frei Otto's Stuttgart Institute for Lightweight Structures (Institut für leichte Flächentragwerke, IL) devoted to interdisciplinary exchange on the 'understanding of nature'.[45] A multifaceted historicization of the concept of nature and of the changing understanding of nature was expressed early on. The history of construction, especially 'natural construction', was handled as a separate area of research from the beginning of CRC 230, for which important preliminary work had already been accomplished in the 1960s from the biological side, as Otto asserted in a critical review: 'Perhaps the most important scientific finding from our work was a new view of the structures of animate nature. With it came a new view of biological developmental history as well. Animal and human behaviourists

Frei Otto's 'Stadt von morgen' (City of Tomorrow) with adaptable single-family houses and residential towers in green spaces, in *Anpassungsfähig bauen/ Adaptable Building, Mitteilungen der Entwicklungsstätte für den Leichtbau (EL)*, no. 6 (1959)

'Vom Pneu zur Technik' (From the Pneu to Technics), illustration from Frei Otto, *Natürliche Konstruktionen. Formen und Konstruktionen in Natur und Technik und Prozesse ihrer Entstehung* (Natural Structures: Forms and Structures in Nature and Technology and Processes in Their Development; 1982)

'Das Ganze' (The Whole), illustration from Frei Otto, *Natürliche Konstruktionen* (Natural Structures; 1982)

were involved. Palaeontologists began to search for impressions of the earliest soft-bodied creatures. Mathematicians, physicists, synergeticists and structural engineers from Berlin, Karlsruhe and Dortmund joined in.'[46] The results of architectural research into construction history, however, would clearly lag behind this interdisciplinary leap in knowledge, as Otto wrote in continuation, 'The historians of buildings have unfortunately not arrived at the present state of our topic, so that there could be no thought of making the desired extrapolation of the historical into tomorrow, although a great deal of remarkable work had been done. I myself failed, as well, when I began to write the history of architectonic inventions and only got from prehistory to antiquity.'[47]

Frei Otto's conceptions of an environmental design close to nature by means of material- and energy-saving lightweight construction were based on an all-encompassing and admittedly subjective understanding of nature that excluded the idea of 'non-nature'.[48] In so doing, he questioned the separation of the natural from the artificial as seen again today under the catchword 'post-natural'. Today, Otto's concept of nature could lead to some problematic, even potentially dangerous conclusions: for example, that separate nature conservation as an obligation of the state is long outdated. Instead, the present-day extent of a misguided anthropogenic environmental design, which has contributed massively to the destruction of the natural foundations of life, makes the clear demarcation of nature worth protecting seem necessary – islands of nature not altogether untouched but largely set apart from further human contact. It is advisable to recognize humankind as an important factor in animate nature, even as an *agent provocateur* of our global common destiny, and locate it within the confines of a sensible, rational design close to nature. An appropriate slogan for our time would be 'environmental protection through environmental design'. Otto himself very likely conceded the possibility of action directed against nature and saw it in the mid-1970s as the rule rather than the exception. At the 1977 celebration held in conjunction with the Schinkel Prize in Berlin, he appealed to his colleagues' professional ethics and vehemently demanded, 'Just stop with building the way you do. It's unnatural.'[49] In his talk, he looked back at the failures of the two decades since the beginning of his own professional career, the decades of a post-war Modernism in which animate nature's ability to repair itself was overstrained: for example, in the peak performance of domestic utilities and an urban space extremely destructive of the environment, as Otto emphasized.[50]

Accessing Frei Otto's cosmos today means placing his concepts of nature and images of nature within their historical context. In the process, we can retrospectively see that his work, extending over six decades, and his understanding of nature, which is variously articulated throughout his career, should not only to be ascribed to the 'alternative' tradition of a 'different' Modernism. In such alternative narratives, opposing points of view are generally ascribed to minor forgotten figures long marginalized in the canonical texts on the history of modern architecture.[51] We now know that neither Otto's buildings nor his questioning of a constantly changing relationship to nature were marginal phenomena of modern architectural discourse. But it cannot be denied that his positions were an open criticism of the prevailing conditions of the post-war decades, their mass consumption society together with the 'Great Acceleration'. Frei Otto belonged to a young generation of visionary architects who understood that what occurred naturally was a complement to the artificially created, not its opposite. They laid the foundation for many of our present-day approaches and, in doing so, were able to draw on central lines of argument and lineages in modern architectural discourse as this introduction has attempted to show. Hope for a desirable preservation or restoration of the unity of the world, about which Riezler wrote in 1927, relied on the convergence of the organic and the mechanical or of nature and technology. The destruction of this unity, felt as a loss, numbers as one of the central global experiences of Modernism, through which the optimistic meaning of Frei Otto's visions as builder, inventor and scientist becomes clear.

1 Frei Otto, 'Meine drei Bilder von Natur', in: *Konzepte des SFB 230*, Universität Stuttgart and Universität Tübingen, no. 3, March 1985, p. 16.

2 Frei Otto in conversation with Juan María Songel, in: *Frei Otto: Conversación con Juan Maria Songel*, Barcelona 2008, p. 27.

3 Bodo Rasch, Frei Otto and Berthold Burkhardt, '50 Jahre Weissenhofsiedlung', reprinted in: Berthold Burkhardt (ed.), *Frei Otto. Schriften und Reden, 1951–1983*. Braunschweig/Wiesbaden 1984, pp. 150 f. See also '50 Jahre jung', in: *Deutsche Bauzeitung*, no. 11, 1977, pp. 27–32.

4 Rasch, Otto, and Burkhardt, '50 Jahre Weissenhofsiedlung', p. 151.

5 Heinz Wetzel, 'Die Werkbund-Siedlung auf dem Weißenhof bei Stuttgart', in: *Deutsche Bauzeitung*, no. 76, 1927, p. 625.

6 Walter Riezler and Wilhelm Lotz, 'Einheit der Welt. Ein Gespräch', in: *Die Form*, 2/8, 1927, pp. 236–248; Wilhelm Lotz, 'Werkbund-Ausstellung Die Wohnung. Stuttgart, 23. Juli–9. Oktober 1927', in: *Die Form*, 2/8, 1927, pp. 249–252; see also Walter Riezler, 'Natur und Maschine', in: *Die Form*, 1/2, 1922, pp. 1–4.

7 Wilhelm Lotz, 'Fotografie und Objekt. Zu den Fotos von Albert Renger-Patzsch', in: *Die Form*, 4/7, 1929, pp. 162–167.

8 Rudolf Schwarz, *Wegweisung der Technik*, Aachen 1929, reprint Cologne 2008, pp. 49 f.

9 Schwarz, *Wegweisung der Technik*, p. 248.

10 Oliver A. I. Botar and Isabel Wünsche (eds), *Biocentrism and Modernism*, New York 2011.

11 Fritz Neumeyer, *Mies van der Rohe. Das kunstlose Wort, Gedanken zur Baukunst*, Berlin 1986, see especially p. 229 with its reference to the correspondence between Mies and Riezler from 1927; in English translation, see Fritz Neumeyer, *The Artless World: Mies van der Rohe on the Building Art*, trans. Mark Jarzombek, Cambrdige, MA, 1991, p. 178.

12 Detlef Mertins, *Mies*, London/New York 2014, pp. 108–113, 328–331, 364–379, 416–419.

13 See Caroline van Eck, *Organicism in Nineteenth-Century Architecture: An Inquiry into Its Theoretical and Philosophical Background*, Amsterdam 1994.

14 Louis Henry Sullivan, 'The Tall Building Artistically Considered', in: *Lippincott's Monthly Magazine*, no. 57, March 1896, pp. 403–409. There, for example, on p. 408 we read, 'It is the pervading law of all things organic and inorganic, of all things physical and metaphysical, of all things human and all things superhuman, of all true manifestations of the head, of the heart, of the soul, that the life is recognizable in its expression, that form ever follows function. *This is the law.*' See Annette Geiger, 'Form follows function als biozentrische Metapher in der Architektur- und Design-Theorie', in: Annette Geiger et al. (eds), *Spielarten des Organischen in Architektur, Design und Kunst*, Berlin 2005.

15 Le Corbusier, *1922. Ausblick auf eine Architektur*, Braunschweig/Wiesbaden 1963, pp. 65, 85, 108, 114, 115, 151, 154, 155, 167, here p. 66; in English translation, see Le Corbusier, *Toward an Architecture*, trans. John Goodman, Los Angeles 2007, p. 136.

16 Hugo Häring, 'Wege zur Form', in: *Die Form*, 1/1, 1925, pp. 3–5.

17 Niklas Maak, *Der Architekt am Strand. Le Corbusier und das Geheimnis der Seeschnecke*, Munich 2010.

18 Le Corbusier, *1922. Ausblick auf eine Architektur*, p. 154.

19 Adolf Rading, 'Neues Wohnen', in: *Die Bauzeitung*, no. 33, 1927, pp. 269–272, here p. 270.

20 Richard Döcker, 'Über Baukunst', in: *Die Volkswohnung*, no. 13, 1923.

21 See, for example, Walter Gropius, *Internationale Architektur*, 2nd ed., Munich 1927, p. 9.

22 Adolf Behne, 'Nationales und Internationales im Neuen Bauen', in: *Moderne Bauformen*, 1931, pp. 209–212.

23 Jacob von Uexküll, *Umwelt und Innenwelt der Tiere*, Berlin 1909.

24 Adolf Behne, *Die Wiederkehr der Kunst*, Leipzig 1919, pp. 57 f., 63, 109, 111. See also Behne, 'Biologie und Kubismus', in: *Der Sturm*, nos 11/12, 1915, pp. 68–71; Behne, *Der Moderne Zweckbau*, Munich 1926, pp. 44, 47 f., 71.

25 Friedrich Dessauer, 'Technik – Kultur – Kunst', in: *Die Form*, 4/18, 1929, pp. 479–486.

26 Bruno Taut, *Die Auflösung der Städte, oder Die Erde eine gute Wohnung*, Hagen 1920, pp. 7, 12, 14. On this, see Manfred Speidel's afterword in the facsimile edition published by Gebrüder Mann Verlag, Berlin 2020.

27 David H. Haney and Elke Sohn, 'Traces of Organicism in Gardening and Urban Planning Theories in Early Twentieth-Century Germany', in: Botar and Wünsche (eds), *Biocentrism and Modernism*, pp. 107–126; Elke Sohn, *Zum Begriff der Natur in Stadtkonzepten – anhand der Beiträge von Hans Bernard Reichow, Walter Schwagenscheidt und Hans Scharoun zum Wiederaufbau nach 1925*, Münster 2008.

28 Martin Wagner, *Das wachsende Haus. Ein Beitrag zur Lösung der städtischen Wohnungsfrage*, Leipzig/Berlin 1932, p. 40.

29 For the history of Wagner's initiative, see Anja Fröhlich, *'Sonne, Luft und Haus für Alle' – Das wachsende Haus. Ein Versuch zur Lösung der Wohnungsfrage unter besonderer Berücksichtigung der Rolle Martin Wagners*, doctoral thesis Bauhaus-Universität Weimar 2008.

30 Arthur Wiechula, *Wachsende Häuser aus lebenden Bäumen entstehend*, Berlin 1926; Arthur Wiechula, *Wie baue ich mir selbst lebende Holzhäuser unter Mitwirkung der Natur?*, Leipzig 1927; see also Ferdinand Ludwig, *Botanische Grundlagen der Baubotanik und deren Anwendung im Entwurf*, doctoral thesis Universität Stuttgart 2012.

31 'Der Wettbewerb "Das wachsende Haus"', in: Frei Otto (ed.), *Anpassungsfähig bauen, Mitteilungen der Entwicklungsstätte für den Leichtbau (EL)*, no. 6, June 1959, pp. 19 ff.

32 Frei Otto, 'Kritischer Rückblick und Aufgaben für die Zukunft', in: Klaus Teichmann and Joachim Wilke (eds), *Prozess und Form 'Natürlicher Konstruktionen'. Der Sonderforschungsbereich 230*, Berlin 1996, p. 220.

33 Hans Scharoun, 'Berlin', in: *Baukunst und Werkform*, no. 1, 1947, pp. 24–26.

34 Hartmut Frank, 'Stadtlandschaften. Rudolf Schwarz' Planungen für Diedenhofen und Köln 1940–1950', in: Jean-Louis Cohen and Hartmut Frank (eds), *Metropolen. Mythen – Bilder – Entwürfe 1850–1950*, Berlin/Munich 2013, pp. 305–329.

35 On this, see Joaquín Medina Warmburg, '(Re)constructores del Mundo. Elegías y elogios de la Tierra en la arquitectura alemana de posguerra', in: *Block*, no. 9, 2012, pp. 84–91.

36 Martin Wagner, *Wirtschaftlicher Städtebau*, Stuttgart 1951.

37 Frei Otto, 'Die Stadt von morgen und das Einfamilienhaus', in: *Baukunst und Werkform*, no. 12, 1956, pp. 642–652.

38 Lewis Mumford, 'The Natural History of Urbanization', in: William L. Thomas et al. (eds), *Man's Role in Changing the Face of the Earth*, Chicago/London 1956, pp. 382–398.

39 See Volker Welter, *Biopolis: Patrick Geddes and the City of Life*, Cambridge, MA, 2002.

40 Lewis Mumford, *Technics and Civilization*, Chicago 1934, pp. 367–373.

41 Frei Otto et al., *Natürliche Konstruktionen. Formen und Konstruktionen in Natur und Technik und Prozesse ihrer Entstehung*, Stuttgart 1982, pp. 85, 104.

42 See George Hersey, *The Monumental Impulse: Architecture's Biological Roots*, Cambridge, MA, 1999, pp. xix–xx; Luis Fernández-Galiano, *El fuego y la memoria. Sobre arquitectura y energía*, Madrid 1991.

43 Philip Steadman, *The Evolution of Designs: Biological Analogy in Architecture and the Applied Arts*, Cambridge 1979.

44 Peter Collins, *The Changing Ideals of Modern Architecture, 1750–1950*, London 1965, pp. 149–158.

45 Otto, 'Meine drei Bilder von Natur', pp. 14–24.

46 Frei Otto, 'Kritischer Rückblick und Aufgaben für die Zukunft', in: Teichmann and Wilke (eds), *Prozess und Form 'Natürlicher Konstruktionen'*, p. 221.

47 Otto, 'Kritischer Rückblick', p. 222. See Frei Otto, *Alte Baumeister. Was könnten die alten Baumeister erfunden haben? Ein Beitrag zur Geschichte des Konstruierens auf dem Weg zur Baukunst, Mitteilungen des Instituts für leichte Flächentragwerke (IL)*, no. 37, Stuttgart 1994.

48 Otto, 'Meine drei Bilder von Natur'.

49 Frei Otto, 'Hört endlich auf, weiterhin so zu bauen wie ihr baut! Es ist widernatürlich', in: *Deutsche Bauzeitung*, no. 5, 1977, p. 8.

50 Otto, 'Hört endlich auf', p. 8.

51 See, for example, Colin St John Wilson, *The Other Tradition of Modern Architecture: The Uncompleted Project*, London 1995.

Competition entry for the multiuse hall Terre-Plein du Portier in Monaco (1969)

Nature

Biology
Ecology
Climate

The Institute for the Development of Lightweight Construction in Berlin 1959

Martin Kunz

Frei Otto's student work already shows that he was not interested in classical architecture but rather in new technologies and architectural concepts of a different kind. Instead of starting to work in an architecture firm after receiving his diploma, he immediately began writing his doctoral thesis focused on the suspended roof. In researching the topic, he came into contact with Peter Stromeyer, the owner of a tent-making factory on Lake Constance. With his support, Otto set out to develop new tent structures whose forms were based on studies of minimal surfaces. With his four-point sail for the German National Garden Show (Bundesgartenschau) in Kassel (1955), Otto demonstrated what large spans were possible in modern tent construction.

To make it clear that his work was not that of a classic architectural office, in early 1958 Frei Otto established the Institute for the Development of Lightweight Construction (Entwicklungsstätte für den Leichtbau, EL) and published the first issue of its report, *Mitteilungen der Entwicklungsstätte für den Leichtbau (EL)*, containing the institute's programme.[1] It indicated that this was to be a research organization that, in addition to its own foundational study and consulting in lightweight construction, would also compile and publish new worldwide developments in the field. To this end, along with specialized technical publications, he planned to issue twelve *Mitteilungen* a year.[2] At the time that the EL was established, Frei Otto had four co-workers in his atelier: Siegfried Lohs, Ewald Bubner, Diether R. Frank and Ingrid Otto, Frei Otto's wife.[3]

At the end of 1958, into early 1959, Frei Otto began planning for an atelier building on the parcel of land at Türksteinweg 5 in Berlin-Zehlendorf.[4] For it, he acquired the front of the plot; at the time of the sale, the site was divided and the back was allotted to the neighbouring property. From the beginning, it was planned that a dwelling for the Otto family would occupy the site in addition to the atelier structure.[5] Detailed planning began in March of the same year, and construction commenced in September. Interior work continued into December.[6] The move into the new atelier quarters began on 18 December 1959 and continued until the new year. In January 1960, the Institute for the Development of Lightweight Construction took up its work in the new building.[7]

The atelier building was a free-standing structure on a rectangular ground plan (5 × 9 m), with the longer side running parallel to the street at the front part of the plot. Constructed as a simple steel edifice, it had eight round supports and wide flange beams for the roof. The flat roof was thermally insulated with diagonal wood panelling. The supports, 105 millimetre thick, stood inside the space, with a filigree glazed outer shell that was visually structured by slender steel T-moulding (45 × 45 mm) alone. All four façades were completely glazed, and there was a door on each of the building's small faces. The interior was a single open space with a walk-in unit along one side lengthwise containing the toilet and a storage room. The space could be subdivided by wooden-slat roller blinds and translucent sliding walls. If these walls were closed an independent space was created within, which could be heated in winter with the surrounding space serving as a climate buffer. In summer, by contrast, window curtains and the sliding walls could create different zones of light and shade, a feature of particular importance for an atelier in which drawings and models were being made. On the garden side, there was a narrow shed panelled with Eternit sheets, housing storage space for garden tools, a workshop cabinet and the warm air heating system.[8]

Frei Otto kept the building's furnishing as flexible as possible. In addition to a writing desk, which he had designed himself, there were tabletops placed on sawhorses. For the most options regarding the illumination, Otto designed ceiling lamps based on the principle of the mobile, with two ball-and-socket joints and counterweights, that could be freely positioned in the space.[9]

In the summer of 1961, plans to build a family dwelling at the rear of the plot became more specific. Frei Otto designed a larger flat-roof bungalow and submitted a planning application to the borough authority, which approved his building project under certain conditions.[10] The addition, however, was never built. It was only after his move to Warmbronn that Otto could realize, on a considerably larger scale, his concept of an atelier along the street, with a residence at the back of the property.

Beginning in 1958, Frei Otto started teaching sporadically in the United States, and consequently, the team in his new atelier became more international. It was first joined by John Koch from St Louis, later by Larry Medlin as well, who had attended Otto's course in Berkeley. For its sixth issue of the *Mitteilungen* on the subject of 'adaptable building', the EL attracted outside authors for the first time, among them Yona Friedman, Antony Herrey and Rudolf Doernach.[11]

When Frei Otto moved with his family to Warmbronn in 1969, the property in Berlin-Zehlendorf was sold and the atelier torn down.[12] In the eleven years of the EL's existence, it published nine issues of the *Mitteilungen* as well as the two professional publications *Zugbeanspruchte Konstruktionen* (vols 1 and 2, 1962 and 1966; *Tensile Structures*). Without the foundational research in lightweight construction carried out in this small building, the tent construction for the German Pavilion at Expo 67 in Montreal would not have been possible at the time. The first important models for the roofing of the Olympic sports venues in Munich were also developed here. The work begun by the EL was later continued at the Institute for Lightweight Structures (Institut für leichte Flächentragwerke, IL) in Stuttgart and the Atelier Frei Otto in Warmbronn.

1 *Mitteilungen der Entwicklungsstätte für den Leichtbau (EL)*, no. 1, 1958. Frei Otto dated the first issue to January 1958, but it is assumed to have been published later, in March.
2 saai, PRESSE/Nachr.-Dienst f. d. Bauwesen/15.3.58/Nr. 10–11, p. 7 f., FO_BE-07.
3 Frei Otto, 'Der zukünftige Ausbau der Entwicklungsstätte', in: *Mitteilungen der Entwicklungsstätte für den Leichtbau (EL)*, no. 1, 1958, p. 13.
4 saai, Werkarchiv FO, Atelier-Tagebücher [Studio Diary], 1957–1960.
5 saai, Werkarchiv FO, Atelier-Tagebücher [Studio Diary], 1957–1960.
6 saai, Werkarchiv FO, Atelier-Tagebücher [Studio Diary], 1957–1960.
7 Frei Otto, 'Entwicklungsarbeiten auf dem Gebiet des Leichtbaus', in: *Mitteilungen der Entwicklungsstätte für den Leichtbau (EL)*, no. 7, 1961, p. 44.
8 Frei Otto, 'Die Entwicklungsstätte in Berlin-Zehlendorf', in: *Mittilungen der Entwicklungsstätte für den Leichtbau (EL)*, no. 8, 1962, p. 47.
9 These lamps were later used in his Warmbronn atelier as well.
10 saai, FO PL A2 003.
11 *Anpassungsfähig bauen, Mitteilungen der Entwicklungsstätte für den Leichtbau (EL)*, no. 6, 1959.
12 Frei Otto, 'Entwicklungsstätte für den Leichtbau', in: *Arch+*, nos 144/145, December 1998, p. 64.

Shell structure of the atelier building (autumn 1959)

Instrument for measuring models in the atelier garden

Frei Otto conducting an experiment

Interior of the atelier with closed sliding walls and open wooden-slat roller blinds

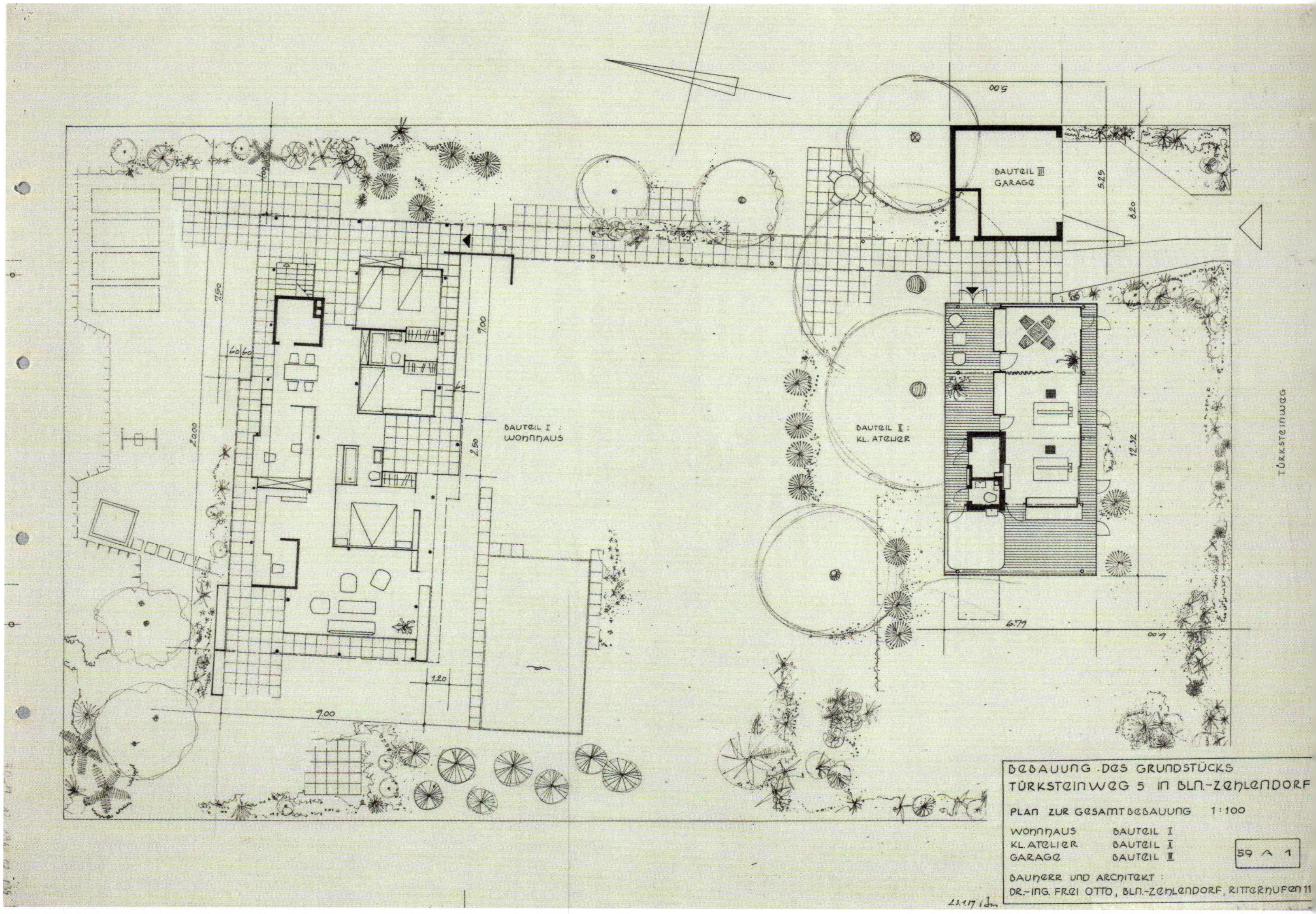

BAUTEIL III
GARAGE
BAUTEIL I:
WOHNHAUS
BAUTEIL II:
KL. ATELIER
TÜRKSTEINWEG

BEBAUUNG DES GRUNDSTÜCKS
TÜRKSTEINWEG 5 IN BLN.-ZEHLENDORF
PLAN ZUR GESAMTBEBAUUNG 1:100
WOHNHAUS BAUTEIL I
KL. ATELIER BAUTEIL II
GARAGE BAUTEIL III
59 A 1
BAUHERR UND ARCHITEKT:
DR.-ING. FREI OTTO, BLN.-ZEHLENDORF, RITTERHUFEN 11

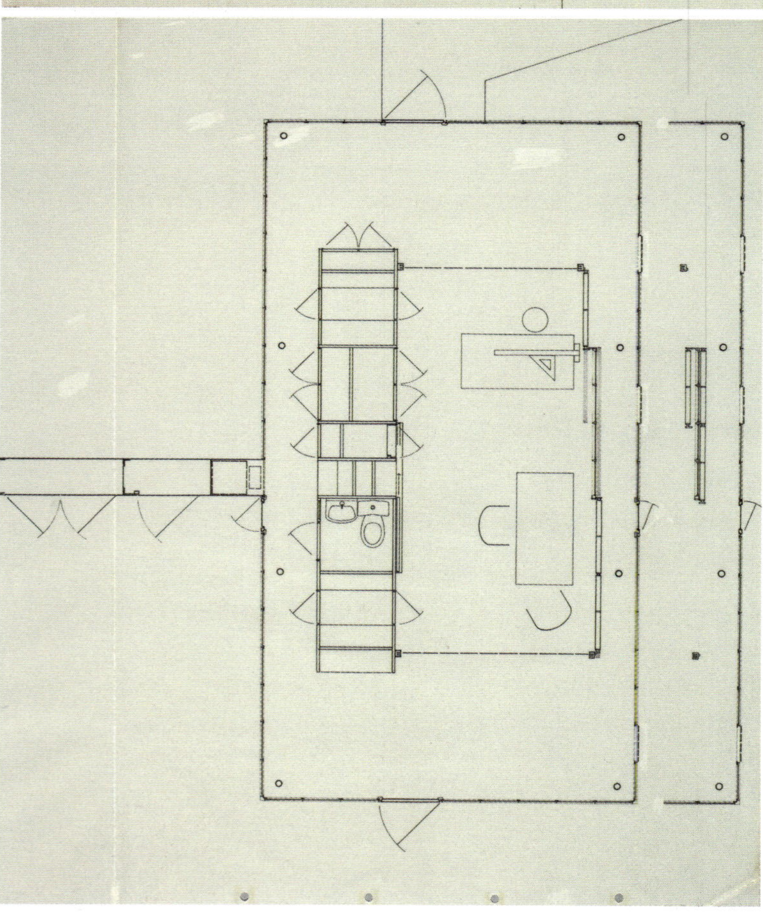

Frei Otto's plan for developing the site at Türksteinweg 5 with an atelier building facing the street and a residence for his family towards the rear (January 1959)

Plan of the atelier building with closed and open sliding walls

57

The atelier building shortly after completion

Frei Otto dictating a text at a table that he designed

Corner of the atelier building

Following double page: the atelier at night in wintertime

Protestant Church in Berlin-Zehlendorf 1959–1963

Mechthild Ebert

The architectural ensemble – consisting of the church, congregation-house, kindergarten and bell tower of the former parish of Schönow – was realized by Frei Otto and Ewald Bubner between 1959 and 1963, and is among the early works of both architects. The site lies along the southern edge of the Berlin borough of Zehlendorf – between Andréezeile towards the northeast and Ramsteinweg towards the southwest, in the immediate vicinity of the Teltower Graben, whose course marks the city limits at this location. Until the division of Berlin after the Second World War, the southern part of Zehlendorf belonged to the town of Teltow. In 1949, the village parish of Schönow was elevated by Provost Böhm to an independent church parish, and with the erection of the Berlin Wall, the parishes in Teltow and Zehlendorf (in East Germany and West Berlin respectively) were finally organized into two separate church districts.[1] Initiated simultaneously in the former parish of Zehlendorf were two additional church building projects: in 1955, Frei Otto took part in the competition for the Kirche zur Heimat, receiving third prize after Peter Lehrecke and Ewald Bubner.[2] The new building was completed in 1957. The Stephanuskirche was realized by the architects Hans Geber and Otto Risse between 1960 and 1961.[3]

Emerging together with the expansion of residential developments in the south of Zehlendorf and the accompanying rise in parishioners was the desire for a new focal point for the religious community.[4] Particularly urgent was a new accommodation for the Protestant kindergarten after the old one had been closed temporarily in 1958.[5]

In a letter addressed to the parish church council, the local synod recommended 'issuing requests to a small number (perhaps three) of suitable architects for a design sketch'.[6] The parish commissioned four architects, choosing one of the designs at the end of the following year.[7] The choice fell upon Ewald Bubner, who realized the project together with Frei Otto, who had also taken part in the internal competition in collaboration with Siegfried Lohs. For the most part, the final design followed Bubner's proposal.[8] Since the available funds were limited, the architects sought a cost-effective and simple solution.

The cornerstone ceremony took place on 27 September 1959,[9] and the topping out ceremony for the church and congregation-house was celebrated together with the dedication of the kindergarten on 31 October 1960,[10] and they were officially opened on 22 May of the following year.[11]

The architectural ensemble is dominated by the church's slate-covered tent roof, which measures 13 metres in height and 20 metres in length and rests on eight three-legged concrete supports, each approximately 1.8 metres in height. The steel roof construction, which is subject to compression and tension, is clad with wood on the inside, with the tension members left visible. The front and side walls are fully glazed, generating the impression of a 'floating' roof and providing a direct connection to the surroundings outside. The nave with its seating, set two steps lower down, was given oak strip parquet and is framed by a continuous bench seat on the long sides. The flooring in the remaining areas of the church was left in grey screed. The church can provide seating for up to three hundred people. The altar, pulpit and baptismal font – each hewn from a block of red sandstone – are raised and constitute space-defining elements. Standing across from them are the organ and choir stall at the end of the church nave.[12]

The church, bell tower and congregation-house enclose a forecourt along Andréezeile. A roofed passageway running parallel to the street provides access to both the church and the congregation-house and continues with the same width as the corridors inside the parish centre. The single-storey flat-roof building that abuts the church contains both the congregation-house and kindergarten. The church vestibule and two parish rooms may be joined by means of collapsible partition walls to form a small reception hall or can be used as additional space during church services. Also located here are the parish office, the pastoral counselling room, two youth rooms (used today by the entire congregation), the sacristy and public lavatories. The building has a partial basement. The kindergarten is accessed via a small courtyard set off Andréezeile. All of its rooms are arranged around a central foyer: three staggered assembly rooms, lavatories, kitchen and office. The assembly rooms are oriented towards the southeast, have expansive windows and enjoy direct access to the garden. The congregation-house and kindergarten were constructed in red brick and are, for the most part, closed towards the street side. The flat-roof building is set at right angles to the church. The buildings are surrounded by a lawn that is used for parish events.

Erected in 1963, following the completion of the church, was the freestanding bell tower, about which Otto and Bubner wrote, 'The dissolved, transparent form of the tower was chosen so as not to overwhelm the nave of the church, either in its size or character, with a bulky form'.[13] A special challenge involved the suspension of the three bells, whose total weight is more than 1.3 metric tons, in such a way that their vibrations would be absorbed by the tower structure with as little material expenditure as possible. The shape and construction of the tower were based on space frame studies with rigid nodes.[14] The truss structure is 24 metres in height and consists of twelve vertically stacked cubes, each measuring 2 × 2 × 2 metres. The sheet steel was cut individually using a curved template and welded together with fillet and butt welds. Depending upon the stress flow, the thicknesses of the sheet steel is reduced from 50 millimetres in the lowest segment to 10 millimetres in the uppermost zone. The steel structure, weighing 16.8 metric tons, is mounted to the reinforced concrete foundation, weighing 60 tons, with four bolts on each of the four anchor plates. The high rigidity of the structure made it possible to assemble the tower in a factory, allowing the welding work to be carried out regardless of weather conditions. Two large mobile cranes and a small holding crane were used to erect the tower, which had been transported to the construction site on a special vehicle. Suspended within the uppermost cube of the tower is a luminous white cross, and below it are the three bells, tuned to the pitches c", b' and a♭'.[15] The height of the tower was intended to visibly signal its connection to the mother parish of Teltow lying beyond the city boundary and the former national border.[16]

The architectural ensemble has been a listed landmark since the mid-1990s. In the early 2000s, the congregation installed a wheelchair lift in order to provide disabled access to the seating area of the church nave.[17]

1 See Kirchenkreis Teltow-Zehlendorf, 'Was wir sind', https://www.teltow-zehlendorf.de/wir/was-wir-sind (accessed on 2 June 2024); Günther Kühne and Elisabeth Stephani, *Evangelische Kirchen in Berlin*, Berlin 1978, p. 337.

2 See 'Kirche der Evangelischen Kirchengemeinde Zur Heimat in Berlin-Zehlendorf', in: *Architektur-Wettbewerbe,* no. 20, *Kirchen und Gemeindezentren*, Stuttgart 1957, pp. 50 ff.

3 See Architekten- und Ingenieur-Verein zu Berlin (ed.), *Berlin und seine Bauten*, vol. VI, *Sakralbauten,* Berlin 1997, pp. 232 f.

4 See Evangelisches Landeskirchliches Archiv in Berlin (ELAB) 1/8840; a transcript by the Protestant Superintendent for Zehlendorf from 25 October 1955 mentions the foundation of a church building association to support the new construction project.

5 See ELAB 1/8847; a letter from the parish church council dated 19 December 1958 mentions that the kindergarten had been closed temporarily in the middle of 1958.

6 ELAB 1/8840; letter from the local synod to the parish church council, dated 27 June 1957.

7 See ELAB 1/8847; letter from the parish church council to the Evangelisches Konsistorium, the city's Protestant consistory, 19 December1958.

8 See 'Glockenturm für die Evangelische Kirche Berlin-Zehlendorf-Schönow', in: *Acier – Steel – Stahl*, no. 2, February 1967, pp. 58 ff.

9 See ELAB 1/8840, report from the press office of the Evangelische Kirchenleitung, the Protestant church leadership of Berlin-Brandenburg, 29 September 1959.

10 See ELAB 63/3807, newspaper article, 'Neue Kirche in Schönow', in: *Der Tag,* 2 November 1960.

11 See ELAB 63/3807, newspaper article, 'Kirche wie ein Zelt', in: *Der Tag,* 19 May 1961.

12 See ELAB 63/3807; letter from the press office of the Evangelische Kirchenleitung on the consecration of the church in Schönow contains a detailed description of the building.

13 ELAB 1/8840, explanatory report on the bell tower by Ewald Bubner and Frei Otto, 9 September 1963.

14 In a test, balloons were squeezed tightly between two plates, and the spaces between filled with plaster. Once the material had hardened, the balloons were removed, revealing the planar and spatial structures with their rounded corners and tapered bridges. See Winfried Nerdinger (ed.), *Frei Otto: Complete Works; Lightweight Construction, Natural Design*, exh. cat. Architekturmuseum der TU München, Basel/Boston/Berlin 2005, p. 207.

15 See Conrad Roland, *Frei Otto. Spannweiten*, Berlin 1965, p. 119.

16 See saai, Werkarchiv FO, 'Gedanken Frei Ottos zum 30-jährigen Bestehen der Kirche', 12 May 1991.

17 See Evangelische Kirchengemeinde Schönow-Buschgraben, 'Unser Haus', https://www.schoenow-buschgraben.de/wir/unser-haus (accessed on 2 June 2024).

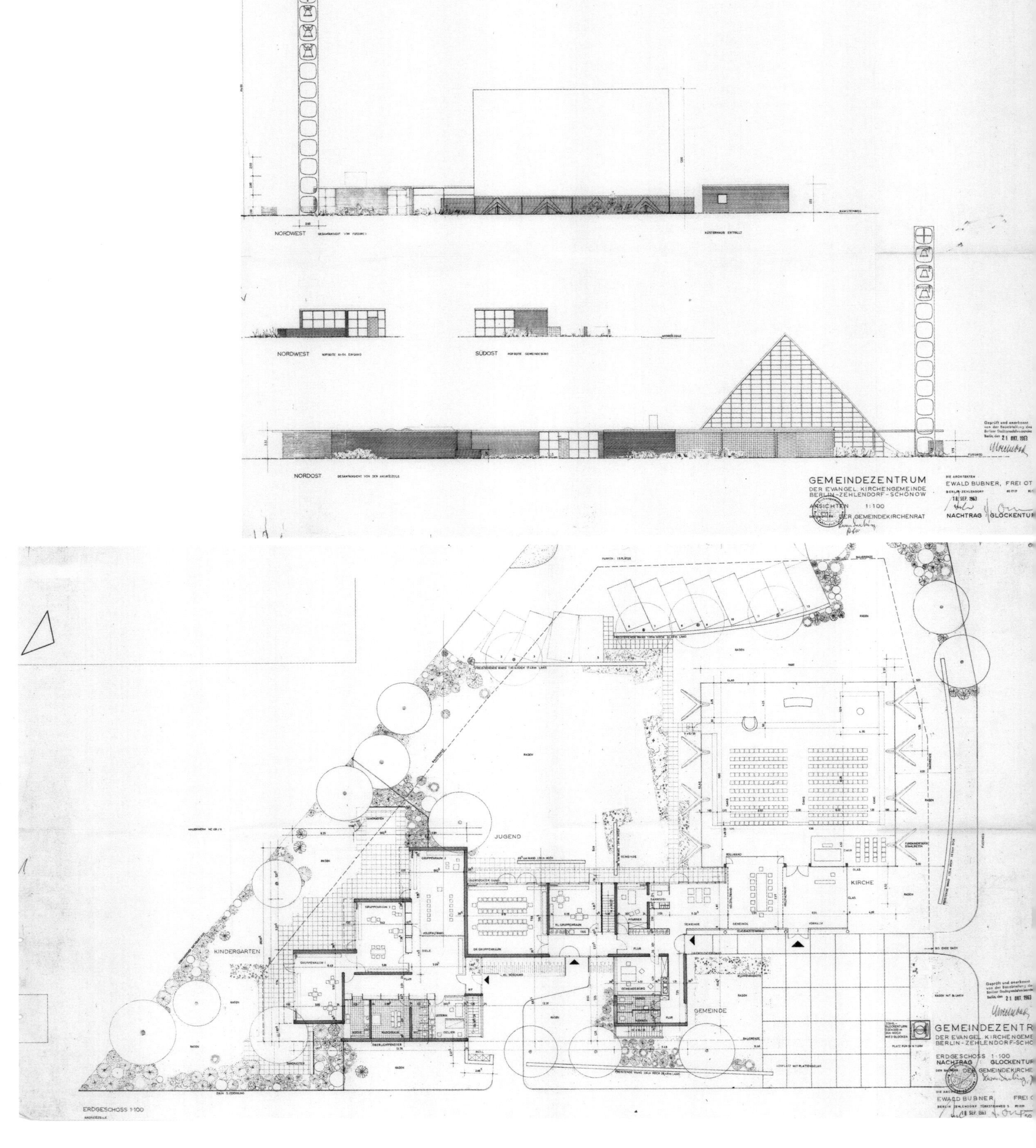

Congregation-house, views and plan of the ground floor (September 1963)

Construction of the church nave

Erection of the tower with the help of two mobile cranes and a holding crane

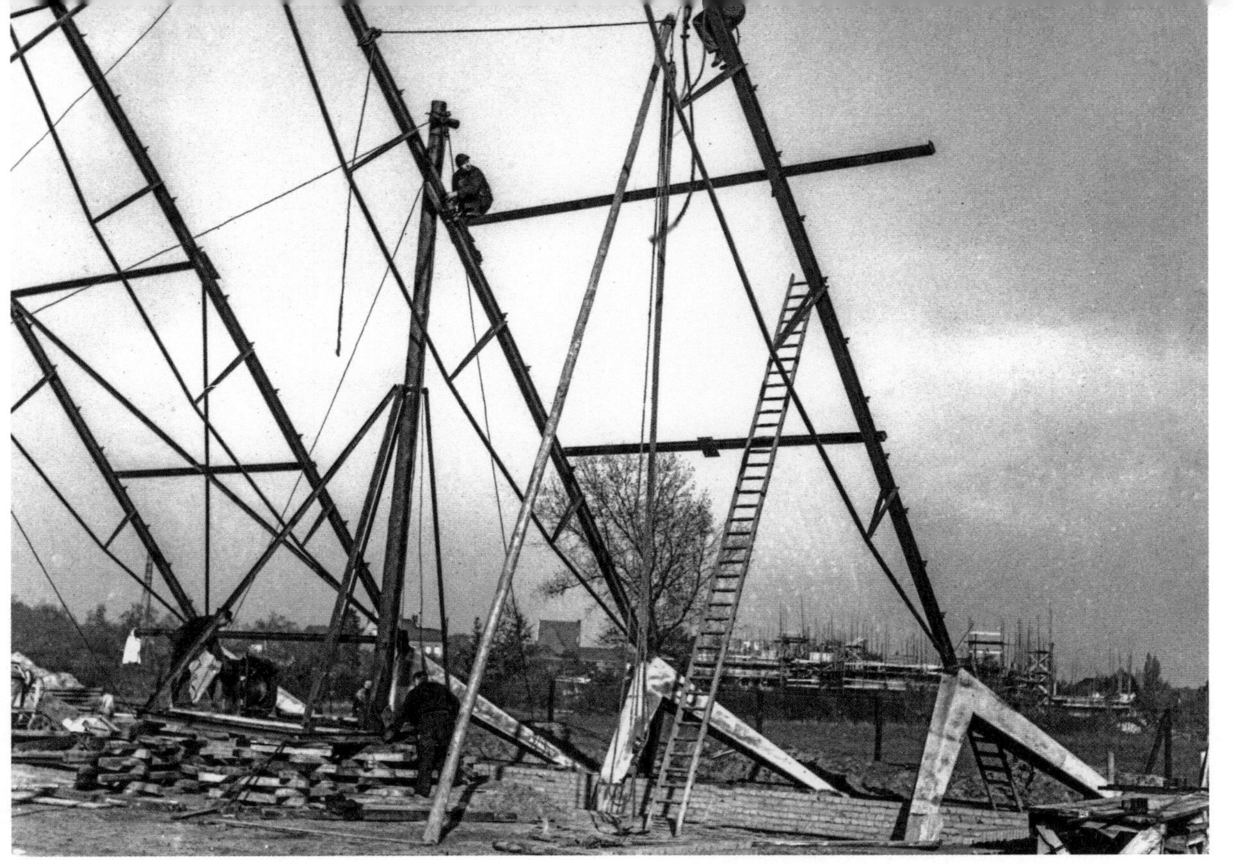

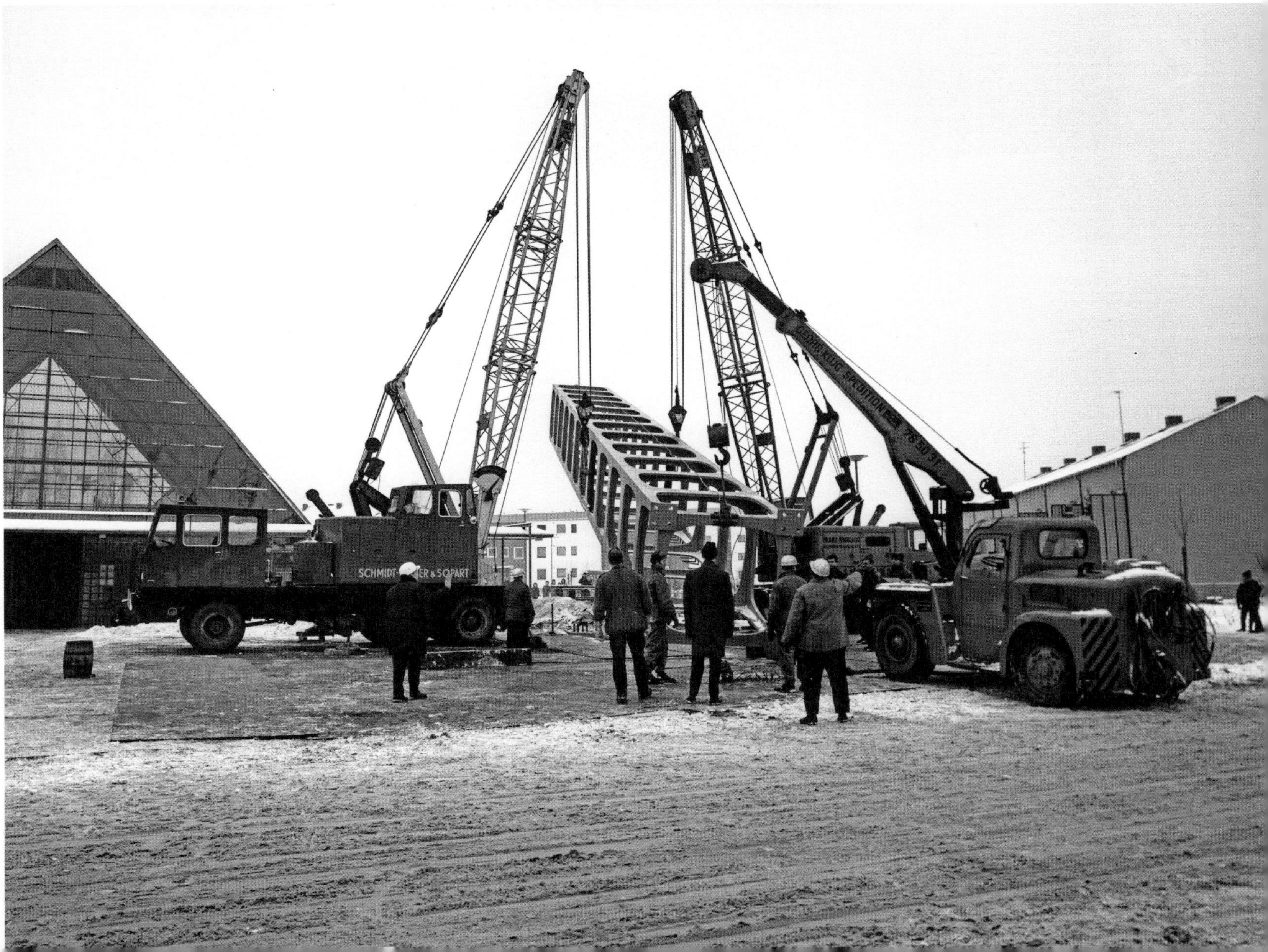
SCHMIDT-
ER & SOPART
GEORG KLUG SPEDITION
76 50 31

The church and bell tower seen from the west

Interior of the nave with seating below

Altar and pulpit in red sandstone

79
75
76
86
139

Otto's House and Atelier in Warmbronn 1966–1971

Jos Tomlow

Once Frei Otto had become more firmly established at the University of Stuttgart, he and his wife, Ingrid, needed to relocate to Baden-Württemberg from their trusted Berlin. The family, soon to be seven in number, required a larger property. Their choice fell upon a parcel on a south-facing slope in Warmbronn, a small village in the township of Leonberg, thirteen kilometres east of the university campus in Stuttgart-Vaihingen. An important factor at the time he was building his house and atelier was that, with such large projects as the German Pavilion at Expo 67 in Montreal and the roof of the Olympic stadium for Munich in 1972, Otto had arrived at a high point in his career. He was thus somewhat flush financially, but his assistants were available for house planning to only a limited extent. Conveniently, just as he was searching for a suitable collaborator, the architect Rob Krier indicated that he was interested in working together with him. Krier moved to Warmbronn with his wife, Gudrun, and set up the architecture firm Architekturbüro Frei Otto in their joint residence. By way of Frei Otto's sketches, which Krier reproduced in finished form, the two communicated about necessary design changes. Fundamental to this discursive design process, in part preserved in handwritten notes on sketches and plans, was Frei Otto's desire to realize his concept of an eco-house (*Ökohaus*) as much as possible.[1] The process therefore revealed Frei Otto's second conceptual focus: in addition to adhering to the principles of lightweight construction and using resource-efficient building methods, he wanted to make use of passive solar energy. In this way, what Frei Otto would later call the 'grandmother of today's passive and solar architecture' was created.[2]

A glass shell envelops the greater part of a two-storey dwelling that was essentially conceived as a bungalow on a sloping site. The children's bedrooms are modules that are partially ventilated – like the living area – through the glass shell. A veritable wealth of plants fills its space with oxygen and fragrance. The volume of the 'great shell' is roughly three times that of the enclosed living spaces. It is like a transparent membrane with which sunlight and the intake of fresh air can be regulated – functioning much like a greenhouse.[3] Even when the sun was at a low angle and at below-zero temperatures in winter, the sun's rays could penetrate deep into the ground-floor living area, so that it sometimes reached temperatures of up to +30°C.[4] In the early evening, the interior garden with its central water basin cooled rapidly, though a shade sail served to moderate this loss of heat. An air heating system assured that the temperature never fell below +8°C, so that condensation was avoided. Previously captured warmth in the living spaces could be kept in by closing the windows, and at night, the temperature in the sleeping modules was kept comfortable by means of heating units specially designed by Frei Otto. With the arrival of summer, ventilation was intensified, and if necessary, the 120 square-metre shade sail could be reeled out at the press of a button. The membrane of the great shell tends to be opened in summer as much as possible, even at night. The opening can be raised between the glass roof and the shade sail to create a 30-square metre opening. Interior sliding doors patterned after those found in Japan remain open in summer.

Two preliminary designs, which could be referred to as 'structural' (February–March 1967) and 'organic-modern' (April–May 1967) were completed in 1967.[5] Likely influences were the Californian Case Study Houses, especially Richard Neutra's bungalows, as well as traditional Japanese houses. The 'structural' preliminary design shows a rigid arrangement of five bays, which was maintained in both the house and the atelier structure. The ten-degree slope meant that the interior space was distributed across different levels, a feature also shown in the 'organic-modern' preliminary design. That had its drawbacks, however, among them the high cost of the foundation. The same design registers Frei Otto's idea of using a grid structure for the great shell. A photograph reveals that the form of the gridshell was checked on the basis of a model Rob Krier produced with wire mesh.[6] The four angled surfaces of the grid are made of 5×5 centimetres wooden strips (made of hemlock) in a module of 75×75 centimetres. Presumably, the curved surfaces were to have been covered with overlapping Plexiglas panes. Architecturally, the purposeful way in which the roof and walls of the house penetrate the membrane suggest that an attempt was made for this 'sheathing' to be invisible.

The dwelling and atelier were constructed between 1969 and 1971 in a cost-saving version without abandoning eco-house principles. Lightweight construction methods were used, with a bearing framework of structural steel for the room modules and 6-centimetre-thick Styrofoam as insulation. Altogether, the house as completed can be seen as an experiment in construction. It is, nevertheless, noteworthy that the family occupied the house over a period of fifty years without any major changes.[7] To be sure, based on the data published by Frei Otto himself, one could conclude that it was not a particularly energy-saving structure. The single-pane glazing of the greenhouse's angled roof meant that the great shell did not retain heat very long.[8] As listed buildings, both structures can be considered problematic, since to prevent permanent damage they have to be regularly tended to, the sunshade unrolled, for example, and the window ventilation and heating checked. Ideally, to make the collection of buildings fully accessible to the public, they would need to be made barrier-free and undergo a thorough restoration. Open-minded discussion of these issues is needed.

1 In the archive of Frei Otto's work at saai there are roughly one hundred drawings and a number of photographs tracing the design process and building of the two structures.

2 'My house and the atelier in Warmbronn are now considered a grandmother of the many solar-powered houses in the BRD [Federal Republic of Germany]': Frei Otto, *Wohn-Be-Reiche im Garten, IBA Berlin 1987. Vorbereitende Studie für das Bauvorhaben 'Ökohaus' Berlin*, Warmbronn 1985, p. 40.

3 Frei Otto applied the term 'great shell' (*Großhülle*), used here, not only to his large urban planning and landscape projects but also to his Warmbronn eco-house. This was probably because its volume was meant to be large in relation to the living area so as to ensure ample ventilation.

4 A measurement made by Frei Otto in February 1985: see 'Atelier und Wohnhaus in Warmbronn Baujahr 1968', in: Otto, *Wohn-Be-Reiche im Garten*, pp. 40 f. The essay includes a table comparing the great shell's temperature with that of the outdoors.

5 A detailed description of the design process is presented in Jos Tomlow and Sebastian Stadler, 'Vorentwürfe eines Ökohauses in Warmbronn. Energetische Studien zu Frei Ottos Ökohaus-Konzept (1967–1969)', in: *Wissenschaftliche Berichte Hochschule Zittau/Görlitz*, no. 136, 2022.

6 For Frei Otto's gridshells, see Christine Otto-Kanstinger, 'Frei Otto: Executing High Tech Concepts', in: *Perceived Technologies in the Modern Movement 1918–1975: Proceedings of the 13th International DOCOMOMO Technology Seminar, Karlsruhe 2013*, special issue, *Wissenschaftliche Berichte der Hochschule Zittau/Görlitz*, no. 120, 2014, pp. 78–83.

7 Small repairs were made, a switch to double glazing in the vertical structures, for example, and the exterior doors were changed to ensure they closed more tightly.

8 See Tomlow and Stadler, 'Vorentwürfe eines Ökohauses in Warmbronn', pp. 40–47, 56–58.

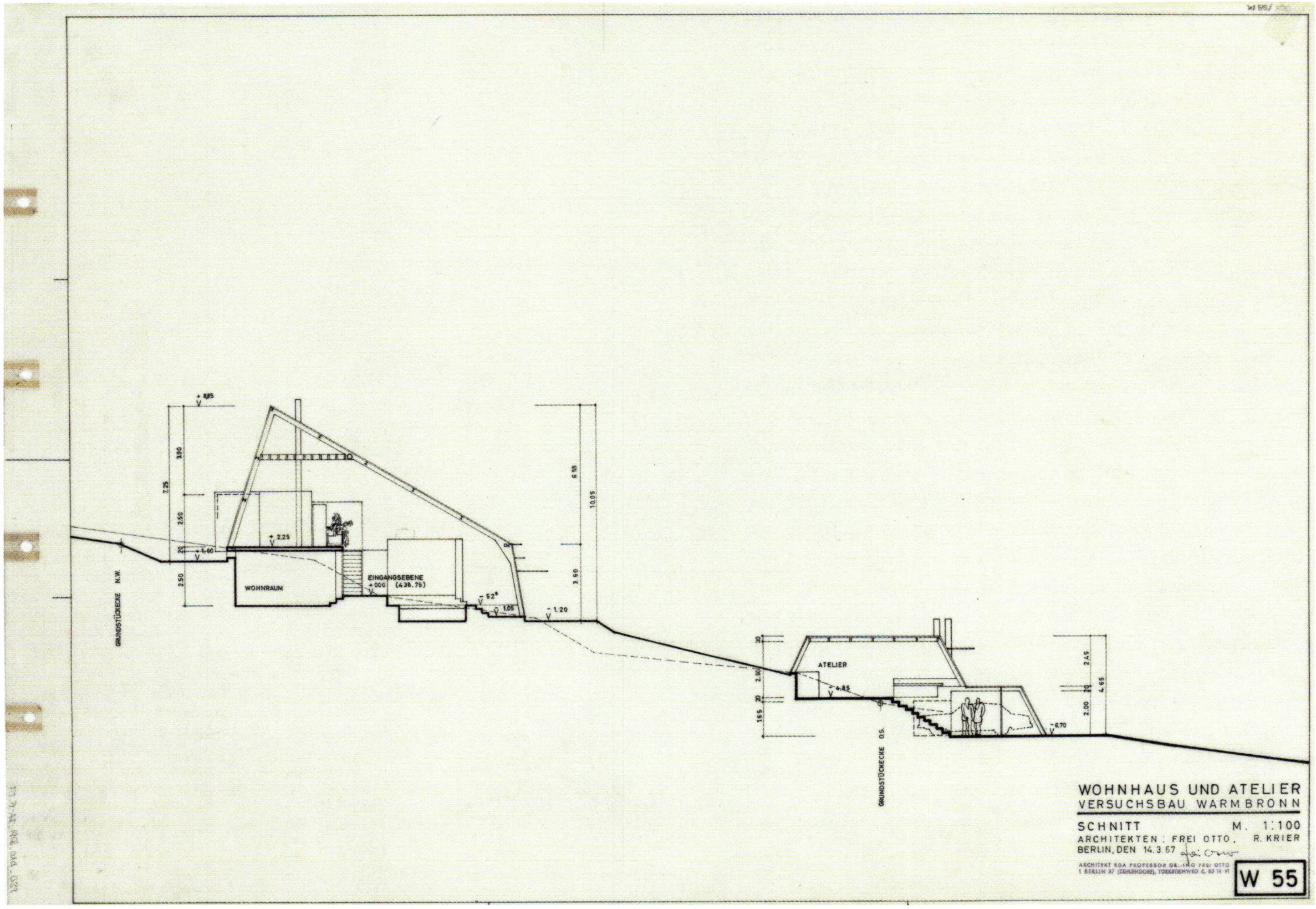

GRUNDSTÜCKSECKE N.W.

WOHNRAUM

EINGANGSEBENE ±000 (438.75)

ATELIER

GRUNDSTÜCKSECKE O.S.

WOHNHAUS UND ATELIER
VERSUCHSBAU WARMBRONN
SCHNITT M. 1:100
ARCHITEKTEN: FREI OTTO, R. KRIER
BERLIN, DEN 14.3.67

W 55

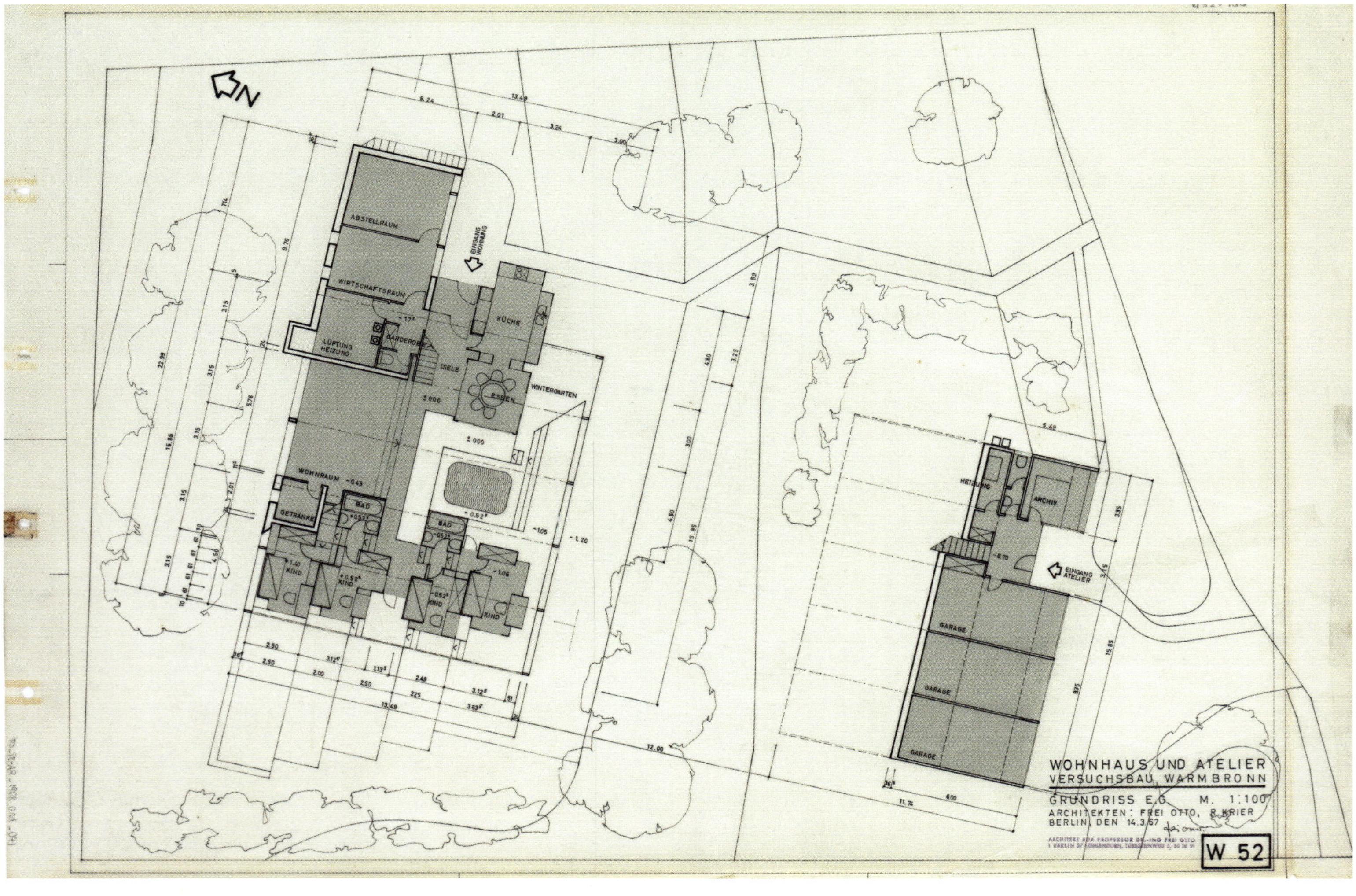

ABSTELLRAUM

EINGANG WOHNUNG

WIRTSCHAFTSRAUM

KÜCHE

LÜFTUNG HEIZUNG

GARDEROBE

DIELE

ESSEN

WINTERGARTEN

WOHNRAUM

GETRÄNKE

BAD

KIND

HEIZUNG

ARCHIV

EINGANG ATELIER

GARAGE

GARAGE

GARAGE

WOHNHAUS UND ATELIER
VERSUCHSBAU WARMBRONN
GRUNDRISS E.G. M. 1:100
ARCHITEKTEN: FREI OTTO, R. KRIER
BERLIN, DEN 14.3.67

W 52

'Structural Design', residence and atelier building, cross-section and floor plan (March 1967)

Rear of the residence with the 'great shell' in wintertime

Path through the garden
from the atelier building
to the residence in wintertime

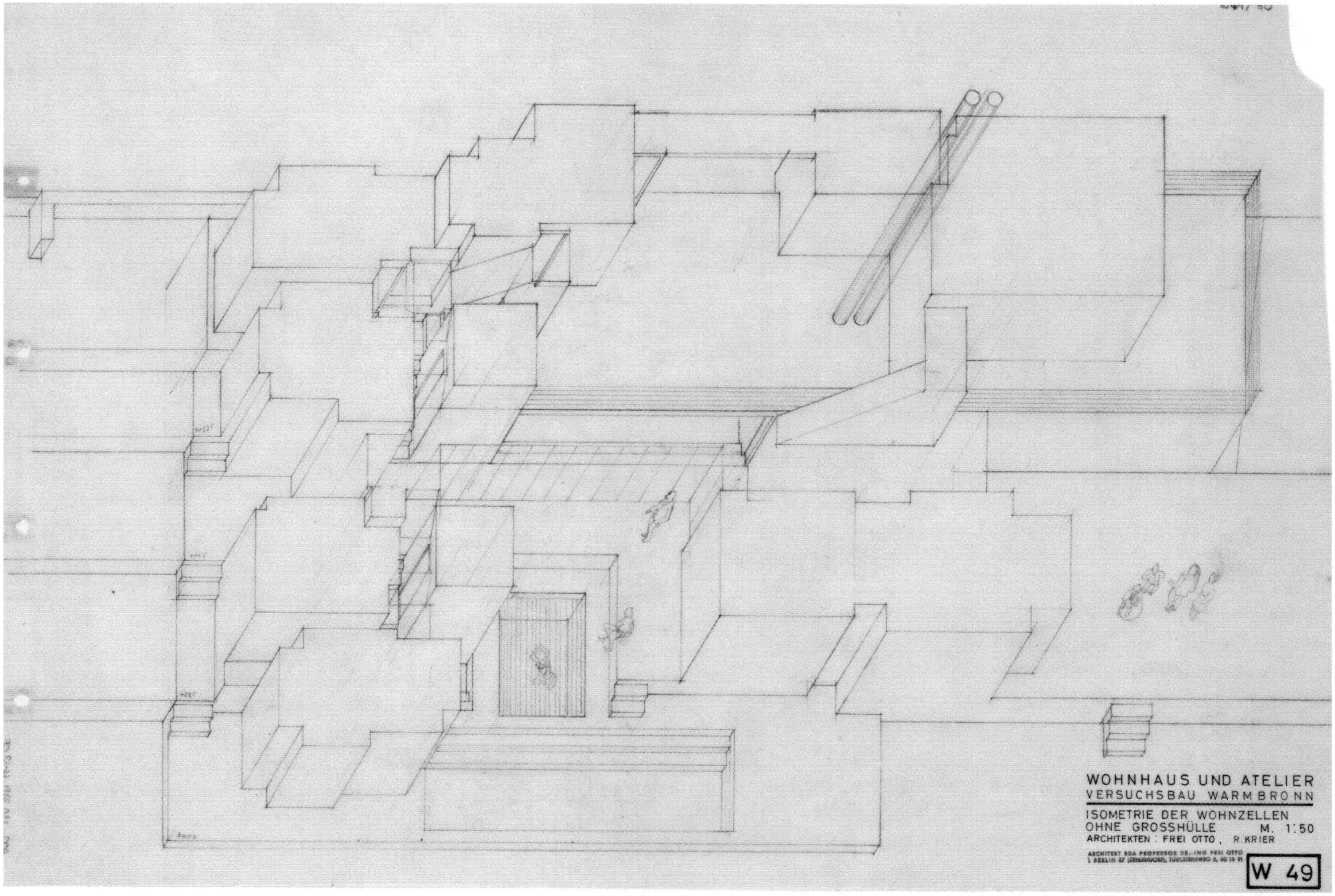

WOHNHAUS UND ATELIER
VERSUCHSBAU WARMBRONN
ISOMETRIE DER WOHNZELLEN
OHNE GROSSHÜLLE M. 1:50
ARCHITEKTEN: FREI OTTO, R. KRIER
W 49

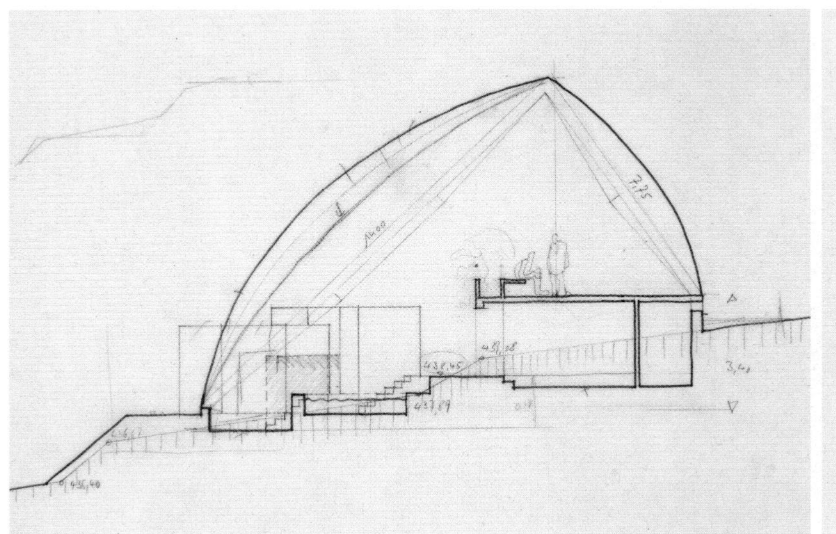

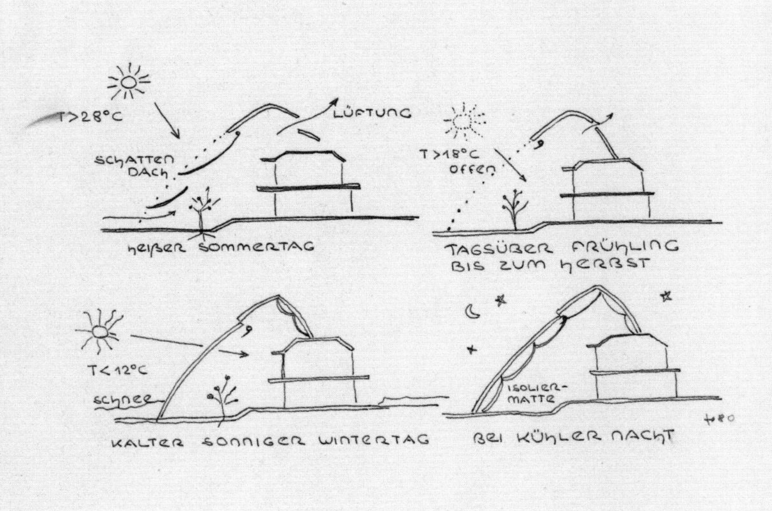

'Structural Design', isometric view of residential modules without the 'great shell'

'Organic Modern Design', cross-section of residence with the 'great shell' and various roof shape modifications

Sketch by Frei Otto explaining the different climatic concepts of the 'great shell' (1980)

The 'great shell' with plants in wintertime

Terrace within the 'great shell' with (empty) water basin

Residence with closed and opened entry from the garden

Frei Otto, Peter Stromeyer and Johann-Gerhard Helmcke: How Does Nature Build, and the Tent-Makers?

Walter Scheiffele

In 1914, during an early phase of modernist lightweight construction, when Paul Scheerbart and Bruno Taut erected their Glass Pavilion at the Cologne Werkbund Exhibition, under the aegis of the programme, 'Ohne einen Glaspalast ist das Leben eine Last' (Without a glass palace, life's a burden), the new building materials and their flexibility and lightweight qualities must have seemed like a prescient view of things to come. One of the places where the future development of lightweight construction would take off – and where it would also reach a peak of excellence – was Stuttgart.

During the National Socialist era, when Albert Speer's monumental stone architecture enjoyed its triumphal heyday, the Stuttgart School under Fritz Leonhardt was already promoting more materially efficient reinforced concrete building. The second phase of lightweight construction began in West Berlin in the 1950s, when Frei Otto turned his attention towards lighter and more mobile materials, and towards the use of textiles, in his doctoral thesis *Das hängende Dach* (The Hanging Roof).[1] In his magnum opus, Gottfried Semper had already offered the unexpected argument that stone architecture had its origin in textile structures.[2] Now, for Frei Otto as well, textile materials represented a transition to a new, mobile building culture. Like Semper, who had called attention to the relationship between the words 'Wand' (wall) and 'Gewand' (garment), Frei Otto posited a close relationship between textiles and construction with the terms 'Haut' (skin or membrane) and 'Dachhaut' (roof covering, literally 'roof skin').[3]

The 1950s and 1960s offered the necessary preconditions for the development of lightweight construction. Fritz Leonhardt was rector of the Stuttgart Institute of Technology (Technische Hochschule Stuttgart, TH Stuttgart) from 1967 until 1969. Peter Stromeyer headed the tent construction firm L. Stromeyer & Co. in Konstanz, attracting attention with his early lightweight structures at the German National Garden Show (Bundesgartenschau) in Kassel in 1955 and in Berlin's Hansaviertel district in 1957. And already beginning in 1961, the biologist Johann-Gerhard Helmcke, a tenured professor at the Technical University of Berlin (Technische Universitat Berlin, TU Berlin), led the research group 'Biologie und Bauen' (Biology and Building) together with Frei Otto.

Concerning his first meeting with Frei Otto in 1954, Leonhardt remarked in his autobiography that Otto's 'ideas fit perfectly with my efforts concerning lightweight building, as I had already presented them in detail in my 1940 essay "Leichtbau, eine Forderung unserer Zeit" [Lightweight Construction, a demand of for our time].'[4] It hardly seems surprising, then, that Leonhardt – who would, in his capacity as an engineer, endow Otto's early membrane structures beginning in 1957 with the requisite stability – pressed for Otto's appointment in Stuttgart: 'In 1964, I succeeded in having him appointed to a permanent teaching position at the University of Stuttgart and setting up an "Institute for Lightweight Structures" (IL) for him, which would become an extremely lively and productive research station. In the beginning, it was, to be sure, far from easy to persuade the evaluators at the German Research Foundation to approve Otto's research proposals. But soon, at my instigation, the University of Stuttgart approved the Collaborative Research Centre 64, devoted to "Lightweight Structures". This also meant that adequate research resources would be available to Frei Otto.'[5]

Just as there is a Siemensstadt in Berlin, there is a Stromeyersdorf in Konstanz. The former factory site on Lake Constance, where the expansive bleaching facilities still stand, accommodated the textile works of L. Stromeyer & Co. GmbH, founded in 1873. In 1976, the Institute for Lightweight Structures (Institut für leichte Flächentragwerke, IL) published the report *Zelte/Tents*,[6] in which Frei Otto shares his vivid memories of Peter Stromeyer, with whom he had developed large tent structures with novel membrane bracing systems over a period of decades. It is a striking homage to a 'tent maker' who was joined to Otto by a close lifelong friendship.

Otto did not, however, enjoy this level of friendship with Fritz Leonhardt, the renowned structural engineer who ensured the structural stability of Otto's large tents, and who had brought him to Stuttgart. About Leonhardt, he remarked, 'I was looking for the engineer for tent building. That was the problem. Many barriers had to be overcome. It took a lot of courage for me to dare to approach him. I succeeded. Fritz Leonhardt did participate, although he did not show his enthusiasm. But the first barrier was overcome. I made a great effort to maintain and strengthen this first link.' All the same, 'There were doubts. Leonhardt was different. He had already built beautiful bridges for the "Autobahn" in the 30s under Todt, during an era which made us young war participants shudder.' Thus, 'a cooperation, which was to last some 12 years, was initiated. Many considered it as an exemplary cooperation between an architect and an engineer, and during that time it was in fact just that.'[7]

But to return to Peter Stromeyer, who in 1952 had taken over the tent manufacturer in Stromeyersdorf. A trained textile merchant, he understood little about tent construction at the time. Nevertheless, in 1953, he offered Frei Otto an opportunity to familiarize himself with their workshops, to use them and to engage there in experimentation, in the process acquiring knowledge together with Otto and becoming a tent builder who would shape an era. Frei Otto commented, 'I shall never forget this week at Constance. It was one of the most productive working weeks of my whole life.'[8] He familiarized himself with operations, getting to know the people 'who designed the large tents, those who built and constructed them, those who sewed them together into large pieces, laid them on the sail-loft and then assembled them into large tents.'[9] This learning process involved a close connection between theory and practice – also a characteristic of future work at the IL: 'But we not only set up theories, we did things. As soon as an idea emerged, it was realized with the help of carpenters, tentmakers, and locksmiths.'[10]

As a tent builder, Stromeyer left his mark on an era during which the chemical industry brought new synthetic fibres onto the market – polyamide (nylon, Perlon), polyester (Trevira), polyacrylonitrile (PAN, Dolan), PVC and PCV, along with fiberglass and many others: 'These new fibers had to be studied to see whether they could be used for tent building and whether they could be woven, coated, and produced in bulk.'[11] Stromeyer 'introduced new ideas and techniques, which right up to the present, are part of the standard procedures of building with resistant fabrics; and he himself has gained a place in architecture. Without Peter Stromeyer's activities, some of the best known building events of the 60s would have been unthinkable, such as the Interbau Exhibit, the German Pavilion at Monteral, the world exposition at Osaka, and the roof of the Olympic Games at Munich.'[12] For Frei Otto and his colleague Berthold Burkhardt, this meant that 'Peter Stromeyer managed to turn tentmaking from a big trade of the textile branch, which was considered to be indecent by engineers and architects, into the art of lightweight architecture. This takes courage and engagement, as an expert, designer and businessman.'[13]

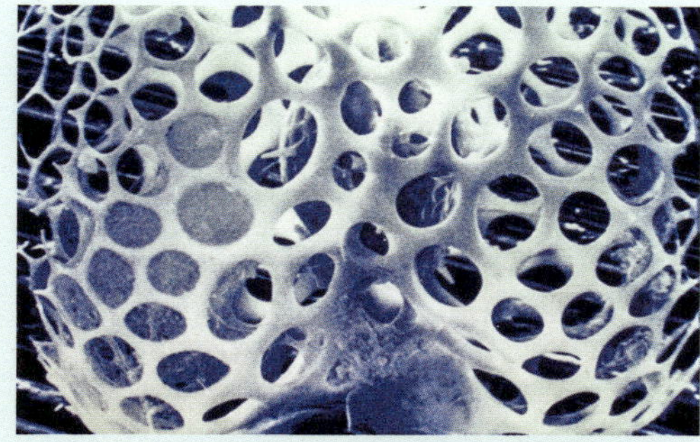

Radiolaria seen through an electron microscope, image from Frei Otto's slide collection (*c.* 1971)

Form study by Frei Otto for an inflatable structure with an interior drainage system, photograph of a plaster model (*c.* 1960)

Membrane from an amoeboid floor plan, experimental construction by Frei Otto for his publication *Zugbeanspruchte Konstruktionen* (*Tensile Structures*), vol. 1 (*c.* 1961)

The degree to which Stromeyer stood for the feasible – as opposed to the conceivable – was documented by Frei Otto during negotiations to finance the German Pavilion in Montreal, when West Germany's highest-ranking building official confronted Stromeyer with the question: '"Do you think this project is feasible?" Stromeyer: "Yes". "Would you act as the general contractor?" Stromeyer: "Yes". Rossig: "How much will it cost?" Stromeyer: "We can only estimate that. Our computation is 2.6 million DM for the net, membrane, masts and erection." Mertz: "Are you prepared to accept the commission on a cost-plus basis and to begin work immediately?" Stromeyer: "Yes".'[14] And yet, 'All manner of distinctions were hung on the breasts of the architects and engineers. Peter Stromeyer, however, was seldom mentioned.'[15]

About her father's relationship to Frei Otto, Gisela Stromeyer wrote, 'My father had a wonderful, loud laugh. He was known for it. Frei Otto, too, loved my father's laugh. They became friends through their collaboration and through pondering over new ideas in tent construction. Both of them valued their work together greatly and remained friends for the rest of their lives. I still remember the beautiful speech Frei Otto delivered at my father's funeral. It was important to him that my father's contribution to tent construction not be forgotten, that people knew that their collaboration had also been enormously important for him. My father regarded the time that he spent collaborating with Frei as one of the most wonderful experiences of his life, and he threw himself into their joint work with openness and enthusiasm.'[16]

While much survives in Konstanz related to the exchange and collaboration between Stromeyer and Frei Otto, the saai | Archive for Architecture and Engineering at the KIT in Karlsruhe also houses extensive material concerning Otto and Fritz Leonhardt. And the Staatsbibliothek in Berlin, the city's State Library preserves the estate of the biologist Johann-Gerhard Helmcke, which contains a wealth of material on the biologist's relationship with Otto, including their intensive correspondence. Their exchanges reflect research into the microscopic natural world, including diatoms and radiolarians, whose structures are well adapted to shaping the materials used in lightweight construction.

At the TU Berlin, Helmcke – who first gained access to the new electron microscopes of Siemens & Halske early on, in 1939 – was able to produce images of microorganisms with a high degree of definition that provided his academic colleagues with entirely new insights into the structural characteristics of organic life. In 1957, he wrote, 'Only now are we able to recognize structures with our own eyes whose existence had hitherto only been presumed, once again enjoying that delight in discovery experienced by the first users of light microscopes at the sight of an unexpected abundance of forms; because in the newly accessed range of sizes, biological objects present a even greater diversity of structures then had been previously assumed. Arising immediately together with the detection of these new structures, however, is the question of the functions they fulfil.'[17] Already among Helmcke's students arouse the first suspicions that their professor's interest in the features of these microorganisms might extend to the realm of architecture, considering he had already spoken of 'brickwork' and 'reinforced concrete' in relation to his investigations of the structure of teeth.

In 1958, Frei Otto founded the Institute for the Development of Lightweight Construction (Entwicklungsstätte für den Leichtbau, EL) in Berlin-Zehlendorf as a private research centre. At that time, he had already begun his exploration of a new region of architecture with his tent structures and the completely novel characteristics of the building materials involved. Later, recalling when he stood with Stromeyer on the membrane of the large tent structure in Montreal, he recognized the entirely singular quality of the construction: 'Suddenly, it began to rise, then stood still, then sunk again. Wow, I thought, we're standing on the belly of a whale, a gigantic whale!'[18] At his EL, Otto undertook his first attempts to make his transparent buildings mobile, lightweight and climate-proof, installing a translucent interior and exterior layer. The interior space was heated in wintertime,

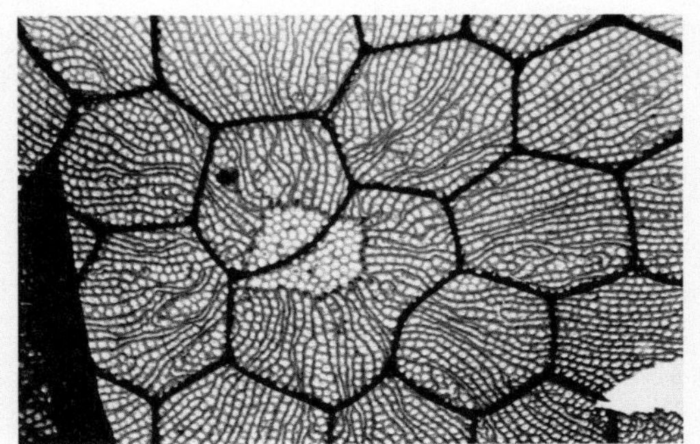

while the outer layer served as a buffer zone. In summertime, by contrast, curtains and mobile wall elements generated various zones of illumination and shade that facilitated his work drafting designs and creating models.

At the TU Berlin, meanwhile, Helmcke sought suitable objects for his research into microscopic realms and – just as users of light microscopes before him – identified organisms in the process that seemed especially well adapted for his needs: 'During the early years of the development and use of the electron microscope, we sought objects with the greatest possible structural precision, with whose help we could test the quality of the electron microscope lenses. At the time, however, there were virtually no objects fashioned by human hands that were fine enough to be adequate to our purposes to have served as corresponding test objects. So we searched the realm of inanimate and animate nature for suitable forms and found them among the same organisms that had also been used for light microscopes in testing high-performance equipment. These delicate, glass-like structures are the outer cell membranes of naturally occurring unicellular plants, which are referred to in the technical realm as kieselguhr, but in biology go under the names of diatoms or Bacillariophyta.'[19]

To build without the involvement of architects – were 'laypeople' capable of that? Together with the growth of leisure time, Frei Otto observed a tendency towards 'do-it-yourself' building. But were the capacities for autonomous, independent building growing as well? Were architects and engineers becoming superfluous? As early as 1957, Otto shared the conclusions of his observations in a lecture delivered at the TH Stuttgart: 'The crystalline building and the restless individual are not compatible. The building must mediate between movement and rest, between the transitory and the permanent. That is the significance of every construction method that enables alterable and adaptable, adjustable and variable buildings. That is the significance of lightweight construction in our time.'[20] And such 'alterable' lightweight construction was beginning to emancipate itself from architects: 'Whether the form is beautiful or ugly, whether a building looks good or bad, is dependent not on the design but on the occupant.'[21] For Otto, one aim of lightweight architecture was 'to reduce everything constructive to a minimum on behalf of living. I can conceive of the ideal structure only in the absence of material [...] With alterable buildings, there is no predetermined, finished form that can be designed or developed, but instead constructed forms emerge simultaneously with the necessary functions, which change together and which disappear together with the function's termination.'[22] The architect will not disappear, but his or her role is to undergo a change: emerging in place of a 'creator' is a supervising 'gardener' or a treating 'physician'[23].

In relation to this newly emerging field, it hardly seems surprising that students of architecture should have developed an interest in biology. In 1960/61, when Otto conducted a seminar in lightweight construction together with the architect Peter Poelzig at the TU Berlin, Thomas Sieverts, a student and seminar participant, called their attention to Helmcke as a 'specialist in lightweight structures'.

The architect and the biologist became acquainted. With Helmcke, Otto got to know an enthusiastic scientist who was prepared to transgress the boundaries of his own field. Addressing the German Research Foundation (Deutsche Forschungsgemeinschaft, DFG), Helmcke once remarked that he had learned, 'to see the shells of diatoms with the eyes of a physical chemist, a crystallographer, a structural engineer, an architect, to understand the observed structures from the perspectives of other academic disciplines.[24] And Otto shared this attitude: 'For engineers and architects, the results of observations made with the electron microscope were stimulating. The shell structures of the diatoms – about which we cannot even assert that they are indeed constructions – resemble some of the most recent developments in the field of widespan, prestressed surface structures that are characterized by their minimal material expenditure. Needless to say, the creators of these outstanding achievements in civil engineering were unfamiliar with diatoms.'[25]

Diatom, image from Frei Otto's slide collection (*c.* 1971)

In the following years, 1961 and 1962, Helmcke's and Otto's advances into the realm of biological building began to bear fruit. In 1961, in issue 7 of the German technical architecture publication *Deutsche Bauzeitung*, which presented the most important protagonists of shell and membrane construction, Otto and Stromeyer wrote about 'Pneumatische Konstruktionen' (Pneumatic Structures), and one year later, Helmcke and Otto authored an article about 'Lebende und technische Konstruktionen' (Living and Technical Structures). In 1962, Jürgen Joedicke, who had begun establishing the field of architectural theory at the TH Stuttgart, published *Schalenbau. Konstruktion und Gestaltung* (*Shell Architecture*), opening his text with a seemingly enigmatic image of an oversized diatom shell drawn from Helmcke's collection of images. It illustrated how closely architecture and nature had converged – and the degree to which research in this area had begun to shift from Berlin to Stuttgart.

Shell structures were to become an important building type of the time. In Stuttgart, a stronghold of civil and structural engineering centred around Fritz Leonhardt, a climate began to develop in the early 1960s that was advantageous for pioneers of lightweight construction like Frei Otto. Helmut Bickenbach, a professor of statics at the TU Berlin, had already referred Otto to Leonhardt in 1955: 'Bickenbach advised me to collaborate with Leonhardt in Stuttgart. Wouldn't it be wonderful if a civil engineer of the highest calibre were finally to develop an interest in tent building and could remove all the limitations that kept tent construction from being taken seriously?'[26] In January 1964, when Otto wrote, 'Unfortunately, in Berlin, I'm always at a disadvantage', the decision to go to Stuttgart was a *fait accompli*.

In Stuttgart, Otto's Institute for Lightweight Structures (IL) was established on the campus for Civil Engineering. The tent-shaped building, a prototype erected in preparation for the German Pavilion in Montreal, rejected all forms of 'correct' architecture – it seemed destined to become a 'centre for crackpots'. Otto remarked, 'At one time, the Bauhaus was a "centre for crackpots" too. It was oriented towards the urgent issues of the 1920s. The formula was simple: bring together a number of capable crackpots with a pronounced feel for the possibilities of their own time. No specific tendency was prescribed. That only emerged later as a result of their findings.'[27] And the urgent issues of the 1970s, Otto was absolutely convinced, would lead towards fresh experimentation: 'The 1970s will bring unconventional, completely new solutions in countless different areas. The 1970s are the great reservoir of the future.'[28]

Membranes and shells were the elementary structures, regarded as fundamental for both nature and technology, that were introduced by Otto and Helmcke through the Sonderforschungsbereich 64 'Weitgespannte Flächentragwerke' (Collaborative Research Centre 64 'Widespan Surface Structures'). Otto said, 'Two-dimensional constructions are of great significance in biology and technology, which is to say, flat surface structures in a variety of forms. We know the two groups: they are membranes and shells. Membranes are soft and flexurally rigid. They can only be subjected to tensile stress. Shells are, in contrast, hard and rigid. They can absorb any kind of load but require for this substantially more material. Shells are usually curved surface structures and are widespread in biology. There are diatoms, radiolarians, seashells, snails, crabs, skullcaps, turtles, insect bodies, legumes, eggshells and much more. [...] In biology, we encounter tensile-stressed, flexible surface structures in skins of all kinds, outer and inner hides, intestines, air and liquid bladders, eggs, larvae, worms and caterpillars. Such skins often enclose tissue – but the webs of spiders in all of their forms belong to this group as well.'[29] It was the inexhaustible inventory of living structures, between membrane and shell, that impelled Otto and Helmcke to undertake so many years of investigation. Ultimately, they were to realize the universal significance of 'pneus'.

The IL regarded itself as standing not just in the tradition of the Bauhaus, but also in parallel with the Ulm School of Design (Hochschule für Gestaltung Ulm,

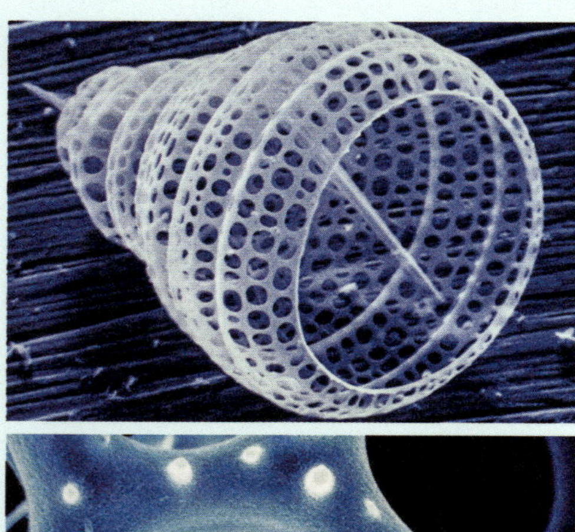

Radiolarians, images from Frei Otto's slide collection (*c.* 1971)

HfG Ulm); during the 1960s and 1970s, the IL developed into one of the most extraordinary research facilities of the Federal Republic of Germany. Central to its activities was a foundation in the connection between biology and building unprecedented in the history of architecture, the two main protagonists here being Frei Otto and Johann-Gerhard Helmcke.

In 1969, when Helmcke again turned his attention towards radiolarians, his letters to Otto reveal unmistakably the degree to which the architect's perspective had shaped his own view of the single-celled forms. He continually alternates between biological and technical terms: 'If we relate the radiolarians to your constructions, it would be possible to derive ideas, such as, installing economical minimal structures, consisting of the finest net, between such masts, corresponding to residential units [...] The spikes need to be of stable material, like the masts of your structures. Yet, with you, the components that emanate from these masts are fashioned from flexible materials (cables or membranes). Why should this be any different with the radiolarians? The soft material, accordingly, must consist of protoplasm, which would of course no longer be present in the dead skeletons examined by the electron microscope.'[30] While Helmcke moves emphatically here into the field of architecture and structural engineering, the avant-garde of lightweight construction would consequently engage in novel and soaring intellectual flights involving domed or tent structures – entire cities, even the Arctic itself, could one day be vaulted over with such constructions.

Such large-scale projects propelled interest in the microcosm, from the inorganic structures of diatoms and radiolarians to the organic – to the pneus. The way in which the term 'pneu' is to be conceptualized and the wealth of empirical material that could be assembled on the topic is illustrated by an extended discussion between Otto and Helmcke, which is among the highpoints of their common understanding of lightweight forms. Taking place in the autumn of 1973 was the colloquium 'Pneus',[31] the contributions for which were collected and published in 1977 in the IL publication *Pneus in Natur und Technik/Pneus in Nature and Technics*.[32] Otto commented, 'This is and will probably continue to be our key publication.'

Between 1972 and 1973, during preparations for the colloquium, Otto and Helmcke struggled with the concept and the empirical aspects of the pneu, and the way in which the two could be brought together. The pneumatic principal, which the two sought to buttress through their investigations, stipulated that a membrane that is subject to stronger inner pressure relative to weaker external pressure is a pneu. But with regard to the jellyfish, which Otto already regarded as a definite pneu, Helmcke objected: 'The interior of the jellyfish does not experience greater pressure than the surrounding environment. The more I occupy myself with the problem of the pneu – and I have gone through mountains of books on the subject in recent months – I am more and more convinced that, in the context of zoology, and when delving into the finest structural elements, the number of unambiguous instances becomes smaller and smaller.'[33]

While the search for images and for real pneus was intensified at the IL in preparation for the approaching colloquium, Otto sought to come to terms with Helmcke's objections, while trying not to become impatient. 'My dear Herr Helmcke!', he wrote out on a manuscript by Helmcke on biology and the topic of the pneu: 'I am inconsolable. Why do you make things so complicated by saying that a ship is *not* an aeroplane. The important thing here is to state what is characteristic. What I miss is a sentence saying that every cell enclosed by a flexible cell wall *is capable* of withstanding high internal pressure, which only rarely reaches the bursting point (and often never). Why don't you also point out that all membranes with an extended area, e.g., the epidermis, are capable of withstanding greater internal pressure/e.g., weight, blood pressure, CO_2, but that their form in a normal state – genetically manipulated – can display only such forms that may be created with pneus.'[34] During this critical phase, the architect took the initiative and bolstered the faltering biologist. In the middle of 1973, Helmcke thanked

Membrane over a star-shaped floor plan, test structure by Frei Otto for his publication *Zugbeanspruchte Konstruktionen* (*Tensile Structures*), vol. 1 (*c.* 1961)

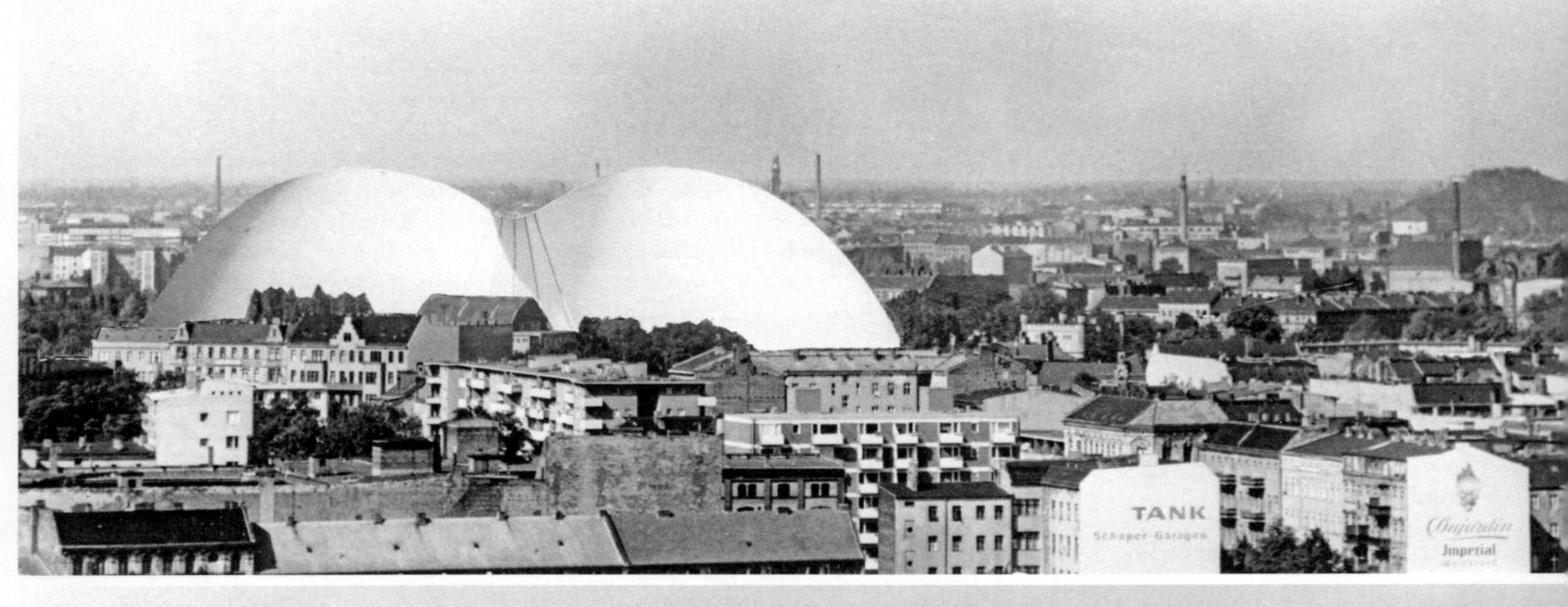

him for recognizing the 'crux of the problem' and calling his attention to the 'problematic as a whole': 'Looking back at my nearly 20 years of activity at the TU, I regard our joint work as having the most interesting and the most productive theme.'[35] But the pneus continued to resist being pinned down definitively as a term, and Helmcke returned to the topic in the autumn of 1973: 'You define the term in a far broader way so that it also encompasses the "presumptive potency", i.e., that a balloon is a pneu, even when it contains no air. There remains the possibility that it be inflated with air, which is to say, it possesses the designated capacity = presumptive potency. For me, a balloon is only a pneu if and when it has been inflated and is subject to greater internal pressure then that from the external environment.'[36] In another letter, Helmcke insists again upon his more restrictive definition of the pneu: 'You say that a duvet cover is a pneu, even when it lies on the ground without any filling. – Then I would have to ask: Is a sail a pneu when the wind blows it, or sucks it in from the lee side? Is a slack sail when there is no wind also a pneu?'[37] For the approaching colloquium, the biologist summarized his questions on the changing forms of the pneu: '1) How does a pneu come to exist? 2) How is a pneu defined to the extent that it has not yet assumed any pneumatic function? 3) From which moment and for how long can we contain a pneu

Large pneumatic structures in an urban setting, photomontages (*c.* 1962); Frei Otto attempted to show how pneumatic structures could be integrated into the landscape

with a genuinely pneumatic form? 4) How does the transition take place from a pneu with a pneumatic function to a static form (e.g., the petrified shell of a diatom)?'[38]

Otto replied to Helmcke with his theses on the pneu: 'Even an open water container, a hot air balloon or even a sail, into which the wind blows, generating a pressure difference between the windward and leeward sides, is by definition a pneu [...] A pneu can be empty, partially filled or stretched to the point of bursting. Even an uninflated balloon is a pneu. It is a membrane structure with the *capacity* to transmit forces.' And, ultimately, 'The non-hardened, living cell is a pneu. The cell is the architectural element of living nature, in multicellular organisms, the cells form the *structure* of the [construction].'[39]

In the end, the biologist and the architect did come to agree. Otto wrote, 'Your essay, excellent, and the courage to say, "in the beginning was the pneu". Many thanks! [...] If only we could make *your* terms and *my* terms identical. [...] If each of us cleave on our, to be sure, similar but also quite differentiated positions with regard to pneus, that wouldn't bother me in the least.'[40]

Helmcke replied to Otto, at the same time outlining the guiding principle of their epoch, which had turned from biology towards architecture: 'Given the reality of constant development, we find it difficult to define our terms all around; for, once we have described a form, an organ, a stage of development, etc., we find that, in most instances, just a moment later, it has already undergone change.'[41]

1 Frei Otto, *Das hängende Dach. Gestalt und Struktur*, doctoral thesis, Berlin 1954.
2 Gottfried Semper, *Der Stil in den Technischen und Tektonischen Künsten oder Praktische Aesthetik. Ein Handbuch für Techniker, Künstler und Kunstfreunde*, vol. 1: *Die Textile Kunst für sich betrachtet und in Beziehung zur Baukunst*, 2nd ed., Munich 1878; translated into English as *Style in the Technical and Tectonic Arts; or, Practical Aesthetics*, trans. Henry Francis Mallgrave and Michael Robinson, Los Angeles 2004.
3 Gottfried Semper, *Die Vier Elemente der Baukunst. Ein Beitrag zur vergleichenden Baukunde*, Braunschweig 1851, pp. 57 f.; in English translation as *The Four Elements of Architecture and Other Writings*, trans. Harry F. Mallgrave and Wolfgang Herrmann, Cambridge, 1989, p. 104.
4 Fritz Leonhardt, *Baumeister in einer umwälzenden Zeit. Erinnerungen*, 2nd ed., Stuttgart 1998, p. 216.
5 Leonhardt, *Baumeister in einer umwälzenden Zeit*, pp. 217 f.
6 *Zelte 1/Tents 1. Bilder ausgeführter weitspannbarer Membrankonstruktionen. Anmerkungen aus der Praxis. Mitteilungen des Instituts* für *leichte Flächentragwerke (IL)*, no. 16, ed. Frei Otto, Stuttgart/Bern 1976.
7 *Zelte 1/Tents 1*, p. 121.
8 *Zelte 1/Tents 1*, p. 117.
9 *Zelte 1/Tents 1*, p. 115.
10 *Zelte 1/Tents 1*, p. 117.
11 *Zelte 1/Tents 1*, p. 122.
12 *Zelte 1/Tents 1*, p. 114.
13 *Zelte 1/Tents 1*, p. 5.
14 *Zelte 1/Tents 1*, p. 134.
15 *Zelte 1/Tents* 1, p. 134.
16 Gisela Stromeyer in an email to the author, 20 April 2024.
17 Johann-Gerhard Helmcke, 'Elektronenmikroskopische Untersuchungen über Einlagerungen und die physiologische Bedeutung anorganischer Hartsubstanzen im Organismus', lecture delivered on 15 May 1957, published in: *Leopoldina, Mitteilungen der Deutschen Akademie der Naturforscher*, no. 3, 1957, pp. 48–52.
18 Louis Saul (director), *Frei Otto. Von Seifenblasen und Zelten*, first broadcast: arte, 22 April 2005.
19 Johann-Gerhard Helmcke, 'Form und Funktion von Diatomeenschalen. Gesetzmäßigkeiten im Kleinen', in: *Beiträge zur Naturkunde Niedersachsens*, no. 12, 1959, p. 3.
20 Frei Otto, 'Die Bedeutung des Leichtbaus in unserer Zeit', lecture delivered on 19 November 1957 at the TH Stuttgart, published in: *Mitteilungen der Entwicklungsstätte für den Leichtbau (EL)*, no. 1, 1958, pp. 4–11, here p. 7.
21 Otto, 'Die Bedeutung des Leichtbaus in unserer Zeit', p. 10.
22 Otto, 'Die Bedeutung des Leichtbaus in unserer Zeit', pp. 8 f.
23 Otto, 'Die Bedeutung des Leichtbaus in unserer Zeit', p. 10.
24 Johann-Gerhard Helmcke to Anita Hoffmann, DFG, 2 November 1981, Staatsbibliothek zu Berlin – Preußischer Kulturbesitz (SBPK), manuscript department, estate of J.-G. Helmcke, Folder 58.
25 Frei Otto, typescript, received 26 January 1965, SBPK, manuscript department, estate of J.-G. Helmcke, Box 28.
26 Rainer Graefe, 'Where Architecture and Civil Engineering Meet', in: Winfried Nerdinger (ed.), *Frei Otto: Complete Works; Lightweight Construction, Natural Design*, exh. cat. Architekturmuseum der TU München, Basel/Boston/Berlin 2005, p. 73.
27 Frei Otto, 'Eine Interbau und ein Spinnerzentrum', reprinted in Berthold Burkhardt (ed.), *Frei Otto. Schriften und Reden, 1951–1983*, Braunschweig/Wiesbaden 1984, p. 95.
28 Otto, 'Eine Interbau und ein Spinnerzentrum', p. 90.
29 Frei Otto, 'Biologie, Klimatologie und die Technik des Bauens', in: *Technisch-Wissenschaftliche Blätter der Süddeutschen Zeitung, der Mensch und die Technik*, 13/181, 28 May 1971.
30 Helmcke to Otto, 30 October 1969, SBPK, manuscript department, estate of J.-G. Helmcke, Box 28.
31 Kolloquium 'Pneus', 3rd interdisciplinary colloquium in the series 'Biologie und Bauen' (Biology and Building), 23/24 February 1973, Institute for Lightweight Structures (IL), Universität Stuttgart.
32 *Pneus in Natur und Technik/Pneus in Nature and Technics, Mitteilungen des Instituts für leichte Flächentragwerke (IL)*, no. 9, ed. Klaus Bach and Eda Schauer, Stuttgart 1977, p. 5.
33 Helmcke to Otto, 1 February 1973, SBPK, manuscript department, estate of I.-G. Helmcke, Box 28.
34 Johann-Gerhard Helmcke, 'Pneus', manuscript with handwritten remarks by Frei Otto, 16 February 1973, SBPK, Box 28.
35 Helmcke to Otto, 1 July 1973, SBPK, Box 28.
36 Helmcke to Otto, 13 September 1973, SBPK, Box 28.
37 Helmcke to Otto, 3 October 1973, SBPK, Box 28.
38 Helmcke to Otto, 18 September 1973, SBPK, Box 28.
39 Frei Otto, typescript, undated, in part with handwritten corrections, SBPK, Box 28.
40 Otto to Helmcke, 5 September 1973, SBPK, Box 28.
41 Helmcke to Otto, 5 October 1973, SBPK, Box 28.

Plural Ecologies: Frei Otto's Integrative Environmental Understanding as an Architectural Avant-Garde

Georg Vrachliotis

'An international building exhibition calls for timeliness, clear proposals and bold initiatives for new ideas. It is indispensable that the handling of ecological problems occupy as much space in the exhibition as is commensurate with its importance for society. It is indispensable that we showcase how this change of consciousness was anticipated by the initiatives of garden and landscape architects, of architects and city planners, as early as the 1920s, before becoming fully active in the 1950s. It is indispensable that the most active tendencies in contemporary architecture are given a voice, tendencies that have enjoyed international success, beginning in Germany, and are now entering Germany once again from the outside. Indispensable is a presentation of the ecology movement in architecture in its broadest tendencies. Clearly, however, our group is confident it can furnish a convincing statement here, since internationally, it has demonstrably worked in this area for the longest period of time and with the greatest persistence (for more than 30 years). This can be substantiated by research, teaching, designs, projects and realized buildings.'[1]

With this incisive demand, Frei Otto opened a publication whose design was as unconventional as the ideas it propagated. The veritable patchwork assembled from a great number of black-and-white photocopies and sundry text fragments in the most diverse typefaces and sizes, it exploded the conventions of traditional book design. With its free, horizontal layout of text and images, handwritten marginalia and glosses, as well as collaged copies, drawings and diagrams, it resembled a scholarly publication less than an experimental zine – a creative manifesto that blurred the boundaries between documentation and activism.

Wohn-Be-Reiche im Garten. Vorbereitende Studie für das Bauvorhaben 'Ökohaus' Berlin (Living Spaces in a Garden: Preparatory Study for the 'Eco-House' Building Project in Berlin) – to give the publication's full title – was presented to the public on 9 May 1985 at a press conference of the International Building Exhibition (Internationale Bauausstellung, IBA) in West Berlin. Originally, the booklet, nearly 150 pages in length and produced in an extremely limited run, was intended for internal use only and had been conceived as a 'research project for the clarification of ecological principles in building'.[2] Its experimental, almost provisional production aesthetic underscored the sense of urgency with which Frei Otto sought to tackle ecological challenges in architecture.

But the study was more than a purely academic project. It was a direct response to the doubts expressed repeatedly during the planning process for the eco-houses (*Ökohäuser*) designed by Frei Otto and Hermann Kendel for West Berlin. Although Josef Paul Kleihues – then director of the division for New Building of the IBA – had explicitly commissioned Frei Otto with the conception and planning of an ecological residential building according to the principle of 'nature and construction', he suddenly entertained doubts about the ecological core of the project. The publication was hence also a strategic reply to the increasing

WOHN-BE-REICHE IM GARTEN · IBA BERLIN 1987

ANPASSUNGSFÄHIG BAUEN

Mit einer Tatsache konnte ich mich nie abfinden daß Architekten Hüllen für andere Menschen bauen, ohne daß diese dazu etwas sagen können. Noch schlimmer: daß sie Fassaden zeichnen, hinter denen irgendwelche Menschen wohnen, zu denen sie keine innere Beziehung haben.

Als Student war ich im Seminar von Hans Freese. Ich fragte meinen Lehrer, ob ich nicht den Entwurf für ein Wohnhaus machen könne - mehrere Geschosse, mit einer Stahlbeton-Skelettkonstruktion -, bei dem jeder Eigentümer seine eigene Wohnung selbst oder mit einem Architekten bauen könne.

Ich entwarf also ein Haus mit vielen Gefachen; bei einer Wohnung stellte ich mir vor, daß sie von LeCorbusier, eine andere von einem Provinzarchitekten, eine dritte von Frank Lloyd Wright ausgebaut würde. →

Freese antwortete mir, daß er sowas zwar nie tun würde, gab mir aber dennoch die Höchstnote. Warum, weiß ich selbst nicht. Gut war der Entwurf nicht. Aber er war ein Weg, den ich nie verlassen habe, obwohl ich nie ein solches Haus bauen durfte.

Ich veröffentlichte aber, hielt Vorträge über anpassungsfähige Architektur, traf mich in Berlin mit Yona Friedman, der die Gruppe 'D'ètudes d'architecture mobile' gegründet hatte, und vertrat in seiner Gruppe das anpassungsfähige Bauen mehr als das mobile.

Als die Entwicklungsstätte für den Leichtbau in Berlin 1958 gegründet wurde, veröffentlichte ich die 'Mitteilungen Nr. 6' dieser Entwicklungsstätte mit vielen Vorschlägen, wie man anpassungsfähige Wohn- und Geschäftshäuser bauen könne - auch die Idee, einen Turmschaft zu machen und die Häuser 'dran anzuhängen, entstand damals: das sog. 'Schaschlik-Haus'. F.O.

ANPASSUNGSFÄHIG BAUEN
ADAPTABLE BUILDING
L'ARCHITECTURE ADAPTABLE
JUNI 1959
6

Titelblatt Mitteilung Nr. 6, 1959
folgende Seite : Faksimile daraus

28

WOHNHÄUSER IN NEW YORK 1960

Nach meinen Eindrücken als Lehrer an der Washington University in St- Louis hatte ich die Idee, für ein freies Grundstück am Central Park in New York ein Wohnhaus zu entwerfen, nicht weit vom Guggenheim Museum (heute schon längst bebaut): drei Treppentürme, an die Wohnungen angehängt sind, Wohnungen mit Dachgärten, individuell gestaltet. Sie hießen bald in meinem Atelier 'die Schaschlik-Häuser'. Gebaut haben wir sie nie.

DIE HORIZONTALE SONNENUHR

Bereits als 14jähriger Junge hatte ich mir einmal einen Kompaß gebaut mit einer Sonnenuhr darauf. Wenn die Sonne schien und ich die Zeit wußte, konnte ich die Nordrichtung mit ihr feststellen - und die Kompaßnadel kontrollieren; wenn sie nicht schien, wußte ich zumindest, wo ich sie mir vorstellen konnte.

Noch als Student, als ich mich mit dem Wohnungsbau beschäftigte, konstruierte ich mit Hilfe eines Bauingenieur-Studenten eine kleine horizontale Sonnenuhr mit einem 1 cm hohen Stift. Eine größere auch mit 2,5 cm wurde gebaut, die man auf Modelle auflegen konnte, die man dann in der Sonne von Hand dreht - und damit den gesamten Schattenwurf von Gebäuden verfolgen konnte. Das Ziel war, daß kein Gebäude einem anderen die Sonne wegnimmt - und daß man erkennen konnte, welche Fassaden wie und aus welcher Richtung beleuchtet sind.

Diese Sonnenuhr wurde für die Berliner Breite konstruiert und hat dann später beim Entwurf der Sozialen-Wohnungsbau-Siedlung 'Alexandra-Stiftung' gute Dienste getan.

Im Jahre 1975 etwa konstruieren wir dann im Atelier Warmbronn eine Besonnungs-Maschine, die ebenfalls mit Sonnenlicht arbeitet. Man richtet sie gegen die Sonne aus und dreht dann das Modell darin - und kann damit die Besonnung schnell feststellen. Dies war eine selbstgebaute, sehr einfache Maschine. Sie wurde später noch mit einer parallelen Lichtquelle, einer Punktlicht-Lampe und einer Fresnel-Linse ausgerüstet. Mit ihr kann man direkt Modelle untersuchen - oder auch horizontale Sonnenuhren herstellen. Wir haben die Sonnenuhren dann in unserem Heft IL 11 veröffentlicht. F.O.

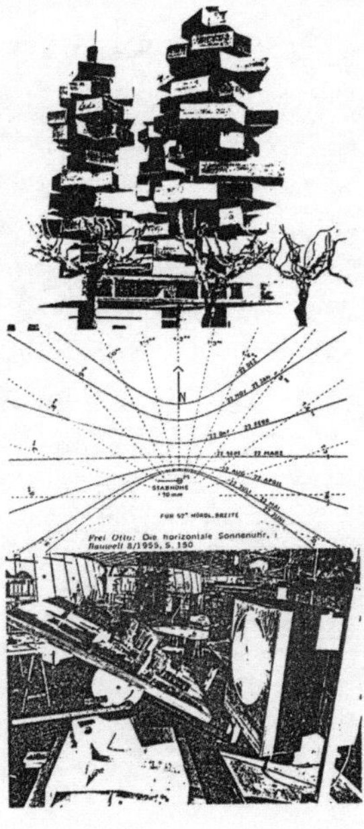

PROJEKT 1
ASKANISCHER PLATZ
1980 - 1981

ETAGENGRUNDSTÜCKE
INFRASTRUKTUR - GERÜST
BAUM - SKELETT
STAPELBARE BAUPLÄTZE
VERTIKALE WOHNSTRAßE
SKELETTKONSTRUKTION
FÜR INDIVIDUELLES
IM GARTEN
AUF DER ETAGE
FÜR STÄDTISCHES
WOHNEN
UND LEBEN
IN DER BERLINER INNENSTADT
SCHREBERGARTEN
SOLARHAUS
ANPASSUNGSFÄHIGE NATURENERGIEHÄUSER
OEKOSOLARISINDIVIDUSTADWOHNBAUM
WOHN(BE) REICHE IM GRÜNEN MIT
MATERIALERSPARNIS
SONNENENERGIE

47

pressure experienced by Otto and his team during the building exhibition and the need to defend their ecological principles in a city that was still firmly tied to traditional building methods. *Wohn-Be-Reiche im Garten* thus symbolized the attempt to build a bridge between visionary ideas and political reality, between the urgency of ecological change and the challenge of implementing and anchoring this change in the urban context of West Berlin.

'Ecological Building'

Illustrated on the front page of this publication, assembled with such a sense of urgency, is an architectural drawing that abolishes the boundaries between the built environment and nature. Positioned at the centre of the illustration is a multi-storey building whose façade, consisting of expansive glass surfaces, conveys a feeling of transparency and lightness. The building resembles a greenhouse designed to allow light to stream in and is, at the same time,

Title sheet and selected pages from Frei Otto's publication *Wohn-Be-Reiche im Garten* (1985) in conjunction with the IBA Berlin 1987

surrounded by luscious vegetation. Particularly noticeable is the green roof, which is not only covered in plant life, but also integrates technical apparatuses such as platforms, wind turbines and solar cells. These elements allude to a sustainable and future-oriented approach to building – an architecture that generates energy while maintaining harmony with nature. The roof is brimming with life: small groups of people are shown moving between various levels of the garden, indicating its collective use. The building's surroundings are densely overgrown, almost like a wild garden, and blend seamlessly into the architecture. The scene is framed by a tree on the left side, along with additional trees in the background, enhancing the impression that the building is not only embedded in nature, but has in fact become a part of it – a vision Otto had pursued in his designs and writings as early as the 1950s, in an attempt to pave the way for his multifaceted ecological understanding of architecture.

Accordingly, the table of contents also reads like a subjective map of ecological architecture and extends from fundamental theoretical deliberations to speculative design ideas, all the way to concrete projects, while also claiming to provide an orienting framework. With his usual concern for fundamentals, Frei Otto begins by elaborating upon his 'ideas about ecology' in the preface. Thus, almost immediately, he seeks to dispose of widespread myths about ecology, many of them traceable to the biologist Ernst Haeckel, in particular. Haeckel coined the term 'Ökologie' (ecology) in the nineteenth century, and well into the twentieth century, he advocated the popular view that nature constituted a kind of 'housekeeping', which is to say that it followed certain principles of 'economy' – a notion Otto emphatically questioned. In Otto's view, it was of central significance to correct this evidently obsolete vision of nature, while nonetheless fostering a scientifically grounded conception of ecological interrelation. He argued that nature was by no means consistently found in a state of equilibrium, underscoring the fact that human action often brought about far-reaching and even irreversible alterations to the natural environment. Otto's intention was nothing less than laying the groundwork for a new, differentiated perspective on the complex relationship between architecture and ecology, one that foregrounded both the inherent dynamism of nature and the responsibilities incumbent upon architects.

The first chapter bears the overarching title 'Ökologisches Bauen' (Ecological Building) and serves as an introduction to the theoretical principles and foundations of an ecologically oriented architecture, which Frei Otto had been investigating, together with his colleagues, during the previous decades. In this section, readers encountered text fragments composed by Frei Otto together with the Dutch landscape architect Louis Le Roy[3] and the Icelandic-Dutch pioneer of ecology Jón Kristinsson. These are presented alongside select projects intended in this juxtaposition to illustrate a new way of thinking in architecture – among them, Martin Wagner's contribution to the working group for a 'wachsendes Haus' (growing house; 1932)[4] and Erik Friberger's experimental residential building assembled from prefabricated sections in Gothenburg (1960).[5] These examples make it clear that Otto did not conceive of architecture merely as a technical craft, but rather that he saw it instead as an integral component of a comprehensive ecological system. These are not simply case studies, but instead guiding principles for the visionary approach to building aspired to by Otto and his team.

Logically enough, this is followed by a section devoted to Frei Otto's own work and to a strategic overview of his multifaceted activities and research projects – from energy and material-efficient construction all the way to ecological insulation materials. This chapter is noteworthy for Otto's structured overview of his own projects, beginning with his studies at the Technical University of Berlin (Technische Universität Berlin, TU Berlin). Of special interest are the three timelines that trace his professional development, at the same time ensuring, clearly with strategic intent, that the reader encounters the appropriate references. Particularly striking here is the timeline on 'Anpassungsfähiges Bauen' (adaptable architecture), which offers deep insights into Otto's lifelong preoccupation with

Model photographs from the first project at Askanischer Platz (1981), contact sheet from the work archive of Frei Otto

flexible and modifiable building concepts. Interestingly, Otto locates its beginning in his experience as an architect in a prisoner of war camp in 1946, which suggests that his early professional experiences had a formative influence on his later understanding of architecture. During the years immediately following his studies, Frei Otto laid down the intellectual foundations for his lifelong preoccupation with participatory and ecological residential concepts.[6] Documented in this meticulously structured timeline are the formative phases of his early career, which already anticipate his later visionary concepts and approaches.

Frei Otto refers, for example, to his 'study for adaptable residential buildings'[7] of 1951, which reflects his early interest in innovative approaches to flexible residential forms, highlighting the fact that his focus had by no means been exclusively on tent structures and lightweight construction. It becomes clear that already at this early date, he had adopted a critical stance with regard to concrete questions of participatory housing structures. This project, one of his earliest surviving works, consists of a series of large-format ink drawings, supplemented by brief handwritten texts. The title of the design is simply 'das übereinandergesetzte Eigenheim' (the stacked private home). Rather than surrendering aesthetic and planning control entirely into the hands of an architect as would be customary, Frei Otto resolved to allow future occupants the greatest possible leeway to participate in the design process. According to this scheme, the role of those producing the architecture is reduced to devising a simple, modular racking system in reinforced concrete within which the individual storeys serve as open platforms. This structure offers residents the freedom to shape and remodel their living spaces according to their own ideas – whether on their own initiative or with the support of professional planners. The 'stacked private home' is hence one of the earliest testimonials to Frei Otto's experimental approach to residential development.[8]

In the timeline, he also mentions his correspondence with Martin Wagner, the former head of city planning in Berlin who had emigrated to the United States. This illustrates first that even early on, Otto sought to engage in dialogue with major architects and urban planners in order to further develop his own ideas. This eagerness for debate continued in 1956 when he wrote a critical essay for the 1957 International Building Exhibition (Interbau) of Berlin, entitled 'Die Stadt von Morgen und das Einfamilienhaus' (The City of Tomorrow and the Single-Family Home), in which he sketches out visionary concepts for future urban housing.[9] A further critical milestone was the establishment in 1958 of the Institute for the Development of Lightweight Construction (Entwicklungsstätte für den Leichtbau, EL) in Berlin-Zehlendorf, which concretized Otto's practical and theoretical approaches to lightweight and adaptable architecture. It seems likely – although this must remain speculative – that Otto also regarded the residential concept he realized in the Hansaviertel near the Tiergarten for the 1957 Interbau in Berlin as insufficiently radical or visionary. He realized, presumably, that if he was to play a central role as an architect in German debates about the urban spaces of the future, he could hardly restrict himself to temporary membrane structures but would be obliged to engage intensively with the question of housing.

Interdisciplinary Challenges

The two concluding chapters, 'Projekt Askanischer Platz' (Project for Askanischer Platz) and 'Projekt Tiergarten-Südrand' (Project for the Southern Edge of the Tiergarten) are devoted exclusively to the development of the convoluted history of the eco-house project.[10] The subjects discussed extend from the 'green concept' and the 'energy concept' to the question of 'shell construction'. Titles such as 'Das Urwaldmodell' (The Primeval Forest Model) and 'Energie und Ökologie' (Energy and Ecology) suggest that Otto conceived of building as a fundamentally interdisciplinary challenge in whose context architecture, landscape

Frei Otto's student project 'Residence for Twelve Families' (1951), perspective

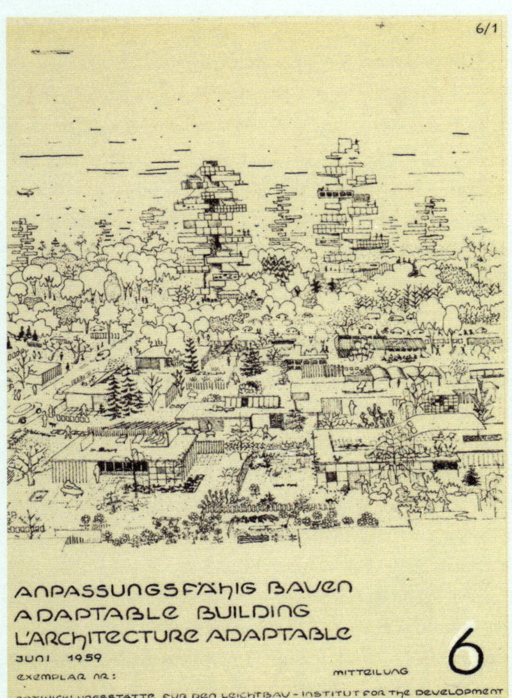

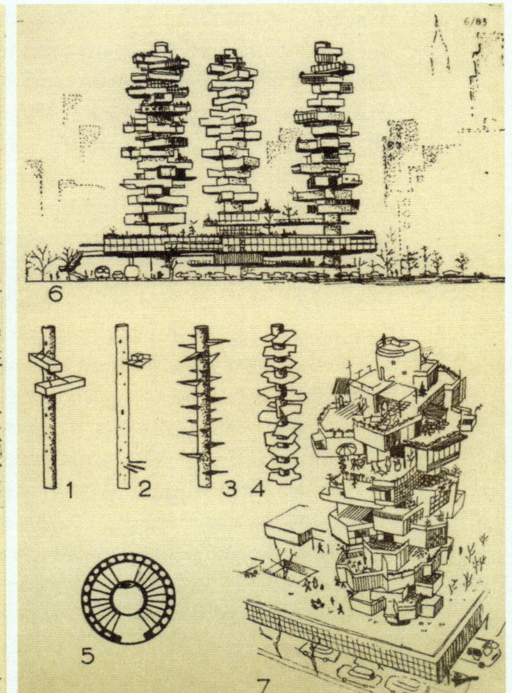

planning, engineering and social factors necessarily intertwine. It thus hardly seems astonishing that this chapter in particular contains such passionate advocacy for ecological architecture when we realize that at that moment Otto was enmeshed in perhaps the most experimental residential project of his entire career. Frei Otto and Hermann Kendel summed things up in a delightful but pointed fashion. They were unmistakable in their insistence on the centrality, for the project, of ecological principles, adaptability and the possibility of self-building: 'In the event that fundamental ecological principles, adaptability and possibility of self-building are decisively restricted, we will no longer be available for the project.'[11] These words are neither vague nor cautious; though they were not directed explicitly against any specific individual, they nevertheless constituted an overt critique of all of those actors who – for whatever reason – lacked the courage to support their visionary project. Otto and Kendel did not see themselves merely as architects, but instead as the guardians of an ecological ideal whose fulfilment they demanded without compromise. Their words were an appeal to the boldness that would be required to defend the project against all resistance, allowing it to be realized as a manifesto of sustainable building. Put differently, *Wohn-Be-Reiche im Garten* reads like a comprehensive glossary of the ecological concepts, key terms and issues that had preoccupied Frei Otto and his team intensively over the preceding three decades – a kind of inventory of his most important practical and research activities. The questions of ecology and participatory building are leitmotifs that pervade his oeuvre as a whole. Otto wove these themes together into a consistent narrative that clarified his architectural vision and his profound understanding of the symbiosis between humanity, nature and architecture building.

By no means did *Wohn-Be-Reiche* simply emerge from nowhere. Rather, it may be regarded as a further development of the sixth issue of the report *Mitteilungen der Entwicklungsstätte für den Leichtbau (EL)* from 1959, which bore the title *Anpassungsfähig bauen* (*Adaptable Building*).[12] This early publication served as a kind of blueprint for the IBA publication that appeared twenty-five years later, and laid the conceptual groundwork for Otto's later ideas and approaches. It follows a similar methodology and contains a list of projects, assembled by Otto, which he regards as exemplary for innovative housing concepts.

Title sheet from *Anpassungsfähig bauen/Adaptable Building, Mitteilungen der Entwicklungsstätte für den Leichtbau (EL)*, no. 6 (1959)

Design for three residential towers off Central Park in New York, from *Anpassungsfähig bauen/Adaptable Building, Mitteilungen der EL*, no. 6 (1959)

Sketch by Frei Otto for a residential tower (1958)

Drawing stimulus from discussions related to the Interbau in Berlin in the post-war era,[13] Otto immersed himself in alternative residential concepts, subsequently developing a booklet that should be regarded less as a finished work then as an open and fragmentary collection of materials. Under the umbrella term 'adaptable building', Otto linked his own remarks, notes and sketches with select contributions and textual snippets by other architects. This early publication is not only a singular compendium on adaptable architecture in the post-war era but also an experimental commentary on the housing question during that period. The spectrum of assembled contributions extends from lesser-known works, such as Antony Herrey's 'Flexibility in the Planning and Design of Structures' (thesis, MIT, 1956/57), all the way to prominent projects, such as Yona Friedman's manifesto on 'l'architecture mobile' and Rudolf Doernach's dynamic residential shell, as well as ideas on industrial building by David Georges Emmerich and Konrad Wachsmann. As in the IBA publication, Frei Otto appears here in a number of different roles: now as an architect and author, now as a managing editor and proofreader. He also composed a series of brief programmatic texts with titles such as 'Die anpassungsfähige Innenstadt' (The Adaptable City Centre), 'Anpassungsfähige Einfamilienhäuser auf gemeinschaftlichem Grundeigentum' (Adaptable Single-Family Homes on Collectively Owned Property), 'Anpassungsfähige Bauordnungen' (Adaptable Building Codes), 'Das autonome Haus' (The Autonomous House) and 'Die dynamische Wohnhülle' (The Dynamic Residential Shell).

Perhaps the most remarkable chapter in this publication is devoted to the project 'Wohnhäuser für New York' (Mansion Blocks for New York). Here, Otto sketches out his vision for three green residential towers off Central Park. Rather than returning to his racking system found in earlier projects, including student assignments and later in the eco-houses, Otto experiments this time with a central mast to which the individual residential levels are attached, making a flexible spatial design possible. 'The building is oriented towards all sides. There will be sunny, shadowed and wind-sheltered spaces. There will be spaces into which no one can look from the outside, not even in this densely populated city',[14] writes Otto, while also emphasizing the ecological dimension as well as the social interdependency between the public and the private – aspects that would later play a central role in his eco-houses.

Ecological Pluralism

Throughout his life, Frei Otto sought to accomplish the radical tour de force of developing a pluralistic and ecological theory of experimental practice that could be implemented on all scales of the built environment. In the process, Otto sought to achieve a balance between romantic assertions concerning human existence and technical innovation in architecture. Or stated differently: he strove to investigate innovative methods of construction for lightweight building while simultaneously developing new social forms of collective life within residential buildings. This continuous process amounted to a search for new foundations for ecological thinking – a search that had already begun during the 1950s and pervades his activities like a leitmotif up to the International Building Exhibition of 1987. That Frei Otto never hesitated to adopt strong positions and to critically question the greats of architecture can be seen already in an early report about his trip through America.[15] Evidently, he saw himself not as a silent observer but instead as a critical thinker, who immediately positioned his observations in a larger context in order to formulate his own position. When an eighty-two-year-old Frank Lloyd Wright guided the young Otto through his studio in Taliesin, Otto's interest was piqued by plans for a residence on a sloping site, which was to be built for the proprietor of the V.C. Morris Gift Shop. Later, in his article 'Ein Besuch bei Frank Lloyd Wright' (A Visit with Frank Lloyd Wright), published in 1952,[16] Otto reflected on his impressions with a mixture of admiration and

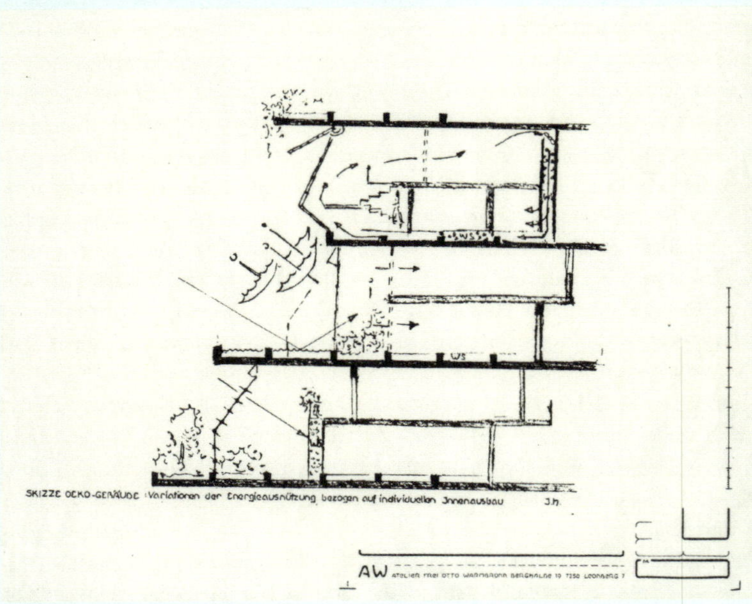

scepticism: 'The house was to be built on a topographically singular and unspoiled site, which I later sought out in San Francisco. Visible from afar, it will hang from the cliff like a swallow's nest. Unspoiled nature is beautiful. Nothing seems more suggestive than to build a house there, to live in such an unspoiled place. Yet you yourself have meanwhile spoiled what had been unspoiled, and all that is left is a harmony that has lost its equilibrium. Rarely, in such cases, is it possible to find a true home. Today, everywhere in the USA, houses are being built in the most beautiful places and, in the process, much is being destroyed. Must people meddle with and destroy everything? Must even Frank Lloyd Wright, who plans to build "organically"?'[17] This little anecdote is among the earliest testimonies of Frei Otto's ecological consciousness. For him, architecture was more than the act of erecting buildings – it was a question of the sensitive equilibrium between humanity and nature. For Otto, it seemed contradictory that Wright, of all people, an advocate of so-called 'organic architecture' and 'natural' houses, should have wished to build on such a fragile site.

Two years later, Otto incisively formulated what he regarded as the essential challenge of modern architecture: 'Today, the task is to develop housing for city dwellers in the technological age.'[18] In order to forestall potential reproaches of naivete or a lack of imagination, he continues, 'We cannot simply take the traditional shell of the farmhouse, layer it, one on top of the next, and densify it, as in the past and present years of rapid industrial expansion in Germany. It is not enough to set the house in a garden and surround it with flowers.'[19] Otto's demands went far beyond mere cosmetic adjustments. In order to do justice to the demands of urban life in the technological age, he argued instead for far-reaching changes in thinking. For him, clearly, it could never be a question of romantically transfiguring earlier forms or simply adapting them symbolically to the reality of present-day circumstances. Required instead were new, radical concepts that took seriously the challenges of the modern city and the needs of their inhabitants.

Otto strove towards an architecture that would go beyond responding to aesthetic or technical questions to open up fundamentally new pathways for urban life in harmony with nature. Running through his lifework is an unbroken thread that leads from the 1950s all the way to the IBA exhibitions, through which

One of the eco-houses with variations in energy use resulting from individualized interior construction (1988), cross-section

First project for Askanischer Platz (1981), model

he linked together questions of living in natural settings with the construction methods of lightweight building, along with his in-part romantic notions of human existence. But his concepts should be grasped less as rigid scientific theories than as a continuous source of inspiration – a never-ending, continuously developing manifesto. And this manifesto is not exhausted in the documentation of technical details or bureaucratic building codes but instead serves as an emboldening resource for the dynamic search for the new ecological lifestyles of the future. His vision resembled an intellectual network of tightly interwoven ideas and experiments that was designed to give expression to his faith in the feasibility of ecological architecture. The way in which he yoked together technology and romanticism, avant-garde and tradition, reflected a pluralistic but also contradictory approach, one that conceived of architecture as a medium of both social and ecological change. In a sense, Otto's ecological way of thinking resembles a prism: depending upon the angle of view, a variety of theoretical approaches, ideas and concepts emerge into the foreground. Seemingly central at times is unspoiled nature and sustainable construction methods, while at other times, it was participatory planning and social responsibility on the part of architects. This prismatic thinking allowed Otto to grasp and to reflect upon diverse facets of ecological and architectural challenges simultaneously without ever fixating on a single theory or demand. Undoubtedly, this intellectual versatility was one of his greatest strengths. But precisely this versatility confronts us with the question of whether Otto's thinking, with all of its contradictions, furnishes the answers he sought, or whether it instead confronts us with the limits of a perhaps excessively open-ended approach.

1 Frei Otto, *Wohn-Be-Reiche im Garten, IBA Berlin 1987. Vorbereitende Studie für das Bauvorhaben 'Ökohaus' Berlin*, commissioned by the Senator für Bau- und Wohnungswesen Berlin, Warmbronn 1985, p. 5.

2 Otto, *Wohn-Be-Reiche im Garten*, p. 2.

3 Louis Le Roy (1924–2012) was known internationally for his radical ecological vision in the design of gardens, parks and cities. Among his most popular projects were the Ecokathedraal (Eco-Cathedral) in Mildam (1964), the garden of his house in Oranjewoud (1962–2012) and the central median of the Kennedylaan in Heerenveen (1965). Le Roy's gardens were less designed then developed organically over a foundation of piled construction waste. His estate is housed in the Netherland's National Collection for Dutch Architecture and Urban Planning in the Nieuwe Instituut, the national museum for architecture, design and digital culture located in Rotterdam.

4 See Joaquín Medina Warmburg, 'Hausanbau. Wachstum als moderne Wohnutopie', in: *Arch+*, nos 198/199, 2010, pp. 122–127.

5 See Jón Kristinsson, 'Light Urban Development', in: Henco Bekkering et al. (eds), *The Architecture Annual 1997–1998, Delft University of Technology*, Rotterdam 1999.

6 Following his activity as a builder in a French prisoner of war camp, Frei Otto resumed his studies in Berlin in 1948. Among his teachers were Hellmuth Bickenbach, Gerhard Jobst and Hans Freese.

7 Frei Otto, *Wohnhaus für 12 Familien*, unpublished study, TU Berlin 1951. The document is preserved in the saai, Werkarchiv FO.

8 Also worth mentioning in this context is Frei Otto's social housing project, realized in 1954, for the Alexandra-Stiftung, a Protestant residential building association. The housing estate is set to the west of Berlin's Tempelhofer Feld and consists of an ensemble of seven- to ten-storey residential blocks. With the help of Otto's horizontal sundial, already developed in 1951, it became possible to minimize the shadow exposure of each individual building based on topography and the position of the sun. See 'Alexandra-Stiftung Residential Complex', in: Georg Vrachliotis et al. (eds), *Frei Otto: Thinking by Modeling*, exh. cat. ZKM | Center for Art and Media Karlsruhe, Leipzig 2017, pp. 292–298.

9 Frei Otto, 'Die Stadt von Morgen und das Einfamilienhaus', in: *Baukunst und Werkform*, no. 9, 1956, pp. 642–652.

10 Otto, *Wohn-Be-Reiche im Garten*, pp. 48 ff.

11 Frei Otto and Hermann Kendel, 'Zusammenfassung von Juni 1985 durch die Architekten des Bauvorhabens', in: Otto, *Wohn-Be-Reiche im Garten*, p. 155.

12 Frei Otto (ed.), *Anpassungsfähig bauen, Mitteilungen der Entwicklungsstätte für den Leichtbau (EL)*, no. 6, June 1959.

13 Frei Otto was represented at the Interbau with a series of experimental tents and also served as an advisor for the roof construction of the central exhibition pavilion. See Sandra Wagner-Conzelmann, *Die Interbau 1957 in Berlin. Stadt von heute. Stadt von morgen*, Petersberg 2007.

14 Otto (ed.), *Anpassungsfähig bauen*.

15 In 1950, Frei Otto received a scholarship from the University of Virginia in Charlottesville and began a trip around the United States that lasted several months, during which he visited Frank Lloyd Wright, Erich Mendelsohn and Ludwig Mies van der Rohe, among others. See Karin Wilhelm, *Portrait Frei Otto*, Berlin 1985, p. 17.

16 Frei Otto, 'Ein Besuch bei Frank Lloyd Wright', in: *Neue Bauwelt*, no. 2, 1952, pp. 24–26. Frei Otto's ecological views consistently amounted to a disguised critique of the functionalism of contemporary architecture, for example when he writes in his article on Wright: 'However, the conviction that it is sufficient for the art of building to simply make a building's functions visible has meanwhile become a widespread and vacuous error from which we have fallen deeply ill.'

17 Otto, 'Ein Besuch bei Frank Lloyd Wright'.

18 Frei Otto, 'Vom Nest zur modernen Wohnstadt', in: *Der Architekt*, no. 12, 1954, pp. 411–414.

19 Otto, 'Vom Nest zur modernen Wohnstadt'.

Climate Shells: Natural Constructions for a Novel Air Architecture

Joaquín Medina Warmburg
Jos Tomlow

Against the background of today's environmental problems, the relevance of Frei Otto's experience in the field of material- and energy-saving lightweight construction seems unquestioned. Yet general recognition of his pioneering achievements towards a lasting, sustainable architecture should not be so one-sided or narrow. In his approaches, Otto followed a considerably more comprehensive environmental design close to nature, one that somewhat found a counterpart in the holistic theories of environmental planning in the 1960s and 1970s. Today, if only from an interest in Otto's work oriented towards problem solving, a critical examination of the entire breadth of his recurring themes is worthwhile. His notions of an adaptable architecture, for example, or his research on macro- and microclimates seem highly topical today. The latter provide important insights for our time, concerned as we are with climate-appropriate structures and urban spaces. The intertwining of these concepts across very different scales – from a single-family dwelling to territorial organization – and their development over time can be traced in Frei Otto's work through the decades.

At the very beginning of Otto's scholarly career, in his 1954 doctoral thesis on the design and structure of suspended roofs, he devoted a brief excursus to the subject of 'house, climate and large shells'. In it, he defined the role of the architect as a mediator between humans and their habitat, which must first be created through technology. He thus construed the house as an artificial, man-made environment that is at the same time a biologically determined, primitive 'nest' and, as such, is built instinctively, therefore impractically. Yet, according to Otto, the architect's main technical task in building a house remains the creation of the climatic environment people need. In this, he conceded that a complete separation from or neutralization of the local climate is not necessarily required; a corrective adaptation of naturally existing conditions was enough. He insisted that a 'consistent paradisical climate' created through complete dependence on technology was indeed not necessarily healthy. He added, 'If outside nature is shut out and the environment is only created technologically, man lacks his eternal partner: flora, which mediates between light and dark, solidity and air. It belongs

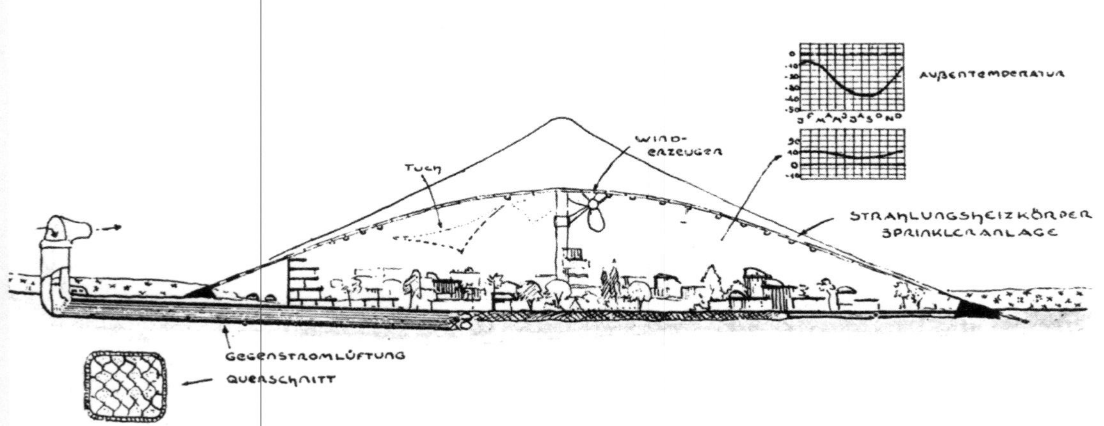

Frei Otto, cross-section of a large transparent living shell in the Antarctic (design 1953)

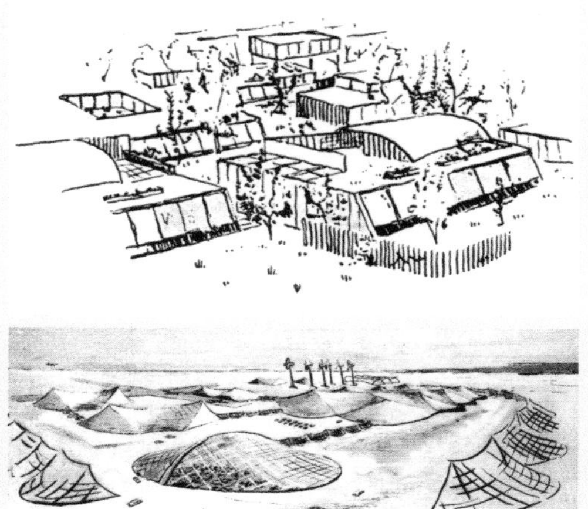

to man like the sun, the basic necessity of earthly life and thus to the house, whether in the city, in the desert or in the eternal ice. [...] It is not the house in the ordinary sense that is architecture but this climate, with which we make the earth as liveable as we possibly can.'[1]

Living Shells and Air Houses

In the course of his early research on hanging roof construction, Frei Otto also developed his first visions of artificial climates in which people would, in future, live and work under large, thin shells of concrete, steel or glass – as in a greenhouse. One of the merits of the roof skins of these novel 'self-heating greenhouses' in their massive dimensions was the fact that they could put an end to the growing disfigurement of the landscape through the unrestricted proliferation of industrial complexes, or such was his hope. But above all, they would make even regions most inimical to life habitable for humans. A huge glass 'living shell' for the Antarctic, for example, conceived as a 'total heat trap', might house a covered green city for labourers and researchers in open-pit polar mining. But he also developed climate shell concepts for the exploitation of altogether different regions with extreme climate conditions like deserts or even outer space.[2] The basic principle of capturing the heat of the sun under glass was thereby scaled upward from the dwelling as a living shell to domed cities, territorial-sized mega-greenhouses or large valleys under roofs. The shifting scales brought with them specific challenges in relation to size: controlling air circulation, for example, or the formation of condensation zones inside the climate shell.[3]

When his book *Das hängende Dach* (The Hanging Roof) was published in the mid-1950s, Otto was already a presence in the trade press with articles on the subject of emerging solar architecture in which he described a projected 'unheated, perfectly warm house'.[4] It is possible that at this point he was familiar with the experimental solar houses being developed mainly by universities in the United States from his study trip in 1950/51, but their progress was also reported in the specialized German press. In 1949, for example, the Berlin architectural journal *Neue Bauwelt* had reported on the 'dwellings heated by the sun', prototypes of which had been tested at the Massachusetts Institute of Technology (MIT) in Cambridge and Boston.[5] That report described how in two of MIT's solar houses hot water was provided as well as various heating systems actuated by solar collectors of black sheet metal behind glass (on the roof of one, on the façade of the other) and how the energy was stored to bridge days with no sun. In conclusion, *Neue Bauwelt* noted that these were only preliminary experiments with many unknowns that would doubtless be economically feasible in Germany in only a few especially favourable locations. The final reference to economic motives touched on the timeliness of these solar houses in the United States, which was then facing a first oil crisis immediately following the Second World War.[6]

To be sure, a retrospective look at historical building types such as orangeries and greenhouses provided numerous valuable instances of the structural realization of artificial atmospheres achieved by simple technological means based on natural principles. In various publications, Otto notably numbered them among 'natural constructions'. 'Klima-Großhülle' (Large Climate Shells) was the title he gave to a brief commentary on the conservatory at Chatsworth House in Derbyshire (Joseph Paxton and Decimus Burton, 1836–1840), which he praised as a pattern worth following in our own day: 'If today anyone had such an assignment, and he could copy this structure by Paxton, he would thereby arrive at virtually our present state of knowledge and at an architecture free of constructive formalism. The task is very topical today. The earth's surface can hardly be made more fruitful. But with the exception of Buckminster Fuller's Climation [*sic*] in St Louis, people are still making "architecture". They are placing plants in "fine parlours", forgetting that the best environment for them is where the construction

Frei Otto, a large living shell in the Antarctic: residential compound on a south-facing slope, sketch; and habitable suspended tension structures, perspective (design 1953)

John F. Haws and the MIT Solar Energy Fund, MIT Solar House in Cambridge, Massachusetts (1948)

of the necessary shell is as invisible as possible, when it has been (further) developed to the point of disappearance. It is not the structure that is architecture, but rather the highly stimulating environment – the "paradise", as the unknown Englishman appropriately called it.'[7]

For his climate shell concept, Otto no less explicitly cited the recent Modernist tradition with examples like Martin Wagner's prototypes from 1932 for an adaptable 'growing' house intended to be largely self-sufficient. Its glass shell over wooden façades painted black produced a thermal buffer zone.[8] Significantly, in 1959, in his discussion of Wagner's model in the sixth issue of his *Mitteilungen der Entwicklungsstätte für den Leichtbau (EL)*, Otto expanded its implied 'natural living space' into a desirable 'growing city' and even a 'growing country'.[9] The same issue reported on Frei Otto's meeting in St Louis with Richard Buckminster Fuller, who was characterized as a champion of the idea of the 'autonomous house'. Fuller's projects also extended from small, movable houses to huge domes and planning on a planetary scale. Rudolf Doernach, a student of Otto's and a Fuller collaborator, later developed the unifying vision of a 'dynamic living shell'. With this, he meant a novel, lightweight and movable architecture suited to the dynamic lifestyle of a new, autonomous type of human. The dynamic living shell of the future would be able to respond to its surroundings, adapting to them by expanding, for example, or by producing and transforming energy. In this way, it would do away with a rigid architecture dependent on supply infrastructures. Doernach also saw in it a structural equivalent of the dynamism of the atomic age and optimistically declared that in the foreseeable future the amount of energy required to produce and maintain these new living shells would not pose a problem.[10]

Everybody was promoting the idea of a 'dynamic' architecture at the time, though interpretations of what that might be were very different. In Udo Kultermann's book *Dynamische Architektur* (Dynamic Architecture; 1959), the adjective 'dynamic' suggested an architecture constantly evolving, in a constant state of becoming, one tending towards immaterialization yet physically experienced, ultimately holding the promise of the freedom for a new way of living. Shell structures, hanging roofs and tent structures were part of the basic repertoire of structural types on the way to this novel architecture, including 'the new, open building style of Frei Otto, the young Berlin engineer and architect who has made a name for himself primarily with his tent structures as well as his investigation of lightweight building methods. The two lines of development appear to proceed independently of each other, yet both arrive at a kind of weightless, suspended structure that can be thought of as a direct precursor of an air architecture.'[11] Udo Kulterman pointed to the originators of this 'air house' idea, namely the artist Yves Klein and the architect Werner Ruhnau. They had proposed using constant streams of air in place of roofs and walls to create temperature-controlled atmospheres protected from the weather. Kultermann did not deny the obvious problems associated with such improvident waste of energy and a foreseeable change in climate with devastating consequences for organic life. For Ruhnau, the integration of the new air architectures into the existing natural conditions was a possible solution, supplementing the natural air currents of a specific spot in the landscape, for example, which Kultermann saw as analogous to Otto's roofed-over valleys: 'Adapting to the natural conditions one could roof over a city lying in a valley and build the individual structures using lightweight construction so that each individual house no longer had to provide protection from the weather.'[12]

Kultermann's book presented Klein and Ruhnau's air architecture as the utopian culmination of dynamic architecture. Frei Otto's membrane structures and climate shells functioned as its real-world preliminary stage: a relatively immaterial architecture in which a central role was actually given to air as an invisible building material. It is therefore unsurprising that Ruhnau's 1960 published lecture 'Klimatisierte Natur. Entwicklung von Architektur und bildender Kunst zur

Yves Klein and Werner Ruhnau, an aerial roof, the decisive element of their 'Architecture de l'air' (1958), photograph

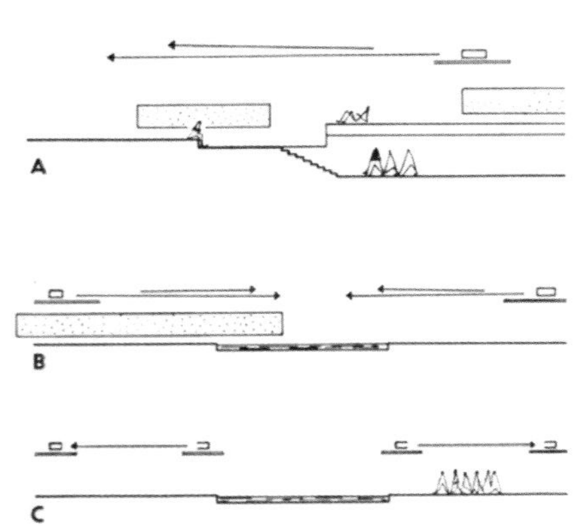

Werner Ruhnau, 'aerial house' scheme for 'roofing without a roof', schematic section in *Deutsche Bauzeitung* (1960)

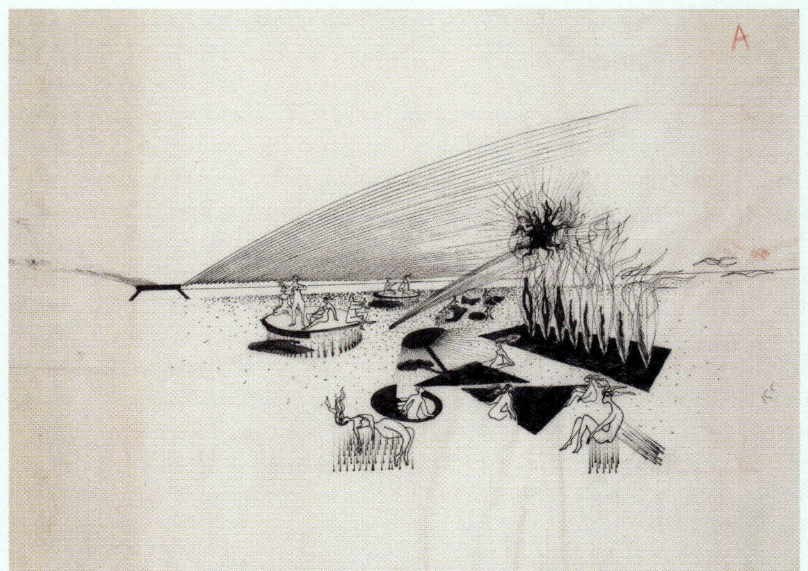

Immaterialisation' (Temperature-Controlled Nature: The Trend Towards Immaterialization in Architecture and the Visual Arts) – a brief historical outline of the development of theatre architecture deliberately culminating in the works of Otto and Ruhnau – also contained extensive documentation of the tent structures realized up to that point by Frei Otto in collaboration with Peter Stromeyer, as well as comprehensive documentation of the glass theatre building realized by Ruhnau in Gelsenkirchen in collaboration with Yves Klein.[13] Also typical of the time was Ruhnau's blatant faith in progress, especially the optimism with which he describes the merits of such development, which is now critically described in environmental history as the '1950s syndrome' or the 'Great Acceleration'.[14] These terms describe the rapid rise in energy consumption and the related rise in the overall standard of living as a result of the establishment of a modern society based on mass consumption within the context of the West German economic miracle, the so-called Miracle on the Rhine. Ruhnau interpreted refrigerators, washing machines, televisions, houses and automobiles as instruments of humanity's liberation and associated them with the atomic age.[15] It was fitting that in 1960 the *Deutsche Bauzeitung* also reported about Buckminster Fuller's dome – a geodesic architectural framework with an aluminium skin – at the American National Exhibition in Moscow (1959), known today primarily because of the so-called 'Kitchen Debate' held there between the Soviet state and party leader, Nikita Khrushchev, and the American vice president, Richard Nixon.[16] Standing before a reproduction of the kitchen of an American suburban model home (the 'Splitnik') Nixon enumerated on camera the advantages of the free world's consumer society.[17]

Yves Klein with Claude Parent, a climatized city with aerial roof, fire walls and air loungers (1961), perspective

Martin Wagner, 'The Growing House' at the Berlin exhibition *Sonne, Luft und Haus für Alle* (Sun, Air and Housing for All; 1932), front façade

Admittedly, the lightweight living shells and air houses of a new 'dynamic architecture' in the early 1960s were full of contradictions and ambivalences with respect to their use of material and energy resources. At that point, they still seem far removed from the 'ecological' discourse of later decades, especially the 1980s. It is therefore somewhat surprising that in 1984 – or long after the second oil crisis of 1973 and shortly after the environmental movement had established itself as a political force with the founding of West Germany's Green Party in 1980 – Frei Otto retrospectively referred to his own works since the beginning of the 1950s as 'early solar architecture'. In them he produced precursors of an economical architecture intended to harvest natural energy and, in that same year, spoke of his own house in Warmbronn (since 1966) as a starting point (literally a 'grandmother') of the new 'eco-house architecture'.[18] In fact, Otto's career exhibits an astonishing continuity with respect to his engagement with active and passive solar systems, demonstrable beyond every political, socio-economic and environmental-historical upheaval and disruption – from the urban planning sunlight studies for his diploma (1952) to his atelier building in Berlin-Zehlendorf (1958) to the Berlin eco-houses of 1984.

Elements of a Prehistory of Climate Shells

In his genealogy of the lightweight membrane house, Walter Scheiffele has convincingly traced a few historical lines of development that explicitly extend further back than Frei Otto's earliest works from around 1950. Among them, as milestones in the history of the notion of the lightweight house, are Bruno Taut's and Paul Scheerbart's visions of glass architecture from around 1914 and especially Siegfried Ebeling's manifesto *Der Raum als Membran* (*Space as Membrane*; 1926).[19] These are not the only preliminary stages with isolated elements or characteristic features of Frei Otto's later eco-house architecture. That genealogy can be expanded with the inclusion of other comparable structures that extend our gaze beyond the boundaries of the German-speaking world.

A Sanitary Building in Yokohama

In addition to Taut's architectural visions, in his 1926 manifesto mentioned earlier, Ebeling named a second, more concrete example of a structure that already conformed to his notion of biological membrane architecture: the 'glass house' of a 'Japanese bacteriologist in Yokohama', which he briefly described, functioned by means of a salt solution between its double-paned glass walls that absorbs the heat of the sun.[20] Ebeling thus introduces the 'sanitary' house of the Dutch physician Dr Wilhelmus Hubertus van der Heyden realized in Yokohama between 1891 and 1893 into the genealogy of membrane structures as a precursor of climate shells. It was an innovative 'model house' designed for the passive use of solar energy.[21] The concept was similar to the principle of a spacesuit, with a hermetic filter system that transforms the quality of air and light in the space between the outside environment and subject. Its background was Van der Heyden's work as an epidemiologist in Japan. His studies were prompted by climate changes observed at the time that suggested a future reduction in habitable regions worldwide. Research by the Australian architect Pedro Guedes concluded that this sanitary dwelling would make healthy living possible even in uninhabitable regions.[22]

The unadorned model house, designed for six people, stood on a slightly slanted base over an underground space covering a still larger area. One entered the house by first descending a flight of stairs and traversing a connecting corridor into the underground space. From there, one ascended into the glass house. The footprint of the above-ground section measured roughly 11 × 7 metres, with a height of 5.20 metres. A photograph of the roomy interior pictures simple Western-style furnishings and a few plants. Grilled openings in the parquet floors

Siegfried Ebeling, *Der Raum als Membran* (*Space as Membrane*; 1926), book cover

point to the provision for air circulation, heating and cooling. The walls consisted of two panes of glass set in steel struts and hermetically sealed. As Ebeling suggested, the aquarium-like space between them was filled with an alum solution. These crystals made the outer walls translucent. But to provide clearer views outside Van der Heyden suggested the integration of a few windows with normal glass. According to the patent, a further pane of glass with an outside wooden frame was meant to heighten the outer wall's insulating effect. The ceiling was also made of two panes of glass with ashes between them. A wooden gable roof protected it from rain and snow. The intention was that only sunlight would enter the house; excessive heat from the sun and other adverse factors would be blocked out. In addition, the interior temperature would remain constant and the air free of dust, bacteria and insects. An eighteen-month test in fact proved that the space was kept at a constant temperature of between 18 and 23°C. Two towers with chimneys next to the model house fulfilled various structural functions. For example, excrement from the toilet on the lower level was immediately burned to render it harmless. Fresh air was drawn from outside the building and fed in through underground pipes, where it was filtered and disinfected. Even the outgoing air was purified. To this end, there was an open glass tank beneath the overhanging roof in which a combination of sunlight and chemical cleansing took place.

The Japanese sanitary house looks like architecture reduced to its translucent glass shell. In its appearance, it resembles Frei Otto's Berlin atelier as well as his eco-house in Warmbronn.[23] All three structures were based on a fundamental physical and climatological analysis as a starting point, paired with a sense and love of experimentation.

A Butterfly Plan in Berlin

As already mentioned, Frei Otto specifically recognized the precedent of historical building types like the orangeries and greenhouses familiar since the seventeenth century. But other features of Baroque solar architecture may also have provided inspiration for his climate shells. For example, one can see the use of butterfly plans as so-called suntraps both in three-wing Baroque structures and residential architecture of early Modernism. Hermann Muthesius briefly mentioned this motif in his three-volume opus *Das englische Haus* (*The English House*; 1904/05) and illustrated it using the example of Edward Schroeder Prior's rural house, The Barn (1896) in Exmouth, Devon. Muthesius adopted its butterfly plan for Freudenberg House (1907/08) in Berlin-Nikolassee, and Bruno Taut and Otto Bartning also produced modern designs based on this prototype or in direct imitation of the English precedents. A butterfly plan is produced when a building's side wings are each angled forty-five degrees away from the main structure's central axis. It was based on the idea that such an arrangement captures sunlight better: not only frontally (facing south as a rule) but also from east and west. A desirable microclimate is thereby created at the front of the house. And such is the case in the Muthesius design, where the house's forecourt, oriented towards the southeast, opens out with its rose gardens. The side wing to the southwest closed off the entire breadth of the house with a conservatory. A counterpart to the sheltered, sun-filled forecourt was the northwest-facing terrace providing a wide-open view of the surroundings. The band of windows in the spacious atelier on the attic floor also shows that, in this case, the angled form responds to the surrounding meadow landscape. Architectural elements like pergolas or loggias function as mediating features.

The butterfly plan designed for optimal sunlight had also been combined with Rationalist architectural approaches even earlier, in the nineteenth century. This is attested by Eugène Emmanuel Viollet-le-Duc's design for a *hôtel particulier* in Paris from 1872. His description shows it utilizing such an arrangement.[24] In line with the period's Positivist, Rationalist approach, Viollet-le-Duc tried to provide greater comfort in his residential architecture with a holistic concept of

Wilhelmus van der Heyden, 'sanitary' house in Yokohama (1891), photograph of interior with double glass walls

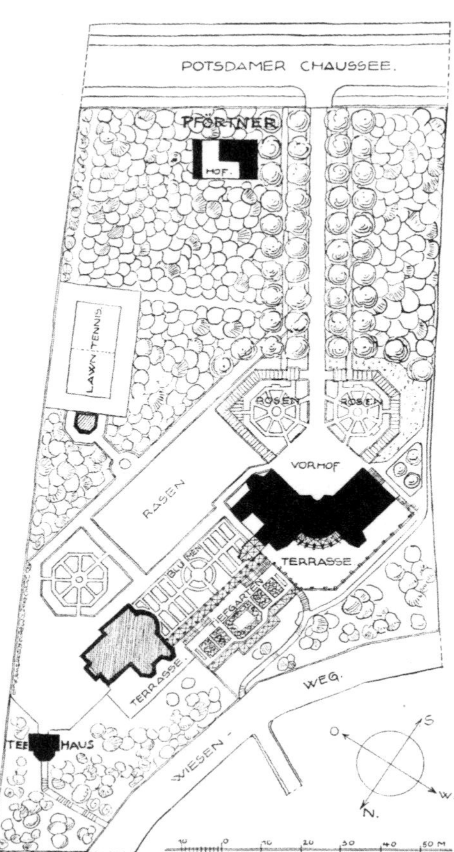

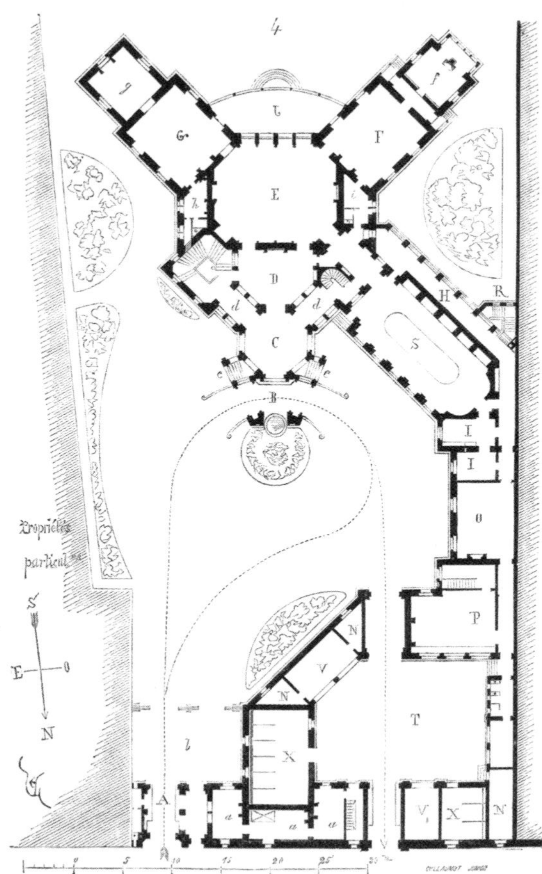

habitation in which design questions of ventilation and heating, as well as issues of social intercourse within a middle-class family and with its guests and servants, were considered. With his design, he criticized the standard imposing *hôtel* with its *cour d'honneur*. Along with its functional disadvantages, for example the great distance between the kitchen and ballroom, which placed a particular burden on the domestic staff, he also noted its inadequate ventilation during receptions and drawbacks with respect to the exploitation of daylight. He described the advantages of the butterfly house in detail: better illumination during the day and improved ventilation, for example, as well as the way sunlight enters the house from the south through the garden side, which moreover helped to keep the courtyard walls dry. Here again the orientation of house and garden towards the sun was accomplished in conjunction with a holistic view of domestic life and needs throughout the day.

A Habitable Greenhouse in Löbau

As for domestic living arrangements, it is possible to identify modern precedents for Frei Otto's climate-shell architecture that go far beyond simply adding such amenities as a conservatory, for example, to the private sphere. In the first third of the twentieth century, Modernist architecture took initial steps towards more comprehensive residential accommodations within a glasshouse. A good example of this is the house in Löbau (1929–1933) designed by Hans Scharoun for Fritz Schminke, the owner of a pasta factory, and his wife and their four children. The house was designed from the inside out and thus responded to the external influences of each cardinal direction. A steel skeleton from the Niesky firm Christoph & Unmack served as the framework for a liberal use of glass for the façades. The elongated main structure was deliberately placed on a north-south axis so that

Hermann Muthesius, Freudenberg House in Berlin-Nikolassee (1907/08), ground floor plan

Eugène Emmanuel Viollet-le-Ducs, designed for a *hôtel particulier* in Paris (published in 1872), ground floor plan

Hans Scharoun, Schminke House in Löbau (1929–1933), interior of the conservatory

the entrance faces the south, where the neighbouring noodle factory blocked the view. To the north, the house opens out to an expansive garden with a round pond with a base of fieldstone.[25] The main staircase in the two-storey entrance hall heightened the open and dynamic effect of the roughly 100-square-metre living area. The lightweight side staircase on the eastern façade, reminiscent of a nautical gangway, matches the house's other visual features suggestive of an ocean liner, like the deck terraces and porthole windows. The parents' bedroom had its own bay window reminiscent of a ship's bridge.

Developed in close consultation with Fritz Schminke and his wife, Charlotte, the house was meant to be a playground for their children that could be used in different ways in winter and in summer, accordingly. Charlotte was greatly concerned about the importance of nature and climate for the house and their desired lifestyle. She wanted to have direct experience of them in every season – even in melancholy autumn. In summer, nine doors gave the family direct access to the outside: whether stepping out on the balconies and terraces or into the garden. The placement of overhanging roofs for shade was determined by Scharoun's precise study of the path of the sun. The varying outdoor temperatures in summer and winter prompted him to provide auxiliary measures for regulating the indoor climate. Central heating, an important feature of the plan, was supplemented by a small stove in the living area. In winter, curtains were drawn across all the glass surfaces, including the ceiling-high sliding door to the conservatory, which owing to its dimensions and the vegetation was more like a year-round habitable greenhouse. On the outer side of the windows, the layer of air between the roller shutter and the glass also provided additional thermal insulation. A sliding door to the entrance hall kept the warmth of the living area from escaping into the height of that two-storey space. In summer, this could generally be opened, leaving one third of the width for the three door segments. The heating design provided for radiators where they were actually needed: for example, behind the long bench with room for the whole family.[26] In the north-facing conservatory, a boiler pipe installed beneath a steel grille countered drafts along its glass wall. Scharoun also incorporated hopper windows in every section of the façade to provide for adequate cross-ventilation. On the upper floor, a row of waist-high cupboards were installed along the corridor beneath the ribbon window. These provided storage for the children's clothes across from their bedrooms. Any number of details make it clear that the children were the house's most important residents. Their toys, for example, were stored right by the entrance in cupboards with doors of a different colour for each child. Low small windows invited them to climb outside. This experience of the 'living shell' – to use Frei Otto's later terminology – was decisive in the economic principle of biological growth set down by other modern residential greenhouses like those of Martin Wagner or Leberecht Migge. Family life in the Schminke House proceeded in harmony with that of plants, inside and out, the kind of cohabitation Otto called for in the passage from his 1954 thesis quoted at the beginning of this essay.[27]

Sliding Glass Walls for a Physiological Architecture in California

Richard Neutra's California bungalow architecture from the post-war decades show him to have been a master at integrating architecture and landscape. As mediating structural elements in his casually designed gardens, he used improvised pergolas (with simple shade-giving planks, for example), low walls, steps, terraces, natural boulders along with suitable vegetation (for example, cacti) but also swimming pools. In California, where it can be used year-round, the domestic swimming pool was not only an imposing luxury. More importantly, it was seen as an integral component of a simultaneously healthy and hedonistic lifestyle. In this way, Neutra expressly distanced himself from the consumerism of the American way of life at the time. His book *Survival Through Design*, which was published in 1954, at the same time as Frei Otto's thesis, *Das hängende Dach*, provided the socio-critical background of Neutra's architecture, which was omnipresent in the trade press of those years.[28] His architecture was, for example, clearly based on a coherent theory of 'biorealism'. Neutra coined that term to describe his physiological-psychological approach according to which architecture not only responds to biological imperatives and provides for the ensuing basic needs but, moreover, intentionally creates a rich experiential space, as he described in a 1955 issue of *Baukunst und Werkform*: 'The designer of the built environment, and that is in fact the architect, is no mere child playing around with shapes, colours and materials, but is, at least in part, a responsible adult, a man who sits behind the scene, as at a precarious switchboard, and there switches on or off all these stimulations, which either upset or promote our inner balance.'[29]

The open-plan spaces of his bungalows, opening visually and physically onto the garden, promised not only freedom and health. Neutra's 'physiological architecture' was also meant to be seen as a system of 'psychotopes', that is to say, spots that create lasting memories or are capable of evoking deep-seated memories from childhood. An open architecture that creates places whose qualities resemble experiences of nature, psychologically and physiologically, or trigger recollections of them, as Neutra postulated in his book: 'The memories of one's youth and of the landscape in which it was spent, seem composed, to a considerable degree, of this sort of vital recollection. There are in each life certain scattered quanta of experience that may have been of small number or dimension statistically but were so intense as to provide impacts, forever essential.'[30]

Neutra's suburban dwellings discussed here, which Frei Otto encountered during his study trip in the United States in 1950/51, can in many respects be seen as anticipating the demands of an 'air architecture'. In any case, that architecture intended to create an atmosphere of intense lived collective experience differed from MIT's solar houses primarily designed for economic efficiency and energy production and from Buckminster Fuller's objectively quantified technical optimization of resources. In Frei Otto's holistically conceived works, there was no contradiction between these two approaches. Technical quantifiability and collective intensity of experience appear to go hand in hand in structures like the Warmbronn dwelling designed for his own family.

Frei Otto's Closing Sentence

The various climate shells Frei Otto designed and, in part, constructed over the course of his professional career can be thought of as realizations of an architectural programme already proclaimed in the closing sentence of his 1954 thesis. There we read: 'In approaching the ideal of WORKING WITHOUT MATERIAL, fulfilling a structure's technical requirements simply with effects, a new sense of space takes shape, one which lies beyond the still palpable, partially or totally closed translucent shell.'[31] With this vision, Otto was not standing alone in a vacuum, as this brief glance at the historical context and a few proceeding developmental stages has tried to demonstrate.

Jörg Gribl and Frei Otto (Atelier Warmbronn), large aviary at Hellabrunn Zoo in Munich (1978–1980)

1 Frei Otto, *Das hängende Dach. Gestalt und Struktur*, doctoral thesis, Berlin 1954, pp. 114–116, here p. 115.
2 Frei Otto, 'Bauen im Weltraum', in: *Bauwelt*, no. 17, 1963, pp. 458–461.
3 See, on this, the chapter 'Großhüllen', in: Conrad Roland, *Frei Otto – Spannweiten. Ideen und Versuche zum Leichtbau. Ein Werkstattbericht*, Berlin 1965, pp. 138–153.
4 Frei Otto, 'Vom ungeheizt schon warmen Haus und neuen Fenstern', in: *DBZ Deutsche Bauzeitschrift*, no. 3, 1955, pp. 228–230.
5 'Wohnhäuser, von der Sonne beheizt', in: *Neue Bauwelt*, no. 24, 1949, p. 375.
6 For the political and economic backgrounds of the MIT solar houses, see Daniel Barber, *A House in the Sun: Modern Architecture and Solar Energy in the Cold War*, New York 2016.
7 Frei Otto, 'Klima-Großhülle', in: *Bauwelt*, no. 27, 1963, p. 759. The commentary referred to a rediscovered anonymous article about Joseph Paxton's Great Conservatory at Chatsworth that appeared in the *Illustrated London News*, 31 August 1844. The erroneously spelled work by Fuller was the Climatron, a greenhouse at the Missouri Botanical Garden in St Louis erected in 1960.
8 See Frei Otto, 'Das wachsende Haus', in: *Anpassungsfähig bauen, Mitteilungen der Entwicklungsstätte für den Leichtbau (EL)*, no. 6, 1959, pp. 19–24.
9 Otto, 'Das wachsende Haus', p. 24.
10 Rudolf Doernach, 'Die dynamische Wohn-Hülle', in: *Mitteilungen der Entwicklungsstätte für den Leichtbau (EL)*, no. 6, June 1959, pp. 86 f. Doernach (1929–2016) had received a Fulbright scholarship after his architectural studies in Stuttgart that allowed him to study in Washington and in 1956 made possible his working with Richard Buckminster Fuller. He later became known primarily for the concept of an ecologically based 'biotecture', which he promoted internationally in seminars and in best-selling books like *Biohaus für Dorf und Stadt. Lebensgemeinschaft von Pflanzen, Tiere und Menschen* (Frankfurt a. M., 1981, together with Gerhard Heid). His papers are also preserved in the saai | Archiv für Architektur und Ingenieurbau of the Karlsruhe Institute of Technology.
11 Udo Kultermann, *Dynamische Architektur*, Munich 1959, p. 73.
12 Kultermann, *Dynamische Architektur*, p. 76
13 Werner Ruhnau, 'Klimatisierte Natur. Entwicklung von Architektur und bildender Kunst zur Immaterialisation', in: *Deutsche Bauzeitung*, no. 2, 1960, pp. 84–88; Frei Otto and Peter Stromeyer, 'Zelte', in: *Deutsche Bauzeitung*, no. 7, 1960, pp. 351–366; 'Theater-Neubauten in Gelsenkirchen', in *Deutsche Bauzeitung*, no. 12, 1960, pp. 664–686.
14 Frank Uekötter, *Umweltgeschichte im 19. und 20. Jahrhundert*, Munich 2007, pp. 56 ff.; John Robert McNeill and Peter Engelke, *The Great Acceleration: An Environmental History of the Anthropocene Since 1945*, Cambridge, MA/London 2014, pp. 155 ff.; Martin Pawley, 'Energie, die Grosse Hoffnung', in: Martin Pawley, *Theorie und Gestaltung im Zweiten Maschinenalter*, Braunschweig/Wiesbaden 1998, pp. 129–152.
15 Ruhnau, 'Klimatisierte Natur', p. 84; see Thilo Hilpert, 'Urban Utopias and Climate Models: Outlining the Paradox of the Future', in: Joaquín Medina Warmburg and Claudia Shmidt (eds), *The Construction of Climate in Modern Architectural Culture, 1920–1980*, Madrid 2015, pp. 187–197.
16 'Geodätische Kuppeln in Paris und Moskau', in: *Deutsche Bauzeitung*, no. 7, 1960, pp. 373–375.
17 On the kitchen as the location of Cold War propaganda, see David Crowley and Jane Pavitt (eds), *Cold War Modern: Design 1945–1970*, London 2008.
18 Frei Otto, 'Frühe Solararchitektur', in: *arcus*, no. 1, 1984, pp. 8 f. See the essay by Jos Tomlow on Frei Otto's house and atelier in Warmbronn in the present volume, pp. 68–77.
19 Walter Scheiffele, *Das leichte Haus. Utopie und Realität der Membranarchitektur*, Leipzig 2015.
20 Siegfried Ebeling, *Der Raum als Membran*, Dessau 1926, republished Leipzig 2016 (Edition Bauhaus, vol. 43), p. 31.
21 Wilhelmus Hubertus van der Heyden, 'Description of a Newly Devised Sanitary Building', in: *Yokohama, Japan Herald*, 1893 (21 pages of text with 2 photographs and diagrams). A copy is preserved in the library of the Delft University of Technology (TU Delft).
22 Pedro Guedes, 'Presciently Translucent in Yokohama, 1891', in: *ARQ: Architectural Research Quarterly*, 9/1, 2005, pp. 69–79.
23 See Frei Otto, *Wohn-Be-Reiche im Garten, IBA Berlin 1987. Vorbereitende Studie für das Bauvorhaben 'Ökohaus' Berlin,* Warmbronn 1985, pp. 39–41, including 'Das Atelier im Türksteinweg 5 in Berlin-Zehlendorf, Baujahr 1959', p. 39, and 'Atelier Warmbronn, Baujahr 1968', pp. 40 f. See also Jos Tomlow and Sebastian Stadler, 'Vorentwürfe eines Ökohauses in Warmbronn. Energetische Studien zu Frei Ottos Ökohauskonzept, 1967–1969', in: *Wissenschaftliche Berichte Hochschule Zittau/Görlitz*, no. 136, 2021, pp. 50–53 (text volume), pp. 63 f. (plate volume).
24 Eugène Emmanuel Viollet-le-Duc, 'Sur l'architecture privée', in: *Entretiens sur l'architecture*, vol. 2, Paris 1872, pp. 253–301.
25 The garden was designed by the landscape architect Herta Hammerbacher, who was married at the time to the landscape architect Hermann Mattern. Both were involved in garden designs for other Scharoun projects. See 'Gartengestaltung durch die arbeitsgemeinschaft Förster/Mattern/Hammerbacher. Häuser und Garten', in: *Bauwelt*, no. 12, 1935, pp. 1–8.
26 Klaus Graupner, 'Hans Scharoun's Schminke House in Löbau (Saxony): Building Science Aspects, Heating and Ventilation Concepts', in: *Climate and Building Physics in the Modern Movement: Proceedings of the 9th International DOCOMOMO Technology Seminar, June 24–25, 2005, Löbau, Wissenschaftliche Berichte der Hochschule Zittau/Görlitz*, no. 88, 2006, pp. 46–49; Jos Tomlow, 'Building Physics and Its Performance in Modern Movement Architecture', in: Theodore Prudon (ed.), *Modern and Sustainable*, *DOCOMOMO Journal*, no. 44, 2011, pp. 24–31.
27 On the subject of plants in Modernist interiors, see Penny Sparke, *Nature Inside: Plants and Flowers in the Modern Interior*, New Haven, CT/London 2020.
28 Richard Neutra, *Survival Through Design*, New York 1954. The German edition appeared two years later under the title *Wenn wir weiterleben wollen ... Erfahrungen und Forderungen eines Architekten*, Hamburg 1956.
29 Richard Neutra, 'Architecture als angewandte Physiologie', in: *Baukunst und Werkform*, no. 1, 1955, p. 15.
30 Neutra, *Survival Through Design*, p. 229. See Joaquín Medina Warmburg, 'A Sliding Door to Life: The Bungalow as Bioreality', in: *Arch+*, no. 217, 2014, pp. 170–175.
31 Otto, *Das hängende Dach*, p. 158.

Design for a flower exhibition pavilion in Rotterdam, Netherlands (1959/60)

Technics

Structures
Methods
Moulds

The German Pavilion at Expo 67 in Montreal 1967

Joachim Kleinmanns

Because time was short, the site was far away and the budget was limited for the exhibition pavilion in Montreal, a structure had to be developed that could be transported and erected quickly and easily. This was promised by the winning design by Rolf Gutbrod and Frei Otto, and the jury recommended that the design be realized. Germany's Federal Construction Directorate (BBD) followed this endorsement despite reservations expressed by the jury's chairman, Egon Eiermann, about its feasibility. The decision to move forward was primarily thanks to the courage of Carl Mertz, Chief Building Director of the BBD. He took a chance on the experiment with only a year and a half left for its planning and execution.

The design's appeal stemmed from the contrasts produced by an asymmetrical, undulating tent roof structure with eight irregularly placed supports, beneath which terraces at different heights within a 1.25 metre grid were arranged to form a spiral. This was accompanied by yet a third element, a wood lattice dome sheltered by the tent serving as a lecture hall. What was distinctly innovative was the deliberate shift from conventional architecture to something (seemingly) makeshift, from the ponderous to the (seemingly) lightweight. Otto and Gutbrod had proceeded on the assumption that an exhibition pavilion, which was meant to stand for only six months, need not be a building structure but rather an improvisation.

The ideas for the tent, the terrace landscape and the wood lattice dome were worked out by Frei Otto and his collaborators at his Berlin-based Institute for the Development of Lightweight Construction (Entwicklungsstätte für den Leichtbau, EL). The basis for the tent was a model of the 'Hoch-Tiefpunkt-Studie' (High-Low Point Study) by Otto and Larry Medlin. As Otto remembered, Gutbrod judged that 'It's wonderful, but can we maybe change some things a bit?', namely 'make the peaks different heights?'[1] That was Gutbrod's crucial contribution to the design. The masts were placed irregularly, given different heights and slanted differently, which lent the tent roof the animated, lively appearance to which the public responded by giving the German Pavilion the nickname 'Swinging Germany'.

The tent skin was made up of anticlastic, curved surfaces (in two directions), the principle of which Otto had worked on since the 1950s and realized on a small scale in 1955 with the four-point sail structure in Kassel. A larger, regular membrane roof with cable-edged elements followed in 1956/57. Together with Medlin, he developed this further in soap film experiments arriving at a version with 'eyes' (cable loops), culminating in 1964 in the study on structural peaks and valleys. The cable loops reduced the stress at the membrane's high and low points, distributing it along the length of the so-called 'eye cable'. These previously developed principles now had to be transferred onto a large-scale tent, and this meant that the membrane had to be supported by a network of steel cable nets.

The final result was a huge, irregularly shaped tent covering an area of roughly 8,000 square metres. It was supported by eight masts of different heights and slanted in different directions. Bolted steel clamps were used to create the 50 × 50 centimetre mesh size of the cable net, which was made of steel cables with a diameter of 12 millimetres. It was prestressed evenly between the eight peaks at the top of the masts, the three hollows inside the tent and the thirty ground anchors around the edges to create a taut, 'bending-unrigid' (*biegeunsteife*) membrane. A waterproof skin made of a Polyester fabric with a PVC coating hung beneath it at a distance of between 35 to 40 centimetres. The area within each cable loop, the 'eyes', was sealed with acrylic glass.

Otto's model of the wood lattice dome was also reworked at Büro Gutbrod from a regular to a more animated form. The structure developed by Otto with Bernd-Friedrich Romberg and first realized in 1962 at the German Building Exhibition (Deutsche Bauausstellung, Deubau) in Essen was modified to form two irregular overlapping domes. They were comprised of 33 × 42 millimetre laths intersecting at 50 centimetre intervals.

The shape was developed with a suspended model by Hermann Kendel in Gutbrod's firm. Even the compression of the lattice grid for transport was tested on the model. In Montreal, it was possible to set up each of the two domes in a mere eight hours.

There was no time for the development of special masts – a fish-bellied grid structure had been considered – so a standard product needed to be adopted: steel pipes with slightly conically tapered ends. Mast A was the tallest at 38 metres and was the only one that had to be transported in two sections. The cable net of hot-galvanized stranded cable was tied together with three-part cross clamps. These had been developed in Otto's EL and some forty thousand had been forged. The engineering firm Leonhardt und Andrä developed the edge clamps. Owing to time constraints, they were die-cut and pressed into shape. The individual strips of the net were assembled by the tent-making concern Stromeyer in Konstanz, rolled up and then eventually clamped together directly at the construction site. The entirety of the membrane itself was divided up into twenty-three sections, each roughly 400 square metres in area. These were also first joined together in Montreal and suspended beneath the cable net. For this, Frei Otto had developed spring ties that distributed the punctual strain across larger surfaces.

The terrace landscape under the tent roof was made up of rigid 24-centimetre-thick steel lattice slabs on a grid with dimensions of 1.25 metres. The construction was developed in Otto's EL and tested on a model. Otto and the Berlin-based manufacturer Steffen & Nölle received a patent for it.

As Frei Otto was most widely thought by the general public to have been the pavilion's author and creator, he tried to set the record straight shortly before the Expo's opening: 'Of late, I have frequently been named on official occasions without further comment as the originator of the German Pavilion's structural design [...] This is a one-sided distinction that I don't deserve'.[2] Otto emphasized that it was a collaborative achievement and that 'The structure was first and foremost the pavilion of Rolf Gutbrod and his team.'[3]

Along with the pavilion's tremendous popularity there were also critical comments about the enormous expense of the anchorages, which belied the supposed lightness of the concept. But this by no means diminished the pavilion's success, as evidenced not only by the fact that the same concept was adopted by Behnisch & Partner for the Olympic sports venues in Munich (1972) and for the wood gridshell of the Mannheim Multihalle (1975). Its success is also reflected in the fact that the pavilion was not dismantled following the Expo's closure as originally planned but rather taken over by the City of Montreal and used for various purposes up until 1972. It was only the need for new structures for the 1976 Summer Olympics that forced its removal. What survived, however, is the test structure erected at Stuttgart-Vaihingen in 1966, with a single mast and a cable eye. After being moved to its final location, it was expanded to house Frei Otto's Institute for Lightweight Structures (Institut für leichte Flächentragwerke, IL).

1 Joachim Kleinmanns, *Der deutsche Pavillon der Expo 67 in Montreal. Ein Schlüsselwerk deutscher Nachkriegsarchitektur*, Berlin 2020, p. 72.
2 Kleinmanns, *Der deutsche Pavillon der Expo 67 in Montreal*, p. 74.
3 Kleinmanns, *Der deutsche Pavillon der Expo 67 in Montreal*, p. 74.

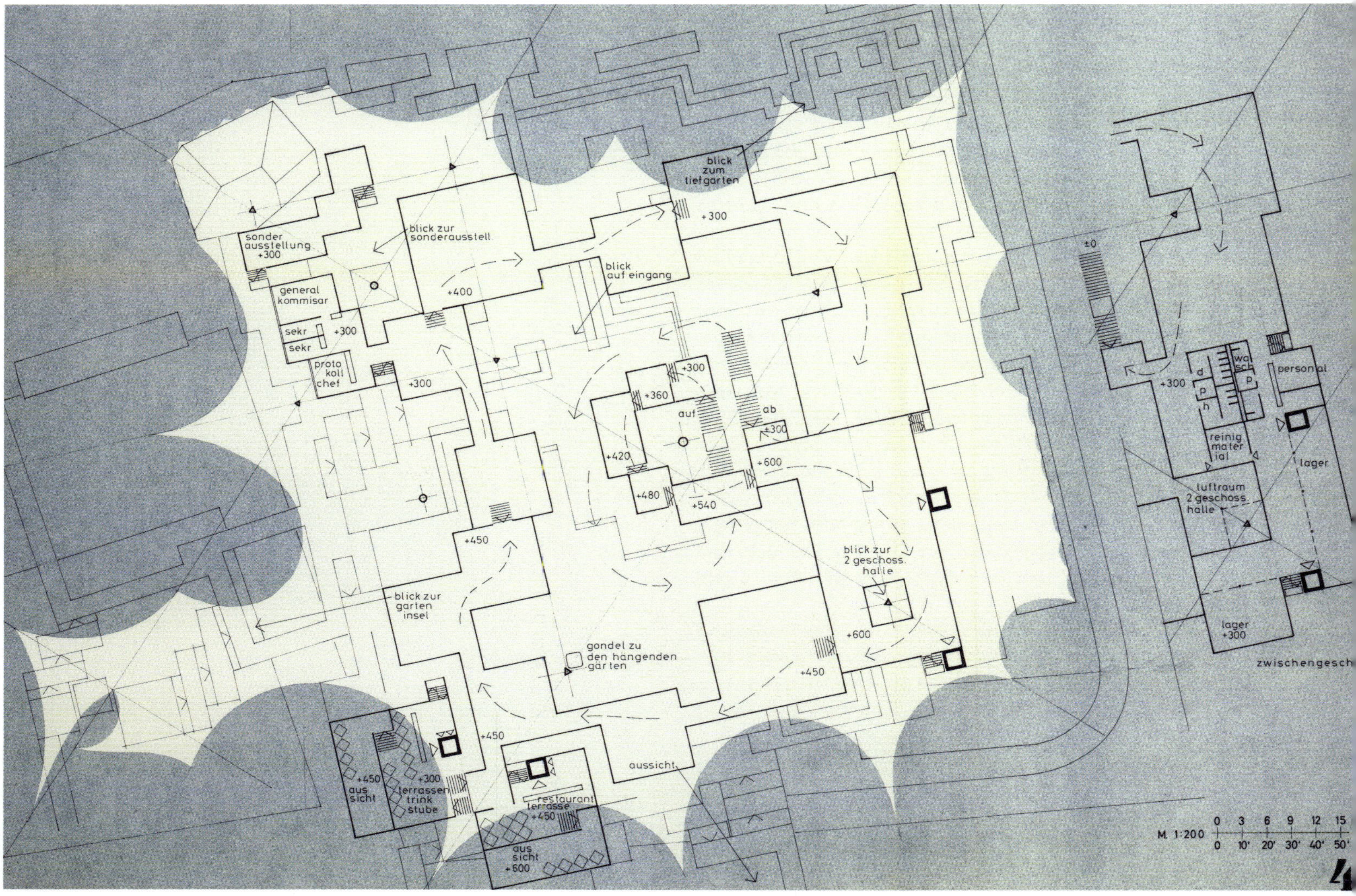

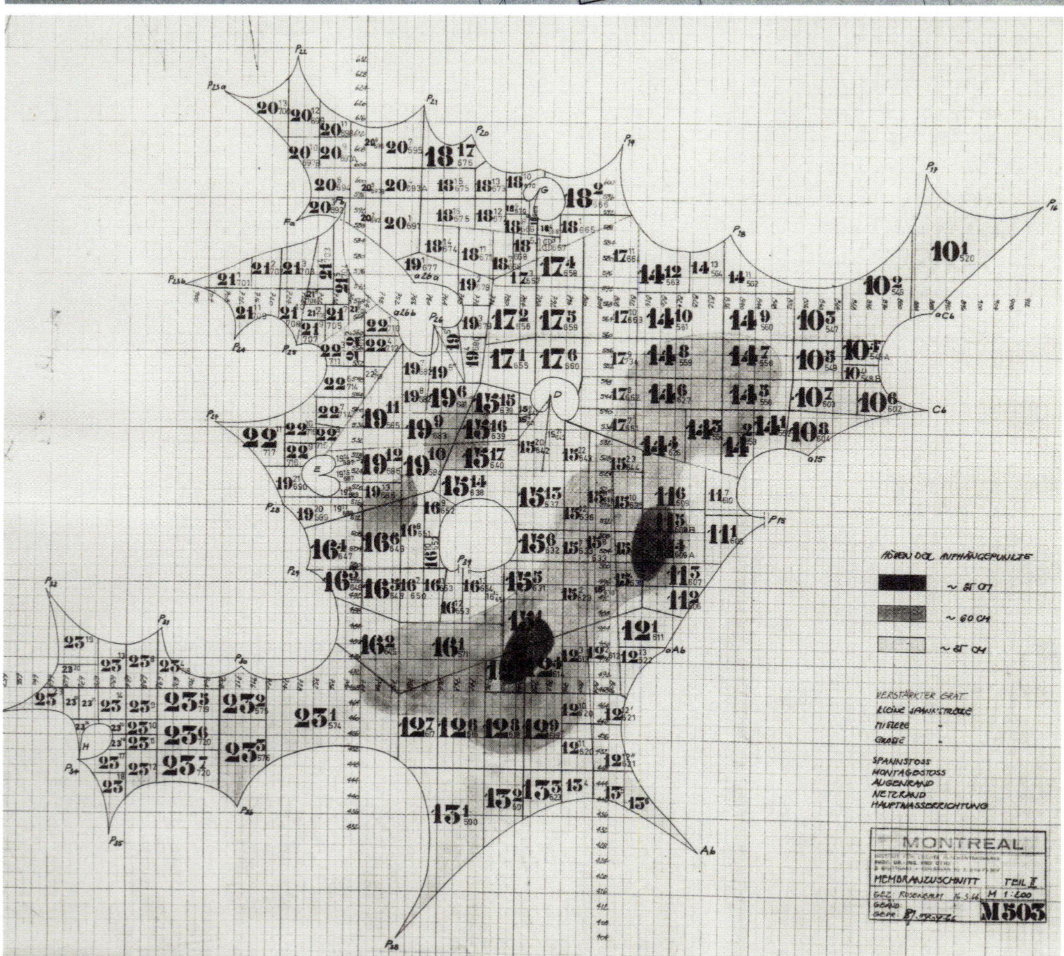

Competition plan, floor plan of the mezzanine and upper level

Overall cutting plan of the tent skin, part III, scale 1:200, drawing: Rosenbaum (March 1966)

Competition model seen
against the Montreal skyline

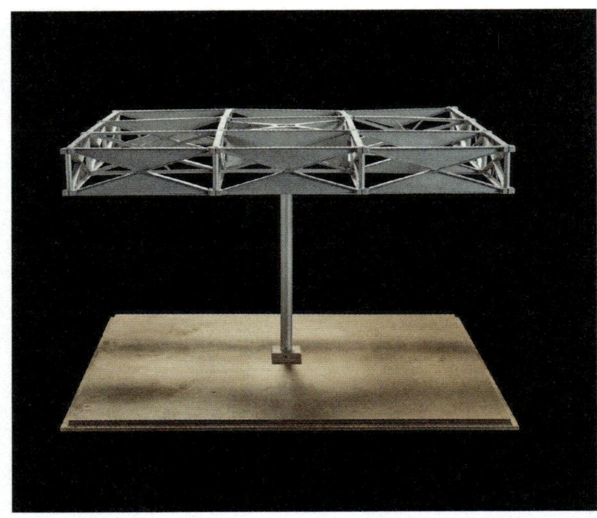

Exhibition terraces in the interior of the German Pavilion (August 1965), model

Cross clamps for the cable net (January 1966), model

Frei Otto with Larry Medlin, tent with uniform high and low points (1964), model

111

Building the interior pavilion terraces (January 1967)

Masthead with cable net structure (1967)

Inside the German Pavilion during the International and Universal Exposition (1967)

Following double page: The German Pavilion at night (April 1967)

Munich Olympic Park 1968–1972

Irene Meissner

When, in Rome on 26 April 1966, Munich was given the nod to host the 1972 Summer Olympics, they were projected to be cheerful, cosmopolitan and filled with goodwill – in distinct contrast to Germany's previous Olympiad of 1936 staged in Berlin as a monumental act of National Socialist propaganda. Six months after the announcement, a competition for the design of the Olympic grounds at Oberwiesenfeld was issued, and in October 1967, it was won by Behnisch & Partner with a concept for roof structures based on Frei Otto's German Pavilion for Expo 67 in Montreal. The large sports venues were to disappear beneath a series of undulating roofs, and the site was designed in such a way that the buildings would be nestled in a landscaped park. The overall design appeared to consist of a single, organically flowing movement. The concept's effective presentation was based, in part, on a clever model that simulated the tent-like structures with the mesh of cut nylon stockings and, in part, on a few expert drawings that provided a clear notion of the idea behind the design.

The jury recommended that the design be implemented. But since the architects had envisioned a roof ten times the size of the one in Montreal, the jury questioned its safety and 'whether the Montreal example can be followed for a roof on this scale'.[1] In the following months, engineers and other experts expressed contrary opinions around the realization of the structural design. A scant five months after the jury's decision, on 1 March 1968, Behnisch & Partner were given the contract for the overall concept – but not yet for the roof. Frei Otto, whom Behnisch had brought onto his team, was finally able to convince the professional community that the roof structure was possible. He divided the large, continuous roof surface into single roofs for the swimming hall, the sports hall and the stadium, with the latter subdivided into nine identical, saddle-shaped net surfaces. A final decision to proceed with the building of the tensile cable net structure was then reached on 21 June 1968.[2] Only then did the team in the 'Roof Planning Group', with its chief members Fritz Auer (Behnisch & Partner), Jörg Schlaich (Leonhardt und Andrä) and Frei Otto, begin its planning work, four years before the opening of the games.

For the realization of the roofs, whose mesh size was enlarged from the 50 centimetres used in Montreal to 75 centimetres, three different technologies were employed.[3] Since the size of the swimming hall roughly corresponded to that of the German Pavilion, it seemed appropriate to construct it at a ratio of 1:1 following the principle of the Montreal roof. That is to say, its shape was derived from models in tulle followed by 'measurement' models (*Messmodelle*) with which the geometry and the forces could be ascertained, and for the pattern, geodetic methods were used to balance out any imprecision in the calculation results. The striking similarity to the pavilion in Montreal can be readily seen from the cable loop, a so-called 'eye', with which the tensile membrane was hung from the mast.

Jörg Schlaich was responsible for the roof of the sports hall. In order to improve the pattern for the hall's roof, which was geometrically more complex than that of the swimming hall, Schlaich already sought an alternative to the measurement models in 1968. He contacted John Argyris, who in 1959 had founded the Institute of Structural Mechanics and Dynamics in Aerospace Engineering (Institut Statik und Dynamik der Luft- und Raumfahrtkonstruktionen, ISD) at the Stuttgart Institute of Technology (Technische Hochschule Stuttgart, TH Stuttgart). Argyris, one of the inventors of the finite element method (FEM), with which the deformation and strain in sections of complex structures can be analysed numerically, found a mathematical solution for the calculation of the net surface, which marked the beginning of computer-based methods for the simulation of lightweight surface structures.

The Olympic Stadium and the intermediate roofs, which were Frei Otto's responsibility, were constructed according to the force density method[4] – a mathematical formula for calculating error compensation – which had been developed under enormous time pressure by Klaus Linkwitz from the Institute for Applications of Geodesy to Civil Engineering (Institut für Anwendungen der Geodäsie im Bauwesen, IAGB) at TH Stuttgart, who had already been on the Montreal team.[5]

Building on the experiences from Montreal, measurement models on a scale of 1:125 (Montreal 1:75) for the stadium, the sports hall, the swimming hall and the connecting roofs were made in Stuttgart at the Institute for Lightweight Structures (Institut für leichte Flächentragwerke, IL) under the direction of Frei Otto.[6] Fish net served to simulate the roof surface. In order to determine the necessary spatial coordinates for the prefabrication and installation of the tensile membrane more accurately, the models were no longer measured mechanically but stereo-photogrammetrically. With the help of double exposures it was thus possible to determine the strain between the load and release of the cables. Gauges hung in the supporting panels registered differences in tension. But because of the small scale of the models it turned out that the target geometry and the target strength condition could be determined only approximately; Klaus Linkwitz calculated the margin of error by means of the force density method. This method for establishing the form of prestressed tensile structures is based on the relationship between the strength and length of a cable.[7] With the help of a specially developed computer programme, it was possible to draw the necessary plans for the shape of the cable net structure.

Since a shadow-free, translucent membrane was required for the stadium's roof to provide the ideal conditions for colour television transmission, it was decided in late 1968 to use a transparent, prestressed and virtually inflammable acrylic glass roofing. The 3×3 metre slabs were cut to size for the tensile structure and the joints between panes made watertight with black neoprene moulding wedged into place in a process developed by Frei Otto.

Carcassing began with excavation of the foundations on 9 June 1969. On the occasion of the commencement of construction, Willi Daume, President of the West German Olympic Committee, declared, 'When – if not for the Olympic games – was such a bold experiment as tent roof construction ever ventured?'[8] A year later, on 23 July 1970, the topping out ceremony took place. On 4 November 1971, the tensile membrane was stretched and on 21 April 1972, four months before the opening of the games, the last Plexiglas pane was set in place. A number of other technological innovations, like the optimization of the steel casting for the cables' deviating points on the mast caps, not only guaranteed the economical and timely completion of the Olympic roof, but were also important for the future development of high-tech architecture.

The Olympic sports venues in Munich not only became a global landmark, but they are also milestones in the development of tensile cable net structures and numerical methods. The park complex fascinates to this day, and the innovative technological solutions worked out in short order are a constant source of inspiration for research.

1 Architekturmuseum der TU München, Sign. alb-42-218: Niederschrift über die Sitzung des Preisgerichtes (1.+2. Richterliche Sitzung), minutes of the jury meeting, the first and second judges' meeting.
2 For a chronology, 1965–1971, see Fritz Auer, *Ein Zeltdach für München und die Welt. Die Verwirklichung einer Idee für Olympia 1972*, Munich 2022, pp. 154–169; Irene Meissner, *Die Olympiastadt München*, exh. cat. Architekturmuseum der TU München, Munich 2022; Elisabeth Spieker, *Olympia München '72*, Berlin 2022.
3 See Kai-Uwe Bletzinger, 'Die Freiheit von Form und Kraft. Das olympische Dach und seine bahnbrechende Bedeutung für die moderne und computerorientierte Simulation', Munich, 4 October 2022: https://www.vdi-sued.de/fileadmin/sn_config/mediapool_vdi/arbeitskreise/technikgeschichte/doc/Olympiadach_Vweb_2.mp4 (accessed April 2024).
4 'Klaus Linkwitz im Gespräch. Modell und Methode', in: Walter Scheiffele, *Das leichte Haus. Utopie und Realität der Membranarchitektur*, Leipzig 2015, pp. 340–351.
5 See saai, Werkarchiv Behnisch & Partner, Olympiaanlagen München 1967–1972, Bauakten/02, Dach/02.
6 For a description of the physical scale models, see *Olympische Bauten München 1972*, vol. 2: *Bestandsaufnahme Herbst 1970, architektur wettbewerbe*, Stuttgart 1970, pp. 22–25; Fritz Leonhardt and Jörg Schlaich, 'Vorgespannte Seilnetzkonstruktionen: Das Olympiadach München', in: *Der Stahlbau*, no. 12, 1972, p. 375.
7 Kai-Uwe Bletzinger, 'Simulationsmethoden im textilen Leichtbau. Die Entwicklung seit 1972 und aktueller Stand', in: *Bautechnik*, no. 11, 2015, pp. 800–805, here p. 801.
8 *Olympischer Grundstein für 1972*, ed. Organisationskomitee für die Spiele der XX. Olympiade München 1972, under the direction of Hans Klein, special issue, 14 July 1969, pp. 24–28, here p. 27.

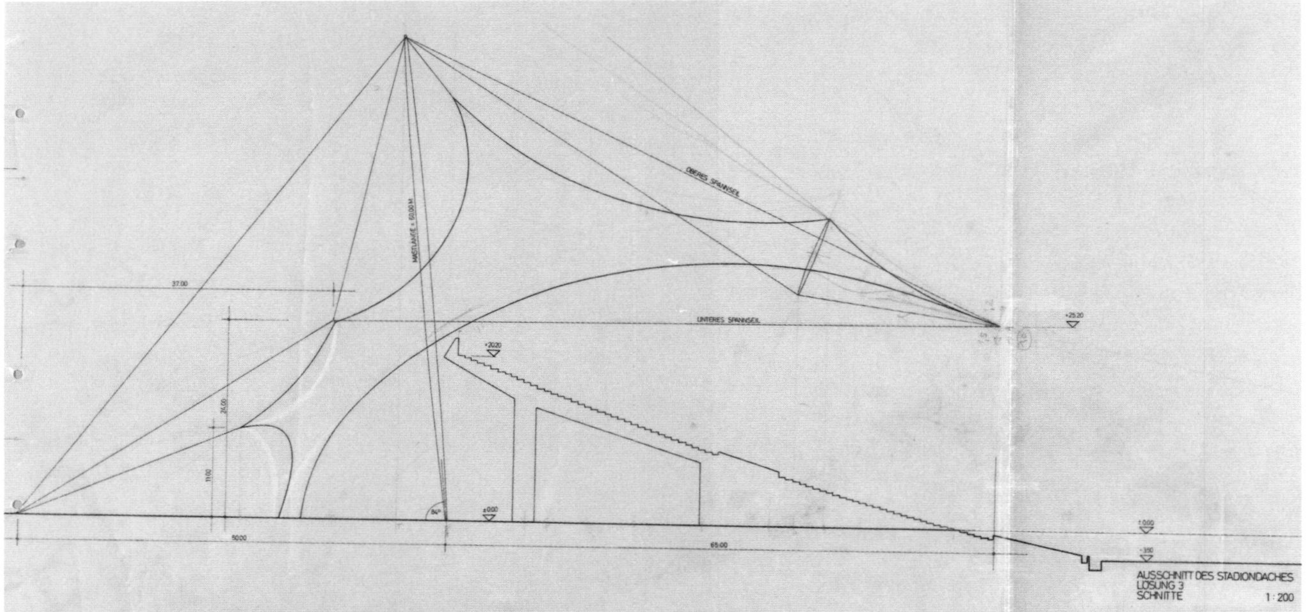

Section through the stadium roof with 'air supports' (April 1968)

Roofing for the temporary stands of the swimming hall, model

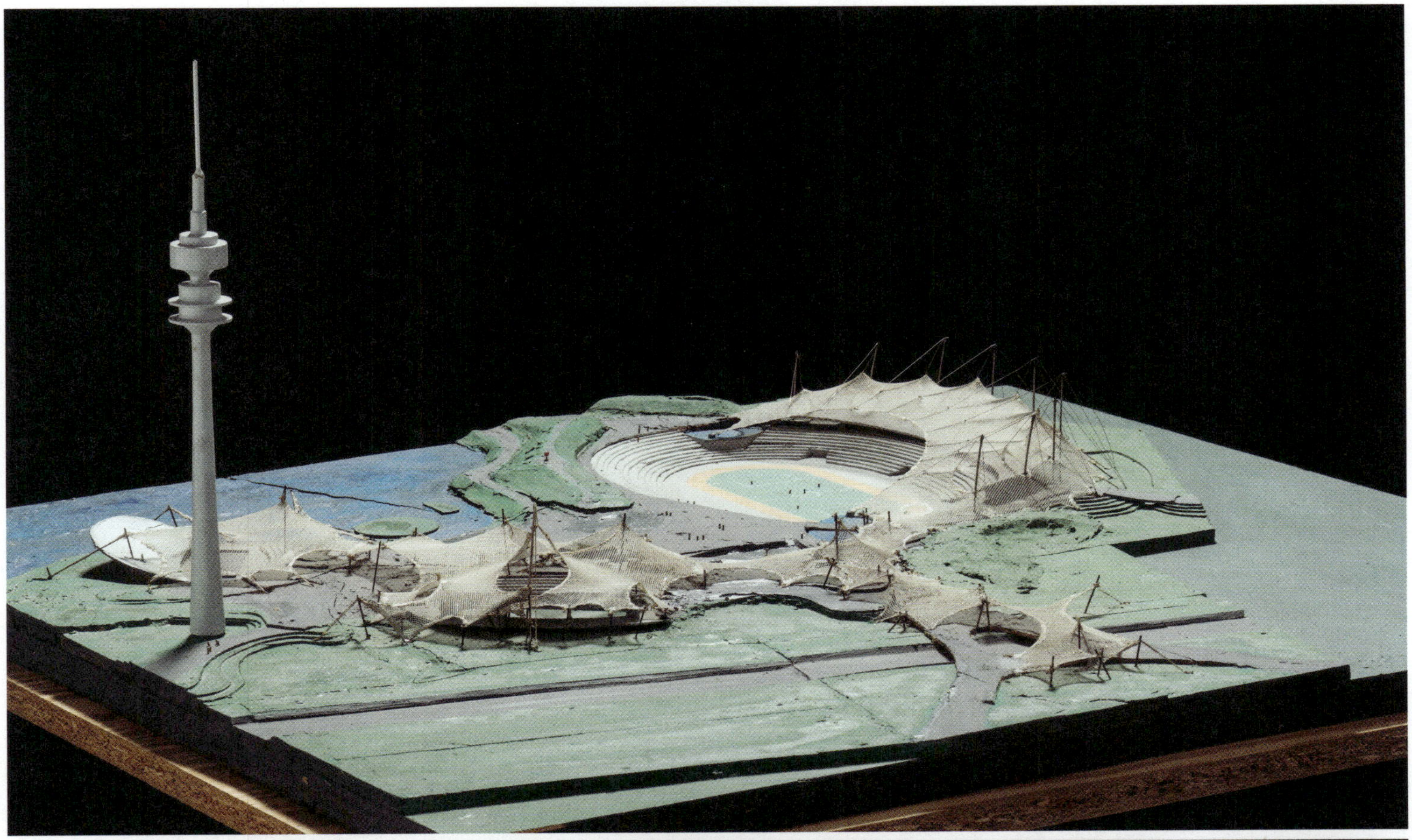

Complete model by Frei Otto (May 1968)

'Measurement' model of the swimming hall

Following double page: Erecting the cable net of the Olympiahalle sports hall

View of the stadium from the roof of the swimming hall

123

Hanging the interior foil
of the swimming hall

View of temporary stands in the swimming hall

Opening ceremony for the Games of the XX Olympiad (26 August 1972)

Following double page: Aerial view of the complex as a whole during the 1972 Summer Olympics

MEXIKO CITY
1968

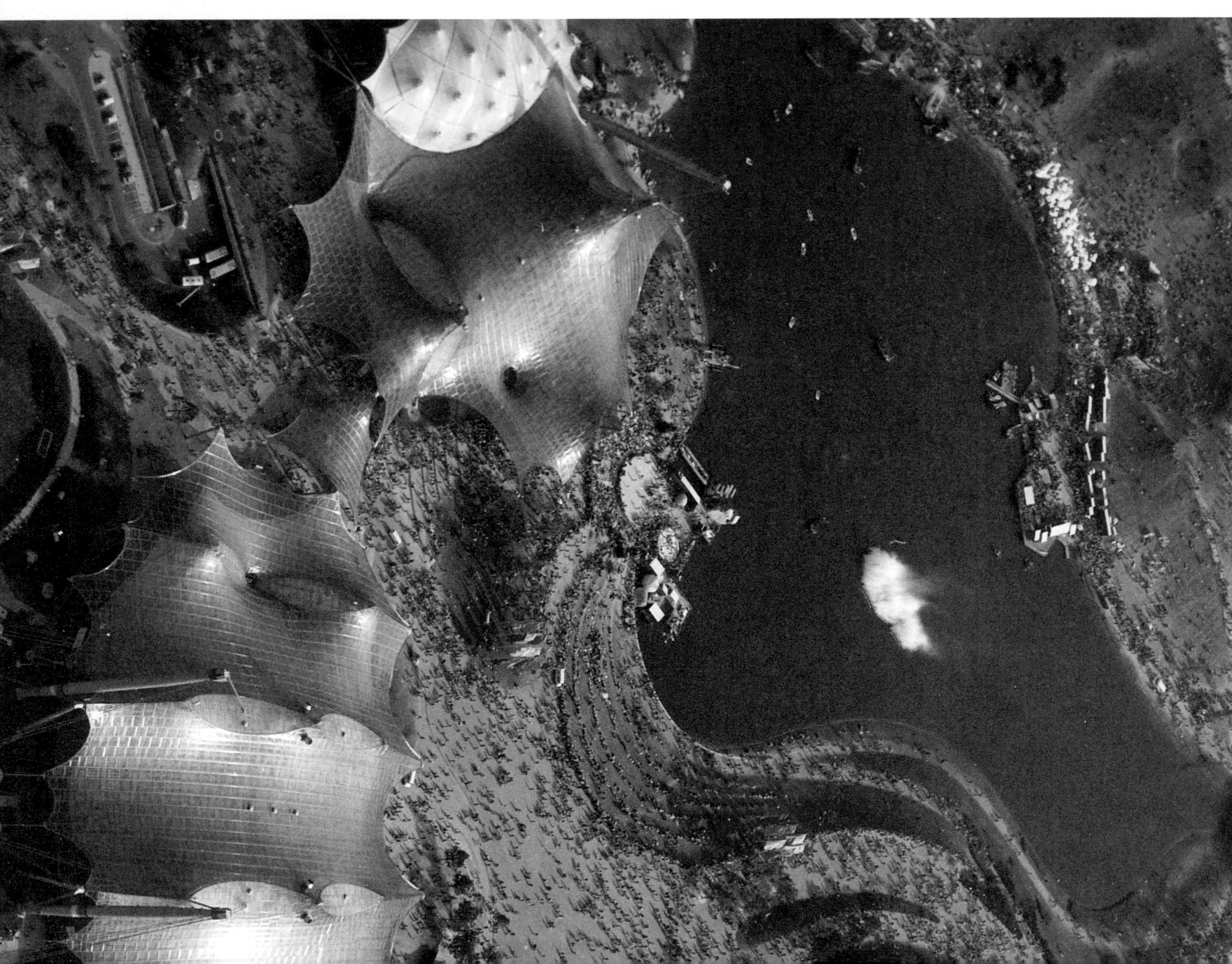

Mannheim's Multihalle 1975

Mechthild Ebert

Once it was decided to hold the German National Garden Show (Bundesgartenschau) in Mannheim for the first time in 1975, expectations for the exhibition ran high; not only would it boost the city's image, but it would also prompt new urban planning, just as the International Art and Great Garden Exhibition (Internationale Kunst- und Grosse Gartenbau-Ausstellung) had done for the city in 1907. The motto, 'Live, Work, Build, Relax in the City', put the relationship between the city and its residents into focus. Two country-wide competitions for the planning were announced. The architecture firm of Carlfried Mutschler & Partners together with the landscape architect Heinz H. Eckebrecht won the contract for the overall planning of the Herzogenried Park quarter. In addition to the design of the garden show site itself, this was to include a housing development with related public buildings.[1] The Multihalle (i.e., multipurpose hall) would be part of the central information axis, which was to lead through the park from the main entrance at the west to the new residential quarter.[2]

When Mannheim's German National Garden Show opened in 1975, it was the 'most complicated simple roof in the world' that attracted international attention.[3] Several other ideas for the design of the roof over the Multihalle and restaurant had been rejected for various reasons: for example, a roof made up of 'an overlapping cluster of large umbrellas [...] suspended from gas balloons.'[4] Then, in 1972, 'somebody remembered Frei Otto's ingenious concept of gridshells' and his realization of one at the German Building Exhibition (Deutsche Bauausstellung, Deubau) in Essen in 1962.[5] At the same time, a Japanese-German research team at the Stuttgart Institute for Lightweight Structures (Institut für leichte Flächentragwerke, IL) was working on geodesic domes under Frei Otto's direction.[6] This research took the term 'gridshell' (*Gitterschale*) to mean a 'grid of wooden slats that is curved twice over its extended area by the bending of the slats and angular twisting at the intersection points.'[7]

Once the client approved the plan, Otto and Ewald Bubner took charge and began making studies of the roof's form in the Warmbronn atelier. The best known of these was the suspended model with fine-linked chains, which solely by its own weight produced the ideal form of the upright roof shell. Measurement of the model and layout details were taken over by Klaus Linkwitz and Hans Dieter Preuss from Stuttgart's Institute for Applications of Geodesy to Civil Engineering (Institut für Anwendungen der Geodäsie im Bauwesen, IAGB). Frei Otto turned to the British engineering firm of Ove Arup & Partners, whose Structures 3 division was headed by Edmund 'Ted' Happold and Ian Liddell, which took on the calculation and dimensioning of the structure.[8]

The most varied experimental models and computer-supported calculations led to a shell construction 'of two resp. four layers of interlaced slats of Canadian hemlock wood, placed 50 cm apart. Each lattice slat is 5.5 cm wide.'[9] In contrast to other lattice domes like the one at Deubau in Essen or at the Expo pavilion in Montreal, the wood gridshell in Mannheim was not set in place with a crane but raised up from below.[10]

The test engineer Fritz Wenzel suggested a load experiment to supplement the theoretical proofs.[11] For it, in January 1975, 205 dustbins were borrowed from Mannheim's Sanitation Department and attached to a partial section of the roof. They were filled with water and placed on concrete cavity blocks. The blocks were gradually removed until finally all the dustbins, with a total weight of 18.45 metric tons, hung from a 406-square-metre section. The measured strain lay just below what had been predicted and assured the structure's safety.[12]

The roof construction consists of two shells, a connecting bridge and ramps – likewise roofed. At a total length of 160 metres and width of roughly 115 metres, the roof structure covers an area of 7,400 square metres. The 9,500-square-metre roof surface was covered with a special mesh – polyester fibres laminated with dark PVC – which was replaced with a white fabric only six years later.[13] The larger of the two domes covers the Multihalle with a free span of 85 metres and a maximum height of 20 metres.[14]

Since 1998, the Multihalle has been a listed monument. In 2016, the structure's upkeep became a matter of debate owing to the high cost of restoration.[15] This sparked a discussion about how to deal with the edifice, which elicited interest and initiatives from various disciplines. In the summer of 2017,

Mannheim City Council determined that financing for the restoration and a concept for the structure's future use should be clarified by the end of 2019. To support this plan, the City of Mannheim together with the Architektenkammer Baden-Württemberg (chamber of architects) established the association, Verein Multihalle e.V., which in 2018, along with the Association of German Architects (Bund Deutscher Architektinnen und Architekten, BDA) of Baden-Württemberg and IBA Heidelberg, Heidelberg's International Building Exhibition, advertised Multihalle – Democratic Umbrella, a global competition for proposals. In 2019, the jury of experts awarded equal prizes to three of the international submissions. After a subsequent workshop, the jury opted for the work of the firms COFO architects and PEÑA architecture and commissioned them to work out a development concept.[16]

According to that concept, the Multihalle is to become a dynamic social space – as envisioned by Frei Otto and Carlfried Mutschler – one that is stimulating, promotes interactions and encourages creativity. Retaining the structural concept, the supporting framework is to be renovated and the halls 'reprogrammed' on a human scale.[17] After approval by Mannheim City Council, nothing more stood in the way of a start to the renovation work. The methodological concept behind the renovation is described as a 'planning-related experimental process' and can be understood in light of the structure's original visionary nature.[18] Ideas about strengthening, restoring and repairing the structure were to be tested on the object itself.[19]

The Multihalle is presented as an outstanding monument, not only because of its varied functions for the German National Garden Show as well as for the City of Mannheim and its inhabitants, but also because of the extraordinary collaboration and 'love of experimentation' between the most varied professions from the worlds of architecture, structural engineering and geodesy. Today, once again, experts from various disciplines are coming together to forge new paths forward. When the German National Garden Show was held in Mannheim again in 2023 it was possible to tour the construction site.[20]

In 1963, in an editorial titled 'Keine Gartenschau ohne ihren Otto' (No Garden Show Without Its Otto), the trade journal *Bauwelt* noted that since Kassel in 1955 'virtually no single National Garden Show in Germany had taken place without one of Frei Otto's lightweight and airy tent structures'.[21] It went on to say that it would be desirable if Otto were sometime given the chance to test his experiments in a more permanent sector.[22]

In 2025, the Multihalle celebrates its fiftieth anniversary, even though it was never intended for permanent use. Despite its transformation into a permanent structure, it has not lost its visionary character, and with its multiple experimental approaches it continues to inspire.

1 See Niels Gormsen, 'Gartenschau und Stadtentwicklung', in: *Bauwelt*, no. 22 (1975), p. 640.
2 See Carlfried Mutschler, 'Grundkonzept', in: *Multihalle Mannheim, Mitteilungen des Instituts für leichte Flächentragwerke (IL)*, no. 13, Stuttgart 1978, p. 21.
3 Manfred Sack, 'Das Wunder von Mannheim', in: *Die Zeit*, no. 21, 16 May 1975.
4 Mutschler, 'Grundkonzept', p. 23.
5 Mutschler, 'Grundkonzept', p. 26.
6 The final report on this research was published in 1974 under the title *Gitterschalen/Grid Shells, Mitteilungen des Instituts für leichte Flächentragwerke (IL)*, no. 10.
7 Winfried Nerdinger (ed.), *Frei Otto: Complete Works; Lightweight Construction, Natural Design*, exh. cat. Architekturmuseum der TU München, Basel/Boston/Berlin 2005, p. 288.
8 Nerdinger (ed.), *Frei Otto: Complete Works*, p. 288.
9 Multihalle Mannheim, 'Architecture', https://mannheim-multihalle.de/en/architecture/ (accessed 3 June 2024).
10 See Nerdinger (ed.), *Frei Otto: Complete Works*, p. 288.
11 Nerdinger (ed.), *Frei Otto: Complete Works*, p. 288.
12 See 'Gitterschale in Mannheim', in: *Deutsche Bauzeitung*, no. 3, 1975, pp. 21f.
13 See Georg Vrachliotis, *Frei Otto. Carlfried Mutschler. Multihalle*, Leipzig 2017, p. 126.
14 See Nerdinger (ed.), *Frei Otto: Complete Works*, p. 288.
15 See Wüstenrot Stiftung, 'Multihalle von Frei Otto in Mannheim', https://wuestenrot-stiftung.de/multihalle-frei-otto-mannheim/ (accessed 3 June 2024).
16 See Multihalle Mannheim, 'Develop', https://mannheim-multihalle.de/en/developing/ (accessed 3 June 2014).
17 See COFO Architects, 'Multihalle Vision', https://cofoarchitects.com/work/multihalle-vision (accessed 3 June 2024).
18 'Die Umsetzung erfolgt als planungsbegleitender experimenteller Prozess': see Wüstenrot Stiftung, 'Multihalle von Frei Otto in Mannheim'.
19 Wüstenrot Stiftung, 'Multihalle von Frei Otto in Mannheim'.
20 See Mannheim Multihalle, Blog Schaustelle Baustelle, https://mannheim-multihalle.de/blog/schaustelle-baustelle/ (accessed 3 June 2024).
21 'Keine Gartenschau ohne ihren Otto', in: *Bauwelt*, no. 18, 1963, p. 495.
22 See 'Keine Gartenschau ohne ihren Otto', p. 495.

Carlfried Mutschler + Partner, conceptual sketch showing the originally planned balloon roofs, competition entry (1972)

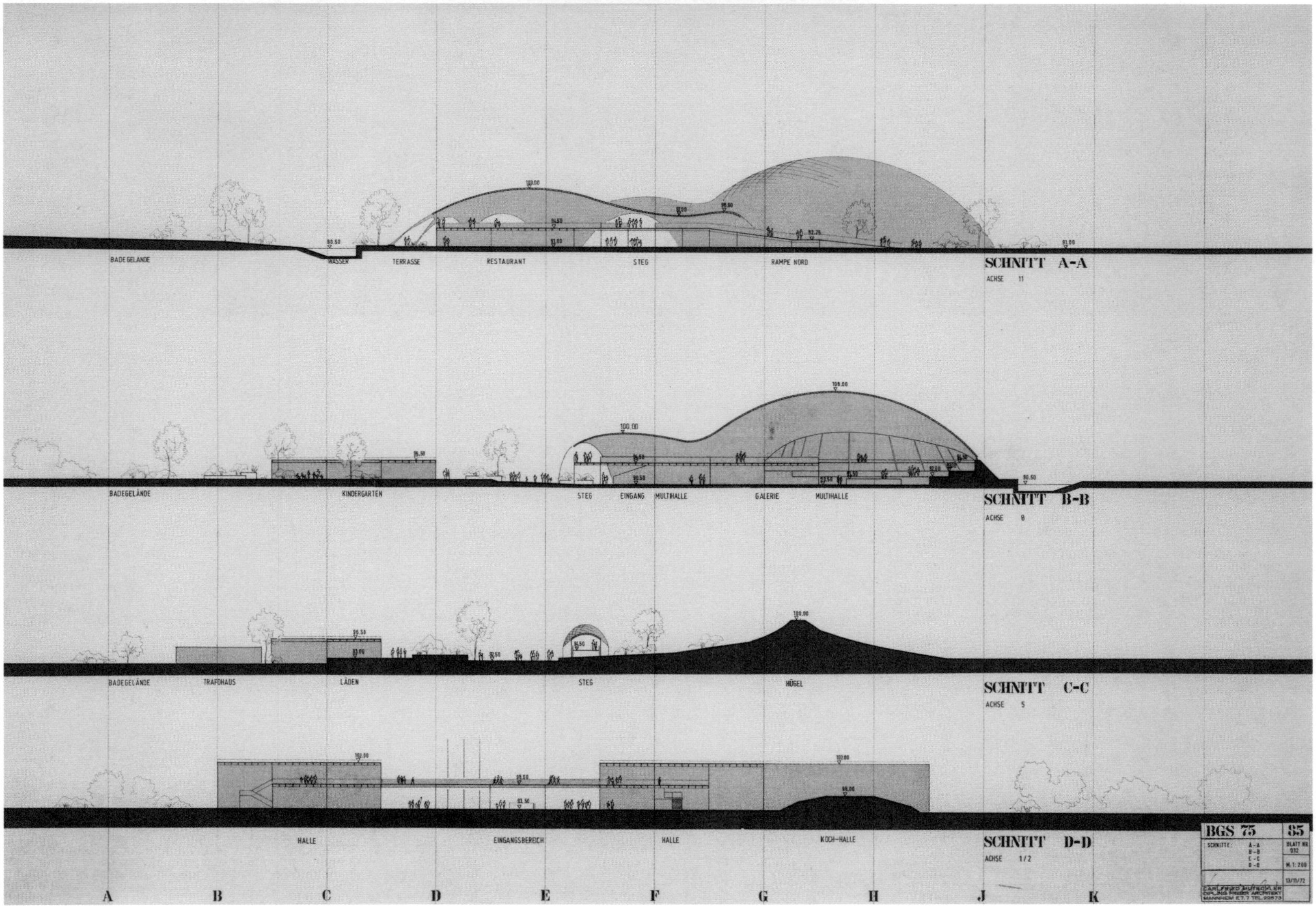

Air currents and flow stimulated in a wind tunnel in order to measure the distribution of surface pressures

Multihalle, cross-section (planning status as of 13 November 1972)

Mounting the textile over the gridshell

Static load tests using dustbins filled with water (18 January 1975)

View across the artificial pond of the restaurant terrace

Ramp entrance from the east

Artificial waterscape

Interior view of the Multihalle after the German National Garden Show (*c.* 1977)

Interior view of the Multihalle during the annual exhibition of the Deutscher Künstlerbund (1976)

Following double page: The Multihalle at night

Lightweight Structures and Roofs: Types and Forms

Irene Meissner

Lightweight construction is the central theme running through Frei Otto's entire career as architect and designer. He worked out the fundamentals of lightweight building decades before its importance became the focus of the architectural world and the broader public. For Otto, 'lightweight' not only meant the minimization of mass, material and energy, but also the solution to structural and constructive tasks in the sense of the self-forming, self-realizing natural processes he studied. According to him, 'lightweight building' was, for one thing, a resource-sparing approach to building in harmony with nature and, for another, a way of building without any claim to 'permanence' or any pretence of grandeur – for after his experiences of the National Socialist period, he decisively rejected any form of grandiosity in architecture. Frei Otto envisioned a variety of forms in lightweight construction: tents and tensile structures with minimal surfaces, gridshells stabilized by inverting tension cables, branching structures free of flexural strength through inversion, pneumatic shells whose form is dictated by pressure relationships and that lie above a landscape like a second skin, and architecture capable of being adapted to any given need and modified again and again. Over the course of his life, Otto developed a comprehensive, holistic and socially minded ideology of lightweight building in which he incorporated all areas of construction: from participative planning processes to bionics, from form-finding following natural laws to the systematic study of processes for self-formation, and from reflections on the origin of life to the ideal form of social cohabitation.[1]

Both scientific and practical engagement with lightweight construction began in the nineteenth century. Among its pioneers were the Russian engineer Vladimir Shukhov, who built lightweight hyperboloid towers and the first doubly curved structural frames; the American polymath Richard Buckminster Fuller, who developed self-supporting edifices and lightweight structures following the principle of tensional construction; the German architect Konrad Wachsmann, who created standardized elements for serial modular construction; and the German engineer Max Mengeringhausen, who in 1939 developed a node with rods that was used internationally in the production of structural frames following the Second World War. A first milestone in the theoretical foundation of lightweight architecture was the essay by the structural engineer and bridge builder Fritz Leonhardt, 'Leichtbau – eine Forderung unserer Zeit' (Lightweight Construction – A Demand of Our Time),[2] which he wrote in 1940 in view of combating resource shortages. But it was Frei Otto, who with his research and experiments, combined with a social-democratic objective, first laid the foundations for the extraordinary development of lightweight construction.

Prisoners of war cemetery at Le Courdray near Chartres, France

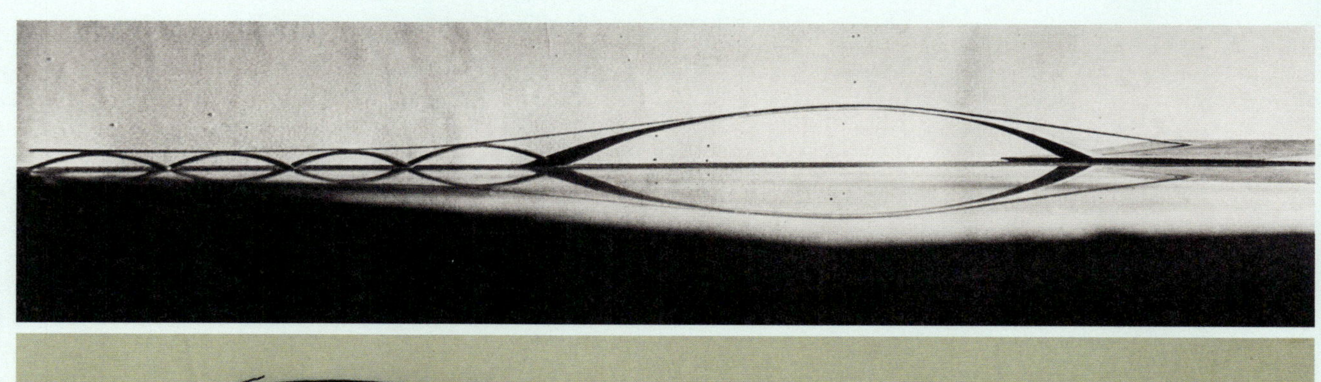

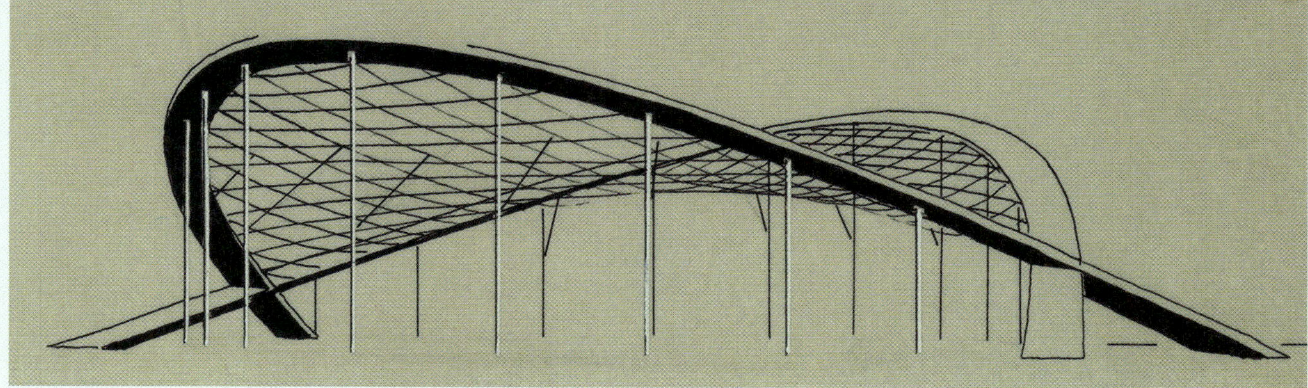

Frei Otto's Path to Lightweight Construction

In his teens, Frei Otto experienced the terror of the National Socialist regime. In 1943, he enrolled at Berlin's Technische Hochschule (technical college) intending to study architecture, but a short time later, only aged eighteen, he was drafted into the Luftwaffe as a fighter pilot. As a flyer, he saw how buildings planned for the 'new eternity' were destroyed in a hail of bombs. 'Burning cities are a bitter introductory course for budding architects',[3] he commented in retrospect. Towards the end of the Second World War, in 1945, he was captured by the French and interned in Le Coudray, on the outskirts of Chartres (Eure-et-Loir). There he found his way to lightweight architecture, his life's calling. With a seminary nearby and surrounded by suffering and death in the prisoner-of-war camp, Otto developed a profound religious commitment; an ethical humanism oriented towards mankind's well-being defined his whole life.[4] It was there that he developed the ideal of taking into account when building that the earth needs to offer living space for future generations, as well as that buildings can disappear again with 'integrity'. Such concern for the *terre des hommes* would mark his life and his work. Since there were virtually no materials in the camp, he was automatically forced into lightweight construction. Because he had a basic knowledge in construction he became the camp architect, laid out the cemetery and was confronted with the task of rebuilding destroyed halls and bridges. The most impressive design from his internment period was his plan for reconstructing a road bridge across the Eure.[5] Since the engineers' plan of using railroad tracks to construct parallel girders would have used up too much material, Frei Otto wondered how he could reduce the weight and, based on the forces involved, hit upon an optimal, material-sparing 'lightweight' structure. The bridge was never built, to be sure, but this first important structural plan laid the foundation for his further studies.

After two and a half years, Frei Otto was released from his imprisonment in 1947. He returned to Berlin and, in the summer semester of 1948, again took up his architecture studies. The next decisive experience on his path to lightweight construction came to Frei Otto in 1950 during a trip to the United States on a grant

Design for a bridge across the Eure River (1946), model photograph

Supporting structure of the Raleigh Arena: cable net suspended between two arches, not prestressed (1952)

Frei Otto, *Das hängende Dach* (The Hanging Roof, 1954), book cover

from the German Academic Scholarship Foundation. In the New York office of Fred N. Severud, he saw the model of the Dorton Arena in Raleigh, North Carolina, that Severud had designed together with Matthew Nowicki. The arena's saddle-shaped roof supported by a structural network of cables stretched between its two parabolic arches was a developmental milestone in the building industry; it marked the turning point from solid, heavy load-bearing structures to light, tensile structures composed of cables and membranes. The arena would be a key influence on Otto's further work.

After returning to Berlin, Frei Otto immersed himself in studies on lightweight construction and, in 1954, submitted his pathbreaking doctoral thesis *Das hängende Dach* (The Hanging Roof),[6] in which he fully rediscovered tents – previously seen as temporary, humble and relatively unstable – for architecture. In it, he summarized the state of current knowledge in lightweight construction methods from the arena in Raleigh (1951/52) and the Swiss Pavilion at the 1952 German Industries Fair in Berlin (Hans Stettbacher and Hans Osterwald) to the Schwarzwaldhalle in Karlsruhe (Erich Schelling, 1953). He illustrated the new potential of these construction methods with designs for large shells built over cities in extreme climate zones. Otto wished to demonstrate with them the global as well as egalitarian benefits of lightweight structures, which for him were bound to the hope that they might also lead to a new, democratic society. Even before he was able to exhibit structures of his own, his thesis published by the Bauwelt-Verlag immediately came to the attention of professional circles.

Lightweight architecture as a symbol of the renunciation of the monumental and heavy structures of National Socialism also helped to define the conversation surrounding the reconstruction of Germany. Lightweight buildings would lend the new society a more democratic appearance. During the talks of the so-called Darmstädter Gespräch, the most important debate on the rebuilding of Germany held in Darmstadt in 1951 – Frei Otto had not been invited – Hans Schwippert explained that people were yearning for lightweight housing, for light, for openness, that instead of fortress-like retreats, simple 'tents' and 'light, open structures' needed to be built.[7] Though during the rebuilding, most modern architects did consequently try to design bright, 'transparent' spaces, massive buildings were ultimately erected by architects not primarily concerned with new structural solutions. The openness and 'transparency' so many strove for was more an expression of the desire to leave monumental building behind than a commitment to dematerialization.

Frei Otto, who sought designs following the laws of nature, had different, wholly new incentives. He advocated 'natural' architectural forms as expressions of a modern, mobile and cosmopolitan generation. He was not concerned with erecting single structures; his work was rather dictated by his vision of creating an architecture for a peaceful society in harmony with nature: 'Less is more, [...] fewer houses, less material, less concrete and less consumption of energy, but building humanely, using whatever is at hand: earth, water, air. Building close to nature and making much out of little [...] Better not to build at all than build too much!'[8] With this he was not only entering new architectural territory; with his concepts of lightweight construction, he was also presenting a new sociopolitical worldview, one that he formulated succinctly: 'With lightness against brutality',[9] against 'the architecture of killing.'[10] He continued, 'We, my generation, which was blasted into adulthood by the war, wanted to help in the reconstruction, wanted to transcend the war, the delusions of grandeur, the cult of the Führer and of personality, wanted to be able to live – but all the while remain humble.'[11] With that objective, he experimented with textiles and air, materials with which it was seemingly impossible to build or which had certainly not been considered building materials heretofore.

Tents and Membranes

Through working on his thesis, Frei Otto came into contact with the tent manufacturer Peter Stromeyer, with whom he realized his first tents in 1955 for the German National Garden Show (Bundesgartenschau) in Kassel. The tent erected for the summer above a music pavilion in front of Kassel's Orangery was Frei Otto's first realized four-point sail structure, which thanks to its aesthetic appeal could also be seen as an artwork, part of the first documenta exhibition taking place in Kassel at the same time. Its planning, fabrication and installation took only six weeks. The simple canopy roof marked a new epoch in membrane construction, as here he realized, for the first time, the principle of a counter-curved saddle-shaped, prestressed membrane with a corresponding form. Since the principal tensions and curvatures were the same in both directions, the roof took up a minimal surface area. The membrane with two peaks and two hollows was made of heavy cotton canvas and extended to a length of 18 metres, much longer than was previously customary in tent construction. In subsequent collaborations with Stromeyer, he produced tent roofs for the German National Garden Show in Cologne and for Interbau in Berlin, both in 1957, with which Otto brought membrane construction to a new level of development and soon made it a recognized structural shape.

Frei Otto's former statics professor Hellmuth Bickenbach recommended that he work with the structural engineer Fritz Leonhardt. Their first collaborative project to reach completion was the entry arch for the German National Garden Show in Cologne – an arch 34 metres wide made of tubular steel with a thickness of only 20 centimetres and spanned by a membrane that simultaneously served to stabilize it. Otto's most famous tent at the Cologne garden show was the so-called Tanzbrunnen (dance fountain), an undulating radial star-shaped tent over a circular dance floor constructed above an artificial water basin. Though planned for only one season, because of its great popularity it was reinstalled over several summers and finally made a permanent fixture. The canopy surface, 1,000 square metres in extent, consists of twelve identical segments corresponding to the principle of the four-point sail structure with a doubly counter-curved surface. The membrane is stretched across six slender cable-stayed masts that define the six peaks, while the cables tied to a central ocular ring establish the six hollows. With numerous other wavy, curving, pointed and peaked tents, Otto developed the potential of membrane structures. A further important developmental step was his first application of a prestressed tensile textile membrane with peaks and hollows for Interbau in 1957 – a protective canopy measuring 17.5 × 22.5 metres created to cover the Symphony Orchestra at the opening ceremony of Berlin's International Building Exhibition. With this peak-and-hollow surface, Frei Otto had found a structural method that could span over large areas. With it, new dimensions were opened up for membrane structures with their finite expanses.

Within a few years, Frei Otto had developed the essential basic forms of modern tent construction and made them important elements within architecture. The lightweight, filigreed, almost floating structures that provided shelter to those beneath garnered worldwide attention and awakened interest in lightweight construction. They were signs of a previously unrecognized stance in German architecture, an architecture that 'danced only for a single summer', as Frei Otto put it, no longer firmly rooted in the ground, but simple and modest.

In 1958, while Frei Otto taught as a guest professor at Washington University in St Louis, Missouri, he got to know the American inventor Buckminster Fuller, another protagonist of lightweight construction with whom he shared a hope of improving the quality of life through lightweight, adaptable structures. Like Otto, Fuller was concerned with achieving maximum efficiency with the least expenditure of material and energy.[12] The two had many discussions, and Otto invited Fuller to Berlin and later to Stuttgart to lecture at his institute. Also in 1958, Otto established his private research institute in his parents-in-law's garden at Berlin-Zehlendorf, the Institute for the Development of Lightweight Construction

Frei Otto, four-point sail at the German National Garden Show in Kassel (1955)

Frei Otto, orchestra canopy at Interbau in Berlin (1957)

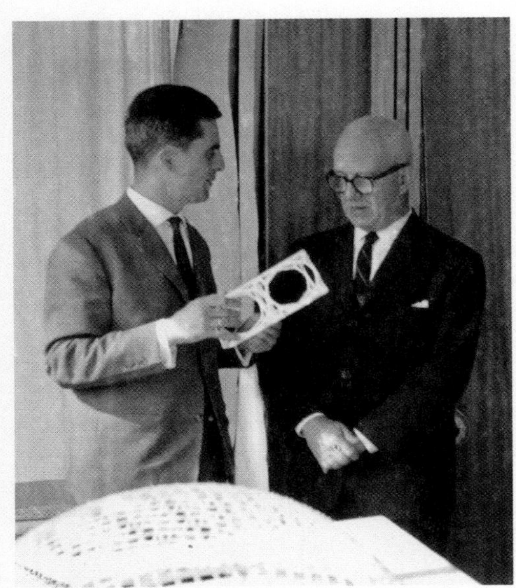

(Entwicklungsstätte für den Leichtbau, EL), where he studied the basics of prefabricated roofs over a broad range of ground plans and experimented with models made of wire, rubber bands and soap films. Experiments and models were his primary tools in his search for the 'proper' form, both in his research and in his designs. Proceeding from soap films, which always form the thinnest surface area, in which the surface tension is identical at every spot and in every direction, Frei Otto immersed himself in the complex subject of minimal surfaces. In order to construct minimal surfaces, understand strength and stress gradients and comprehend processes of self-formation, he developed any number of models with which he ingeniously studied these problems and which he could alter until optimal statics and space requirements were achieved. Measurement of his models then served to dictate the forms of his designs.

Frei Otto's working method was characterized by constant alternation between theory and practice. In 1958, in the first issue of the periodical he edited, *Mitteilungen der Entwicklungsstätte für den Leichtbau (EL)*, he started by listing the tasks of lightweight construction research: 'If lightweight construction is to move beyond its current state of wildly flailing about, it is imperative that appropriate research work be initiated on the broadest scale. [...] For this work, so extremely important for human development and evolution, comparable work must begin like that presupposed at the academies of the quantitative sciences (physics and chemistry).'[13] He went on to explain that 'With a sparing use of high-quality building materials and the full utilization of the tensile characteristics of areal systems, lightweight, movable structures without significant weight of their own are created. The structure contracts to what is absolutely necessary. [...] Technological development leads, as we hope, from anti-nature technology to nature technology. It leads from the analytic to the holistic apprehension of complex relationships.'[14] Frei Otto's goal was nothing less than the synthesis of architecture, technology and nature. He then published a first summation of his architectural concepts in 1959 under the programmatic title *Anpassungsfähig bauen* (*Adaptable Building*). To him, adaptability meant building modifiably and thus 'ephemerally' – lightweight structures deliberately conceived in such a way that they can be altered and dismantled again. Another important influence on Frei Otto's concept of an adaptable architecture were the studies by Konrad Wachsmann, who in his pioneering publication *Wendepunkt im Bauen* (*The Turning Point of Building*; 1959) demonstrated how, through industrialization of building, wholly new paths could be taken in this direction.

Cable Nets

In 1962, Frei Otto published, in collaboration with the engineer Rudolf Trostel, the first volume of his *Zugbeanspruchte Konstruktionen* (*Tensile Structures*), and in 1966, its second volume with Friedrich-Karl Schleyer. In this pathbreaking publication for lightweight construction – translated into English in 1967 and 1969 – Otto discussed basic principles, typologies, models and construction examples as well as the analysis of cable structures, cable nets and membranes, and thus summarized what was then known about tensile structures.

At the recommendation of Fritz Leonhardt, who recognized the young Frei Otto's abilities and hoped for support from him in his own efforts pertaining to lightweight construction, in 1964 Otto was offered a post as Director of the Institute for Lightweight Structures (Institut für leichte Flächentragwerke, IL), newly established for him at the Stuttgart Institute of Technology (Technische Hochschule Stuttgart, TH Stuttgart). There he was able to continue his research on a larger scale, and the institute became one of the central research facilities for lightweight construction methods and 'natural' structures. Since a membrane's stress tolerance and span are both limited owing to the minimal material strength of foils and textiles, Otto now experimented with lightweight support structures, creating large nets out of steel cables. He linked the horizontal and vertical cables together as nodes with special fasteners and secured the nets at

Frei Otto and Richard Buckminster Fuller (1962)

the edges with reinforced cables. The weight was borne solely by the cables' tensile strength. As with membranes, stretched, prestressed and saddle-shaped curves make the cable nets rigid enough to serve as support structures. In his research, Frei Otto proceeded in a strictly scientific manner. He made observations and developed such apparatuses as the soap film machine for the geometrical analysis and measurement of soap film models. Over the years, for different steps in his work, he created, through immense effort and with the greatest artisanal skill, a variety of model types encompassing form-finding, design and scale models with the most diverse techniques and materials, amassing a 'magical microcosm of his own'.[15]

Beginning in the 1960s, multiple projects were undertaken at the IL as well as at Otto's atelier in Warmbronn, which aimed to enlarge the span of lightweight surface supports and that can be seen as precursors of the German Pavilion in Montreal. In the design for a harbour roof in Bremen (1961), which was never realized, nineteen masts served to support a large surface roughly 1,500 × 380 metres in size. Another precursor of the Montreal structure was the second design for Ulm's Medical Academy (1965). This project, like the German Pavilion, also presents a free form for an irregularly shaped cable net with a uniform grid and interior masts of differing heights.

The breakthrough to the new cable net structures came when, with Rolf Gutbrod, Frei Otto won the competition for the German Pavilion at Expo 67 in Montreal. After preliminary stages with Vladimir Shukhov's exhibition rotunda in Nizhny Novgorod (1896) and Matthew Nowicki's Raleigh arena (1952), a new epoch in lightweight construction began in Montreal. An astonishing development since between Otto's first four-point sail structure in 1955 and the erection of the German Pavilion in Montreal there had been only twelve years, during which he had studied its potential on the basis of various types of prestressed membrane structures and cable nets. One study model in which a canopy roof was stretched by means of eye-shaped cable loops, rhythmically alternating from above and below, provided the fundamental structural form for the tensile construction in Montreal, which spans 8,000 square metres. The large, lightweight tent offered 'visitors a kind of exhibition landscape that conveyed the promise of a highly appealing and in every way engaging impression'.[16] The pavilion was celebrated nationally and internationally as one of the main attractions of the exposition, and the swooping tent was also widely interpreted as an architectural symbol of Germany's transformation into a peaceful democracy. Rudolf W. Leonhardt wrote in the weekly newspaper *Die Zeit* of a 'stroke of genius' on Frei Otto's part: 'It stands there as an airy, yet sheltering structure that displays modesty and grace, clearly a temporary guest, laying no claims to Canadian soil. Canadians have coined the title "Swinging Germany" to describe it, and this is a lovely compliment.'[17] In Montreal, the tent structure stood next to Buckminster Fuller's geodesic dome, and the editors of the *Whole Earth Catalog* wrote of the combination, 'The only pavilion of Expo 67 more beautiful than Fuller's U.S. Dome was the West German tent, designed by Frei Otto. He is currently the master of structures whose flexible skin is the prime structural element.'[18] With Montreal, Frei Otto became the representative of a lightweight, people-friendly architecture – recognized the world over as 'the tentmaker'.

For the internationally celebrated structure with minimal surfaces, as well as a cable net stretched over high and low points, an experimental structure was first erected that would become the seat of the famous Institute for Lightweight Structures at the University of Stuttgart and a centre of research on lightweight construction. At the institute, within the framework of the DFG-Sonderforschungsbereichs 64 'Weitgespannte Flächentragwerke' (Collaborative Research Centre 64 'Widespan Surface Structures'), extensive studies were carried out that formed the basis for the cable net roofs at Munich's Olympic Park, with which lightweight construction attracted worldwide attention.

Rolf Gutbrod and Frei Otto, German Pavilion at Expo 67, the International and Universal Exposition of Montreal (1967)

Press reports on the German Pavilion tent in Montreal prompted the architects at the firm of Behnisch & Partner to propose cable net structures in their competition entry as roofs for the Olympic sports venues in Munich. Though Behnisch & Partner won the competition, the realization of a lightweight roof hovering above the landscape was possible only with Frei Otto. A team of experts put together by Otto, among them Fritz Leonhardt and Jörg Schlaich, worked out the fundamentals for constructing the cable net roofs. At Otto's Stuttgart institute, physical scale models were built, and measuring devices as well as test facilities were further developed and adjusted. At the same time, Jörg Schlaich and John Argyris from the Institute of Structural Mechanics and Dynamics in Aerospace Engineering (Institut Statik und Dynamik der Luft- und Raumfahrtkonstruktionen, ISD) at the University of Stuttgart developed numerical models that would simplify a representation of the cable net by means of computer-supported methods. Frei Otto played a major role in the creation of the suspended roofs, but it was also an outstanding collaborative effort by all the planners and staff members involved. To be sure, in the stadium roof, Frei Otto missed the 'lightness of a cloud floating above the landscape', as 'the great complexity of cables, masts and construction elements interferes with the realization of an idea that can only have its effect if the construction itself seems inconsequential and all that matters is the sheltered landscape. In relation to the "roof and landscape" problem, the Olympic roof is still an experiment in an early stage of development. It provides the hope that soon more advanced propositions may perhaps be hazarded with new projects.'[19] This hope would not be fulfilled, for lightweight construction was pursued in Germany to only a very limited extent. But in retrospect, Frei Otto's new form of lightness and freedom found its culmination in Munich as a contrast to 'brutality in stone'[20] – 'Here they have not let grass grow over the past, but rather with shrewdness and lightness and a joy of life, they realized a radical alternative to the monstrous, cold stone worlds of someone like Albert Speer; here, then, in full awareness of a criminal past, a garden was created that was meant to represent a peaceful future.'[21]

A Panorama of Developments in Construction

Retractable Roofs

The theme of adaptable architecture led Frei Otto to retractable roofs, to canopies that could adapt to changes in the weather, creating sheltered areas in short order. Adaptability can be achieved either by gathering up the roof skin – the Romans had already developed *vela* (sails), which could be extended by hand as protection against the sun for their amphitheatres – or through movement of the support structure. Such awning structures were among the oldest forms of adaptable, retractable roofs. Frei Otto was one of the first architects to again focus on such methods of construction. He planned his first large electronically operated roof skin for the terrace of a casino at Cannes in 1965. A short time later, he produced a similar roof over the abbey ruins at Bad Hersfeld. Retractable membranes over swimming pools in Paris, Lyon and Regensburg followed. At the German National Garden Show in Cologne in 1971, he introduced large calyx-shaped umbrellas. In a further development of this type, for the American tour of the rock band Pink Floyd in 1977, Frei Otto designed ten retractable umbrellas, each of them 4.5 metres in diameter, which could be folded up and lowered into the stage floor. Their considerable aesthetic appeal led the musicians to integrate the shades into their show and make their opening and closing a fixed feature of their concerts.

Gridshells

In a further development of membrane and cable net structures, Frei Otto turned to the motif of arches, gridshells and domes. He had already recognized in the

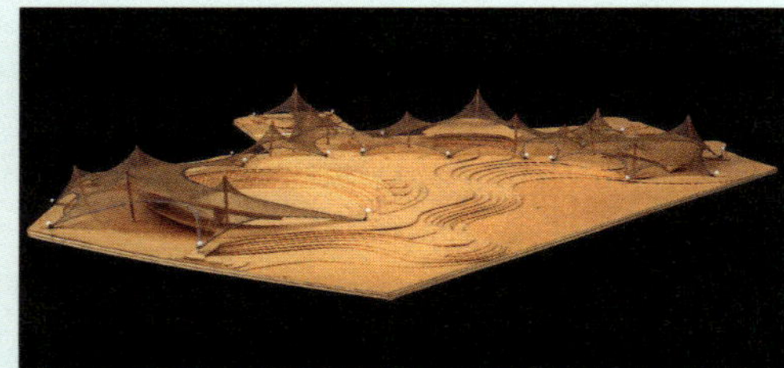

Behnisch & Partner, Olympic complex, competition entry (1967), model on a scale of 1:1000

Tulle model of the Olympic Stadium and large measuring table at the Institute for Lightweight Structures (Frei Otto on the right)

1960s that self-forming processes of tensile construction could be applied to compression loading: 'I also began to experiment with the reverse principle – to develop hanging vaults. It is easy to dip a cloth in plaster and hang it up, let it harden and invert it. I had the experience of this from my father. I had not yet heard of Gaudí [...] With the chain standing as an arch and the inversion experiment, it seemed as if the entire world of domes and vaults was opening up to me.'[22] This new building type developed by Frei Otto – an ultralight, standing structure – also makes do with only a fraction of the previously standard material costs. The construction method is based on two principles: the so-called inversion principle and the strain of an originally flat lattice grid into a doubly curved shape that is subsequently hardened. Behind the inversion principle is the fact that free-hanging cables, chains or entire nets passively attain their form according to the laws of nature. By inverting these tensile, suspended forms, arches, vaults and domes result that are only compressed and not bent under the pressure of their own weight. Frei Otto presented his first experimental structures in 1962 at the first German Building Exhibition (Deutsche Bauausstellung, Deubau) in Essen with a dome of thin wooden laths, and in that same year, he developed gridshells of simple carbon steel with students from the University of California, Berkeley. Beneath the cable net at Montreal, two gridshells also arched over the lecture hall and the foyer. The most remarkable application of this principle, however, was the Multihalle conceived by Frei Otto in collaboration with Carlfried Mutschler and Joachim Langner for the German National Garden Show in Mannheim in 1975, a gridshell roof structure with a surface of 9,500 square metres. Its striking design and innovative construction were comparable to the cable net structures from Montreal and Munich and attracted national and international attention.

Branching Structures

At the German National Garden Show in Cologne in 1957, Frei Otto had exhibited his first branching structure for a concave 'humpbacked' canopy roof. Since a simple mast would threaten to pierce the thin stretched membrane, he fanned out the mast cap in order to distribute the load and lessen the framing structure's mass. Frei Otto also developed a number of other branching solutions on the suspension model in order to achieve bend-free structures through inversion. Although in contrast to tree branches in nature these do not bend, they are generally referred to as tree supports. In the mid-1970s, Frei Otto proposed such branching forms in combination with gridshells for a government centre in Riyadh. In parallel with these application-oriented designs, Frei Otto also studied the processes leading to branched structures in animate and inanimate nature. These played a central role in the interdisciplinary Collaborative Research Centre 230 'Natural Structures'. Along with branching structures in nature, there are branched solutions in human technology. For traffic and transportation infrastructures, such as streets, rails or conduit systems, either minimally or direct branching path networks are developed. Depending on the demand, the most diverse branching forms can be optimized with various mathematical and physical models.

Pneus and Hydros

In 1960, when Otto's studies of membranes filled with air or water had reached a first plateau, he became acquainted with the biologist and anthropologist Johann-Gerhard Helmcke, then teaching at the Technical University of Berlin (Technische Universität Berlin, TU Berlin), who held the view that biological entities develop through physical processes of self-formation, independent of their genetic makeup. In his collaboration with Helmcke, the structures Otto had investigated in his experiments with soap bubbles, rubber skins, nets and *pneus* now assumed a natural, biological basis. In 1961/62, the two established the research group 'Biology and Building' and declared, 'In the beginning was the Pneu.'[23] All objects in nature are accordingly power-transmitting structures that are either 'genuine' fluid-filled pneus composed of membranes and fibres under internal

Frei Otto, changeable roof above the terrace of the Palm Beach Casino in Cannes (1965)

Hanging model in the Warmbronn atelier for finding the form of the gridshell of the Multihalle in Mannheim (1973)

pressure or else their subsequent hardening lead them to form bodies with high compression strength.[24] According to this theory, all forms of animate nature arise out of the 'fibre net-supported pneu'. On this basis, Frei Otto became increasingly engaged with the emergence of forms and structures in nature and technology. He thereby wanted to understand natural processes and structures and to bring their principles into harmony with supporting structures for buildings. It was not that forms from nature were to be imitated, rather that knowledge of nature's laws of form should help us to better understand nature so as to ultimately create an architecture whose structural and bearing principles stand 'in harmony with nature'. In his book *Tensile Structures*, Otto pointed to air as the lightest of all building materials. He subsequently worked out numerous designs based on the principles of pneumatic structures, among them his 'City in the Arctic' conceived with Kenzo Tange and engineers of Ove Arup in 1971. Since a large percentage of the earth's raw materials lie in inhospitable climate zones, the producer of dyestuffs Hoechst underwrote a project study investigating how to create better climatic conditions for people working in such zones. A flattened dome with a span of 2,000 metres was to shelter a city for a maximum of 40,000 inhabitants. The pneumatically supported shell consists of two transparent plastic skins with a net of cables running between them. Admittedly, the design remained only a vision.

Collaborative Research Centre 64 was still primarily supported by engineers, but nets, pneus and shells in nature and technology were worked on in subprojects, since 'expansive and expandable surface structures – like the structures of animate nature – build on the "principle of lightweight construction" to an equal extent'.[25] In 1978, Johann-Gerhard Helmcke became a corresponding member of CRC 64, and together with him, Otto initiated the largest Collaborative Research Centre in the history of the Federal Republic of Germany, SFB 230

Kenzo Tange with Frei Otto, project study for City in the Arctic (1971), model photograph

Frei Otto, public bathing place on Lake Geneva (design 1960)

'Natürliche Konstruktionen – Leichtbau in Architektur und Natur' (CRC 230 'Natural Structures – Lightweight Construction in Architecture and Nature'). In a unique worldwide collaboration, international scholars from various fields exchanged ideas, experiments and research results, exploiting synergies. A number of symposiums and publications provided food for thought and made Frei Otto's institute the most vital and creative research centre in Germany and the one with the greatest international impact.

Frei Otto was far more than a pioneer in lightweight construction, he was a seer in his time and changed the perception of German architecture after 1945. Norman Foster accurately summarized Otto's importance in 2005: 'As much, then, as his extraordinary sequence of works altered the nature of architectural form in the twentieth century, his environmentalism, intelligence and foresight have established the defining architectural mentality for the twenty-first. He is an inspiration.'[26] This is still true two decades later. Frei Otto's urgent appeal for humane construction and his engagement in our built environment are more relevant today than ever.

1 See Winfried Nerdinger, 'Frei Otto: Working for a Better "Earth for Mankind"', in: Winfried Nerdinger (ed.), *Frei Otto: Complete Works; Lightweight Construction, Natural Design*, exh. cat. Architekturmuseum der TU München, Basel/Boston/Berlin 2005, pp. 8–15; Winfried Nerdinger, 'Frei Otto. Internationale Repräsentant der deutschen Architektur', in: *Bautechnik*, no. 10, 2015, pp. 730–732.

2 Fritz Leonhardt, 'Leichtbau – eine Forderung unserer Zeit. Anregungen für den Hoch- und Brückenbau', in: *Die Bautechnik*, nos 36/37, 1940, pp. 413–423; reprint with a commentary by Jörg Schlaich, in *Bautechnik*, no. 12, 2013, pp. 825–838.

3 Frei Otto, 'Stuttgarter Architektur – gestern, heute und morgen, 1979', reprinted in Berthold Burkhardt (ed.), *Frei Otto. Schriften und Reden, 1951–1983*, Braunschweig/Wiesbaden 1984, p. 157.

4 See Frei Otto's letters to the camp priest Wilhelm Delbeck from the neighbouring seminary from the years 1947 and 1948, private property of the Delbeck family, author's copies.

5 *Prinzip Leichtbau. Form–Kraft–Masse 4/Lightweight Principle: Form–Forces–Mass 4, Mitteilungen des Instituts für leichte Flächentragwerke (IL)*, no. 24, ed. Frei Otto, Stuttgart 1998, p. 7; Catalogue of Works, cat. 1, in: Nerdinger (ed.), *Frei Otto: Complete Works*, p. 172.

6 Frei Otto, *Das hängende Dach. Gestalt und Struktur*, doctoral thesis, Berlin 1954.

7 Hans Schwippert (lecture speech), in: Otto Bartning (ed.), *Darmstädter Gespräch. Mensch und Raum*, Darmstadt 1952, p. 86.

8 Frei Otto, *Architektur-Natur*, Warmbronner Schriften 7, Christian-Wagner-Gesellschaft, Warmbronn 1996, p. 4.

9 Frei Otto, 'Mit Leichtigkeit gegen Brutalität', in: *Allgemeine Bauzeitung*, 1976, reprinted in Burkhardt (ed.), *Frei Otto. Schriften und Reden*, pp. 128–132.

10 Frei Otto, 'Die Zeit der vielen Architekturen', in: *Allgemeine Bauzeitung*, 1972, reprinted in Burkhardt (ed.), *Frei Otto. Schriften und Reden*, p. 123.

11 Frei Otto, 'Subjektives und Kritisches zu dem, was andere als mein Werk Bezeichnen', in: Karin Wilhelm, *Architekten heute. Portrait Frei Otto*, Berlin 1985, pp. 132 f.

12 Irene Meissner, 'Frei Otto, Buckminster Fuller, Yona Friedman. Anpassunsfähige Architektur für eine freie und mobile Gesellschaft', in: Winfried Nerdinger (ed.), *L'Architecture engagée. Manifeste zur Veränderung der Gesellschaft*, Munich 2012, pp. 296–302, here p. 296.

13 *Das Programm. Mitteilungen der Entwicklungsstätte für den Leichtbau (EL)*, no. 1, ed. Frei Otto, Berlin 1958, quoted in Walter Scheiffele, 'Die Entwicklungsstätte für den Leichtbau. Vorlesugen zu Biologie und Bauen in Berlin', in: Walter Scheiffele, *Das leichte Haus. Utopie und Realität der Membranarchitektur*, Leipzig 2015, pp. 302 f., here p. 303.

14 *Das Programm*, quoted in Scheiffele, 'Die Entwicklungsstätte für den Leichtbau', p. 303.

15 Rainer Graefe, 'Where Architecture and Civil Engineering Meet', in: Nerdinger (ed.), *Frei Otto: Complete Works*, pp. 70–79, here p. 76; for his models, see also 'Experimente / Experiments', in: *Mitteilungen des Instituts für leichte Flächentragwerke (IL)*, no. 25, ed. Frei Otto, Stuttgart 1990; Rainer Barthel, 'Natural Forms – Architectural Forms', in: Nerdinger (ed.), *Frei Otto: Complete Works*, pp. 16–31.

16 *EXPO '67 Montreal – Deutscher Pavillon. Dokumentation über das Bauwerk*, published in collaboration with the Bundesschatzministerium (Bundesbauverwaltung), Düsseldorf 1967, p. 3.

17 Rudolf W. Leonhardt, 'Swinging Germany. Der Geniestreich des Architekten Frei Otto setzte den Maßstab', in: *Die Zeit*, 12 May 1967, quoted in Irene Meissner, 'Lightweight Construction Versus a Display of Prestige: From Montreal '67 to Munich '72', in: Georg Vrachliotis et al. (eds), *Frei Otto: Thinking by Modeling*, exh. cat. ZKM | Center for Art and Media Karlsruhe, Leipzig 2017, pp. 37–48, here p. 47.

18 *The Last Whole Earth Catalog: Access to Tools*, Harmondsworth 1971, p. 106, quoted in Walter Scheiffele, 'Eine neue Kette, Finsterlin – Joedicke – Otto in Stuttgart', in: Scheiffele, *Das leichte Haus*, p. 293.

19 Frei Otto, quoted in Rainer Barthel, 'Mit Leichtigkeit gegen Brutalität. Zum Tod von Frei Otto', in: *Stahlbau*, no. 5, 2015, pp. 367–370, here p. 369.

20 Alexander Kluge and Peter Schamoni, *Brutalität in Stein*, short documentary film, 1961.

21 Gerd Heidenreich, 'Ein Dach der Welt. Warum der Olympiapark den Ehrentitel Weltkulturerbe braucht', inaugural event of the association Aktion Welterbe Olympiapark e.V. at Munich's Volkstheater, 2016, which is labouring to have the Olympic Park recognized as a UNESCO World Heritage Site; reprinted with the kind permission of the author for the exhibition 'Die Olympiastadt München' at the Architekturmuseum der TU München, at the Pinakothek der Moderne, 2022.

22 Frei Otto, 'Subjektives und Kritisches zu dem, was andere als mein Werk bezeichnen', quoted in Wilhelm, *Architekten heute*, p. 137.

23 Ulrich Kull, 'Frei Otto and Biology', in: Nerdinger (ed.), *Frei Otto: Complete Works*, pp. 44–55, here p. 47.

24 Frei Otto, 'Was wir Johann-Gerhard Helmcke verdanken', in: *Diatomeen II. Schalen in Natur und Technik III, Mitteilungen des Instituts für leichte Flächentragwerke (IL)*, no. 38, ed. Ulrich Kull and Klaus Bach, Stuttgart 2004, pp. 6, 141–143, quoted in 'Pneus/Hydros', in: Nerdinger (ed.), *Frei Otto: Complete Works*, p. 150.

25 Walter Scheiffele, 'Das Institut für leichte Flächentragwerke und der Sonderforschungsbereich 64, "Weitgespannte Flächentragwerke"', in: Scheiffele, *Das leichte Haus*, pp. 316 f., here p. 316.

26 Norman Foster's contribution to an 'Homage to Frei Otto', in: Nerdinger (ed.), *Frei Otto: Complete Works*, p. 363.

‘I cannot trust the pure calculation, if this cannot be verified with a model’: Frei Otto and Model Statics

Christiane Weber

Frei Otto’s architecture is based on the principle of lightweight construction: spanning the largest possible area with the least possible material. Such structures had already been envisioned as expansive shells and cable structures in the interwar period, but it was only after the Second World War that Frei Otto was able to realize these ideas in architectural buildings. In the 1960s and 1970s, Frei Otto was supported in this by a whole team of engineers involved in the realization of his lightweight architectural visions. Since it was difficult to represent these complex structures geometrically before the arrival of high-performance computers, and their statics could only be calculated with great effort, the engineers relied on model statics: a method for designing the structures and determining their dimensions using small scale models.

In 2010, before Frei Otto’s death, the Southwest German Archive for Architecture and Civil Engineering (Südwestdeutsche Archiv für Architektur und Ingenieurbau, saai) at the Karlsruhe Institute of Technology (Karlsruher Institut für Technologie, KIT) took over the collections from his atelier in Warmbronn, the successor to Otto’s Berlin-based research Institute for the Development of Lightweight Construction (Entwicklungsstätte für den Leichtbau, EL) Included in these holdings are more than four hundred models – the saai thus has one of the largest collections of models of all of Germany’s architecture archives.[1] For Frei Otto and his team, models were a medium for architectural design in all phases of a project: as working models to test and visualize decisions in the design process and as presentation models made to convince clients and competition juries. Models continue to serve these functions despite the many possible 3D visualizations that have since become possible. What is special about the Frei Otto collection at saai is the enormous number of form-finding models for architectural designs based on natural form-finding processes. Of particular interest, however, are the models used not only to arrive at a given shape, but also to determine and even calculate the structure. In structural engineering this type of physical model is called a *Messmodell* (measurement model) in German.

Frei Otto and Fritz Leonhardt

With what Frei Otto called ‘natural constructions’, applying his analysis of growth and development processes in animate and inanimate nature to architectural principles, he created his first tent structures in the 1950s, which followed the principles he understood as pertaining to lightweight structures.[2] In 1957, shortly after earning his doctorate at the Technical University Berlin (Technische Universität Berlin, TU Berlin) with his thesis *Das hängende Dach* (The Hanging Roof; 1953/54), he began experimenting at his private institute, the EL in Berlin. With his tent structures for the German National Garden Shows

(Bundesgartenschauen) in Kassel in 1955 and Cologne in 1957, he attracted such admiring recognition that he was simultaneously offered professorships at several universities, including the technical institutes and universities of Karlsruhe and Berlin, as well as Harvard and the University of California, Berkeley, in the United States. In 1964, he chose to join the Stuttgart Institute of Technology (Technische Hochschule Stuttgart, TH Stuttgart). His choice was based on the fact that in Stuttgart the internationally acclaimed structural engineer Fritz Leonhardt,[3] also Dean of the Faculty of Civil Engineering, had done all he could, pulling out all the stops to see that Otto was appointed at Stuttgart. The former TH Stuttgart (now the University of Stuttgart) did not offer Frei Otto a mere professorship but rather an interdisciplinary research institute specially created for him and his research interests: the Institute for Lightweight Structures (Institut für leichte Flächentragwerke, IL). Fritz Leonhardt and Frei Otto already knew each other and had successfully worked together for a long time: Leonhardt's Stuttgart office Leonhardt und Andrä (L+A, later LAP) was responsible for calculating the statics of Otto's lightweight, temporary tent structures. At the German National Garden Shows these were publicly accessible structures, and even though used only temporarily, they had to satisfy strict safety requirements. That Fritz Leonhardt, a professor in solid construction at TH Stuttgart, was also greatly interested in lightweight construction may be seen from a 1940 article he wrote under the influence of the wartime economy, 'Leichtbau – eine Forderung unserer Zeit' (Lightweight Construction – A Demand of Our Time).[4] Leonhardt's office not only designed Stuttgart's slender television tower, but also a number of long-span suspension and cable-stayed bridges.[5] The best known of these are in Düsseldorf: the so-called Düsseldorf Bridge Family, three elegant cable-stayed bridges over the Rhine. The Stuttgarter's expertise in the building of cable structures would provide an important, presumably even the decisive basis for the realization of Frei Otto's lightweight structures in the coming years.

The Principle of Lightweight Construction and the Soap Film Machine

The principle of lightweight construction on which Frei Otto based not only his new institute in Stuttgart but also his experimental designing style called for the greatest possible span with the least possible material. Today one would call it 'resource efficient'. Among the many innovative approaches in Otto's experiments were tests based on the fact that soap film always automatically assumes the smallest possible surface area within the given limits.[6] Otto had started to perform experiments with soap film earlier in Berlin in 1958,[7] and in 1963, he began to develop the so-called Minimalwegegerät (minimal paths apparatus).[8] In Stuttgart, this experimental device was further developed into the so-called soap film machine, which can be seen to this day in the pavilion of the IL (now the Institute for Lightweight Structures and Conceptual Design; Institut für Leichtbau Entwerfen und Konstruieren, ILEK) at the University of Stuttgart's Vaihingen campus.[9] This machine was refined to the point that ephemeral soap films were protected from gusts of air in a special chamber; in addition, the form-giving frame was no longer lifted out of the soap film solution, but rather the container of soap solution was lowered. Also, there was an air cooling and humidifying device to prevent the shapes from bursting as long as possible. Only in 1987 did the team present the apparatus retrospectively in the eighteenth issue of the institute's own publication, *Mitteilungen des Instituts für leichte Flächentragwerke (IL)*.[10] Soap bubbles had already been mentioned in the ninth issue, titled *Pneus in Nature and Technics*,[11] and the researchers now devoted the entire eighteenth issue to the subject of soap bubbles, publishing, among other things, ideas for pneumatic structures with which Frei Otto pursued his goal, formulated early on, of roofing large spaces with the least possible amount of material.[12] Unlike his designs for tents and gridshells, these experiments, which Frei Otto

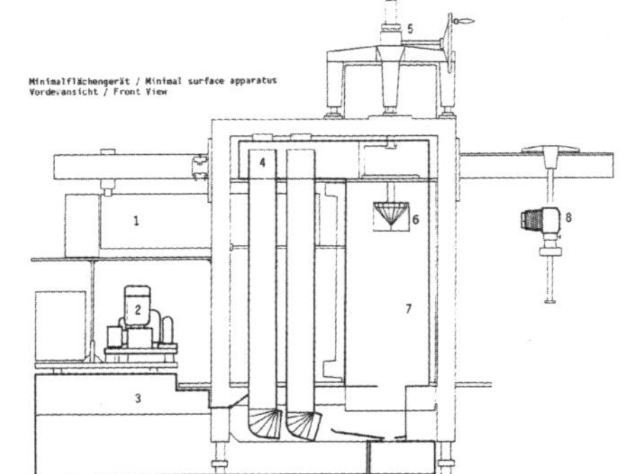

Soap film machine as testing device at the Institute for Lightweight Structures (IL) in Stuttgart-Vaihingen, drawing and photograph from *Mitteilungen des Instituts für leichte Flächentragwerke (IL)*, no. 18 (1988)

documented on paper in numerous visionary drawings as physical shells over cities and landscapes, did not lead to realized projects.

Particularly difficult in these form-finding experiments with soap films was documenting such ephemeral, evanescent membranes. They could not be measured 'by hand', for touching the soap film would instantly burst it. Their shapes could thus only be captured in photographs, for which reason the TH Stuttgart's Institute for Applications of Geodesy to Civil Engineering (Institut für Anwendungen der Geodäsie im Bauwesen, IAGB),[13] under the direction of Klaus Linkwitz, was enlisted for help. IAGB worked out a photogrammetric method for the contactless measurement of the physical soap membrane. For this, Otto and his assistants developed a parallel light projector with an optical instrument called an optical bank so as to photograph the soap films without distortion. When the IL researchers noticed that the shape of the soap film reacted intensely to surrounding conditions in temperature, starting in 1973, the soap film machine was further refined so that the objects of research could be produced in a special environmentally controlled chamber under optimal conditions, that is to say, with the highest possible humidity.[14] An attachable wind tunnel also made it possible to test soap film shapes under wind loading – one of the greatest challenges to tent structures. The photo-optic measuring method developed by the engineers around Klaus Linkwitz produced such precise photographs that the measured data could be scaled and served as the basis for further structural planning.

'Measurement' Models at the IL in Stuttgart and the Warmbronn Atelier

The natural forms discovered with the aid of the soap film machine served as patterns for numerous tent structures designed through the 1960s by Frei Otto and his team at the EL in Berlin, at the IL in Stuttgart and in his Warmbronn atelier. The first larger and the world's best-known example was the German Pavilion at the International and Universal Exposition, Expo 67 in Montreal. Frei Otto's Stuttgart connections played a role in its design. In December 1964, he and the Stuttgart architecture professor Rolf Gutbrod were announced as the winners of the competition for the national pavilion.[15] Its freely swooping tent roofs would become an emblematic structure of post-war Modernism, one that architecture critics praised as a structural rebuke to the monumental classicism of National Socialist architecture intended to overwhelm. The realization of Rolf Gutbrod and Frei Otto's design would not have been possible without a whole team of additional engineers at TH Stuttgart, above all the structural planners from the office of L+A. They relied on the model statics method, focussing on the use of physical scale models made with technically similar materials and with

Physical model for the German Pavilion in Montreal with suspended load weights (1965)

comparable geometry in load tests to assess deformation and stress distribution. The resulting data could then be extrapolated, that is to say, scaled to the intended structure. This method had been introduced in the United States in the first decades of the twentieth century and was very soon adopted worldwide for projects whose structures were so complex that load calculation would be highly labour-intensive and time-consuming and accordingly very expensive.[16] Notably, among such structures were concrete shells and cable constructions like the aforementioned suspension and cable-stayed bridges. In the late 1930s, a German centre for such research had been created at the TH Stuttgart's Materials Testing Institute (Materialprüfungsanstalt, MPA), which Leonhardt largely helped to shape. From 1938 on, substantial research funds were granted to the MPA Stuttgart in connection with grand National Socialist construction projects, for example the suspension bridge for the Reichsautobahn (motorway) at Cologne-Rodenkirchen. The Stuttgart engineers had thus acquired expert knowledge that they were able to draw on and further develop after the end of the Second World War in the planning of suspension and cable-stayed bridges like those in Düsseldorf. Particularly the MPA's physical scale models for cable bridges can be seen as technologically groundbreaking.[17]

For the German Pavilion project at Expo 67, Gutbrod and Otto had proposed a cable net structure. Since, as part of the 1964 competition for the project, Germany's Federal Construction Directorate (BBD) had specified that the structure be prefabricated and transported to Canada by ship, the minimization of material played a major role.[18] Up to that point, Frei Otto had only realized temporary textile tents with manageably sized spans. The stipulated size of the German Pavilion could not have been covered with a purely textile structure, so at the IL, a cable net was developed with a mesh size of 50 centimetres. A pavilion was erected for it as a test structure in a scale of 1:1; with this, it was possible to refine details like the cross connectors at the cable intersections and especially to determine the necessary prestressing of the cables. Such prestressing is essential in tent constructions to prevent unwanted, hazardous fluttering. With its dreaded blizzards, Canada was particularly problematic territory in this respect. Responsibility for calculating the supporting structure was again taken over by the office of L+A.

For the 'measurement' model tests at the IL, a 1:75 physical scale model in technically similar materials and with comparable geometry was made of thin steel wire. Creating the net out of steel wires was extremely labour-intensive as each of their intersections had to be fixed by hand. With this model, it was then possible to undertake load tests to determine the deformation under load. The physical model was analysed photogrammetrically, in part by means of double exposures, by Klaus Linkwitz's team at IAGB. Special gauges, the so-called Montreal-Messbügel (Montreal micrometre), had to be developed additionally to determine the tensile stress in the cables. These were based on the three-point support principle, testing the tensile cable's resistance to deflection; if the cable is under stress, the needle on the semicircular scale deflects. With the help of data thus derived from the physical model, the engineers at L+A were able to plan the support structure and determine the cables' cross-section. The actual cable net was produced by the firm Stromeyer & Co. in Konstanz, with which Frei Otto had worked since the early 1950s. It was fabricated in sheets, as designed, and rolled up so that it could be transported to Canada by ship. On site it was possible to hang the cable net from the eight masts in three weeks, and in another five weeks, it had been prestressed. To prestress the cable net, L+A's engineers resorted to methods from prestressed concrete bridge construction. The roof skin was hung at a distance below the cable net. This membrane was no longer made of cotton like the temporary tent structures at the German National Garden Shows but a polyester fabric laminated with PVC. Previously, material tests had also been done on this new textile substance at the MPA in Stuttgart. In the twentieth century, the MPA played an important role in the innovative developments in construction, and its importance for the Stuttgart school of structural engineering

Test structure for the German Pavilion at its first location in Stuttgart-Vaihingen (1965)

Physical model for the IL pavilion with detail of the Montreal micrometre (1964/65)

cannot be overstated. Additional models were necessary for wind tunnel tests, for which wooden models were built on a 1:200 scale. They were fitted with 150 measuring points at which pull and suction loads could be measured with a manometer. Wind tunnel tests simulate aerodynamic loads, and along with seismic and acoustic tests are an area in which physical scale models are still used today in engineering.[19]

The German Pavilion realized by the Stuttgart architects and engineers was the most-admired contribution to Expo 67, one that the press celebrated with the phrase 'Swinging Germany'. It was said that with this architecture alone at the International and Universal Exposition a new image of the Federal Republic of Germany had been created. Another successful Stuttgart project was based on this positive, popular tent structure: the roofs over the Olympic venues in Munich.[20] As designed by the Stuttgart architects Behnisch & Partner, the dimensions of the areas covered by the free-floating tents were nearly ten times as large. In addition to this leap in scale, there was the fact the cable net roofs planned for the Olympic Games were not intended to be used only temporarily but to remain in use permanently. Here the pavilion in Montreal provided important insights for the German builders, for owing to its popularity, the pavilion continued to be used as an event venue by the city of Montreal after the close of the world's fair – this ran contrary to the original plan, which had only taken into account a service life of one year, and thus it needed only to withstand a single Canadian winter. It was not until seven years after Expo 67, after regular maintenance had been discontinued, that the structure collapsed. Notably, this maintenance had included melting snow off of it in winter, a common practice before the oil crisis but now unimaginable. The extended service life of the Montreal tent provided the engineers with extensive research material. One learns from a 1970 IL report, for example, that 'for the roof structure in Munich, the German Pavilion at Expo 67 should certainly be considered one of the most informative structures'.[21] A delegation, which included representatives of the firm Behnisch & Partner, Jörg Schlaich from L+A and Berthold Burkhardt, who had advised on the pavilion's installation on the part of the IL, carefully studied the structure in 1969 and took samples. It was hoped that findings of corrosion, and thus the durability of the construction, would be of use in the design of the Olympic roofs, which were meant to be permanent installations. Realization of the spectacular design for the Olympic Park roofs would also have been impossible without a whole team of engineers.[22] Again the most important figures were Fritz Leonhardt and, especially, his project director at the office of L+A, Jörg Schlaich, Leonhardt's eventual successor at the University of Stuttgart.

As in Montreal, the cable support structure for Munich was developed on the basis of models made at the IL of technically similar materials and with comparable geometry. The physical models, up to 4 metres long, could be loaded and tested on the specially built-in measuring table in the IL pavilion – parts of it are still preserved at the present-day ILEK. During test calculations, various measurement methods were employed simultaneously so as not to subject the fragile models to too frequent loading and unloading. At the time, these were called 'multimedia tests' (*Multimediaversuche*) – not to be confused with our present sense of the term 'multimedia' – which imply the parallel use of both the mechanical Montreal gauges and Linhof cameras for photogrammetry, in a technique developed by IAGB. To measure the tension in the boundary cables, electronic strain gauges were used in the same load tests to calculate the prestressing. This electronic measurement method, which can be used only on stronger dimensioned components, had been further developed at Stuttgart's Institute for Model Statics (Institut für Modellstatik) – a centre focused on model statics in Germany. The physical models constructed for the multimedia tests were at a scale of 1:125 since the size of the IL's measuring table limited them to a maximum of 4 metres in length. They were also intended to determine the actual cutting patterns for the roof surfaces. Given the free form of the tents this was impossible to

The German Pavilion in Montreal as a model for wind tunnel testing, scale of 1:200 (1965)

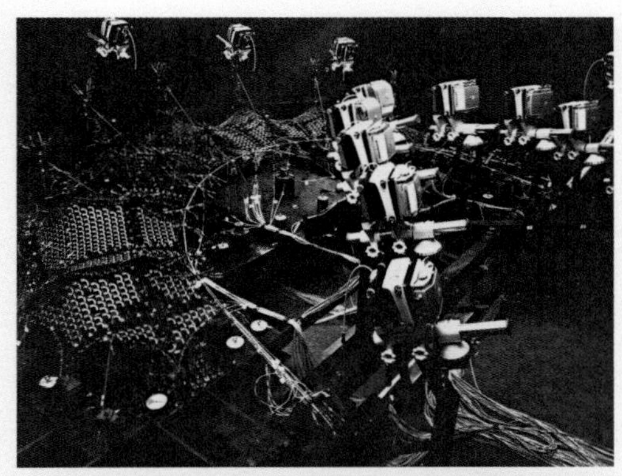

plot from traditional graphic representations of ground plans and cross sections, for which reason physical models had already been used to establish the shape of the Montreal tent. With regard to the accuracy of the patterns, the greatest care was required to ensure precise fabrication of the roof cladding for Munich – which, after long discussion, was to be executed in Perspex. For this, IAGB under Klaus Linkwitz again performed photogrammetric measurements of the wire models. However, it turned out that the scale of the available models made the necessary precision impossible and more detailed models were needed to ensure the required accuracy essential for defining the final cutting patterns. One such model, at a scale of 1:25 for the low point T2 over the swimming hall, is still preserved at ILEK in Stuttgart.[23]

When it became clear during the design phase that the precision of these models would probably still not suffice, Klaus Linkwitz and his Stuttgart colleague John Argyris from the Institute of Structural Mechanics and Dynamics in Aerospace Engineering (Institut für Statik und Dynamik der Luft- und Raumfahrtkonstruktionen, ISD) decided to determine the geometry of the cable net with the help of a computer. For this Argyris employed the finite element method (FEM) he had co-developed and the University of Stuttgart's first mainframe computer. To visualize the assembly of the cable net's many differing connection points to the boundary cables as free from distortion as possible, at a scale of 1:10, Linkwitz developed two computer-assisted solutions with which he then produced patterns for the 3,800-square-metre roof using two different types of drawing machines – one of the first applications of computer-assisted design (CAD) in the construction industry. The British construction historian Bill Addis has therefore spoken of the design of the Olympic Park roofs in Munich as a 'hybrid model analysis', a combination of digital and physical models.

This hybrid method of model statics was also used in 1972 during the design of Mannheim's Multihalle, a gridshell structure of wood laths planned as temporary for the 1975 German National Garden Show.[24] In the development of the structure, following a plan Frei Otto produced together with the architecture firm Carlfried Mutschler + Partner, Otto worked with a so-called inversion model to design and refine its form.[25] For it, a purely compression-loaded form is generated out of a two- or three-dimensional, purely tensile-loaded suspended form by mirroring it along the horizontal axis. In other words, the suspended form is 'frozen'.[26] This inversion principle had long been known; Galileo Galilei first experimented with catenaries in around 1600,[27] and in the nineteenth and early twentieth centuries, Heinrich Hübsch and Antoni Gaudí had employed suspended models.[28] Frei Otto had been working with this principle since 1946 – because in suspended models only tensile forces are involved and in the inverted shell only compression forces, the shell produced can be built with as little material as possible. In response to criticism of the Munich cable structure, which had required heavy concrete foundations as counterweights to absorb the tensile forces, for the construction of the amorphous shell in Mannheim, Frei Otto proposed a lattice structure of wooden laths, a solution minimizing material in the extreme.[29] The suspended model of the Mannheim net,[30] which is now in the collection of the German Architecture Museum in Frankfurt am Main,[31] is not a 'measurement' model in the strict sense to be used for calculating forces on the structure.[32] With this model made of 15-millimetre chain links on a production scale of 1:98.5, the geometry of the free-form structure was refined. Several sections of the net, painstakingly linked together by the hands of Frei Otto's assistants, are mounted on a marble slab free of deformation. Measurement of the form was again carried out by IAGB under Klaus Linkwitz using photogrammetry.[33] With these analogue data, engineers from the office of Edmund 'Ted' Happold in Bath, England, then produced a three-dimensional digital model with the CDC 6600, the earliest supercomputer. With it, it was possible to calculate the lengths of the laths used for the gridshell. A programme had to be written for this that translated the data into graphic illustrations. These drawings could then be plotted and printed with

Physical model for the Olympic roof in Munich in the so-called 'multimedia test', scale of 1:125

Physical model for the low point of the Olympic swimming hall in Munich, scale of 1:25

a so-called ZUSE Graphomat, then known as a 'drawing machine'.[34] This machine was one of the first computer-based drawing systems in the construction industry. As a German technical innovation, the ZUSE Graphomat had even been exhibited at the German Pavilion in Montreal in 1967. The actual structural planning for the Multihalle in Mannheim was done at the London firm Ove Arup & Partners. Since Otto had only realized two shells as structural precursors up to that point – one for the 1962 German Building Exhibition in Essen, the second for the lecture hall under the lightweight tent roofs in Montreal – the engineers at Ove Arup & Partners rebuilt the Essen shell to scale in order to determine its static behaviour. A scale of 1:60 was chosen for the gridshells ultimately realized. Load tests on this physical model revealed that to ensure that it was rigid enough the gridshell needed to be formed of two layers. Ove Arup & Partners had experience with digital models, and in these tests were already working with hybrid model analysis. In the process, automated measurement control of the strain gauges was accomplished with the help of the first analogue computer.

Frei Otto Maintains His Faith in Models...

Frei Otto's projects in Munich and Mannheim mark a turning point in the use of physical models in structural engineering: in the early 1970s, structural engineers had already begun to exploit the potential of digital methods. To be sure, for the Alster swimming pool project in Hamburg, for example, after a design by the architects Niessen & Strömer at Stuttgart's Institute for Model Statics, an imposing 'measurement' model more than 4 metres in length was built that is still preserved and can be viewed at the Stuttgart-Vaihingen campus.[35] Even so, engineers from the office of LAP worked simultaneously with digital and computer methods.[36] The project director, Jörg Schlaich, reasoned in retrospect that model tests can only serve to disprove hypotheses and are to be evaluated with great caution. One can take this statement as an indication of a turning away from physical models on the part of engineers. The fact is, already in the following years, ever faster and more powerful computers obviated the expense of laborious model tests, which led to the use of digitally generated models in the dimensioning of structures instead of physical models. Nevertheless, Frei Otto did not go along with this development and even in the following decades remained true to thinking in terms of models.[37] He continued to design his structures on the basis of countless form-finding models, many of which are preserved in the saai collection. 'Measurement' models, like those known from the Montreal pavilion project, the IL pavilion and the Olympic roofs in Munich, were no longer used, however. In the following years, Frei Otto also produced a number of presentation models to show and win over clients and agencies. Particularly for Stuttgart's underground train station project – for which he developed, together with the architect Christoph Ingenhoven, the expressive funnel-shaped columns – more than 120 different design, working and presentation models of the columns were made, on the basis of which it is possible to trace the entire process leading to their final form. Frei Otto, thus, went his own way. Beginning with the Multihalle project in Mannheim he mainly worked with the Structures 3 division of Buro Happold,[38] yet he himself remained convinced that to understand the distribution of forces one needed physical models. Even in 2012, he still affirmed, 'Ich traue der reinen Rechnung nicht, wenn diese nicht am Modell überprüft werden kann' (I cannot trust the pure calculation, if this cannot be verified with a model).[39]

Hanging model for the Multihalle in Mannheim in the Warmbronn atelier, scale of 1:98.5 (1973)

Physical model for the Multihalle in Mannheim at the offices of Ove Arup & Partners in London, scale of 1:60 (1973/74)

1 KIT, press release no. 109, 29 June 2011, p. 1.
2 Winfried Nerdinger (ed.), *Frei Otto: Complete Works; Lightweight Construction, Natural Design*, exh. cat. Architekturmuseum der TU München, Basel/Boston/Berlin 2005.
3 Joachim Kleinmanns and Christiane Weber (eds), *Fritz Leonhardt 1909–1999. Die Kunst des Konstruierens/The Art of Engineering*, Stuttgart/London 2009.
4 Christiane Weber, *Fritz Leonhardt, 'Leichtbau – eine Forderung unserer Zeit. Anregungen für den Hoch- und Brückenbau'. Zur Einführung baukonstruktiver Innovationen im Leichtbau in den 1930er und 1940er Jahren*, Karlsruhe 2011. According to Berthold Burkhardt, Frei Otto was unaware of Leonhardt's essay.
5 Kleinmanns and Weber (eds), *Fritz Leonhardt 1909–1999*.
6 Siegfried Gaß, *Form–Kraft–Masse/Form–Force–Mass 5 (Experimente/Experiments), Mitteilungen des Instituts für leichte Flächentragwerke (IL)*, no. 25, Stuttgart 1990, p. 0.15
7 Klaus Bach, Berthold Burkhardt and Frei Otto, *Seifenblasen/Forming Bubbles, Mitteilungen des Instituts für leichte Flächentragwerke (IL)*, no. 18, Stuttgart 1987, p. 15.
8 Berthold Burkhardt, *Experimentelle Ermittlung von Minimalnetzen. Mitteilungen des Instituts für leichte Flächentragwerke (IL)*, no. 1, 1969, pp. 12–14; Bach, Burkhardt and Otto, *Seifenblasen/Forming Bubbles*, p. 320.
9 Only the whereabouts of the attachable wind machine are unknown. See Christiane Weber, 'The Last Witnesses: Physical Models in Architecture and Structural Design', in: Brian Bowen et al. (eds), *Proceedings of the Fifth International Congress on Construction History*, vol. 3, Chicago 2015, pp. 569–576.
10 Bach, Burkhardt and Otto, *Seifenblasen/Forming Bubbles*.
11 Klaus Bach and Eda Schaur, *Pneus in Natur und Technik/Pneus in Nature and Technics (IL)*, no. 9, Stuttgart 1977.
12 Frei Otto and Rudolf Trostel, *Zugbeanspruchte Konstructionen*, Frankfurt a. M./Berlin 1962, pp. 10–168.
13 Wolfgang Faig, *Vermessung dünner Seifenlamellen mit Hilfe der Nahbereichsphotogrammetrie*, doctoral thesis, Universität Stuttgart, Munich 1969.
14 Bach, Burkhardt and Otto, *Seifenblasen/Forming Bubbles*, p. 328.
15 Christiane Weber, 'Der Deutsche Pavillon auf der Weltausstellung 1967 in Montréal', in: Klaus Jan Philipp (ed.), *Rolf Gutbrod. Bauten in den Boomjahren der 1960er*, Salzburg 2011, pp. 68–83.
16 Bill Addis, 'Toys that Save Millions: A History of Using Physical Models in Structural Design', in: *The Structural Engineer*, no. 4, 2013, pp. 12–27.
17 Benjamin Schmid et al., 'From Leonardo Da Vinci to Fritz Leonhardt: The Role of Physical Measurement Models in Bridge Engineering', in: *Conference Proceedings of IABSE*, Istanbul 2023, pp. 928–935, https://doi.org/10.2749/istanbul.2023.0928 (accessed June 2024).
18 Bundesbaudirektion (ed.). *Expo '67 Montréal – Deutscher Pavillon. Dokumentation über das Bauwerk*, Düsseldorf [1967].
19 Bill Addis, Dirk Bühler and Christiane Weber, 'Versuchsmodelle im Ingenieurbau. Geschichte, Bedeutung, Erhaltungsperspektiven', in: Ædificare*: Revue internationale d'histoire de la construction*, 2/12, 2022, pp. 205–266.
20 Elisabeth Spieker, 'Die Planung des Olympiadachs in München. Fritz Leonhardts Mitwirkung und Impulse', in: Kleinmanns and Weber (eds), *Fritz Leonhardt 1909–1999*, pp. 118–125.
21 Berthold Burkhardt, 'Besichtigung und Untersuchung am Deutschen Pavillon EXPO 67 Montréal (Kanada) 7.11.69–14.11.69', in: *Mitteilungen des Instituts für leichte Flächentragwerke (IL)*, no. 3, Stuttgart 1970, p. 1.
22 See, most recently, Benjamin Schmid and Christiane Weber, 'The Experiments on Measurement Models for the Munich Olympic Site', in: João Mascarenhas-Mateus et al. (eds), *History of Construction Cultures*, vol. 1, *Proceedings of the Seventh International Congress on Construction History (7ICCH)*, Lisbon 2021, pp. 625–631, with additional bibliography.
23 This model could be retro-digitalized and virtually rebuilt as part of the priority programme funded by the German Research Foundation (DFG) 2255: Last Witnesses. Benjamin Schmid et al., 'Die Seilnetzmodelle zur Olympiadachlandschaft in München. Letzte Zeugen der Modellstatik. Ein Bericht aus dem DFG-Schwerpunktprogramm "Kulturerbe Konstruktion"', in: *Bautechnik*, no. 5, 2024, pp. 335–340.
24 Frei Otto, *Multihalle Mannheim, Mitteilungen des Instituts für leichte Flächentragwerke (IL)*, no. 13, Stuttgart 1978, p. 33.
25 Frei Otto, *Natürliche Konstruktionen. Formen und Konstruktionen in Natur und Technik und Prozesse ihrer Entstehung*, Stuttgart 1982, p. 48.
26 Rainer Graefe, 'Gewölbe und Kuppeln, Schalen und Stabtragwerke, Gitterschalen. Beispiele aus der Baugeschichte', in: Frei Otto (ed.), *Gitterschalen, Mitteilungen des Instituts für leichte Flächentragwerke (IL)*, no. 10, Stuttgart 1974, pp. 20–25.
27 Karl-Eugen Kurrer, *Geschichte der Baustatik*, Berlin 2002, p. 126.
28 Gaudí's suspended models for the Church of Colònia Güell have disappeared; they were painstakingly reconstructed by those working for Jos Tomlow at the IL. See Jos Tomlow, *Das Modell: Antoni Gaudis Hängemodell und seine Rekonstruktion. Neue Erkenntnisse zum Entwurf für die Kirche der Colonia Güell, Mitteilungen des Instituts für leichte Flächentragwerke (IL)*, no. 34, Stuttgart 1989.
29 Graefe, 'Gewölbe und Kuppeln, Schalen und Stabtragwerke, Gitterschalen'.
30 See, most recently, Baris Wenzel et al., 'The Hanging Model for the Mannheim Multihalle and Its Digital Twin', in: *Conference Proceedings of IASS/Apcs 2022: Innovation, Sustainability and Legacy*, Peking 2022, pp. 2834–2843, with an additional bibliography.
31 The collection of the German Architecture Museum (Deutsches Architekturmuseum, DAM) in Frankfurt a. M. has the second largest collection of Frei Otto models, after the saai. The museum's founding director, Heinrich Klutz, first exhibited Frei Otto's designs and models in the exhibition *Vision der Moderne* (1986). In 2012, a special section was dedicated to his work in the exhibition *Das Architekturmodell. Werkzeug, Fetisch, Kleine Utopie/The Architecture Model: Tool, Fetish, Small Utopia*, exh. cat., ed. Peter Cachola Schmal and Oliver Elser, Zurich 2012, including Christiane Weber, 'Frei Otto. Experimentelle Modelle/Experimental Models', pp. 45–50.
32 Benjamin Schmid and Christiane Weber, 'From Physical to Digital: The Form-Finding and Measuring Models of the Mannheim Multihalle', in: *Proceedings of the Ninth Conference of the Construction History Society*, Cambridge 2022, pp. 485–495.
33 Lothar Gründig, Ulrich Hangleiter and Hans D. Preuss, 'Berechnung des Hängenetzes und Zuschnittsermittlung', in: Frei Otto, *Multihalle Mannheim*, pp. 41–50.
34 Gründig, Hangleiter and Preuss, 'Berechnung des Hängenetzes und Zuschnittsermittlung', p. 41.
35 See, most recently, Benjamin Schmid and Christiane Weber, 'Das Messmodell für die Alster-Schwimmhalle Hamburg. Ein interdisziplinäres Zusammenwirken Stuttgarter Bauingenieure auf dem Gebiet der Modellstatik', in: *Schriftenreihe der Gesellschaft für Bautechnikgeschichte*, vol. 5, Petersberg 2021, pp. 207–222, with an additional bibliography.
36 Rolf Kayser et al., 'Das Hyperschalendach des Hallenbades Hamburg Sechslingspforte', in: *Die Bautechnik*, 65 (1970), no. 9, part I (Leonhardt and Schlaich), 'Entwurf und Tragverhalten', pp. 207–215; no. 10, part II (Müller and Kayser), 'Modelluntersuchung', pp. 245–249; no. 11, part III (Voßbein and Lehmitz), 'Bauausführung', pp. 261–264.
37 Georg Vrachliotis et al. (eds), *Frei Otto: Thinking by Modeling*, exh. cat. ZKM | Center for Art and Media Karlsruhe, Leipzig 2017.
38 Christian Brensing, 'Frei Otto and Ove Arup: A Case of Mutual Inspiration', in: Nerdinger (ed.), *Frei Otto: Complete Works*, pp. 102–108; Michael Dickson, 'Frei Otto and Ted Happold: 1967–1996 and Beyond', in: Nerdinger (ed.), *Frei Otto: Complete Works*, pp. 110–123.
39 Frei Otto in conversation with the author, 12 December 2011.

'Ähnliche Prozesse': Natural and Cultural Self-Formation

Sean Keller

A flickering constellation of terms, in two languages, hovers over the course of Frei Otto's long career: form (*Form*, *Gestalt*), force (*Kraft*), finding (*finden*), self-forming (*selbstbilden*), form-finding (*Formfindung, Gestaltwerdung, Formentstehung*). Looking back at his writings, one has to recognize that Otto did not deploy these terms with the precision or consistency of a pure scientist or an analytic philosopher. Rather he used them as motivational concepts for his experiments in materialized form – we might say that their use was justified by this experimental work rather than by their conceptual precision. The ambiguity of these key concepts also pointed towards the main goal of his career: to (re)connect the natural and human realms. In this way they also played a crucial role in the wider success of his work, especially as it reached beyond his research centre and into realized works of architecture.

While these concepts themselves contain powerful ambiguities, the worldview that Otto constructed from them was remarkably consistent over the course of six decades. Perhaps the most complete version of his understanding was offered by the publications associated with the exhibition *Gestalt Finden* (*Finding Form*) created by Otto and Bodo Rasch on the occasion of their receipt of the Deutscher Werkbund Bayern Prize in 1992. Through their texts and images, Otto and Rasch construct a grand interpretation of the world in which the chronology of the universe's development leads to, and is embodied by, present categories of existence (as such it resembles pre-twentieth century *Naturphilosophie* more than contemporary science). The concept of form plays the central role in their narrative, as they wrote:

> Material objects acquire their form through processes that shape form.
> Forms originate in all natural spheres:
> – in inanimate nature
> – in animate nature
> – in animal and human technologies
> – in art[1]

Here as throughout his work, Otto does not see these categories neutrally or as a trajectory of progress. Instead, there is – implicitly and explicitly – a sense that something has been lost or corrupted as we crossed the border separating the natural from the human. The troubling factor, which we can easily extrapolate but which Otto rarely identifies, is nothing less than free will. While the relationship of process and form is spontaneous and unmediated in the natural world (whether inanimate or animate), it becomes open to wilful manipulation by humans in the realms of technology and art – the point at which roads, cities and buildings enter the pictorial history Rasch and Otto present. As they describe it:

Animal and Human Technologies

For about half a million years highly developed and mobile animals have been using technologies for shaping products.
Techniques used by insects and spiders, whose forms and constructions are anchored genetically, are old in terms of biological development.
Genetic anchoring is increasingly replaced by learning from parents in higher animals and those that are younger in terms of biological development. Tools and materials that are part of the body are supplemented by found items or tools the animal makes itself.
Finally man invents and develops technical objects according to his own targeted optimization processes with self-reproducing tools that create products from self-made materials in any quantity and only exceptionally relate to animate natural objects or animal technologies.
Technical objects age and become superfluous. They are replaced by technically improved items. Art objects are produced using technologies.

They are frequently a very great distance away from all nature. They do not need models, rules or conventions. They develop very little or not at all.

1 Animal technologies
spiders' webs, devices for catching food, overall genetically anchored
2 Spiders' webs in detail
hardened forms of viscous thready masses
3 Birds' nests
houses for vertebrates, built from found materials
4 From inside a termite city
three-dimensional light construction
5 Wasps' nest
miniature city built of self-made paper

Genetic anchoring [of construction techniques] is increasingly replaced by learning from parents in higher animals [...] Tools and materials that are part of the body are supplemented by found items or tools the animal makes itself.
Finally man invents and develops technical objects according to his own targeted optimization processes [...] Art objects are produced using technologies. They are frequently a very great distance away from all nature. They do not need models, rules or conventions. They develop very little or not at all.[2]

We can understand Otto's entire career as a series of efforts to bridge or overcome this break between the natural and artificial realms by returning us to processes of self-formation – what he calls 'Self-formation Processes Used by Man'.[3] Otto's hope was that 'Tomorrow's architecture will again be minimal architecture, an architecture of the self-forming and self-optimization processes suggested by human beings.'[4]

The same impulse was present almost four decades earlier in the introductory words of his dissertation where his advocacy of suspended roofs is grounded on a claim that such structures are, somehow, not technical but natural:

> The instinctive drive that inseparably belongs to life not only directs that dwellings are to be built, but also how they are to be built. The tent is fundamentally of a biological, non-technical or ur-technical nature. (In contrast, the vaulting of stone buildings is surely a technical act, invented by individuals, grown into a model, and taken up by everyone and used everywhere.)[5]

Otto's long exploration of suspended roofs was for him, therefore, not a mere interest in one category of building technology among others. It was the development of a way of building that could reconnect us to the natural world and its own processes of form generation. (The deep contradictions of this view are also apparent: how are the highly complex suspended roofs that Otto helped develop less technical than masonry or any other construction method?)

This advocacy for 'natural construction' pushed Otto into a unique role within the architecture community, since rejecting the entire lineage of 'the vaulting of stone buildings' meant turning away from the greatest portion of the discipline's history (at least in the West). For Otto, writing in West Berlin in the aftermath of the Second World War, this rejection was highly intentional. It was a rejection of architecture as the representation of power and of anti-democratic politics. This context also suggests a deeper reading of his fascination with the self-forming processes of nature: in a century in which free will was so often deformed into a grasping will-to-power, Otto sought out prelapsarian design

'Techniken der Tiere und des Menschen' (Animal and Human Technologies), double pages from Frei Otto and Bodo Rasch, *Gestalt finden. Auf dem Weg zu einer Baukunst des Minimalen* (*Finding Form: Towards an Architecture of the Minimal*; 1995)

methods in which the spontaneity of nature replaced the corruptible judgment of human actors.

While certainly unique in the specifics of his approach, Otto was not alone in the post-war decades in seeking to displace architectural authorship away from its traditional, and seemingly necessary, reliance on judgment. As I have discussed elsewhere, the 1960s and 1970s saw the emergence of diverse research programmes dedicated to the development of 'automatic' architectural design methods.[6] While other figures may have relied on the new field of electronic computation (Christopher Alexander and Lionel March) or a radicalized formalism (Peter Eisenman), they shared with Otto a sceptical attitude towards individualized architectural judgment, as well as the sense that architectural modernism – in the period of its apparent triumph – had already devolved into a tool for bureaucrats or mere stylists. (Here we might note that, despite his well-known antipathy for computational design methods, Otto's interest in form-finding methods became, along with these other approaches, an important precursor to contemporary computational-based design.)

By centring his thinking around the concepts of form and forces, Otto was also connecting – knowingly or not – with long lines of discourse in philosophical aesthetics and biology. For instance, the Goethe scholar David Wellbery argues that the concept of form lies at the heart of a cluster of terms that are 'central both to Goethe's aesthetics and to his scientific studies'.[7] In Wellbery's analysis, Goethe's understanding of form, though varying across his works, was in fundamental respects similar to the picture given by Otto in which form is the emergent result of a force-driven process. In contrast to both Platonic and constructivist notions of form, Wellbery sees Goethe working out an idea of what he calls 'endogenous form':

> [...] which understands form as a lawful process of formation actualized in an interplay of invariance and variation. Form thusly conceived is a genesis from within, a self-shaping governed by an inner principle. The relation of form and material is no longer one of opposition, but rather of interpenetration. While conceptually distinguishable, form and matter are not separable.[8]

Which is not of course to suggest a precise alignment of Goethe and Otto, or even to suggest that Otto was conscious of the conceptual parallel – again, he was an experimenter not a philosopher. Nonetheless it remains important to recognize that his ideas of form have deep echoes within the European cultural context.

Even more directly relevant to Otto's view is the argument put forward by Malika Maskarinec in her recent book *The Forces of Form in German Modernism*. Building on the observations of David Summers, Maskarinec describes how, since the Enlightenment, 'form has no longer been a preexistent idea that defines how a specific exemplum develops; instead form emerges over time under the direction of a progressively unfolding force [...] continually fashioned in an ideally autonomous process of *Bildung* (formation or development). Form and force become inextricable.'[9] This belief was central to philosophers, artists, writers and scientists from the late-eighteenth to early-twentieth centuries. Of the last group, the most influential individual on this topic – and one who surely stood as a model for Otto – was the Scottish biologist D'Arcy Wentworth Thompson, who in *On Growth and Form*, first published in 1917, stated clearly that 'the form of an object is a "diagram of forces" [...] from it we can [...] deduce the forces that are acting or have acted upon it.'[10] Otto's research project – what he often referred to as the 'reverse path' – was essentially to invert Thompson's observational method into a generational one by setting up experiments in which forces would create forms within the setting of his hybrid laboratory/studio.

This experimentation was crucial in differentiating Otto's work from that of many other artists and architects (and certainly philosophers and writers) who worked within the wider milieu described by Maskarinec for whom the 'forces' creating form are almost always metaphoric. By borrowing aspects of a scientific laboratory, Otto generated forms from literal, physical forces – while also, crucially, maintaining their metaphoric resonances. He also enacted his belief that form provided the connection between the natural and artificial spheres through his collaborations with biologists and other life scientists, from his early work with Johann-Gerhard Helmcke to the founding of the Sonderforschungsbereich 230 'Natürliche Konstruktionen' (Collaborative Research Centre 230 'Natural Structures') at Stuttgart, which ran from 1984 to 1995. We might say that Otto translated an understanding of natural science and aesthetics that stretched back to Goethe into the organizational structures (and funding opportunities) of late-twentieth century academic research.

Out of this hybrid context of laboratory and atelier came Otto's richest explorations of form-finding and its dilemmas: his experimental models. And among decades of experimentation with chains, blocks, sand, rubber sheets and magnets, it is the long run of soap film models that stand as the epitome of his form-finding aspirations. These models were spontaneously created, and then remained in existence, due to the physical forces of tension within the films and with their boundaries. Moreover, before the development of computational calculation and visualization of these geometries – which would be invented during the design of the roofs for the 1972 Summer Olympics in Munich – the soap film models 'found' forms that were otherwise unknowable. These models were not just replicating known forms or forms that could be devised by humans, they were finding mathematically correct solutions to the forces acting on them that were (at that moment) beyond human reach. The interaction of invisible forces in these models are revealed by the thin, shimmering surfaces of soap film that hover on the border between the physical and the purely optical. It is easy to see why these qualities created a magical fascination for Otto as they revealed a way to use the spontaneous reactions of physical forces as a creative power within design – a way to create the 'Self-formation Processes Used by Man' described by *Gestalt Finden*.

However, we should also see that the seeming immediacy of the physical models – what Otto would see as their connection to nature – was bracketed, on one side, by the highly artificial laboratory conditions that allowed them to occur and, on the other, by the distinct and very human architectural contexts to which they might be applied. Granting the inevitability and centrality of these cultural tensions brings the character of Otto's process into sharper outline: Otto's model-based techniques can be understood as distancing devices – limiting and shifting his role within the design process so that he is not designing directly but by establishing the conditions in which form-finding can occur and be utilized. In this regard, the soap film models again offer a particularly intensive example: shaping one of these minimal surfaces through manipulation of its edge condition redoubles the role of the form-finding techniques by allowing Otto to achieve compositional action at a distance.

Understanding the fundamental ambiguity of Otto's explorations also helps us resolve the contradiction raised by the fact that, despite the minimalist rhetoric, his portfolio of full-scale works is largely comprised of projects that are rather extravagant and almost purely symbolic: exhibition tents for garden festivals, multipurpose halls, pavilions and roofs for sports venues. From a stringent functionalist standpoint, these projects do not literally conserve resources, but rather are symbolic performances of conservation and of the spontaneous efficiency of nature itself.

Arguably the richest and most coherent of the built works was the pavilion designed by Otto and Rolf Gutbrod to represent West Germany at the Expo 67 world's fair in Montreal. While echoing the lightweight, and light-hearted, vocabulary of a festival tent, the pavilion was in fact a work of unprecedented technical complexity, built at the limit of existing architectural methods. Rhetorically intended to stand for the open, post-war attitude of West Germany, its tensioned

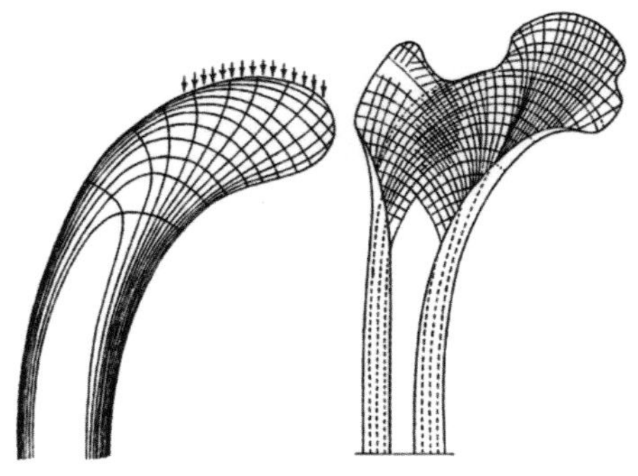

D'Arcy Wentworth Thompson, comparison of lines of force in a mechanical crane head and a human femur, after Culmann and H. Meyer, in *On Growth and Form* (1917)

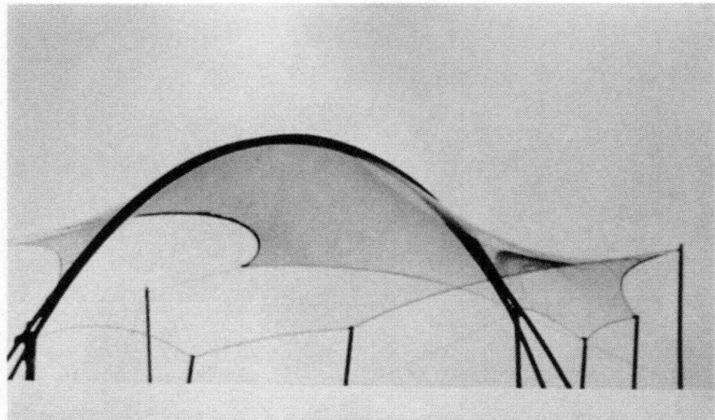

Frei Otto at the Institute for Lightweight Structures (IL), soap film model of an arch tent (1970)

cables and PVC-coated polyester skins demanded great precision of planning and fabrication, which the very 'naturalness' of its picturesque roof made enormously difficult. Expo 67 was the ideal realization of Otto's interest in using form-finding to (re)connect architecture to nature. Beginning with the small soap-film models that 'found' the correct minimal surface for the roof, the project advanced through many technical challenges to be realized as a lightweight, temporary structure that was immediately compared to a landscape.

In Expo 67 and elsewhere, Otto's unusual use of models had remarkable effects. For, more than any other architecture, it seems reasonable to say that his realized pavilions were themselves models – larger but entirely continuous with the elaborate studio versions that preceded them. This was one important way in which they were set apart from the long tradition of compressive architecture – from the world of stone, as Otto would put it. While the model of a traditional structure will look like that building, we take for granted that it does not act like its full-size counterpart. In contrast, Otto and his team painstakingly created models that not only looked like but, more importantly, acted like the full-size buildings they represented. Or, more accurately, as we have seen, it was only through the performance of the many development models – through their spontaneous response to physical forces – that the final, full-size projects came to exist. By thus dissolving the boundary between representation and object, Otto's design method created a continuum between models and buildings.

The symbolic role that the West German Pavilion needed to perform was surely as complex as its technical aspects. First, it needed to avoid monumentality and any obvious nationalism, both of which were strongly tainted by associations with National Socialism. This was achieved by conceiving of the pavilion as a landscape project, with a garden running through it and only a 'very light roof' overhead. (This vision is far more evident in the proposal models, constructed with highly transparent fabric nets, than in the realized pavilion, where the open cable net was necessarily supplemented by an opaque membrane of PVC-coated polyester.) Sounding a theme that ran throughout his career, Otto's proposal was that the West German Pavilion could avoid architecture by merging with nature.

Yet an essential aspect of the pavilion's role nearly overturns this first direction. While the project needed to avoid national dramatics by being 'natural', it also needed, by definition, to still perform as an instance of national self-presentation. Given Germany's history, the 'unconventional Germany' that the pavilion represented was precisely a nation trying to move beyond nationalist representations of itself. Otto's success in this projection of self-effacement depended on automatic methods of form generation to fulfil a rhetoric of transparency, lightness, naturalness and efficiency in a project of great technical novelty and complexity. His roofs were important not just technically, but because they advanced a new, and acceptable, formal vocabulary for large-scale national structures, a vocabulary reached through form-finding processes that did not achieve some impossible mission of escaping design and representation but that were themselves representative of a new attitude towards design and its relationship to power. The conflation of the organic and the technological, the flexible and the rigid, the minimal and the elaborate, the automatic and the composed, the natural and the political, endowed Otto's projects with symbolic stresses that redoubled their structural tensions and were the key to their success as representations of post-war West Germany. Around the issues of monumentality, national expression and technology, this architecture offers a series of incomplete negations, of concepts under erasure. The result was a symbol of a new Germany and, paradoxically, of an attitude towards design and building that struggled to move beyond symbolic representation, beyond nationalism and, in some sense, beyond architecture itself.

Finally, to return to my opening theme, we should recognize that it was precisely the ambiguity of Otto's central concepts – finding, form, forces – that enabled the great achievement reached by the best of his full-scale constructions.

Rolf Gutbrod and Frei Otto, West German Pavilion at Expo 67 in Montreal (1967)

German postage stamp issued by the Deutsche Post depicting the West German Pavilion at Expo 67 in Montreal, from the four-stamp series titled 'Deutsche Architektur nach 1945' (German Architecture post-1945) issued in 1997

Most crucially was the doubled status of these terms as they referred both to literal, physical conditions and to metaphoric, allegoric ones. This ambiguity allowed a cultural activity – architecture – to be reframed as a quasi-scientific one based on 'finding' forms in nature. For a national culture that, in the post-war period, had good reason to doubt its judgment, this displacement of the architect's authorial role offered an attractive solution to the dilemmas of representation. This productive elusiveness, and its symbolic importance, was wonderfully captured by the postage stamp depicting the Expo 67 pavilion, which was issued by the Deutsche Post in 1997. The commemorative pane for 'Deutsche Architektur nach 1945' (German architecture post-1945), in which the stamp was issued, includes a quotation from Otto: 'Wir suchen jene Baukunst, die aufgrund ähnlicher Prozesse entsteht, wie die Konstruktionen der Natur' (We seek an architecture that arises through similar processes as the structures of nature).[11] The exploration of this idea of 'ähnliche Prozesse' – of (re)unifications, or perhaps synchronizations, of the cultural and natural spheres – was the engine of Otto's entire career not despite, but because of, its rich and fundamental contradictions.

1 *Frei Otto, Bodo Rasch: Finding Form; Towards an Architecture of the Minimal*, Sabine Schanz (ed.), exhib. cat., Villa Stuck, Munich 1995, p. 23.
2 *Finding Form*, pp. 34 f.
3 *Finding Form*, p. 41
4 *Finding Form*, p. 14.
5 Frei Otto, *Das hängende Dach: Gestalt und Struktur*, Berlin 1954, p. 9; translated here by the author.
6 See Sean Keller, *Automatic Architecture: Motivating Form After Modernism*, Chicago/London 2018.
7 David Wellbery, 'Form (Form)', in: *Goethe-Lexicon of Philosophical Concepts*, 1/1, 2021, pp. 45–52, https://doi.org/10.5195/glpc.2021.38.
8 David Wellbery, 'Form (Form)'.
9 Malika Maskarinec, *The Forces of Form in German Modernism*, Evanston 2018, p. 6.
10 D'Arcy Wentworth Thompson, *On Growth and Form*, abridged edition edited by John Tyler Bonner, Cambridge 1961, p. 11.
11 An unfortunate consequence of the pane's design is that it strongly suggests that Otto was the sole architect of the pavilion, excluding Gutbrod entirely. The precise source of the quotation is also not given and remains elusive. It most likely comes from a speech.

Large shades at the German National Garden Show in Cologne (1971), model

Society

Ethics
Participation
Networks

Project Study 'City in the Arctic' 1971

Szilvia Gellai

In his book *Space as Membrane* (1926), Siegfried Ebeling asserted that the 'climatological differentiation of architecture' represented altogether 'new territory for continental architecture'[1] and that the 'elementary conditions'[2] in architecture mainly needed to be considered with a fresh and scientifically informed eye. According to Ebeling, hollow spatial entities (*Hohlraumkörper*) maintain complex interrelationships through their shells, first with the ground, second with the elemental medium of the outside air and third with the living creatures inside, so that in each of the three components, individually, diverse currents and radiances preside. Walls thus functioned like climate-regulating membranes. Ebeling offered an especially illuminating example of the transvaluation of architectural values by pointing to tropical and polar regions. In his opinion, places with extreme variations in temperature and solar radiation posed challenges to the design of spaces not only 'because they could very soon become important geopolitically for our own vibrant economic development, but also purely as a geo-social act.'[3]

Ebeling's deliberations provide a revelatory foil for critical consideration of the project study 'City in the Arctic'[4] presented by Frei Otto during a press conference in April 1971, for they help us address the tension between the 'utopia and reality of membrane architecture'.[5] The prototype of a domed city was created for geographical regions extremely rich in natural resources like oil, uranium and ores but lying in harsh climate zones of the polar circle. The proposal calls for opening up these regions with urban centres for roughly 15,000 to 45,000 inhabitants where they would be protected from extreme temperatures by climate-regulating shells and be able to live and work under the conditions of a continental climate. The roof was to be a pneumatic tensile structure in the form of a shallow dome installed before the city was built. Once the building site was graded and a ring-shaped foundation excavated, the prestressed shell would be anchored to this ring and inflated from within. It would thus provide suitable conditions for the continued construction work. With a diameter of two kilometres, the dome would cover a surface area of 3.14 square kilometres and rise to a height of 240 metres. The dome membrane itself was to be elastic and consist of two layers of transparent synthetic foil, while between them was stretched a supporting grid of cables made of polyester fibre. The mesh size of his net would be 10 metres, with the cables having a diameter of 27 centimetres. The membrane would be supported from inside by a light air pressure, like a balloon.

The study was commissioned by the Hoechst chemical concern and carried out by an international collaboration of the Stuttgart team led by Otto and Ewald Bubner working together with the London engineering firm of Ove Arup & Partners and the Japanese team of Kenzo Tange and URTEC. While the London engineers conducted the analyses and calculations of the dome's statics, the Tokyo architects dealt with aspects of urban planning and environmental design. Of top concern in the concept was the establishment of a high quality of living. Plans included, for example, silently moving pavements connecting a recreational area and green spaces with the residential area as well as the administrative and business centres. In the winter months, a powerful artificial sun would travel on rails beneath the roof and provide adequate light, also for the plant life. So that the city would not feel hermetically cut off from the outside world, fluctuations in the polar climate would still be felt. Provisions for air circulation and transportation were therefore constitutive elements of the architectural plan. They would be relegated to two subterranean storeys beneath the pedestrian level of duct systems and logistical tunnels. Motor vehicles would be restricted to the first level, where exhaust fumes could be directed outside. The second level would in turn serve the intake of fresh air, drawn in with energy from an atomic power station outside the city, warmed and distributed citywide.

Similar tunnel systems are often found in the domed city visions of the post-war period, promising urban surroundings free of automobiles, noise and emissions.[6] In the 1960s, settlement concepts were produced, especially for the Arctic, and primarily by Canadian, Soviet and Swedish architects. During the Cold War, the cryosphere increasingly became the target of geopolitical ambitions that went far beyond economic concerns. Since the visionary concept of domed climate shelters bounced back and forth between the blocs, analysis reveals differing responses to local factors. What strikes the eye in plans for a settlement in the extreme north by the Soviet architect Konstantin Agafonov, for example, is the elevation of the buildings, some 3 metres above the permafrost, to avoid warming it through contact.[7] Even in Alaska and Canada, pipelines are frequently carried on specially cooled supports to avoid cracks in the metal or surface instability during periods of thaw. A definite blind spot in Frei Otto's Arctic City concept was its failure to address the issue of permafrost. According to the project report, no difficulties were expected in the creation of foundations owing to the location.[8] Otto's argument for the placement of the thought model in cold zones was simply 'heating is easier than cooling'.[9]

His primary focus was on the spectacular membrane construction and its behaviour in wind and weather. This was also in line with his client Hoechst's priorities. And here the interconnections between architecture and economy indicated by Ebeling come into play. As the historian Christian Marx has pointed out, West German chemical companies anticipated the forthcoming energy crisis long before the oil shock of 1973, for energy costs had already been rising since the late 1960s.[10] Hoechst was dependent on crude oil as both a source of energy and a raw material, but was also looking for alternatives. For a time, the company even considered building its own nuclear power station. The main considerations behind 'City in the Arctic', like the exploitation of new resources and the use of atomic power, were responses to this situation. At the same time, the study's centrepiece – a faithful model on a scale of 1:2000 – was displayed at the Hanover Industrial Fair a few days after the press conference and provided an elaborate display opportunity for one of Hoechst's most important products: the polyester fibre Trevira, which like Nylon and Perlon was most closely linked to West Germany's economic Miracle on the Rhine and was used far beyond the fashion industry. Trevira-Hochfest-Fasern, a specially impregnated, high-strength variant of the product, played a central role both in the model and in the city concept, since the grid to which the roof's transparent membrane was to be attached would be made of this material.

The genealogy of the Arctic City project is not only intertwined with the petrochemical industry, however. To a greater degree, it rests on the problematic notion that in the Arctic land for building 'does not cost anything',[11] which implies a wholesale consideration of these regions as *terra nullius*, one whose resources can be exploited at will. It was first and foremost this colonialist and imperialist premise that made the future realization of the prototype appear 'not only possible but even economical'.[12]

1 Siegfried Ebeling, *Der Raum als Membran*, reprint, Leipzig 2016, p. 19; in English translation as *Space as Membrane*, trans. Anna Kathryn Schoefert, London 2010.

2 Ebeling, *Der Raum als Membran*, p. 36.

3 Ebeling, *Der Raum als Membran*, p. 18.

4 Bernd Oleiko and Einar Thorsteinn, *Projektstudie Stadt in der Arktis/Project Study City in the Arctic, Mitteilungen des IL*, no. 2, Stuttgart 1971; trans. W. Woodson Hand, Gary L. Bostwick, Bernd Oleiko.

5 Walter Scheiffele, *Das leichte Haus. Utopie und Realität der Membranarchitektur*, Leipzig 2015.

6 Szilvia Gellai, 'Minnesota Experimental City, oder: Zukunft als Experiment', in: *Technikgeschichte*, 88/1, 2021, pp. 43–78.

7 Ekaterina Kalemeneva, 'Arctic Modernism: New Urbanisation Models for the Soviet Far North in the 1960s', in: Nina Wormbs (ed.), *Competing Arctic Futures: Historical and Contemporary Perspectives*, Cham 2018, p. 228.

8 Oleiko and Thorsteinn, *Projektstudie/Project Study*, p. 34.

9 EB, 'Himmel aus Kunststoff', in: *Kölner Stadt-Anzeiger*, 21 April 1971, p. 31.

10 Christian Marx, 'Failed Solutions to the Energy Crises: Nuclear Power, Coal Conversion, and the Chemical Industry in West Germany Since the 1960s', in: *Historical Social Research* 39, no. 4, 2014, pp. 251–271, here p. 252.

11 Oleiko and Thorsteinn, *Projektstudie/Project Study*, p. 7.

12 Oleiko and Thorsteinn, *Projektstudie/Project Study*, p. 7.

in the arctic'
airport
glass-roof above dwelling city
Mining area covered with cable-net structure
153 x 73
wind shelter

City in the Antarctic (1953), design sketch

Urban landscape under a large shell in the Arctic (1971)

Visualization of the climate shell for the City in the Arctic, model photo

Model photo

Model for City in the Arctic
without the large shell

Residential development beneath a climate shell

Frei Otto and his team photographing the model

Frei Otto's team testing the membrane

The Eco-Houses in Berlin 1980–1991

Georg Vrachliotis

As part of the International Building Exhibition (Internationale Bauausstellung, IBA) held in Berlin in 1987, Frei Otto was charged by Josef Paul Kleihues – then director of the division for New Building of the IBA – with a pioneering task: to design a residential complex that would embody the principles of sustainable and natural building. The project was not only a technical challenge, but also a social and ecological milestone for the Building Exhibition, one that was intended to redefine the future of urban living.

The parcel of land originally proposed for the project was at Askanischer Platz in Berlin-Kreuzberg, a historically and symbolically charged site that had lain fallow since the Second World War and stood just a few steps from the Berlin Wall. By virtue of belonging to a neighbourhood that had been characterized for decades by the division of the city, the location invested the project with special urgency and significance. The vision developed by Otto for the property was radical and forward-looking: a 'three-dimensional garden city', as he called it, that would blur the boundaries between private and public spaces, facilitating the intimate interweaving of nature and urban life. This concept – which goes back to an experimental project Frei Otto produced as a student in 1951,[1] as well as early designs from 1959 for a parcel off New York's Central Park[2] – was characterized by its innovative use of space and resources.[3] The core concept of the eco-houses (*Ökohäuser*) encompassed not just the integration of green areas into the city's fabric, but also the active participation of residents in the construction of their own homes: ecological aspects converged here with participatory strategies. In order to safeguard both principles, Frei Otto envisioned a low-density settlement that would allow inhabitants to design their own flats according to their individual needs and conceptions, at the same time minimizing the ecological footprint.

In order to realize this vision architecturally, Frei Otto imagined buildings that were conceived and ordered as tree-style structures and consisted of two monumental concrete skeletons, each approximately 35 metres wide and some 60 metres tall. These shelf-style loadbearing structures, which would be interconnected on the lower levels, were to form the basis for about fifty one-or-two-storey residential units, each of which would be designed and realized by the future occupants in collaboration with architects, ecologists and energy consultants.

Despite these ambitious plans, Kleihues and the Berlin Senate decided to shift the eco-houses project to a alternative smaller, less prominent piece of land at the edge of the Tiergarten, along the course of the Landwehr Canal. This decision was made in deference to a comprehensive urban planning measure that envisioned a perimeter block development under the direction of Oswald Mathias Ungers. One can only speculate about Kleihues's reasons for displacing Frei Otto's project to this relatively out-of-the-way location. Though he was presumably in accord with the basic ecological concept of the design, it seems likely that he regarded the informal appearance of the eco-houses as an aesthetic impertinence, especially in comparison with the postmodernist principles of order governing the other designs. In place of the 'perimeter block' and of 'critical reconstruction', Frei Otto proposed – so to speak – the principles of the 'platform' and 'nature'. The project 'would be a great tree with dwellings on all of its branches. [...] According to current aesthetic rules, what I am striving towards would certainly not be more beautiful, but it is more natural', wrote Otto in a critical letter addressed to Kleihues.[4]

The change of location had a direct impact on the project's overall conception and presented the project team around Frei Otto with a fundamentally new design challenge. Compared with the initial concept, the second design had to be reduced considerably in height and extent. While the drawings and model photos for the urban context at Askanischer Platz display high-rise style structures with spacious living surfaces and densely landscaped terraces, Frei Otto was now obliged to conform to the heights of the surrounding IBA buildings and to orient himself in relation to the existing tree population. By virtue of the uneven topography, the irregular shape of the parcel and its dense stock of trees, the new site – formerly the location of the Vatican's Apostolic Nunciature – represented an enormous architectural challenge.

Frei Otto and project architect Hermann Kendel, therefore, opted for an ensemble consisting of three multi-storey blocks of flats that would function as open platforms and have heights of between 6 and 12 metres. Since the project was subject to the demands of social housing development, all of the units would have to be virtually the same size. Each building consists of an open reinforced steel skeleton with a constructive core that accommodates the centralized utilities. This ensured the future occupants the greatest possible design freedom when configuring and designing their individual units along ecological lines. The glazing on the south side and the installation of solar panels would allow the harvesting of solar energy. At the same time, the landscaped roof and the greening of various building surfaces would allow the structures to retreat optically behind a garden landscape.

Construction finally began in 1988, after a planning and waiting period lasting over eight years. Work on the buildings continued until 1991.[5] Hermann Kendel was responsible for directing and coordinating overall planning and contributed to the designs of three residential units as well. The artificial building footprints, consisting of simple concrete platforms and supported by solid pillars and beams, were intended to offer occupants maximum individual freedom in laying out their homes. Despite an emphasis on self-construction and individualized design options, the stringent requirements of social housing development restricted the diversity of the living spaces to a considerable degree, interfering with the desired mixture of social levels. In the end, given political realities and the less than fully mature developmental state of certain methods, the original aspiration of linking together experimental residential forms with a range of ecological concepts could be realized only to a limited extent. As an overall concept, nonetheless, the eco-houses offer residents a remarkable level of quality of life at a central location in the city while differing markedly from the postmodernist style of the neighbouring IBA buildings. In a fascinating way, the project exemplifies the capacity for architecture to go beyond providing living space in order to transgress social and ecological limits. Today, nearly forty years after the IBA, the eco-houses remain a forward-looking prototype in the history of experimental residential development and an international icon of alternative architecture of the late 20th century.[6]

1 Frei Otto, *Wohnhaus für 12 Familien*, unpublished study, TU Berlin 1951, saai, Werkarchiv FO.

2 *Anpassungsfähig bauen, Mitteilungen der Entwicklungsstätte für den Leichtbau (EL)*, no. 6, June 1959.

3 On this, see the essay by Georg Vrachliotis in the present volume, pp. 86–93 [editor's note].

4 Letter from Frei Otto to Josef Paul Kleihues, 30 July 1980, printed in Frei Otto and Hermann Kendel (eds), *Wohn-Be-Reiche im Garten, IBA Berlin 1987. Vorbereitende Studie für das Bauvorhaben 'Ökohaus' Berlin*, Warmbronn 1985, pp. 48 f. My thanks here to Fee Kyriakopoulos for calling my attention to this letter, as well as for a friendly discussion about the eco-houses.

5 Engineering services were provided by the Buro Happold in Bath, represented by Edmund 'Ted' Happold, Derek Clements-Croome, Michael Dickson and Peter Buckthorp. The team received support from the Büro Gutbrod in Berlin and Stuttgart, to which H. Henning, Hermann Kendel and B. Riede belonged. Frei Otto was joined by many years of collaboration to both Buro Happold and with Gutbrod, stretching back all the way to the 1960s.

6 See 'Otto and the Open System: Georg Vrachliotis in Conversation with Jean-Philippe Vassal', in: *uncube Magazine*, no. 33, Frei Otto, 2020, www.uncubemagazine.com/sixcms/detail.php?id=15508949&articleid=art-1429001789303-71c8ac75-dcca-4664-8331-3fb42d523bb0#!/page41 (accessed on 13 July 2020).

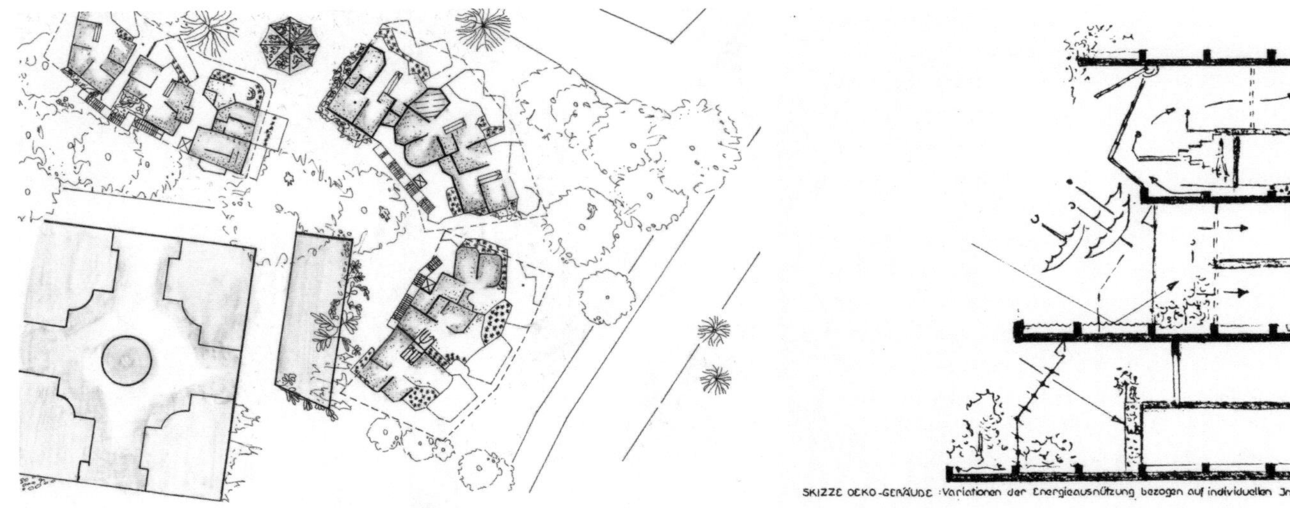

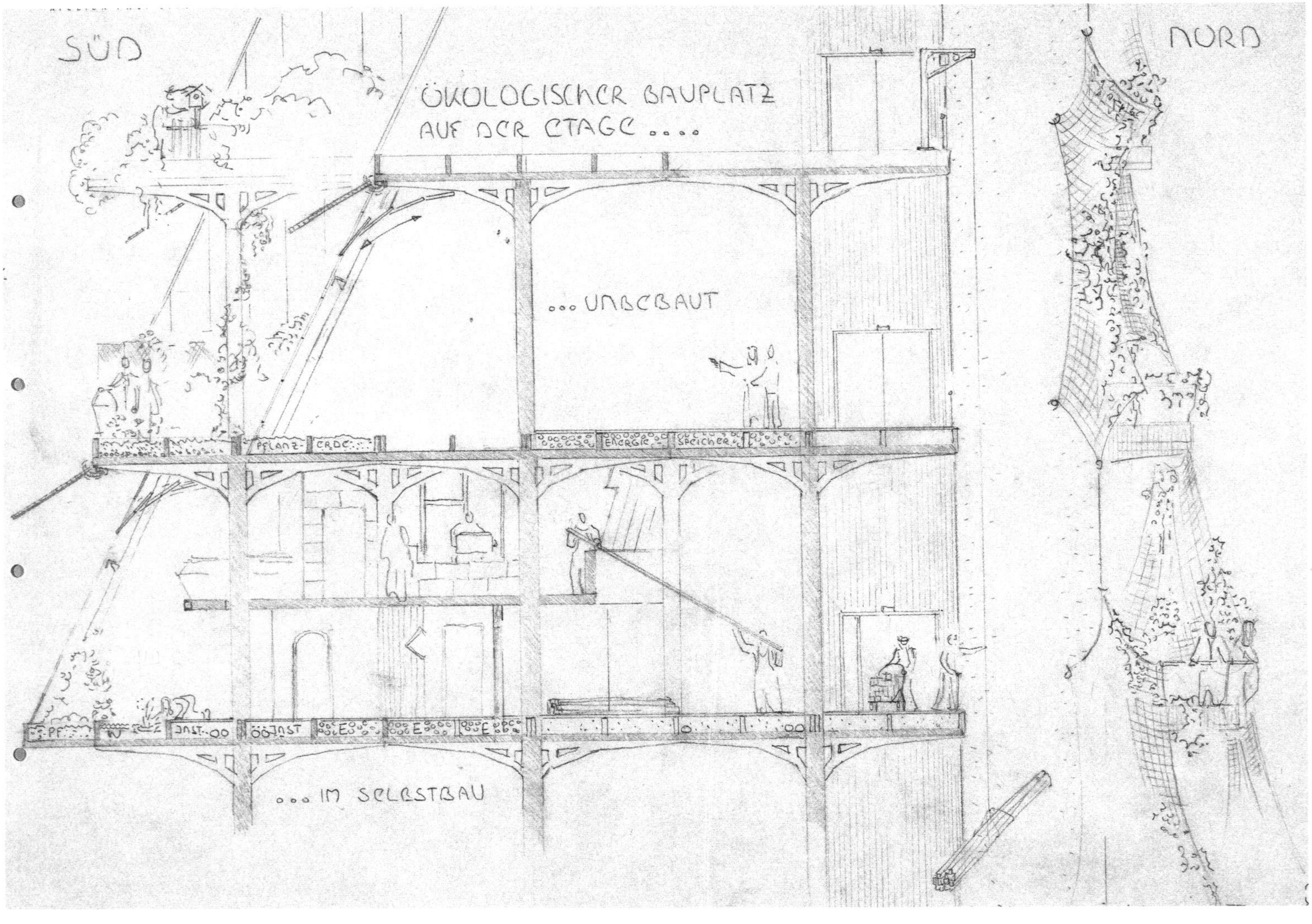

The project as realized in the Tiergarten, site and floor plans

Eco-house with variations of energy use through individualized interior construction (1988), cross-section

Eco-house with individual interior finishings by residents (1981), cross-section

Device at the IL for simulating sun and shade with the model of the eco-houses at Askanischer Platz

Model of the realized design for the Tiergarten (above) and the model of the project for Askanischer Platz (bottom and opposite)

Following double page:
The eco-houses in Tiergarten, seen from Corneliusstraße

Diplomatic Club in Riyadh 1980–1986

Martin Kunz

After Frei Otto, together with Rolf Gutbrod, scored one of the two first places in an invitational competition for a conference centre and hotel in Riyadh in 1966, Otto maintained close ties with Saudi Arabia, planning as well as realizing several projects for the House of Saud. In the second half of the 1970s, he was involved in two large projects there. Starting in 1974, he planned, together with Büro Gutbrod, the construction of a new governmental centre in Riyadh. Two years later, the two designed a sports hall for King Abdul Aziz University in Jeddah, which was built the following year. In all these projects, Edmund 'Ted' Happold was involved as engineer.

It was therefore unsurprising that Frei Otto received an invitation when the Ministry of Foreign Affairs announced a competition for a Diplomatic Club in Riyadh. In March 1980, Otto submitted a design developed together with the American firm Sprankle, Lynd & Sprague and Buro Happold in England. It envisioned a central area with common rooms surrounded by an extensive hotel complex made up of rows of separate domes.[1] With its submission, the team was able to clinch the competition. However, realization of the design was prevented by differences of opinion regarding conditions of the contract, and Sprankle, Lynd & Sprague withdrew from the project.[2]

Yet Frei Otto as well as Edmund Happold indicated that they remained interested in the project's realization. They were informed that in the next stage it was expected that the Saudis would get back to them, but that at the moment, conversations were being held with the other competition participants.[3] In early March 1981, Edmund Happold and Frei Otto were informed that the Saudis would happily proceed with them in the realization of the project. At the same time, it was suggested that they rework the design together with Omrania, a firm from Riyadh, which had also participated in the competition.[4] They both agreed, and already in April of that year, a new proposal had been worked out. It had been inspired by the so-called 'desert rose', which is why the design was given the name 'Wall and Roses'. A first sketch shows an organically undulating wall along which rose-like blossoms seem to flower. In a further development, the roses became tents and the wall attained the necessary thickness so that it could accommodate rooms and corridors. An oasis was created in the interior courtyard it enveloped. This concept was approved before the end of April.[5] Work on the project intensified in the next few months. The physical layout and use of space was once again reworked as the result of a survey taken of the diplomatic missions in Riyadh regarding their expectations and desires for the building complex.[6] The concept for the design ultimately realized was fixed in December 1981.[7]

In the further development of the project, there was a dispute between Frei Otto and Nabil Fanous of Omrania about the height of the wall. Frei Otto wanted to make it at most 8 metres, or two storeys high, so as not to detract from the beauty of the landscape and because he feared that it would look too much like a fortress.[8] But since a large number of different functions had to be accommodated in the wall, Frei Otto was unable to assert himself in this point.

The completed complex occupies an area of 24,000 square metres and consists of a large, sinuously curving wall whose cross section was determined by Frei Otto on the basis of a suspended model. The wall is a reinforced concrete structure faced with local reddish yellow sandstone, so that its colour blends with that of the desert plateau on which it stands.[9] Thanks to its exposed position, the ensemble of buildings is visible from afar – a massive structure rising up out of the desert landscape and surrounded by lightweight, radiantly white tents. The design combines two elements typical of Arab architecture: an artificial oasis surrounded by a massive wall and the lightweight nomadic tent.

Outside the wall are three white tents housing the restaurant, the lounge and a sports facility. In the interior courtyard are two tent structures fitted into niches and clad with glazed blue ceramic tiles. These accommodate the foyer and a banquet hall. The wall is accessible throughout its entire length of 500 metres. It begins as a single storey on either side of the north entrance area and step by step rises to a full four storeys in height. On the ground floor, it is 12 metres thick and increasingly narrows to a diameter of roughly 4 metres at the top. In one section of the wall, terraced towards the desert, is a hotel with forty beds.[10]

Inside the wall lies an interior courtyard filled with plants, in the centre of which, between palms, rises what is called the 'Heart Tent'. It is the smallest tent in the complex with a diameter of roughly 18 metres and its surface is made of colourfully painted glass tiles. Frei Otto had originally planned it as a textile structure, but that idea was rejected since the colours would have quickly faded and yellowed under the desert sun. For that reason it was decided to use float glass painted with ceramic glazes in several firings. Its design was produced by Frei Otto's daughter Bettina and was meant to evoke Paradise with all kinds of imaginary flowers and plants. A fountain beneath the tent invites guests to linger for a while.[11]

The complex is now known as the Tuwaiq Palace. In 1998, it was distinguished with the Aga Khan Award for Architecture. The building ensemble was renovated in 2022.

1 saai, Werkarchiv FO, brochure on the concept behind the competition, 1980.
2 saai, Werkarchiv FO, several letters between Otto, Happold and Sprankle, 1980.
3 saai, Werkarchiv FO, telex from Mohamed Alsheik to Happold, 6 July 1980.
4 saai, Werkarchiv FO, telex from Mohamed Alsheik to Happold, 4 March 1981.
5 saai, Werkarchiv FO, telex from Ahmed Salloum to Happold, 27 April 1981.
6 saai, Werkarchiv FO, DQDC programme in report Appendix 4, August 1981.
7 saai, Werkarchiv FO, DQDC conceptual design, December 1981.
8 saai, Werkarchiv FO, fax from Otto to Nabil Fanous, 1 June 1982.
9 German-language reports generally call it 'Sandstein' (sandstone), at times 'Naturstein' (natural stone). In English articles, it is sometimes referred to as 'limestone'.
10 Johannes Fritz, 'Architekturbericht Diplomatic Club Riad', in: *Der Architekt*, no. 1, 1987, pp. 37–40.
11 'Gläsernes Kunstzelt im Diplomatischen Club in Riyadh, Saudi-Arabien', in: *Glasforum*, no. 4, 1986, pp. 19–24.

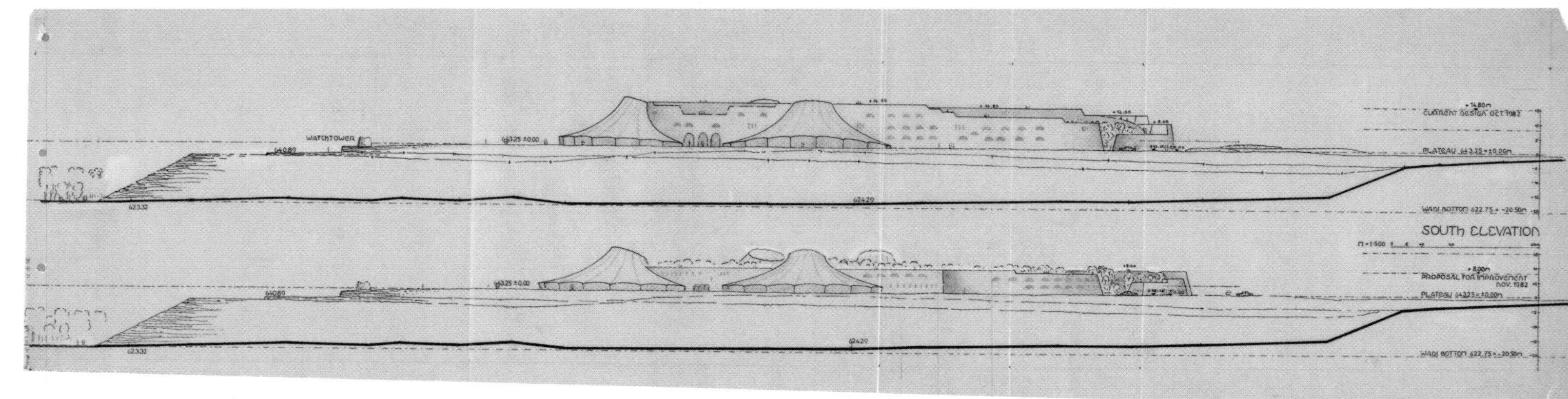

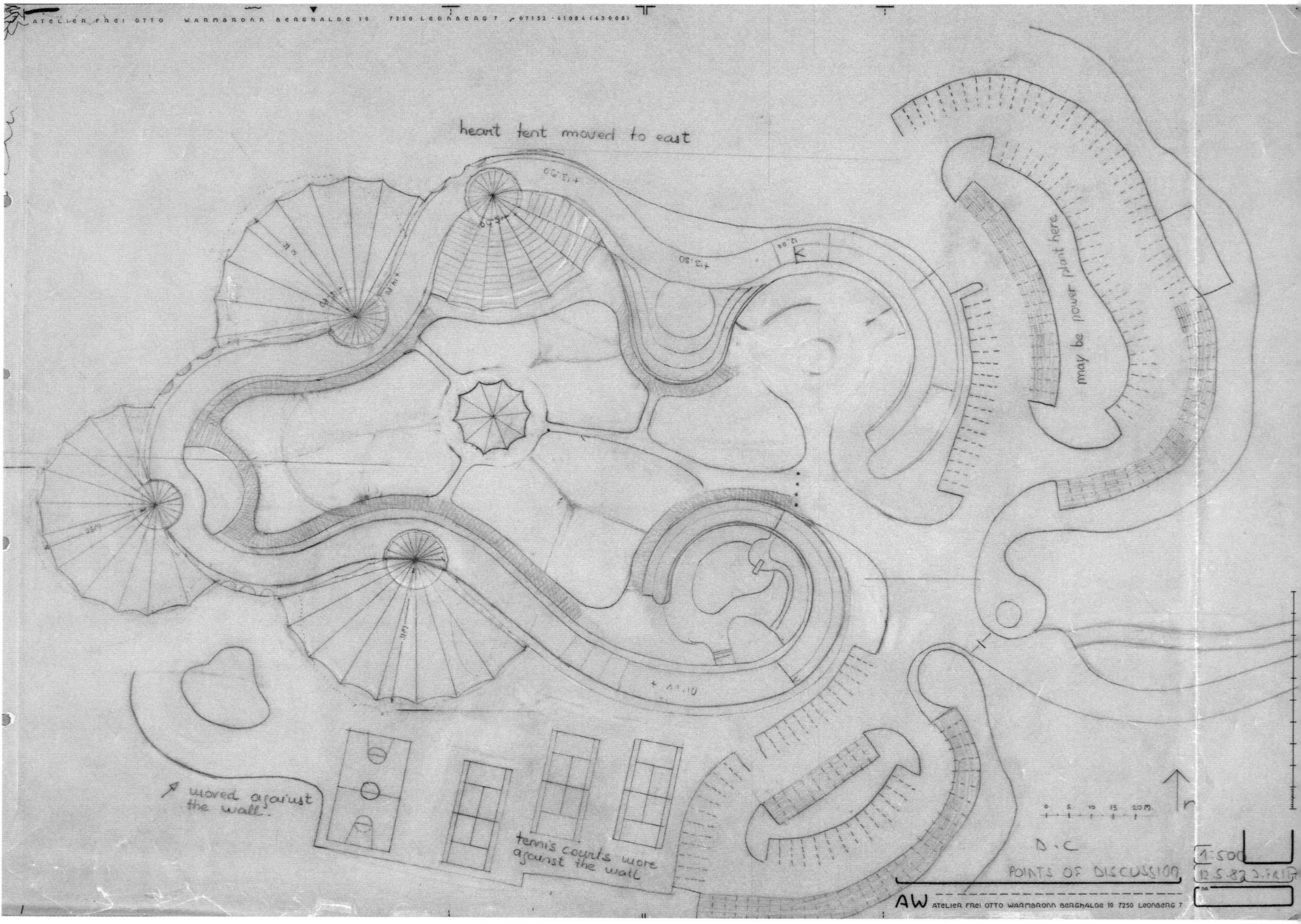

View of the complex as a whole with a terrain profile of the high plateau: above with the high, finished wall; below with Frei Otto's proposal for a lower wall topped by tents.

Site plan of the entire complex

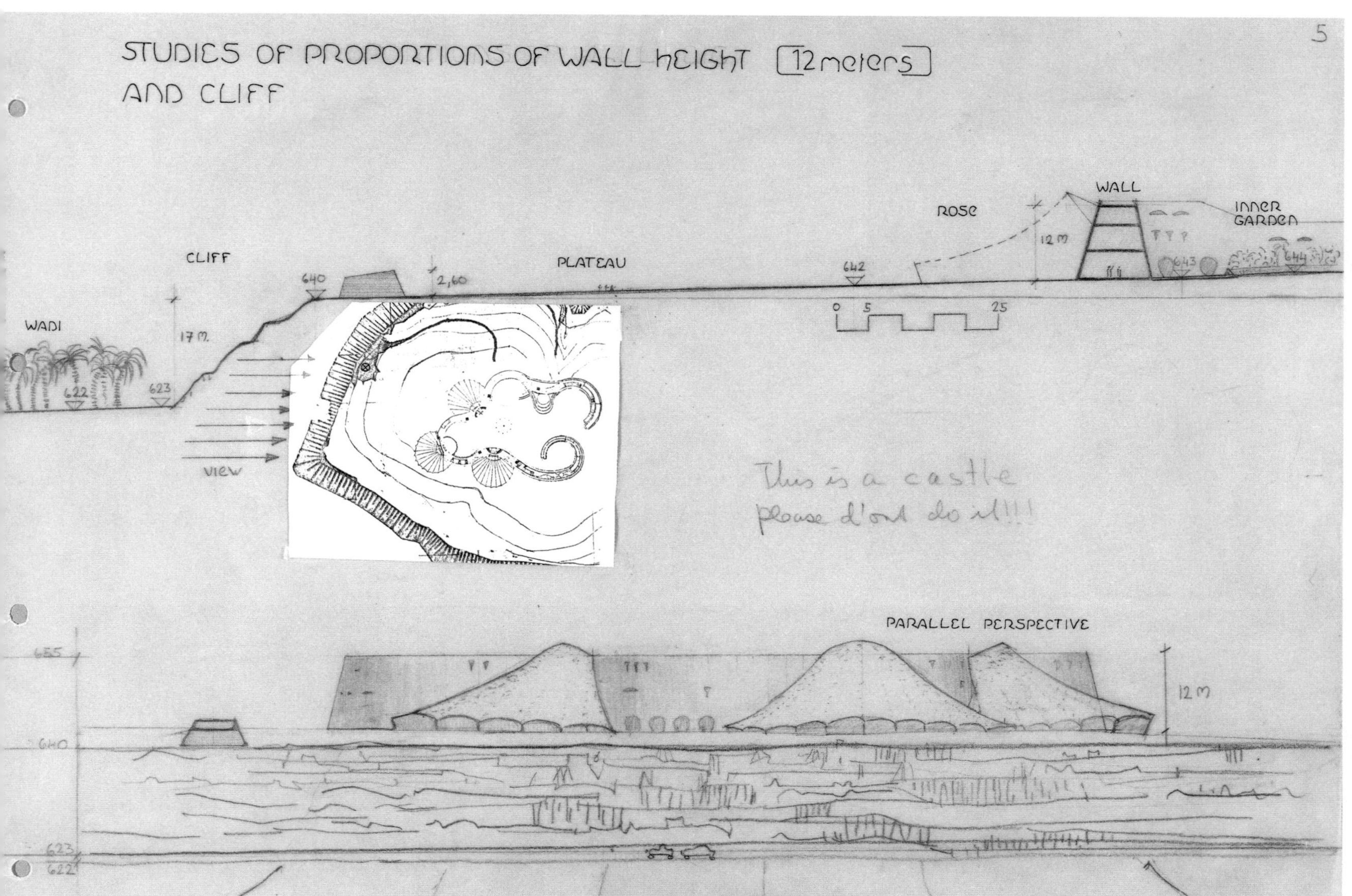

Studies for the proportions of the wall

Hanging model for determining the form of the wall and cross-sectional model of the wall

Diplomatic Club with plants in the inner courtyard, model

Following double page: External view from the high plateau

Road leading to the entry gate

Connection between tent structure and wall

Following double page: Inner courtyard seen from the Heart Tent and view of the Heart Tent structure

Thresholds of Calculation: The Material Experiments of Frei Otto

Daniela Fabricius

Those looking for the built architecture of Frei Otto today will find relatively few structures. The ones we have been left with are famously light and airy; in some cases, they have been in danger of disappearing altogether, like the 1975 Multihalle in Mannheim. Otto strove to create an ephemeral architecture that would leave the smallest possible trace on the earth. He nevertheless left behind physical artefacts: delicate models created at the Institute for Lightweight Structures (Institut für leichte Flächentragwerke, IL), but also ephemera produced by research – projections, photographs, time-based experiments, graphs and publications. Because of the near immateriality of the objects created by Otto and his researchers, the tools and devices used at the IL were of particular importance: these scientific and media instruments translated between real and incalculable matter, and models, equations and systems used to measure, simulate and predict. This essay will focus on these processes of measuring, representing and calculating using instruments and media, and how these marked the threshold between the material and immaterial in Otto's work.

The difficulty of representing or 'capturing' lightweight forms was a theme in Otto's work from the beginning. In his 1953 doctoral thesis on the 'hanging roof', *Das hängende Dach*, he wrote:

> Hanging roofs cannot be designed. When every impure tone is avoided, one can help them unfold. They suggest a peculiar beauty that is perhaps closest to the plastic trace of the spider web: an appearance that one cannot draw or explain, which will discreetly elude us.[1]

For Otto, an ideal structure unfolds by itself. Not only can these structures not be designed, they cannot really be represented. The spider web – which was a form that preoccupied Otto throughout his career – was the ultimate example of this: a structure so minimal and light that it is beyond representation or analysis.

Otto was describing a kind of sublime. But even if Otto insisted on their elusiveness, he nevertheless tried to represent and measure such minimal forms. I would like to investigate what lay behind this contradictory process of measuring and calculating what he believed were 'incalculable' structures. For Otto, the range of incalculable phenomena included not only minimal forms but also the bodily interiors of animals and humans, structures like planets and atoms that were too large or small to accurately measure, optimized pathway systems and forms that were considered aesthetically 'taboo', like sexual organs. Otto believed that these elusive objects could expand what he considered to be the limited imagination of modernist architecture.

These incalculable objects were also evidence of Otto's conflicted relationship to architectural authorship. Like many of his contemporaries in the 1960s who worked with automation, cybernetics or intelligent machines, Otto was

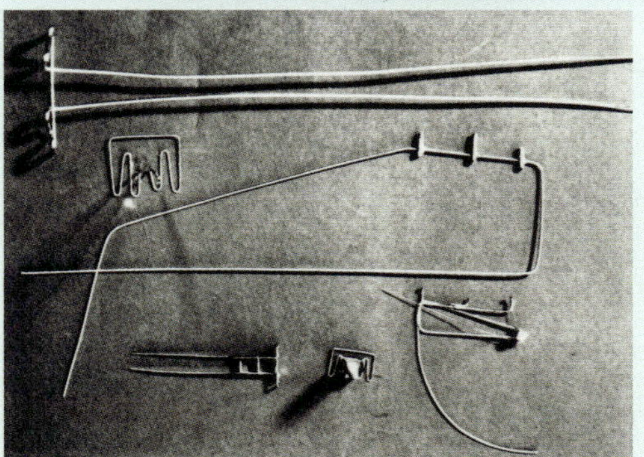

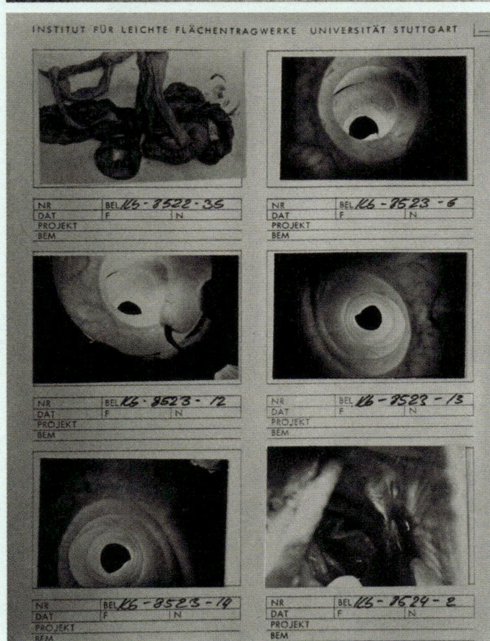

interested in self-forming structures, or the idea of the autopoietic. In Otto's case, however, this interest was tied to the behaviour of organic and inorganic matter, and not to computation. He idealized self-formed structures as born from the intelligence (and what he assumed was the goodness) of nature, as opposed to the limited capacity and potential brutality of the human imagination. This view of the elusive lightweight forms created by chemical, biological or physical processes was directly related to his condemnation of National Socialist monumentality and the concrete architecture of post-war reconstruction.

Otto was also suspicious of the mathematics of engineering and was ambivalent towards the emerging field of computer-aided design. He considered the calculation of statics used by engineers to be 'coarse' and based on 'inexact assumptions'.[2] He writes that these calculations 'will never have the same meaningfulness as the de facto testing of a real object by real forces', and that 'until today there are buildings which cannot be grasped mathematically, meaning that they are – to use the exact term – "incalculable" (*unberechenbar*)'.[3]

Otto's questioning of calculation can be viewed as part of a more general ambivalence towards scientific culture in post-war West Germany, which persisted in spite of the scientization (*Verwissenschaftlichung*) of architecture in the 1960s. This apprehension was famously expressed in *Dialectic of Enlightenment*, where Theodor Adorno and Max Horkheimer described the domination of nature as achieved in part through mathematical description: 'Nature [...] is what can be registered mathematically; even what cannot be assimilated, the insoluble and irrational, is fenced in by mathematical theorems.'[4] Otto and his team arguably had a conflicted relationship to rationalism. They were reverent of the natural world as a source of knowledge and of cultural and ethical legitimation; but the work at the institute was, at the same time, largely based on the objectification of nature through scientific methods.

In spite of their scientific intentions, it was not so easy to measure the forms created at the IL – whether fragile soap films or natural objects. In the 1960s and 1970s, researchers at the IL arrived at ways of making and measuring form that were arguably proto-digital, but the process of translating matter into numerical data was definitely analogue. Experiments took place in physical spaces and not the immaterial 'space' of the screen. Unlike other experiments with computation in the 1960s that unfolded within the black box of the computer, here the interaction between matter, objects and data took place in physical laboratory and workshop spaces.

Capturing the Ephemeral

One example can be seen in the evolution of devices used to measure soap film models. Otto's early years of free experimentation with soap film had yielded a collection of attractive photographs and speculative ideas. But for the soap film models to be measurable, they had to become more durable, which could only be accomplished by controlling their chemistry and atmospheric conditions. They also had to be placed within a framework in which space itself was already constructed as measurable, where a total and precise coordination between object, camera and lighting was possible.

The first soap film device at the IL was thus constructed in 1965 to study minimal path systems.[5] It consisted of a glass plate with a matrix board of pins suspended over a soap tank. When the device was dipped in the solution, the soap film would 'find' the most efficient path between the pins. The entire device was installed on a concrete slab in order to avoid vibration and featured a glass cover to protect it from dust and evaporation, which apparently allowed for fragile soap membranes to be kept stable for up to three weeks.[6]

As Otto's team continued to develop a series of devices for soap film structures, these devices became increasingly larger and more complex. More

Soap film machine experiments (*c.* 1977)

Device used to measure strain in the Montreal pavilion model (*c.* 1966)

Photographs of pig intestines taken by an IL researcher (*c.* 1973)

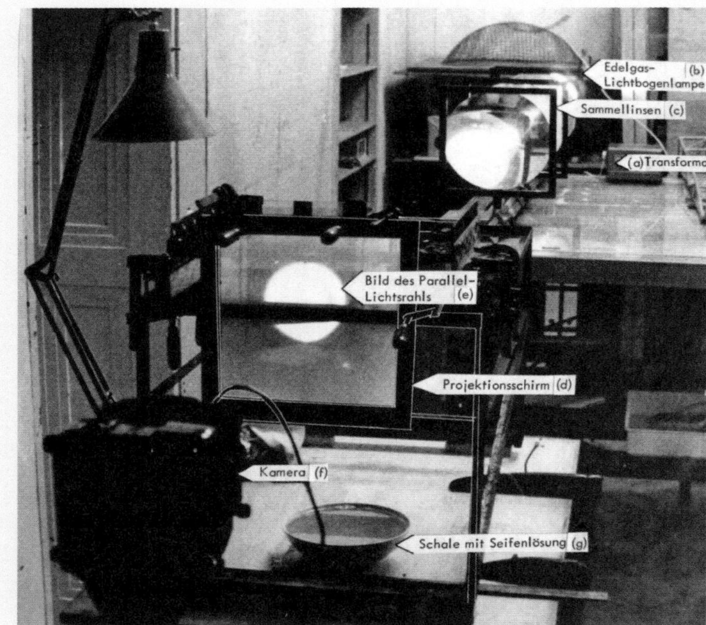

Soap film model measurement setup with optical bench, IL student research project (1967/68)

Soap film machine at the IL

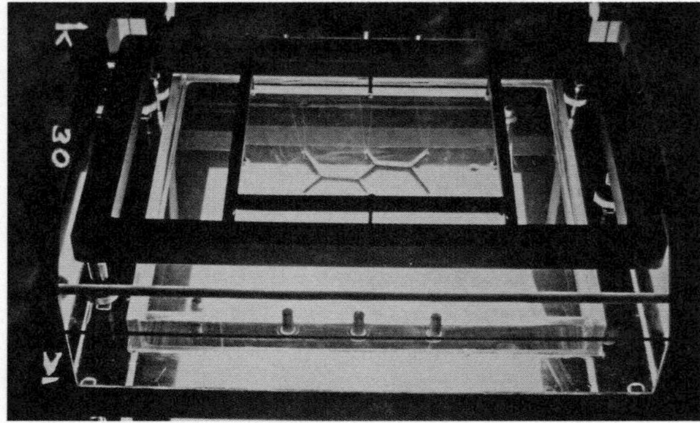

Minimal path device at the IL (1965)

significantly, these apparatuses integrated ways of capturing the models photographically, using special lights, plates and lenses. It was the photograph that allowed the model to be measured. Jürgen Hennicke, who for years collaborated with Otto, has confirmed that photography was 'the central medium' of the work at the IL.[7] Indeed, by 1970 the archive held 25,000 negatives and 8,000 colour slides and films.[8] The goal in these experiments was not to come up with a variety of forms – in fact, the form remained the same – but instead to improve the documentation.

In one setup, the soap film model was placed on an aluminium ring below a rotating turntable. A light source, located at the considerable distance of 15 metres in order to approximate parallel light waves, illuminated the model as a sheet of photo paper was inserted behind it. This created a photogram of the model. Photos were taken with rotations of the model in increments of 10 degrees, allowing for a 'scan' of the form. By now it is clear that another shift had taken place: the apparatus for creating and documenting the model had become larger and far more difficult to produce than the model itself.

The most elaborate apparatus, which can still be seen at the IL today, was first developed in 1973. The comical-looking machine, which I have had the privilege of operating, is a large assemblage (about 2 metres tall and 2.7 metres deep) of acrylic basins, rubber and plastic tubes, dials, steel frame supports, a spindle, a light box and a camera. Aesthetically, it calls to mind the air- and machine-based fantasies of the avant-garde of the 1960s. It is a similarly utopian idea of a device that harnesses technology to create instant, adaptable and autonomous architecture. It is also not unlike the self-contained world of the computer, in which model-creation, measurement, calculation and output are enclosed in one machine.

Here the model is housed in an air-conditioned chamber surrounded by glass and acrylic. A camera is mounted on an adjustable support in front of the chamber. The support for the soap film model can be fully manipulated to not only adjust the height but also rotate and tilt the model. This recalls the disorienting space of the digital model, in which it is no longer the viewer who moves around the object, but the model that is manipulated in space according to its axes.

In these devices, the onus of representation is placed on the apparatus that documents and measures the model, and not the model itself. Otto's ideal of the disappearing spider web is realized: the object is overwhelmed, and eventually disappears, as it is measured and converted to data.

The Calculated Eye

As these devices became more sophisticated, it was clear that the image had gained prominence over the object. As a result, the experiential and phenomenological aspects of image-making and observation were emphasized. For instance, a 1973 IL publication included a groovy pair of 3D glasses for the reader to use in order to view anaglyphic images printed in red and green at the centre of the book.[9] The 3D images show a hanging chain net model, photos of a diatom taken with an electron microscope, the structure of veins in human legs and a geodesic image of a topographical landscape. The reason for using this technology was surprisingly tied not to questions of perception but to precision: the IL researchers argued that these images are more 'realistic' spatial representations, without distortions, unlike two-dimensional drawings, which they viewed as inadequate to describe new forms that do not follow 'simple geometric laws'.[10]

While the measuring photographs had attempted to capture an object in order to flatten it into data, these anaglyphic images virtually maintained the object in three dimensions. Research was done on the distance between a human's eyes, the ability of the brain to perceive depth and the desired focal distance and angle so as not to create blind spots. In this significant step towards simulation (and computer modelling), the traditional architectural drawing and its outdated technology of perspective were seen as no longer sufficient. These images suggest something closer to a simulated image, and one that, unlike the fragile models, could be stored, reproduced and transferred as media.

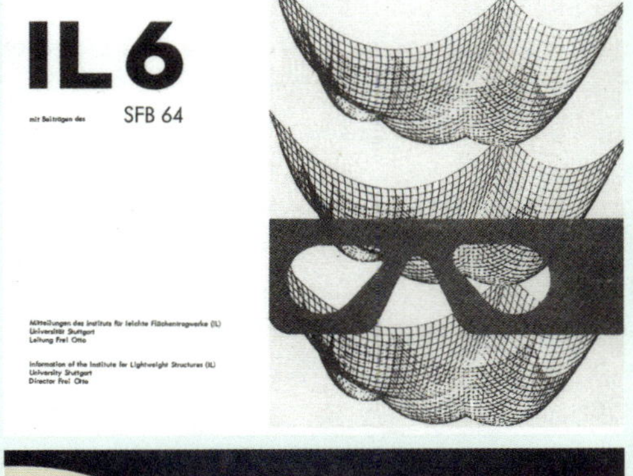

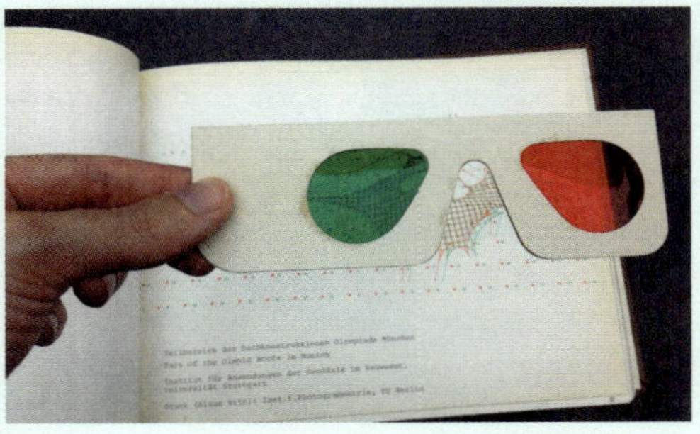

'Ten thousands of "data at a glance"'

In theory, Otto celebrated the immeasurable ideal of a universal, optimized structure, but his built projects demanded precise measurement and calculation. Special measurement models were created to yield numerical information about stresses that were difficult to comprehend visually and impossible to calculate mathematically. Otto had constructed measurement models and form-measuring devices as early as the 1950s but needed more sophisticated methods when he was commissioned to work on large cable net projects, beginning with the West German Pavilion for Expo 67 in Montreal. Unlike the nearly immaterial liquid surface of soap film, cables and connections on a matrix allowed for the isolation of individual points. These fixed points made it possible to position these forms within the coordinates of Cartesian space and eventually allowed for Otto's work to be digitally modelled.

The forms for these models were arrived at through inductive methods using soap film and fabric. But paradoxically, once an optimal form was found, the model lost its mutability as the complexity of minimal surfaces required a very precise structural solution. This was especially the case for structures with inconsistent loads, like the cable net roofs used for the 1972 Summer Olympics.

Biologie und Bauen 3/Biology and Building 3, Mitteilungen des Instituts für leichte Flächentragwerke (IL), no. 6 (1973), cover and the 3D glasses for viewing the anaglyph images

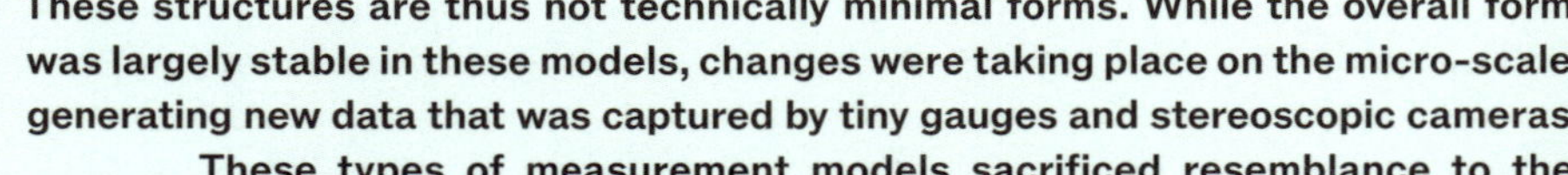

These structures are thus not technically minimal forms. While the overall form was largely stable in these models, changes were taking place on the micro-scale, generating new data that was captured by tiny gauges and stereoscopic cameras.

These types of measurement models sacrificed resemblance to the building in favour of a 'picture' of the building in numbers. As in the soap film experiments, a physical model was combined with a method of precisely documenting it. What makes these models so impressive is not only their scale (the largest was 1.9×4 metres) but also their machine-like precision. One could describe these as a form of physical computing; nothing in the construction of the models was arbitrary, and all of the performance variables were scaled down. For instance, spring wire, dimensioned and cut to scale, was prestressed proportionally according to the real cables.

The measurement of the model took place in stages. First, the overall geometry and position of the coordinates were determined by the use of a measuring table. This was a large structure, a kind of virtual Cartesian space, that was able to trace and measure the geometry of a complex model through the use of a plummet. This method, like the soap film model drawings, resulted in an indexical 'scan'; the data obtained could even be read and stored in the form of punch cards.

Next, another level of information was obtained by the use of photography combined with special measurement devices. Whereas increasingly larger devices were used for the soap film models, here the development was towards ever-smaller tools that were, in effect, sensors embedded within the model. Measurement was less a question of dimension than it was one of performance. Individual wires were hung with number tags so that they could be identified in photographs as the model was pulled at by means of chains and weights simulating different loads.

While the soap film models had been photographed in their entirety, these models were photographed in close-up sections. The enormous quantity of data contained in the model, not yet translated into digital information, could be documented only with the camera, and only in parts. Not only single instances, but also multiple layers of information were recorded through time-lapse photographs that showed the model change under strain. These jittery images document a blurred landscape of grids, dials and numbers. With these images we return to the early modernist desire to capture form in motion and change through time. But however similar the effect, the objective was different: to control movement, rather than release its potential energies; to predict the future of architecture mathematically, rather than to imagine it.

One of the most difficult tasks was the reiterative process of manually tensioning and re-tensioning thousands of wires until equilibrium was reached at every point in the structure. This non-linear series of protocols, based on feedback from the model, resembles the command-based process of computing. In contrast to this careful adjustment over time, an immediacy was evident in what was called the 'multimedia test'. The great sensitivity of the Olympic stadium model made it vulnerable to imprecision if too many subsequent tests were run. The researchers thus devised a snapshot of the model in which as much data as possible was collected at once. This photograph shows what looks more like a performance stage than a model. Hundreds of instruments were attached to the model, and the weights that hung from it were all suspended at once as the pneumatically controlled floor below dropped. Surrounding the model in a manner resembling a television studio is a battery of cameras from which bundles of wires emerge. This setup was a composite object made up of both the model itself and the devices that measure, adjust and document it. The two become indistinguishable, together forming an architecture that is as much about information as it is about form. Information was viewed not with one eye but with many cameras, multiplying the observation experience so that the object could be seen from all sides at once. With this assemblage of architecture and devices, the panoptic quest to capture 'ten thousands of "data at a glance"' was achieved.[11]

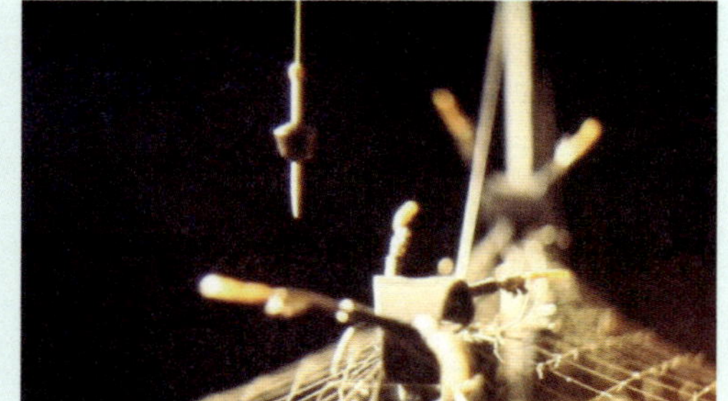

'Measurement' model for the Olympic buildings in Munich (*c.* 1968), detail

Measuring table at the IL (*c.* 1968); screw spindles to move the x, y and z axes are operated by electric motor, and measurements could be printed directly onto coded punch tape

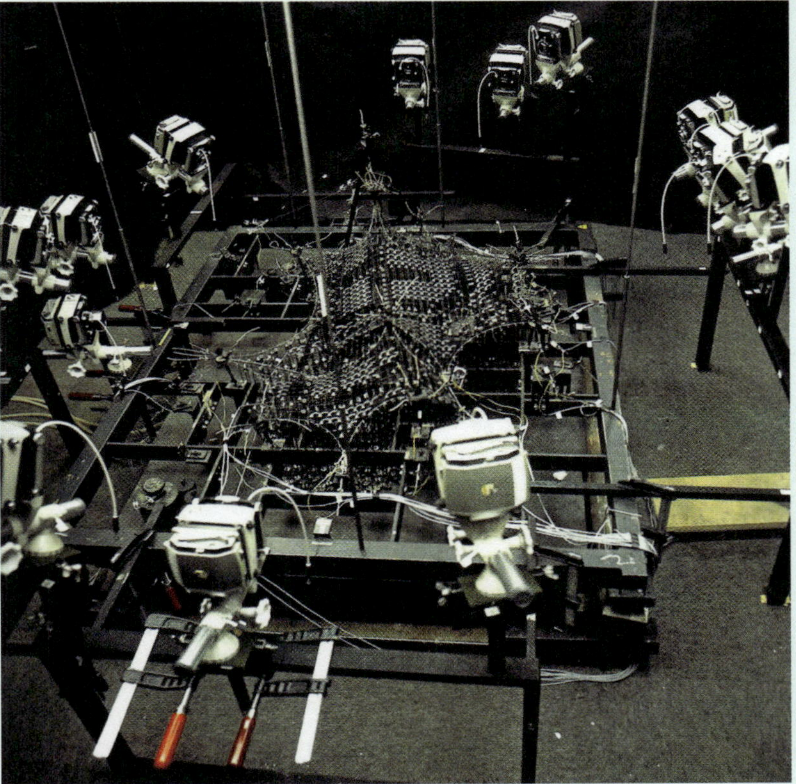

But how accurate was this data? As computer models were increasingly able to calculate complex structures, it became clear that the analogue technologies used here were in some ways primitive. The measurement models of the IL generated patterns for cable lengths, which were directly translated to the manufacturing and construction process, and yet the patterns were simply not accurate enough. Incredibly, an error of .007 millimetres in the model could result in a cable being 0.8 millimetres too long or too short, which when stretched would become 5 centimetres, which would mean that the tension would be off by fifty percent.[12] This was an intolerable risk.

Thus, at the same moment that the measuring models were constructed to replace traditional calculation, they were being replaced by a newer form of computation. At the University of Stuttgart, the teams of both John Argyris at the Institute of Structural Mechanics and Dynamics in Aerospace Engineering (Institut Statik und Dynamik der Luft- und Raumfahrtkonstruktionen, ISD) and Klaus Linkwitz at the Institute for Applications of Geodesy to Civil Engineering (Institut für Anwendungen der Geodäsie im Bauwesen, IAGB) separately worked on methods of calculating the structure using computers. These calculations, some of which required equations with up to eight thousand unknowns, were processed on a CDC 6600, which was a supercomputer originally used for nuclear physics research.[13]

Double exposure shot of the 'measurement' model for the Olympic Park in Munich under load, and detail (*c.* 1968)

'Multimedia' test at the IL: simultaneous measurements of the Olympic roof model using 6 × 6 cameras, miniature cameras and gauges (*c.* 1968)

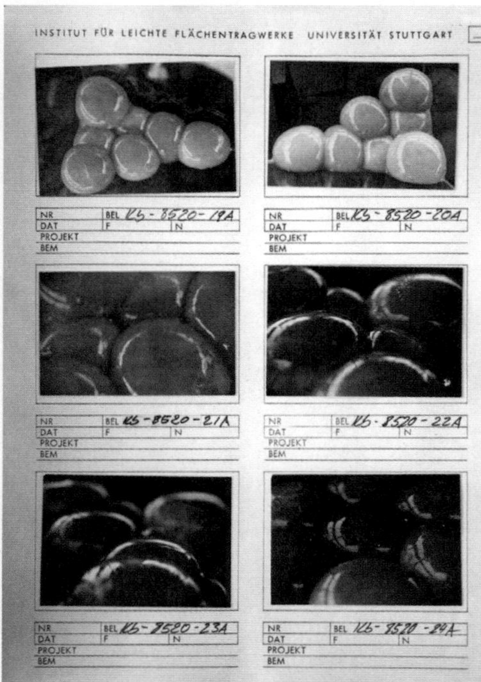

The transition from relying on Otto's physical models to calculating the information on computers took place very quickly. By this time, it was also clear that Otto had distanced himself from the process. The large, intricate models built by the IL were brought to the construction site, but the engineers did not know what to do with them. Otto had created a form of architecture so dense with information and potential risk that it could probably only have been executed by using computers. But this use of computation changed the architecture itself, creating a rigid and inefficient structure that ended up far from Otto's ideal of lightness and adaptability.

The Pneu

Not all form-finding at the IL took place within the carefully controlled space of the measuring apparatus. We have seen how photographs of models served more as the basis for measurement than the discovery of new forms. Beyond the lab and in the 'field', however, the quest to collect and document new and incalculable forms led to a very different use of photography. At the intersection between forms found in experiments and those found in nature lay Otto's theory of the *pneu*.

The pneu represented what was perhaps the furthest limit of the immeasurable and incalculable. 'Pneu' refers to pneumatically strained membrane structures, but also to other envelopes (like shells or the inside of bones) that result from the hardening of moist membranes. Otto viewed the *pneuma* as a universal concept of enclosure found in all of nature and believed that the pneu was tied to the origins of life. 'Am Anfang war der Pneu' (In the beginning was the Pneu), he wrote.[14] Pneus not only represented some of the lightest forms in nature, but were also considered the most optimized.

One of the things that made the pneu a difficult object of study (and what links it to the soap film experiments) is that it is attributed to living, mutable things and is thus difficult to capture. Otto's interest in these 'highly unstable' transient qualities of life (or the utterly ephemeral), and their unique structural properties, can be linked to his early interest in adaptable building envelopes. But unlike the finicky precision of the technical models, the study of the pneu was looser and less exact, more focused on observing and classifying structures than on measuring them.

Otto discovered the concept of the pneu while working with the biologist Johann-Gerhard Helmcke at the Technical University of Berlin (Technische Universität Berlin, TU Berlin). At the time, Otto had been working on pneumatic structures but had little familiarity with the natural sciences or biology. Helmcke's microscopic images of radiolaria – in other words, the perception of structure at a scale invisible to the human eye – revealed the idea of the pneu. In his work with Helmcke, Otto's physical experiments became structurally and conceptually linked to the world of nature:

> I saw the animated world with different eyes. In all living things I saw the form of 'my' pneumatics, of 'my' bubbles, fibers, and nets. At first I could hardly believe it and asked myself whether I was imagining it all. But it became even worse: even those objects of living nature which are not pneumatics such as bones, shells, spines, and timber, exhibited these forms.[15]

The pneu would eventually become the basis for what Otto saw as a universal order. Otto began organizing found 'pneu' forms into a system based on resemblances found mostly in photographs and material experiments. With this system he claimed to be able to account for every form in nature.

This project of form-finding in nature was not a side interest but was fully integrated into the IL's activities and eventually became a separate, nationally

Pages from photographic studies of 'pneumatic' forms, from the IL archive, taken by researchers at the IL (mid-1970s); above: egg yolk, below: animal innards at a slaughterhouse

funded research project in 1984.[16] To demonstrate the theory of the pneu, Otto's research team became more playful with form-finding experiments, using threads, fabric, foam and balloons. But more significant were the photographs taken by the IL team members at zoos, slaughterhouses and indoor markets, or those acquired from science publications. The photograph became the vehicle through which the natural and the architectural could be placed within the same conceptual system. The great amount of material gathered seemed to have no possible limits, and as a result, the definition of 'pneu' seemed just as boundless.

Images collected under the title 'pneu' were extensive and heterogeneous, and included unusual and 'taboo' subjects. There were 'found' structures like upholstery cushions and fishing nets, but also pig intestines, microscopic images of pollen, frog spawn, icicles, car tires, amoebas, a human egg 'a few instances before fertilization', clouds, algae colonies, seahorse skin, a cow's heart, a Venus flytrap, multiple exposures of a human penis becoming erect, a pig's bladder, 'the testicles of a 20-year-old man', a slug, a human brain and skull, an embryo inside a uterus and a naked pregnant woman with two children.[17]

The special interest in the anatomy of human reproduction hints at the idea that the human is somehow privileged in this collection. It is as if the origins of the human body itself – as represented by eggs, sperm, the uterus, the penis, the foetus – offer a kind of new beginning for architecture. The theory of a universal membrane was so expansive that it was able to contain these images of seemingly unrelated objects. It is only through the framing devices of the photograph and the juxtaposition of images that the scientists could hope to put together a theory. The objective was to universalize the pneu theory, producing an alternative encyclopedia of possible forms and structures to provoke and question the boundaries of what is permissible within architecture.

For Otto, the question of the taboo object, the object that cannot be represented or measured, is also tied to a theory of an ideal structure – both are transgressive within their relative domains. Otto thought that conservative moral responses to these unusual and 'taboo' subjects were analogous to the resistance to new forms and geometries in architecture.[18] Thus, the incalculable is also that which is taboo, and the 'inhibitions' (*Hemmungen*) he describes limit both architecture and science. Otto knowingly evoked the anti-rationalist tradition of expressionist architecture: 'Strange biological cavern systems have been discovered in stomachs, intestinal tracts, and bones, which are similar to the visions of inhabitable caves of the architects in the 1920s.'[19] For Otto, the goal was less to disturb an existing order through this formless materialism, but rather to establish an expanded formal order, a system that is able to assimilate all forms and find within them a unifying principle of optimal structure.

As the IL researchers moved further into the terrain of biology, they allowed themselves greater imprecision. To avoid recourse to the Euclidian geometry used to describe 'known' forms, everyday objects (spider webs, human bodies, etc.) had to be defamiliarized to allow for the recognition of potential structural forms. And yet, Otto suggests that these too might eventually be integrated into a mathematical framework: 'Simple forms require hundreds of datum to permit their adequate description. Complex forms often require millions of datum so that the form can be stored with certainty and recognized reliably by many people.'[20] Thus as the complexity of the forms increased, so did the amount of information needed to capture and reproduce them.

Otto's use of models was of great significance for the beginnings of digital architecture, but to frame these experiments only within this technological history would miss the opportunity to speculate more broadly on the potentials of the assemblages of matter, form, information and image that they suggest. Science promised to make uncertainty knowable, such that the calculability of risk gave authority and legitimacy to institutions like the IL that could claim to produce a mapping of the future world. With his concept of the pneu however, Otto tried to open up the possibility of the incalculable and unknowable. This was a

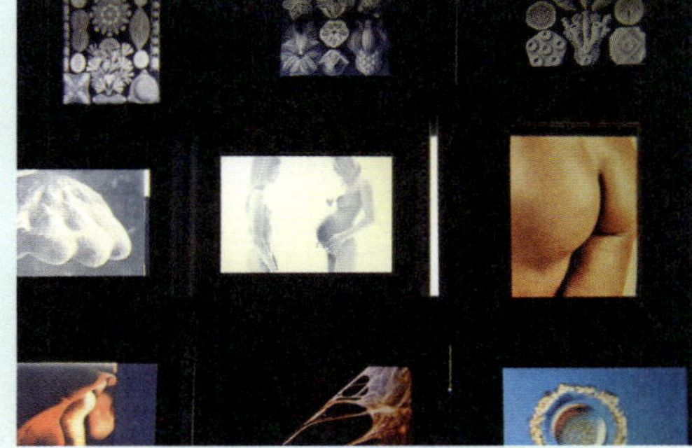

Studies of 'pneus' from the IL archive, including photographs of a pregnant woman (centre) and plates from Ernst Haeckel's *Kunstformen der Natur* (*Art Forms in Nature*)

threshold of calculation. Could a space for this kind of radical uncertainty be created in architecture? In the case of the 1972 Olympics project, uncertainty was intolerable, and a clear calculation and management of the complexity of the risks eventually had to be carried out by other means, namely by computation.

But Otto saw other risks in relying on mathematics alone. One could go so far as to ascribe a moral imperative to Otto's insistence on physical evidence. Calculation, especially with the more sophisticated tools of computation, may displace the hubris of authorship, but its programmed rationality also displaces accountability and blame. While it was Otto's project to move beyond the confines of calculation, his limitation was to constantly return to it as structures and forms had to be translated into numbers. The idealization of the incalculable and ephemeral was also, it turned out, an idealization of complex and possibly risky forces that had to be simulated and measured. The ethical architecture of the minimal – light and unbound envelopes, adaptable forms, living nature – also became examples of a new kind of rationality.

1 Frei Otto, *Das hängende Dach: Gestalt und Struktur*, Berlin 1954, p. 158. This is the published version of Otto's dissertation, which was completed in 1953 at the TU Berlin.
2 *Prinzip Leichtbau. Form–Kraft–Masse 4/Lightweight Principle: Form–Forces–Mass 4, Mitteilungen des Instituts für leichte Flächentragwerke (IL)*, no. 24, Stuttgart 1998, pp. 33 f.
3 *Mitteilungen des Instituts für leichte Flächentragwerke (IL)*, no. 24, pp. 33 f.
4 Max Horkheimer and Theodor W. Adorno, *Dialectic of Enlightenment: Philosophical Fragments*, trans. Edmund Jephcott, Stanford 2002, p. 18.
5 The first soap film device was featured on the cover of *IL 1*: see *Minimalnetze/Minimal Nets, Mitteilungen des Instituts für leichte Flächentragwerke (IL)*, no. 1, Stuttgart 1969.
6 *Mitteilungen des Instituts für leichte Flächentragwerke (IL)*, no. 1, p. 12.
7 Jürgen Hennicke (Instructor, IL, now called the Institute for Lightweight Structures and Conceptual Design; Institut für Leichtbau Entwerfen und Konstruieren, ILEK), in discussion with the author, February 2013.
8 'IL Archiv. Teil 1', IL Bericht 06/70. *Mitteilungen des Instituts für leichte Flächentragwerke (IL)*, Universitätsarchiv Stuttgart.
9 *Biologie und Bauen 3/Biology and Building 3, Mitteilungen des Instituts für leichte Flächentragwerke (IL)*, no. 6, Stuttgart 1973.
10 Berthold Burckhardt, 'The Problem of Form Presentation', in: *Mitteilungen des Instituts für leichte Flächentragwerke (IL)*, no. 6, pp. 54 f.
11 *Grundlagen. Form–Kraft–Masse 1/Basics: Form–Force–Mass 1, Mitteilungen des Instituts für leichte Flächentragwerke (IL)*, no. 21, p. 16.
12 Mick Eekhout, 'Frei Otto and the Munich Olympic Games', in: *Zodiac*, no. 21, 1971, pp. 12–73, here p. 45.
13 Eekhout, 'Frei Otto and the Munich Olympic Games'.
14 'Der Pneu ist die wesentliche Grundlage für die Formenwelt der lebenden Natur' (The pneu is the essential foundation for the world of forms within living nature): *Pneus in Natur und Technik/Pneus in Nature and Technics, Mitteilungen des Instituts für leichte Flächentragwerke (IL)*, no. 9, Stuttgart 1977, p. 5. Johann-Gerhard Helmcke apparently first wrote the phrase 'Am Anfang war der Pneu.' 'Lieber Herr Helmcke, das wird ja immer noch spannender. Ihr Aufsatz, toll, und der Mut zu sagen "am Anfang war der Pneu". Vielen Dank!' (Dear Mr. Helmcke, this is becoming ever more exciting. Your essay, excellent, and the courage to say, 'in the beginning there was the pneu'. Many thanks!), letter from Otto to Helmcke, 5 September 1973, TH Stuttgart Universitätsarchiv, Bestand 137, no. 50B.
15 *Diatomeen II. Schalen in Natur und Technik III/Diatoms II: Shells in Nature and Tecnics III, Mitteilungen des Instituts für leichte Flächentragwerke (IL)*, no. 38, Stuttgart 2004, p. 141.
16 Sonderforschungsbereich Natürliche Konstruktionen, Leichtbau in Architektur und Natur, *Beiträge zum I. Internationalen Symposium des SFB 230 'Natürliche Konstruktionen – Leichtbau in Architektur und Natur'*, Stuttgart 1989.
17 Published in *Mitteilungen des Instituts für leichte Flächentragwerke (IL)*, no. 9 and *Wachsende und sich teilende Pneus/Growing and Dividing Pneus, Mitteilungen des Instituts für leichte Flächentragwerke (IL)*, no. 19, Stuttgart 1979.
18 *Mitteilungen des Instituts für leichte Flächentragwerke (IL)*, no. 9.
19 *Biologie und Bauen 1/Biology and Building 1, Mitteilungen des Instituts für leichte Flächentragwerke (IL)*, no. 3, Stuttgart 1971, p. 10.
20 *Mitteilungen des Instituts für leichte Flächentragwerke (IL)*, no. 21, p. 17.

Frei Otto Teaching Architecture: Form-Finding for Society

Anna-Maria Meister

Frei Otto only accepted his chair in Stuttgart at the Institute for Lightweight Structures (Institut für leichte Flächentragwerke, IL), established especially for him, with the guarantee that 'he be released from the obligation of academic teaching for the rest of his life', as his successor, Werner Sobek, relates.[1] To be clear, Otto was never a full professor, never had a full teaching load nor did he teach any required core courses. Then to what can Frei Otto's teaching in architecture have amounted? How did he influence the teaching of architecture, specifically in higher education and especially in the 1960s? For, despite all the missing pieces and institutional questions, there is indeed a Frei Otto School, and students clamoured explicitly to study under his tent roof in Stuttgart.[2] And this was not least owing to the nature of Germany's research funding: as the second Collaborative Research Centre, CRC (Sonderforschungsbereich, SFB), in architecture of the German Research Foundation (Deutsche Forschungsgemeinschaft, DFG), CRC 64, titled 'Weitgespannte Flächentragwerke' (Widespan Surface Structures) and created in 1969 at the University of Stuttgart with Otto as its founding director, the centre would influence generations of architecture students.[3] Otto not only instructed students, but also the peers succeeding him, his collaborators and guests, his cooperating partners as well as his wider readership – or better, they all learned together with and through him. As researcher, architect, writer and partner, in 1964, he began to create a centre in Stuttgart that had a wide-raging influence as a 'school' – within a structure that perhaps taught just as much as Otto did himself.

But what did such a Frei Otto School stand for? On the one hand, it stood for the integration of humanity, nature and technology, as these concepts were understood within the context of the 1960s. On the other hand, however, or at least for Otto himself, it represented an adaptable, open architecture, which was not imposed by a few on all others – a concept that he would further develop in the 1970s and 1980s with his eco-houses (*Ökohäuser*). According to his own retrospective point of view, what was important was first of all a new conceptual model. In a speech at a national convention of the Association of German Architects (Bund Deutscher Architekten, BDA) in 1967, Otto asserted that an outdated planning concept had been followed and taught far too long in architecture, 'even though it has not worked for a long time'.[4] This had to be changed in teaching practices, Otto maintained, since 'the architect's main tool, what we have learned in school up to now, our conceptual model, has become as useless as a dull wood plane'. At the same time, according to Otto, 'new development-oriented conceptual models' had been emerging for a long time, that 'demand technology for adaptable architecture [*anpassungsfähiges Bauen*]'.[5] This adaptability, which Otto considered essential for building, he also demanded in teaching.

In addition, he diagnosed the necessity of easing a 'cramp', as he put it, in order again to 'study intently with joy (but without schoolmasters)'.[6] His diagnosis makes sense if one considers it in relation to Otto's own history with the various Stuttgart Schools. Whereas the first famous Architecture Faculty in the interwar period, with architects like Paul Schmitthenner, Paul Bonatz and Martin Elsaesser, rather aggressively pushed a conservative modern design approach, after 1945, the second Stuttgart School, with pupils from the first one (like Richard Döcker, Rolf Gutbrod, Rolf Gutbier and Ludwig Schweizer, and later Hans Kammerer, Peter C. von Seidlein, Jürgen Joedicke and Klaus Humpert), changed its orientation towards a post-war modernism.[7] Much as Otto was 'personally beholden to the pioneers of the twenties and was on friendly terms with almost all of those still alive' and felt 'unalterably, greatly indebted to this time', he asserted, 'Whether I like it or not, the time of "Modernism" has past.'[8] What he diagnosed about the position of the faculty in the 1960s was an increasing dogmatism among the students in comparison to their teachers. Otto criticized their interpretation of a historic architecture in the Second School as a watered-down version of a German building tradition 'with its delicacy and quiet elegance', calling it a formalistic misunderstanding; simply being against 'uniformity', which Otto himself criticized again and again, was not enough, as 'form is not yet architecture'.[9] For Otto, form was dependent upon rules, not only the forms whose laws Otto himself sought and found in nature, but also the historical forms of a past architectural idiom.

The so-called Third Stuttgart School, at which Otto taught, was the University of Stuttgart's reorganized Department of Architecture, resulting from the academic reforms in 1968. The intermediate 'forgotten' Stuttgart School, the reform movements that had already begun there in the mid-1960s and the resulting alterations to the entire faculty and university, merged into this Third School.[10] Otto ascertained in it 'ideological foundations and also vast gaps', which he welcomed, while at the same time also missing the open critical verbal exchanges that he highlighted as characteristic of the Second School. As always, for Otto it was a matter of a larger social vision: in this case, 'first about the future of architecture and only then about the future of this school. Without an overriding goal it has no foundation.'[11] Yet, how did Otto see himself as a teacher in this Stuttgart School? What he had aimed for and encouraged about every Stuttgart School was a diversity of positions and the willingness to negotiate them – a teaching method based on a multiplicity of approaches and that stood in constant exchange with them.

The Seminar 'Adaptable Architecture' at the Ulm School of Design

As a place for discussion and research, the Ulm School of Design (Hochschule für Gestaltung Ulm, HfG Ulm) played a role for the Architecture Faculty at the University of Stuttgart early on. Peter Dietze, the architect and co-founder of the magazine *Arch+*, and who studied architecture in Stuttgart in the 1960s, asserted that the HfG Ulm was even able to fill 'a vacuum' at the University of Stuttgart with regard to a broader, more comprehensive social conscience and the emerging scientific nature of design.[12] Exchange between the two institutions took place by way of the HfG Ulm's publications (its official journal, *ulm*, and its student magazine, *output*) as well as through teachers like the philosopher and mathematician Max Bense and then also Frei Otto. Both had taught at the HfG Ulm before coming to Stuttgart.

In January 1959 – some nine years before he organized CRC 64 at Stuttgart and just as long before the start of student protest movements in Germany – Otto taught a seminar at the HfG Ulm as a guest lecturer.[13] It was held in the Department of Industrial Building, in which at that time twenty-five second- to fourth-year students were registered – since in the Bauhaus tradition, the first year was devoted to fundamentals in a Preliminary Course. Because some were studying abroad and others on leave, seventeen of them were present and probably in Otto's seminar. Otto had been in the war himself, and after being a prisoner of war in France and completing architecture studies at the Technical University

Frei Otto at the HfG Ulm speaking with a student (1959)

of Berlin (Technische Universität Berlin, TU Berlin), he had followed a similar path and was a similar age as many of his students. This was another reason why he published their work along with his own and that of famous colleagues, like Yona Friedman, in his own journal, *Mitteilungen der Entwicklungsstätte für den Leichtbau (EL)*.

The HfG Ulm, one of the best-known institutions for design in West Germany after the Second World War, had been founded in 1953 by Inge Aicher-Scholl, Otl Aicher and the Swiss architect Max Bill, and in 1955, moved into a building designed by Bill on the Kuhberg near Ulm. Originally conceived as an adult education centre with a focus on the humanities, under Bill's influence, the school became an institution where 'good form' (*die gute Form*) was to contribute to a democratic Germany.[14] As a school of higher learning for students who already had degrees (today it would be a postgraduate course), the HfG Ulm was, in spite of its relatively brief existence, an international pathbreaking institution over fifteen years. After its closure in 1968, amid protests from students and teachers alike, the HfG Ulm continued to influence design and teaching methods for decades (and not only in West Germany). The so-called 'Ulm Model' – the intrinsic and curricular combination of theory and practice – was adopted by national and international institutions, and the inclusion of diverse disciplines like mathematics, sociology, philosophy and psychology created the foundation for an unusually eclectic and wide-ranging spectrum of teaching that went far beyond the notions of design in the 1950s.

With his technical, rational and interdisciplinary approach, as well as his design methodology, Otto – who in 1957 had established his Institute for the Development of Lightweight Construction (Entwicklungsstätte für den Leichtbau, EL) in his Berlin atelier in Türksteinweg, was an ideal candidate for a guest lectureship at the HfG Ulm. There, projects and modules of every and all sizes, from teacups to roof structures, were shaped and designed. During a study trip to the University of Virginia in 1951, Otto was able to collect experiences of an education system in another country; this was also the case during his lectureship at Washington University in St Louis in 1958, which in view of the unusually high percentage of international students at the HfG Ulm, and the school's American sponsorship and campus-style layout, was surely an advantage. Indeed, in the year following his Ulm appointment, Otto would again teach in the United States, this time at Yale University. At the same time, Otto was a person who employed scientific form-finding, a method which placed him squarely between the polar design camps of the HFG Ulm during the late 1950s: between Max Bill's legacy of 'good form', for one, and the cybernetic approaches of Horst Rittel and Max Bense, as well as the semiotic and process-oriented approaches of Tomás Maldonado.

Otto clearly structured the assignments to be given to the students in his seminar. First the fundamentals were to be established, from an analysis of the existing situation – 'an assessment of the suitability of current structures for adaptable architecture' and of 'available serially produced products from the construction industry' – to a 'study of a family's changes over the course of its entire lifetime.' Then 'thoughts and considerations for supplementing the survey analysis' were to be compiled and 'ideas about the preferred dimensions of windows, doors and wall panels within a modular principle' were to be deliberated. Next were the 'study of a village/an industry/a building' and 'design suggestions for structures that need to be especially adaptable'. The leap in scale in urban planning was to be accomplished by way of the 'influences of adaptable architecture', and the potential of do-it-yourself building, with its 'special requirements and possibilities', was tested. Then came the question of 'mobile building[s]' and the related urban planning problems, and finally 'thoughts about humankind's sedentary nature' and to what extent that was 'stabilizing or inhibiting'.[15] An ambitious programme for a guest lecturer's seminar, yet the students turned in ground plans and diagrams, essays and survey catalogues. Otto made no written comments on their submissions, but he did let the students' projects become part of the

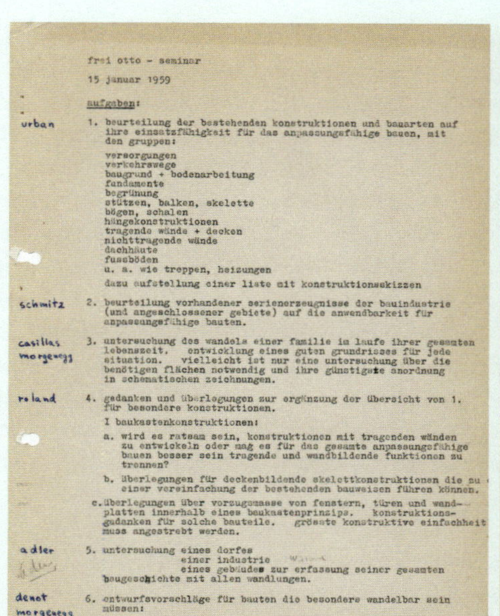

frei otto - seminar

15 januar 1959

aufgaben:

urban — 1. beurteilung der bestehenden konstruktionen und bauarten auf ihre einsatzfähigkeit für das anpassungsfähige bauen, mit den gruppen:

versorgungen
verkehrswege
baugrund + bodenarbeitung
fundamente
begrünung
stützen, balken, skelette
bögen, schalen
hängekonstruktionen
tragende wände + decken
nichttragende wände
dachhäute
fussböden
u. a. wie treppen, heizungen

dazu aufstellung einer liste mit konstruktionsskizzen

schmitz — 2. beurteilung vorhandener serienerzeugnisse der bauindustrie (und angeschlossener gebiete) auf die anwendbarkeit für anpassungsfähige bauten.

casillas, morgenegg — 3. untersuchung des wandels einer familie im laufe ihrer gesamten lebenszeit. entwicklung eines guten grundrisses für jede situation. vielleicht ist nur eine untersuchung über die benötigen flächen notwendig und ihre günstigste anordnung in schematischen zeichnungen.

roland — 4. gedanken und überlegungen zur ergänzung der übersicht von 1. für besondere konstruktionen.

I baukastenkonstruktionen:

a. wird es ratsam sein, konstruktionen mit tragenden wänden zu entwickeln oder mag es für das gesamte anpassungsfähige bauen besser sein tragende und wandbildende funktionen zu trennen?

b. überlegungen für deckenbildende skelettkonstruktionen die zu einer vereinfachung der bestehenden bauweisen führen können.

c. überlegungen über vorzugsmasse von fenstern, türen und wandplatten innerhalb eines baukastenprinzips. konstruktionsgedanken für solche bauteile. grösste konstruktive einfachheit muss angestrebt werden.

adler — 5. untersuchung eines dorfes
einer industrie
eines gebäudes zur erfassung seiner gesamten baugeschichte mit allen wandlungen.

denot, morgenegg — 6. entwurfsvorschläge für bauten die besonders wandelbar sein müssen:

geschäftshaus in der innenstadt
industrieanlage
mehrgeschossiges wohnhaus
eingeschossiges wohnhaus

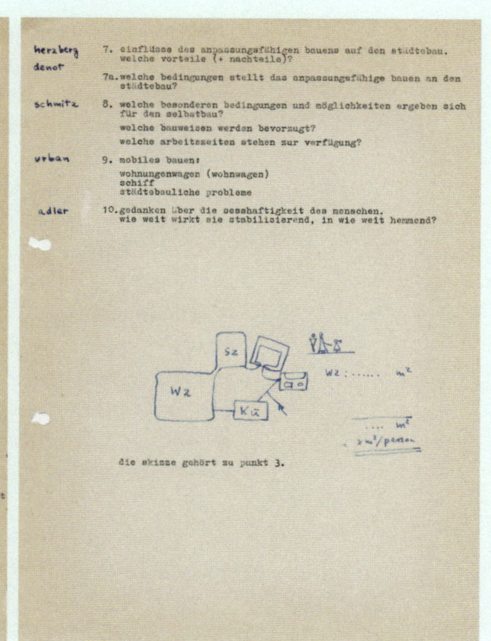

herzberg, denot — 7. einflüsse des anpassungsfähigen bauens auf den städtebau. welche vorteile (+ nachteile)?

7a. welche bedingungen stellt das anpassungsfähige bauen an den städtebau?

schmitz — 8. welche besonderen bedingungen und möglichkeiten ergeben sich für den selbstbau?

welche bauweisen werden bevorzugt?

welche arbeitszeiten stehen zur verfügung?

urban — 9. mobiles bauen:

wohnungenwagen (wohnwagen)
schiff
städtebauliche probleme

adler — 10. gedanken über die sesshaftigkeit des menschen. wie weit wirkt sie stabilisierend, in wie weit hemmend?

die skizze gehört zu punkt 3.

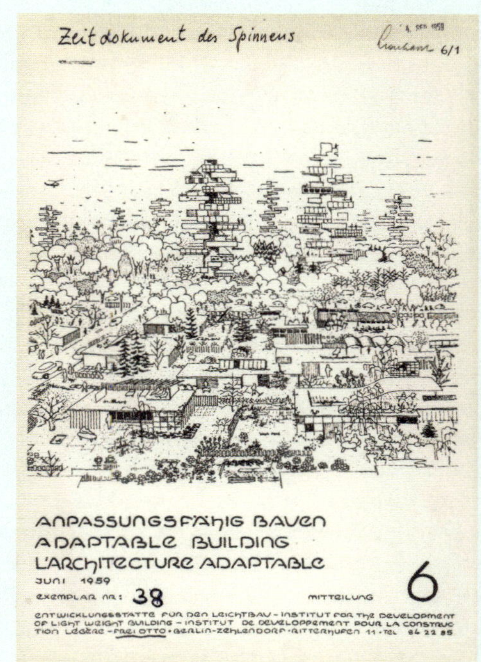

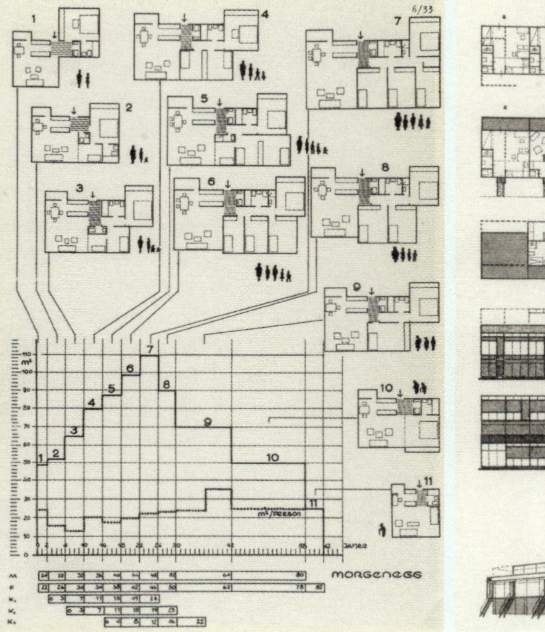

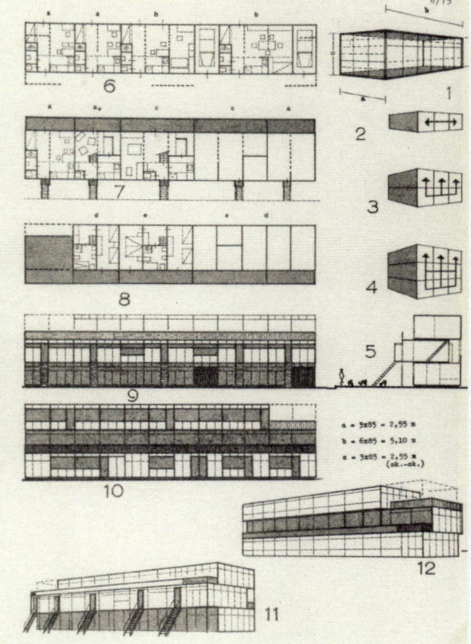

Mitteilungen journal that he published. Teaching became research, and research, ultimately, became practice.

Otto liked to formulate in networks and relationships, whether those of teaching, research and practice or the tenets of his thoughts on the triangle between humankind, nature and technology. The latter was significantly influenced by post-war discussions about a German future. The so-called Darmstädter Gespräche, in which well-known figures from architecture, politics, history and philosophy with, in part, fundamental differences of opinion met in Darmstadt to debate over the role of 'Man and Space' (1951) or 'Man and Technology' (1952) – and, years later, 'Man and His Future' (1967) – had a particularly lasting influence on architectural discourse. But these core concepts about humanity and what was human, what technology could and ought to be, and even the concept of

Frei Otto's seminar plan for adaptable building at the HfG Ulm with hand-drawn sketch and annotations (1959)

Anpassungsfähig bauen/ Adaptable Building/L'Architecture adaptable, Mitteilungen der Entwicklungsstätte für den Leichtbau (EL), no. 6 (1959), title page with handwritten notes

Excerpts from student works by Siegfried Morgenegg (left) and Roland Lindner (right) for Frei Otto's seminar at the HfG Ulm, published in the *Mitteilungen der EL*, no. 6 (1959)

nature were subjected to massive changes over the decades of Otto's career. For Otto, however, the basic understanding of the relation itself underwent little change but rather the division of tasks among those players in the networks – and their formal manifestations. As his student Max Herzberg wrote in his seminar paper on adaptable architecture, 'it is commonly maintained that man's needs change. We would rather say that they do not change so much in their nature as in their form'.[16] Yet the view of humanity itself changed as well, especially with regard to the needs of tenants. As Kirsten Wagner describes, in the 1920s these were still the universal subject to be formed by the Neues Bauen (New Building); it was only in the 1950s that the modern subject became an individual who takes possession of their apartment.[17] For Otto, from the 1950s onward, this meant that the more passive his houses became – Otto referred to his home in Warmbronn as the 'grandmother of today's passive and solar architecture'[18] – the more active tenants would become, up to the do-it-yourself construction of his eco-houses in Berlin in the 1980s.

A Teacher (or A Didact) Rooted in His Time and Place

Otto was and is said to have been a progressive visionary, and if one looks at the themes of his speeches from the 1960s and 1970s they resonate with many a new professor at this or that institution of higher learning nowadays. In his own time, Otto spoke about and researched subjects ranging from cross-species design to open processes, from multipolar institutional structures to 'adaptive living' and 'sensuous architecture', themes which in the following decades completely disappeared from many architectural faculties only again to reemerge in the twenty-first century. Nonetheless, his radical thinking was rooted in his time and place. If one considers the educational landscape of the 1960s in Germany and beyond, Otto was a visionary of another kind. Unlike figures who wished for radically different politics, societies and, ultimately, worlds through architectural education, Otto focused his observations and foresight on the form and function of architecture for a society that already existed instead of fundamentally questioning it.

His intense consideration and subsequent solutions to such questions was also revealed with a light hand – and minimal material – in his projects. Otto built a pavilion as shelter from rain in the Volkspark Rehberge, a public park of Berlin, a gridshell 'with only a hint of eroticism in is overall form', since 'lovemaking but also the possibility of physical aggression are linked to such places'.[19] And 'not recognizing the role they play in a society would mean misunderstanding architecture'.[20] Even the installation of the concave 'humpbacked' tent, which Otto had designed for the German National Garden Show (Bundesgartenschau) in Cologne in 1957 and later reprised for the Inselcafé on Lake Zurich in 1958, not only served as an example for him of resource-efficient construction par excellence, but moreover a 'symbol of the ongoing struggle of the women of Switzerland, who in 1958 were still campaigning for the right to vote'.[21] For Otto, architecture was 'not humane per se. Architecture can make people ill, can terrorize them, can kill them'.[22] Rather, he thought of architecture as a responsibility most of all, a recognition that would reappear in scholarship only decades later.

In 'Begegnung' (Encounter), Else Lasker-Schüler wrote that Otto was committed to the human scale. She felt that his architecture offered a counter-design to the approach of Adolf Loos, who wanted 'to establish order in the worlds here below, in the world which man, aspiring away from himself, permits the architect-man to create, yet into which he does not fit'.[23] She uses the next sentence in her critique of Loos as Otto's motto: 'How many sit and sweat in the four skins of others, for the walls of our private chambers should be our best fitting garment, they should bear the traces of our breath.'[24] One could say that Otto was committed to 'man, the measure of all things', a slogan long upheld in architectural history.[25] Yet Otto saw this human scale as an alternative concept to the thinking of Ernst Neufert: whereas Neufert classed humans as an abstract unit of measure in a standardized system, to Otto they were a formal, sensual inspiration.[26] Nor was Otto's human scale one that sought in monumentality 'eternal values of the contrasting scale' as Hugh Stubbins put it in his self-defence against Otto's vehement criticism of his design for Berlin's Kongresshalle conference hall in 1957.[27] Otto's scale also differed from the global, universal one of the architecture of Richard Buckminster Fuller, whom he met at Washington University in St Louis in 1958. Otto quarrelled with Fuller about the dimensions of the latter's domes and asked the university's dean at the time, whether 'Bucky even knows the maximum dimension of his domes?'[28] Otto also reported – not without a certain amount of smugness – that Fuller had had an insight and had learned something from their exchange. Despite much emphasis to the contrary, Otto was simply someone who liked correcting others.

Otto later said about teaching, 'Sometimes – it appears – a teacher (and I don't like being a teacher, instead I always see myself as a student) can learn more than his pupil.'[29] Like a number of his contemporaries, he appears to mirror the radical theories of Jacques Rancière, James Baldwin or June Jordan, who described the act of teaching as a form of dumbing down and instead propagated the emancipatory logic of learning and questioned the traditional hierarchies between instructor and student in the production and spread of knowledge.[30] But if one questions his former students and collaborators, many of them freely describe Otto as being cooperative, open-minded and curious; he is said to have had charisma and the ability to inspire, yet combined with a 'certain stubbornness'.[31] Although he openly shared his intellectual insights and made his intellectual property freely available, former collaborators also tell of his constant efforts to gather all achievements under his own name and of his bitterness over what he perceived as inadequate recognition – especially in Germany.[32]

Peter Hübner describes his time as a student assistant to Otto – who was a 'monomaniac, a brilliant visionary, with enormous charisma' – as being characterized by unbelievable euphoria and a faith in technological progress. This faith was not placed in engineering but specifically and especially in architecture. To Hübner that was no coincidence, for 'only people like architects' can answer the urgent question of how 'to solve the world's problems' because 'with their tremendous hubris, their naivete and their belief in their own abilities, they are still in a position to uproot trees and move mountains'.[33] Like Hübner, others remembering Frei Otto the 'teacher' often focus on his research and his projects, not on his actual teaching. Recalling what he thought of Otto as a teacher, Jürgen Bradatsch said nothing about how Otto taught but described a lecture on lightweight construction and how it led him to apply for a job in Otto's atelier. Engaged students readily morphed into working collaborators, so that here too questions about teaching, research and practice became inseparably intertwined. What began as teaching became research, and what was tested in research was played out in teaching.

Which Pedagogy, Which Architecture?

Werner Sobek laid out in *Bauwelt* that, from the beginning, Otto 'resisted being categorized as an architect' – and that, in fact, Otto constantly moved between the boundaries and conventions of different disciplines. Yet if one looks at the radical experiments of architecture schools in the 1960s more closely, one discovers that at that time, at least, such a classification had little categorical value. To many people 'architecture' was an open discipline, as opposed, for example, to urban planning or engineering or even fine art. The field was open to new types of thinking, practice and responsibility, as well as to new forms of perception, of solidarity and communication.[34] Alternatives were more than welcome, especially when it came to refuting the traditional teaching methods of polytechnic institutions, schools of fine arts or modernist practice of lecturing outside one's own faculty. If in Florence, Adolfo Natalini, a member of the Global Tools movement, could present archaeological bone finds or artefacts such as walking sticks in a lecture hall as a seminar on architecture, and in Chile, Godofredo Iommi could stage poetry performances on the beach, architecture as a course of study had long since ceased to be restricted to the principles of construction or design.[35] Designing spaces had become a social-technological project – what mattered now was how one imagined new spaces for different societies.

Otto's influence as a teacher was not primarily the result of modules, seminars or lectures. It derived from his collaborations, his publications, from the methodology in his atelier and, only at times, literally from the actual practice of teaching. And this was the case even when his teaching engagement itself was limited to a few days and a few students, as was the case at the HfG Ulm in January 1959. His seminar was only to take place there once – he was at Ulm as a guest, as a initiator, not part of the regular curriculum. And yet, that seminar had widespread repercussions. For example, some of the students from his 1959 seminar would later expressly write their dissertations under Otto, like Roland Lindner and Winfried Wurm with their project on the 'Planning of a Flexible Airport' completed in 1961. Lindner had previously attended Otto's seminar, and his student research project was published, with reference to the HfG Ulm seminar, in Otto's publication, *Mitteilungen*.

In other cases, Otto was not listed among a graduate's instructors, yet his influence is obvious. Dominique Gilliard, a student in architecture at the HfG Ulm and later professor and eventually rector of the École d'architecture de l'Université de Genève (EAUG), graduated in 1960 with a dissertation on the 'Development of Residential Units as Additive Elements of Horizontal Living Groups'. The subject, which appears to seamlessly relate to Otto's seminar on adaptable architecture, had been a focus for Otto in the late 1950s and early 1960s. For Otto, and thus for his students as well, it was *the* social question of the time, how housing could adapt to people – not the other way around. Max Herzberg, a French architect and another seminar attendee, wrote a multipage essay on the social urgency of this new architecture, which would not only face such questions but would have to respond to them in terms of planning.

This social urgency is also constantly reflected in Otto himself. In speeches, essays and his atelier diaries – mixed in with reminders on the order of 'organize studio' or 'clean up' – he regularly noted the pressing issues of his time: How are we to live, how can we use energy and resources sustainably and, in this vein, how are we to construct social spaces accordingly? These were questions he mulled over through his writing, designing and, above all, research. In the spring of 1958, he wrote in his *Mitteilungen der Entwicklungsstätte für den Leichtbau (EL)*, 'Although we tried very hard, we have not yet managed to receive any research funding for work in the field of adaptable architecture'. Still on July 18 of the same year, he recorded in his atelier diary, 'Letter to the German Research Foundation', and only seven days later, the same diary has an entry about receiving a commissioned research report from the Federal Construction Directorate (BBD) on 'adaptable architecture'.[36] And what of his teaching? A look at Otto's work and his academic activities reveals that for him teaching was never a separate occupation, nor did it occupy a separate category, but rather, it was one approach out of many, a way of working out and testing his ideas and methods. In his papers, his notes on the seminar at the HfG Ulm are mixed in with his thoughts for the sixth issue of his *Mitteilungen*, *Anpassungsfähig bauen* (*Adaptable Building*). His student's papers are mentioned in letters to his collaborators, included in illustrations and published projects, and bound in with his own sketches and letters.

Did Otto's approach continue to have an effect, or was it Otto who had been so perfectly suited to the agenda of the HfG Ulm that they progressed together in the same direction? What they shared was an approach that would

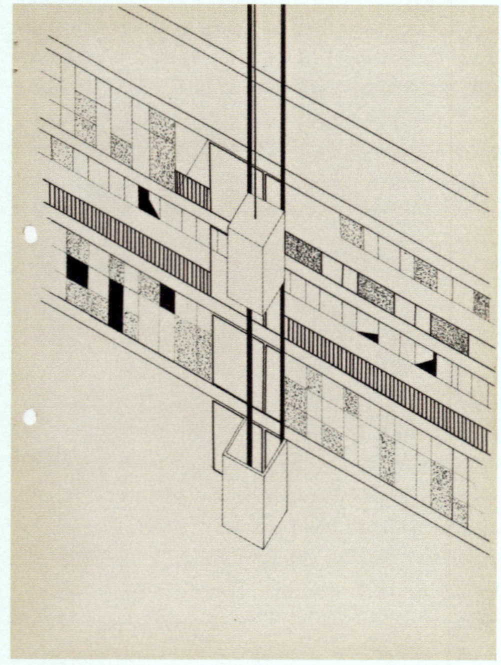

Lift detail for a 'particularly adaptable office building', study project by Horacio Denot for Frei Otto's seminar at the HfG Ulm (1959)

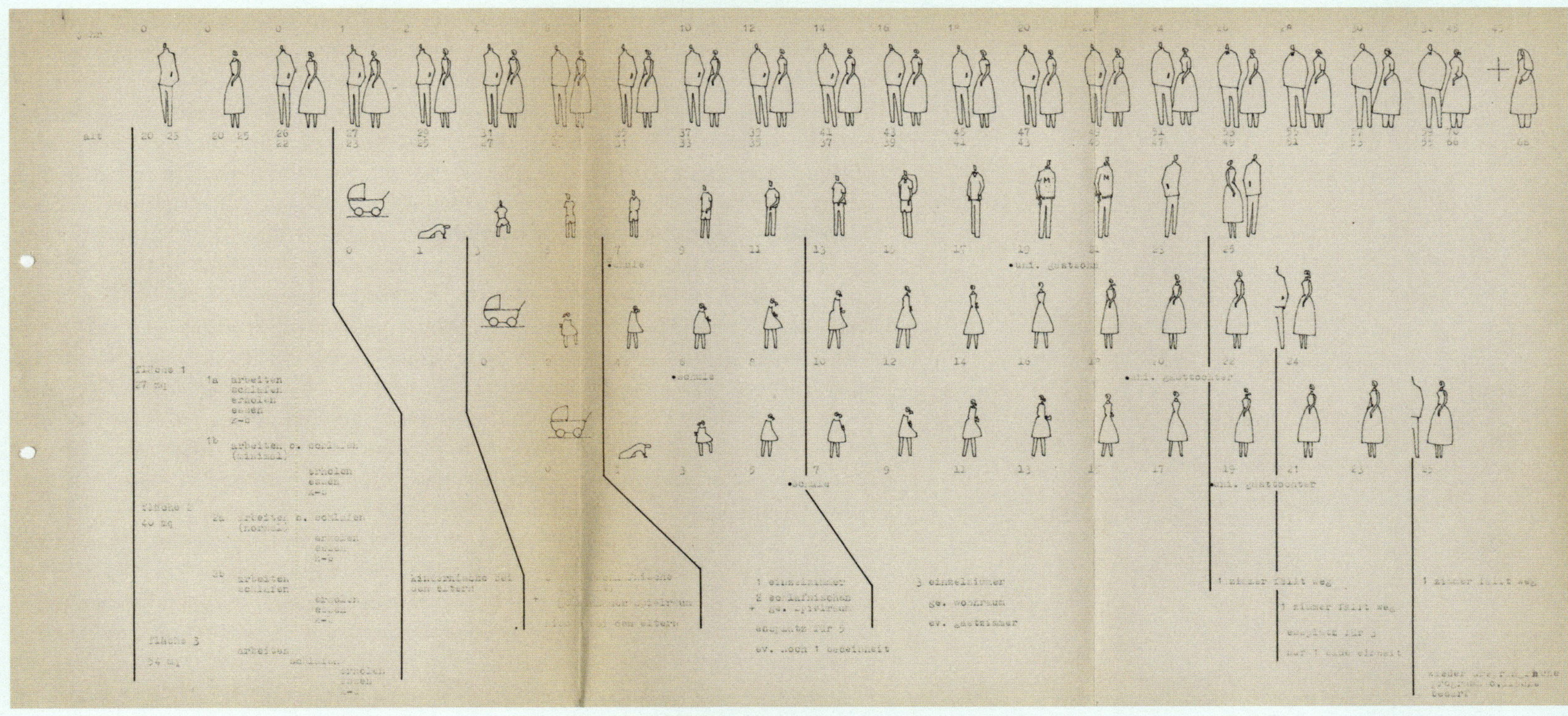

later become known as the 'Ulm Model': the joint development of theory and practice, without the use of causality or formal determinism. Not least, Otto's teaching had an impact on the curriculum. In a file memo of the HfG Ulm from 1960, the point is made that 'the Department of Industrial Building lacks permanent lecturers' and 'it is folly to hope to construct a course of study around such guest lecturers'. Frei Otto's teaching was a success, indeed so successful that the pedagogical committee of the HfG Ulm determined that 'new lecturers are required: 1) an engineer specialized in structural issues, if possible with experience in lightweight construction. 2) architects to direct the work of the department. 3) a sociologist dealing intensively with the social issues in building'. If one reads Herzberg's student essay and is aware of Otto's proven expertise in lightweight construction, one already finds both aspects – sociology and lightweight construction – in this request for a permanent faculty member from the year following Otto's guest lectureship.

Architectural Pedagogy as Form-Finding for a New Society

Otto's success and influence on subsequent generations as a teacher, whether as a guest at Washington University in St Louis or the HfG Ulm or as an honorary professor in the University of Stuttgart's Architecture Faculty, can be seen as the establishment of his own 'school' – perhaps even in the sense of a 'radical pedagogy'[37] from the 1960s and 1970s. Internationally, the battle against patriarchal and oppressive structures frequently began at the very same institutions that had initiated them. Student movements, often in association with like-minded teachers, not only protested against the status quo but also proposed radical alternatives: for example, separate architecture schools were established for women so that they could be trained on an equal footing.

Otto also had a few female collaborators, and the HfG Ulm had female students – but in the Department of Industrial Building, there were only men on the list given to Otto of students enrolled in his January 1959 seminar. Otto's IL, the University of Stuttgart as well as the HfG Ulm were institutions of their time – their radicalism lay elsewhere. They were radical in their promotion of broad

Correlation between housing needs, age and family status, student project for Frei Otto's seminar at the HfG Ulm, probably by Andrés Casillas de Alba (1959)

interdisciplinary studies, which first had to be set up, and radical in their intensive search for form-finding outside of architectural conventions. In Germany, the protests of the 1960s were differently charged: the protesting students' famous slogan in Germany, 'Unter den Talaren – Muff von 1000 Jahren' (Under the academic gowns – mustiness of a thousand years), was directed at the problematic number of professors from the Nazi era who still held or had returned to their posts. The power structures of the 1940s were deeply intertwined with their institutions, and student protests and reform movements wanted to dismantle them. Yet there were also regional differences. 'Schools and academic chairs burned in California, England, Japan and Paris. Not in Stuttgart',[38] but in the same West German state, there were fierce disputes, demonstrations and protests in 1968, even at the HfG Ulm. This institution, which had been founded in response to the need for change after the Nazi regime and was devoted to a different way of teaching, was already the more political of the two schools of higher education before 1968. At the University of Stuttgart – 'Stuttgart was not conservative after all' – according to Otto, people were 'relatively progressive ideologically and their arguments were mild',[39] and above all it was 'greatly reformed'.[40]

The reforms left their trace upon the University of Stuttgart, and the Architecture Faculty was broken up into specialized disciplines. The HfG Ulm was closed down in 1968. These two cases illustrate the range of radical pedagogical experiments of their time between absorption and dissolution.[41] Some failed after a few years, others were absorbed by their institutions. However, it is not easy to define success or failure in these cases. The majority were only short-lived, but does that mean that they failed? And if so, was this failure not a boost to later success? Think of the HfG Ulm, whose closing led to the spread of the Ulm Model as the bases of a new curriculum, while its approach to product design would define the German 'look' for decades. Because, in spite of their supposed failures, these short-lived projects often drastically influenced the structures that sought to absorb them and changed the discipline for the following decades. Their ideas survived, as did the networks that connected them.

What they shared was the conviction that complex social questions could be resolved by the teaching of architecture, that the teaching of architecture should be different in many ways, that a radical pedagogy should attempt to free itself from conventional institutional definitions. Yet, instead of pitting extreme positions against conventional conservatism, a whole spectrum of critical attempts were employed – from resistance to reinforcement, from covert activism to open political protest. In many cases, there was a gradual change in pedagogy from within that would have a lasting influence on both teaching and learning. Otto shared this faith in architecture – and not simply engineering knowledge – as an instrument for social change. And he believed in teaching as a field for experimentation, testing and of further thought, along with other disciplines and generations. What is today promoted at universities as research-centred teaching or, from the point of view of students, as research-centred learning, was common practice for Otto. While with his eco-houses in the 1970s he surrendered more design responsibility to residents – and, in doing so, accepted aesthetic and formal compromises – in the late 1950s, his teaching had already reflected his belief that society was in transition and that architecture needed to be able to adapt. As he said in an interview, it was 'not a matter of designing a future society, but rather planning in such a way that this society was given the chance to design itself'[42] – in a dramatically changing environment. Frei Otto's teaching of adaptable architecture was accordingly an attempt to gradually provide methods to future societies that could be of help to them in this design process. It was, if you will, instruction in social form-finding.

1 Werner Sobek, 'IL wird ILEK', in: *Bauwelt*, no. 20, 2015, pp. 14–17.
2 Daniela Fabricius, 'A Spinner in His Web', in: Beatriz Colomina et al. (eds), *Radical Pedagogies*, Cambridge, MA, 2022, pp. 318–322, here p. 318.
3 SFB/CRC 64 'Weitgespannte Flächentragwerke' (Widespan Surface Structures) ran from 1970 to 1985. A year before it ended, another research centre was approved in 1984, SFB/CRC 230 'Natürliche Konstruktionen' (Natural Structures). In its first phase, the centre concentrated on the integration of theory and practice, and the implementation of theory in practice, but in its second phase, Otto increasingly focused on structures of animate and inanimate nature.
4 Frei Otto, 'Wie werden wir weiterleben?', in: *Wie werden wir weiterleben? Dokumentation der Referate und Diskussionen, 42. Bundestag des BDA*, Hanover 1967, reprinted in Berthold Burkhardt (ed.), *Frei Otto. Schriften und Reden, 1951–1983*, Braunschweig/Wiesbaden 1984, pp. 72–79, here p. 73.
5 Frei Otto, 'Stuttgarter Architektur – gestern, heute und morgen', lecture at the University of Stuttgart on 27 October 1978, reprinted in Burkhardt (ed.), *Frei Otto. Schriften und Reden*, pp. 154–168, here p. 162.
6 Otto, 'Stuttgarter Architektur', p. 162.
7 Klaus Jan Philipp, Kerstin Renz and Iñaki Bergera, *Architekturschulen. Programm – Pragmatik – Propaganda*, Tübingen 2012; Johann Jessen and Klaus Jan Philipp (eds), *Der Städtebau der Stuttgarter Schule*, Berlin 2015.
8 Otto, 'Stuttgarter Architektur', pp. 162 f.
9 saai, Werkarchiv FO, Ateliertagebuch [studio diary], entry *c.*1962; Otto, 'Stuttgarter Architektur', p. 161.
10 Nina Gribat, Philipp Misselwitz and Matthias Görlich, *Vergessene Schulen. Architekturlehre zwischen Reform und Revolte um 1968*, Leipzig 2017, pp. 10 f.
11 Otto, 'Stuttgarter Architektur', p. 162.
12 Peter Dietze in conversation with Nina Gribat, Philipp Misselwitz and Matthias Görlich, in: Gribat, Misselwitz and Görlich, *Vergessene Schulen*, p. 36.
13 I am especially grateful to Martin Kunz at the saai Archive for his help in my search for materials in the Werkarchiv FO.
14 René Spitz, *HfG Ulm. Der Blick hinter den Vordergrund. Die politische Geschichte der Hochschule für Gestaltung, 1953–1968/HfG Ulm: The View Behind the Foreground; The Polical History of the Ulm School of Design, 1953–1968*, Stuttgart/London 2002.
15 Seminar programme for 'Anpassungsfähiges Bauen' [Adaptable Architecture], saai, Werkarchiv FO, 'Anpassungsfähiges Bauen'.
16 Max Herzberg, 'Influence de la construction adaptable sur l'urbanisme, ses avantages et ses inconvénients', paper for the seminar 'Anpassungsfähiges Bauen' [Adaptable Architecture] at the HfG Ulm, 1959, saai, Werkarchiv FO, 'Anpassungsfähiges Bauen'.
17 Kirsten Wagner, 'Von den Akteuren des Wohnungsbaus zu den Akteuren des Wohnens. Philosophische und soziologische Bestimmungen des Wohnens in den 1950er- und 1960er-Jahren', in: *Architekturen*, ed. Regine Hess, vol. 43, Bielefeld 2018, pp. 45–62.
18 Cornelia Escher and Kim Förster, 'Ich war Dr. Zelt. Frei Otto über Anpassungsfähigkeit, Ökologie und Ökonomie im Bauen', in: *Arch+*, nos 211/212, 2013, pp. 72–80.
19 Karin Wilhelm, *Portrait Frei Otto*, Berlin 1985, p. 145.
20 Wilhelm, *Portrait Frei Otto*, p. 163.
21 The tent was part of the Swiss Exhibition for Women's Work (Schweizerische Ausstellung für Frauenarbeit, SAFFA); see Escher and Förster, 'Ich war Dr. Zelt'.
22 Otto, 'Stuttgarter Architektur', p. 166
23 Else Lasker-Schüler, *Essays*, Berlin 1920, pp. 32 f.
24 Lasker-Schüler, *Essays*, pp. 32 f., and Else Lasker-Schüler, 'Begegnung', in: Wilhelm, *Portrait Frei Otto*, p. 11.
25 Anna-Maria Meister, 'Ernst Neufert's Lebensgestaltungslehre: Formatting Life Beyond the Built', in: Angela Creager, Mathias Grote and Elaine Leong (eds), *Learning by the Book: Manuals and Handbooks in the History of Science*, in: *BJHS Themes*, vol. 5, 2020, pp. 167–185.
26 See Frei Otto, 'Sinnliche Architektur', in: Wilhelm, *Portrait Frei Otto*, pp. 162 f.
27 Wilhelm, *Portrait Frei Otto*, p. 23.
28 Wilhelm, *Portrait Frei Otto*, p. 145.
29 Frei Otto, 'Subjektives und Kritisches zu dem, was andere als mein Werk bezeichnen', in: Wihelm, *Portrait Frei Otto*, p. 165.
30 Jacques Rancière, *The Ignorant Schoolmaster: Five Lessons in Intellectual Emancipation*, Stanford 1991, p. 13, trans. by Kristin Ross from *Le Maître ignorant. Cinq leçons sur l'émancipation intellectuelle*, Paris 1987; James Baldwin, 'A Talk to Teachers', lecture from 16 October 1963, first published as 'The Negro Child – His Self-Image' in: *The Saturday Review*, 21 December 1963.
31 For the latter, see Wilhelm, *Portrait Frei Otto*, p. 16.
32 See the interview with Jan Knippers and Achim Menges in this volume, pp. 228–239.
33 Gribat, Misselwitz, and Görlich, *Vergessene Schulen*, p. 235.
34 Beatriz Colomina et al. (eds), *Radical Pedagogies*, Cambridge, MA, 2022, p. 11.
35 Valerio Borgonuovo and Silvia Franceschini (eds), *Global Tools, 1973–1975: When Education Coincides with Life*, Rome 2020; Sony Devabhaktuni, Patricia Guaita and Cornelia Tapparelli (eds), *Building Cultures Valparaiso: Pedagogy, Practice and Poetry at the Valparaiso School of Architecture and Design*, Lausanne 2015.
36 saai, Werkarchiv FO, Ateliertagebuch, Skizzen und Notizen [studio diary, sketches and notes].
37 Colomina et al. (eds), *Radical Pedagogies*.
38 Otto, 'Stuttgarter Architektur', p. 160.
39 Otto in Burkhardt (ed.), *Frei Otto. Schriften und Reden*, p. 160.
40 Otto in Burkhardt (ed.), *Frei Otto. Schriften und Reden*, p. 160.
41 Colomina et al. (eds), *Radical Pedagogies*.
42 Escher and Förster, 'Ich war Dr. Zelt'.

Otto the Educator: Formative Experiments in the USA

Rob Whitehead

Of all the roles that define Frei Otto's career, perhaps 'educator' fits best. From the beginning of his working life, Otto defied the conventional expectations for what an educator should do and in what forums this instruction should occur. He operated simultaneously as a designer, researcher, builder, author, orator, publisher and artist. Work in one realm was immediately generative to other realms, and new knowledge was persistently shared openly.

Otto's connection to education and research is primarily associated with his decades as the Director of the Institute for Lightweight Structures (Institut für leichte Flächentragwerke, IL) at what was then the Stuttgart Institute of Technology (Technische Hochschule Stuttgart). Yet many of the IL's foundational qualities and the ideologies that shaped Otto's career can be traced to the formative years between 1950 and 1964 and his experiences in the United States. Reciprocally, Otto's brief, but intensive experiences as an educator in America contributed to the broader evolution of architectural educational methods in that country.

Otto's Education and Inspiration from the USA, 1950–1953

Otto's journey as an educator was consistently influenced by his experiences as a learner. From 1948 to 1952, he studied architecture at the Technical University of Berlin (Technische Universität Berlin, TU Berlin). Students in postwar West Berlin faced many challenges, but their technical studies were mostly routine. Otto's work relied heavily on knowledge of technical assemblies and construction methods more than design experimentation. His student notebooks reveal a training method firmly based on a 'case study' method of learning. Annotated hand-drawn images of traditional building assemblies and orthographic drawings for properly sized structures are thoroughly documented.[1] In a few cases, Otto explored design ideas for nontraditional assemblies like structural shells and laminated wood forms. Overall, the importance of iteration, obedience to tradition, attention to detail and technical correctness is evident throughout the work – as was Otto's magnificent commitment to craft.

In 1950, he won a scholarship to study in the United States at the University of Virginia.[2] He contacted many high-profile architects living in America and arranged visits: Eliel and Eero Saarinen, Mies van der Rohe, Erich Mendelsohn, Frank Lloyd Wright and Charles Eames. Upon his return, he wrote articles reflecting on his visits with Wright, Mies and Mendelsohn.[3] His most formative trip, the one to see the renowned structural engineer Fred Severud, however, was not on his initial agenda.

Upon the recommendation of Eero Saarinen, Otto visited Severud's office in New York City. They shared many interests. Severud was an expert in tension structures, yet he maintained an accessible ability to explain structural principles to others. In his 1945 article, 'Turtles and Walnuts, Morning Glories and Grass', he explained how natural forms could influence the design of building structures, including cable structures and pneumatics. These lightweight structures could 'meet the demand for more efficient, more economical and more attractive structural forms' in a post-war world.[4] This argument aligned with Otto's most commonly expressed ideologies for the remainder of his career.

According to Otto, his favourite moment of his trip occurred when Severud showed him a physical model of the Dorton Arena in Raleigh, North Carolina. The arena was designed by Matthew Nowicki in 1950; despite the fact he had died tragically that year, the project continued. They discussed the logical formal relationship between the outward leaning concrete arches and the saddle-shaped hanging mesh of tension wires that sagged between. In a letter to Severud upon his return to Germany dated 20 March 1951, Otto called the model, 'One of the most interesting things that I have seen in the U.S.'[5] He asked for more information so he could give a lecture to his class at the TU Berlin about engineering advances in the United States. Severud politely deferred the request to the firm's architect, William Henry Deitrick, with the explanation that the roof had not yet been installed.[6] Otto was both inspired and anxious to learn more but did not wait. For an article published in *Bautechnik,* in October 1951, Otto wrote about the 'Raleigh arena' and presumptuously created his own drawings in an effort to explain, to the best of his ability as an undergraduate architectural student, how the building structure worked.[7]

Creating drawings and writing about a building that interested him, of course, followed what Otto had learned in his undergraduate studies about the benefits of a case study methodology: to learn how something works, one studies it and documents it. He was inspired in other ways, too. For the remainder of this undergraduate and graduate education, Otto also used concrete arches and cables nets as central design elements in several of his own ensuing design projects as a student (e.g., Concert Hall on the Lietzensee, 1952, and Mining Town, 1953).[8]

As Otto transitioned from his undergraduate to his Doctorate in Engineering (Dr.-Ing.) programme at the TU Berlin between 1952 and 1953, he began years of regular letter correspondence with Severud. He sent updates about

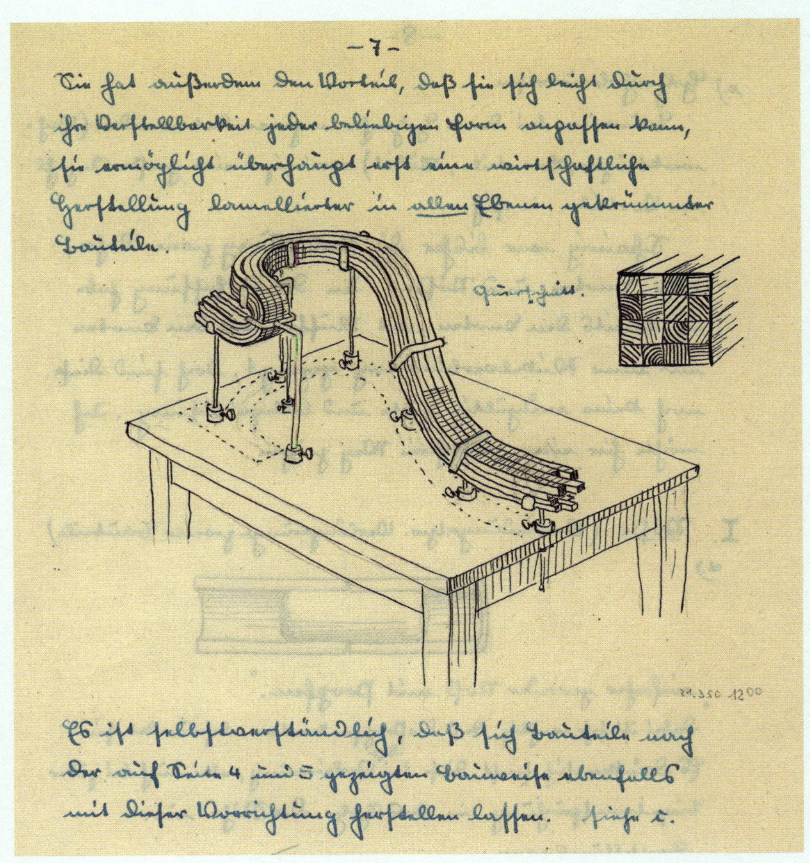

Sketch from Otto's student notebook on the possibilities of shaping wood into new forms through physical modelling

tension structures in Germany, discussed historic structures and solicited information. Otto claimed to be, ‘currently compiling everything that has ever been done in the field of the “hanging roof” in book form to publish it as a dissertation’ and asked for help.[9] Otto valued Severud’s input and humbly submitted that ‘I am also an architect, not trained as a civil engineer. I am just trying to summarize this new field.’[10]

Initial Connections, Emerging Expertise and Costly Criticisms, 1954–1958

Otto finished his doctoral thesis on the ‘hanging roof’, *Das hängende Dach*, in October 1953 and elected to have the Raleigh arena on the book cover. He sent one of only five bound copies to Severud along with a letter of thanks: ‘You gave me the inspiration to write this book. I will always be grateful to you for that.’[11] Months later, when Severud responded, he was quite praiseful: ‘All the way through your book we found useful information [...] there is almost nothing in any other existing literature that gives information of this kind.’[12] Severud and his primary tension design expert, Igor Voshinin, agreed to do a joint article together with Otto for Bauwelt-Verlag. Their professional collaborations seemed bound to continue.

In March 1956, Severud co-authored the cover article, ‘Hung Roofs’, in the prestigious international publication *Progressive Architecture*. After explaining basic principles of tension structures, Severud added, ‘I should like to introduce Frei Otto [... he] has done a great amount of work in this field.’ He explicitly recommended *Das hängende Dach* and assured readers that, ‘we are certain to hear from him again’.[13] This was a very high-profile introduction to a broad international architectural audience from America’s pre-eminent designer of tension structures.

In a fateful twist, the article also included drawings of the Berlin Congress Hall, which Severud had designed with American architect Hugh Stubbins. This roof garnered Otto’s attention. Not only was the project an incredibly prominent, symbolic and politically sensitive building, but the roof looked similar to the Raleigh arena. When asked, Severud invited Otto to, ‘Please feel free to comment in any way that you see fit’ as part of an exchange of ideas which they normally shared in letters.[14] Unfortunately, Otto criticized the building publicly in a magazine article for *Bauwelt*; he questioned the building’s structural design logic, calling it expensive, overdesigned and monumental.[15] Although Otto may have intended to start a debate about architectural form and structure, these critiques generated unwanted negative attention.[16]

At this time, Otto was actively looking for a teaching position in the United States. After learning that Eduardo Catalano, an engineering professor at North Carolina State University, had designed a house with a roof form similar to the Raleigh arena, Otto struck up a regular correspondence with him beginning in 1956. Eventually, Otto learned that the only opportunity to teach at NC State would be contingent upon him teaching engineering (not architecture) for a full-year term. This was not what Otto wanted.[17] Catalano left to teach at the Massachusetts Institute of Technology (MIT) in mid-1956 and, in a later letter, informed Otto there were no teaching opportunities for him there either.

In an effort to repair his relationship with Severud, Otto partially apologized in 1957 for the public nature of his comments, while still insisting on the correctness of his assessment. He also updated Severud about his future prospects: ‘I have now given up teaching at an (American) school. I am currently working on founding a development center for lightweight construction methods, which will first and foremost have the task of collecting all documents about groundbreaking work in the field of lightweight construction and making them available to the wider public.’[18] Weeks later when he responded, Severud instead included a memo, written by him and Stubbins, refuting Otto's criticisms with language that was harshly critical of Otto's understanding of design from both an architectural and engineering perspective.[19] Severud never wrote to Otto again and their relationship came to an abrupt end.

In 1958, Otto's career opportunities in practice and teaching were diminished.[20] He founded a small private research group, the Institute for the Development of Lightweight Construction (Entwicklungsstätte für den Leichtbau, EL) in West Berlin. This quasi-practice/research centre filled many important 'educator' roles. It provided a creative outlet, a home for ongoing research work and a forum from which Otto could publish updates on his continuing projects: *Mitteilungen der Entwicklungsstätte für den Leichtbau (EL)*, issues one to nine, from 1958 to 1963.

But Otto was still interested in teaching. In early 1958, in a letter to Catalano, Otto reminded him that the 'year is still unoccupied for me', making himself available to accept any teaching invitation that might become available in the United States.

Changes in Architectural Education in the USA, 1950s–1960s

When Otto received an offer to teach later that year at Washington University in St Louis, Missouri, he found himself in the middle of the largest shift in architectural education in a century.[21] At this time, architectural schools in the United States were engaged in a contentious debate about what it meant to teach *and learn* architecture. Progressive schools were moving beyond a rigidly controlled, practice-based pedagogy towards programmes that reflected the new post-war perspectives about the social, cultural and technological obligations for design.[22]

Design studios turned away from their long-standing alignment with engineering and professional practice. Project briefs and expectations for 'practice-based' presentations quickly gave way to creative experimentation. From 1951 to 1958, a rebellious group of instructors at the University of Texas at Austin, known as the 'Texas Rangers' argued that students should be given opportunities in studio for 'personal voyages of exploration and discovery' intended to stimulate their spiritual and intellectual growth.[23] To fit in with this new educational context, Otto could not simply teach structural design, he would also be expected to reflect more broadly on ways that building structures affected humanity.

In the United States, a few high-profile schools built the identity of their programmes around the ideologies of their celebrated studio instructors from abroad including Walter Gropius (Harvard University) Mies van der Rohe (Illinois Institute of Technology, IIT) and Konrad Wachsmann (University of Southern California, USC).[24] Given these conditions, Otto's selection to teach his first architecture studio at the age of thirty-three was apt *and* opportunistic.

'Nature and the Architect', New Opportunities at Washington University, 1958

Like Otto, the person that hired him, Dean Joseph Passonneau, was also educated as an architect and engineer. As dean (1956–1967), Passonneau developed a reputation for supporting innovative programmes and for hiring internationally renowned faculty.[25] In an article for *Washington University Magazine* entitled 'Nature and the Architect', he provided a thorough summary of what Otto's studio did and how these unique activities were rooted in deeper progressive ideologies.[26] Similar to Severud's 1945 article, Passonneau discussed the importance of considering natural forms in structural design in order to create 'a humanist architecture'. He emphasized the need for discovery in architectural education as a means of awakening excitement and understanding through 'direct and sensory experience'. Otto's ideology was clearly viewed as progressive and that his form-finding model-making approach was seen as a positive evolution to design studio education.

The actual content of Otto's first academic lectures would no doubt have been surprising to those expecting a highly technical presentation. Instead Otto argued that designers needed to 'build in a humane manner'.[27] He parsed differences between art, architecture and structures, and called for the critical deployment of science and technology towards architecture. He mentioned 'lightweight structures' only at the end of the lectures. He noted their inherent ability to optimize material efficiency as a means of increasing access, availability and adaptability for humanity.[28] Despite the thoroughly technical nature of his thesis and his reputation as being one of only a few people in the world that could creatively design membrane structures, there is no portion of his lecture that describes how to design them. He simply wanted students to commit to the journey of looking for lightweight structures with him.

Model Making and Analysis

Model making was the centrepiece of Otto's career and, unsurprisingly, this is where he began as an educator.[29] Form-finding modelling would have been a new experience for all the students because, at this time, it was primarily for representational purposes. Otto's approach elevated model making to a generative role in design. These models, created from cables and membranes, were inherently embued with technical information about their structural performance and material behaviour.

Otto asked his students to begin modelling using a process that he learned in school: the use of case study. He assigned different structural forms to each student (e.g., hanging shells, pneumatics, cable nets and membranes) and asked them to create the lightest structure they could devise through a modelling process. The model's forms were clearly provided by Otto as they resembled illustrations from his thesis, practice and writings. As his students built the models, they realized that lightweight structures were 'self-forming'. Otto had written that, 'Hanging roofs cannot be designed [...] one may be able to help them develop.'[30]

At the end of the semester, his students had created design proposals for a concrete shell, a suspension bridge, an arch and cable net greenhouse, a large up-down membrane roof, an aviary and a study about adaptable structures for families and factories. Interestingly, nearly all of the projects, except the shell, were revisited by Otto in later years. According to Berthold Burkhardt, this fit a pattern of 'upcycling' ideas and forms that Otto (or others he had worked with) had found.[31]

These models represented more than designed proposals – Otto expected students to learn about the inextricable relationship to the forces within as well. Although the behaviour of tension forces is intuitive as a hanging chain, Passonneau described the difficulty that architecture students would have in analysing them from a purely engineering perspective; he praised the analytical benefit of using modelling to 'simulate the action of full-scale structures' particularly as the forms evolved to the third dimension.[32]

Three main 'measurement' models were created. The first was a gridded rubber membrane that had been hung inverted in a wood frame and loaded regularly with nails. Students measured and documented the final double-curved form, stiffened it with plaster and inverted it to create a free-standing shell. The second measurement model was a simple 'two-high, two-low' gridded rubber membrane that looked like Otto's Music Pavilion at Kassel (1955). Students were expected to accurately measure models and produce scaled drawings that could be used for fabrication. Otto introduced students to the plumb bob measurement and plotting system he had developed years earlier.

After constructing a form-finding model, a student prepares the documentation and measurements of the form, Washington University (1958)

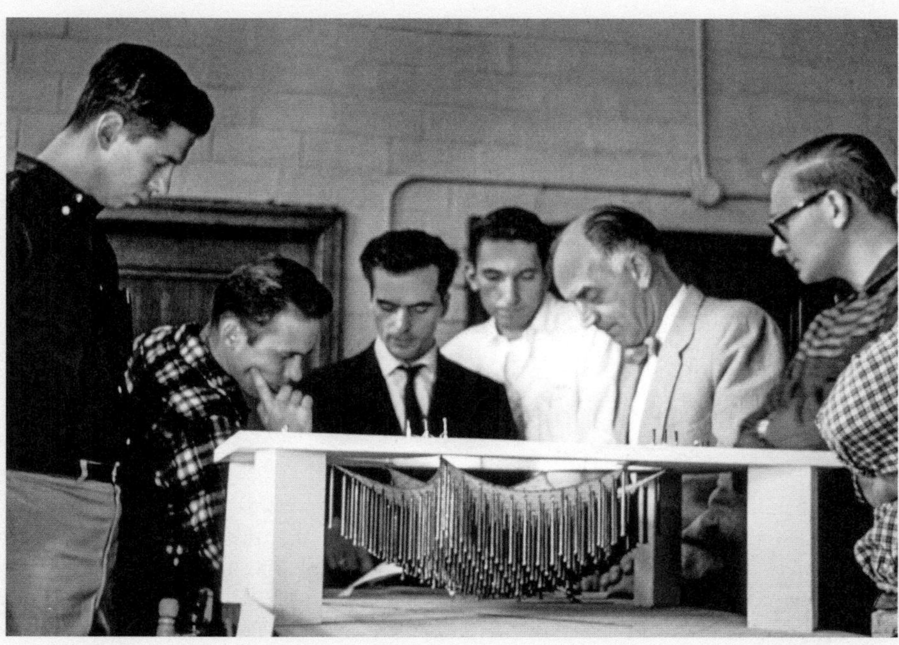

The third measurement model was created by a student named John Koch (1937–2004). It was a high-low tent system based on Otto's Berlin concert hall entrance canopy from 1957. Koch's work was so thorough that Otto asked him to write and illustrate a 2,700-word essay in the seventh issue of the EL publication, *Mitteilungen*, detailing the step-by-step method used to model, measure and analyse the behaviour of the roof.[33] Upon graduation in 1960, Koch joined a handful of people at the EL in Berlin, where he completed several hanging chain study models for shells using a method that was later used for the Mannheim Multihalle model in 1973. Koch also devised the deployable wooden gridshell system for the pavilion at Essen (1962) which became the prototype for the interior lecture spaces within the German Pavilion (1967).[34] Koch eventually returned to Washington University and retired as an Associate Professor of Architecture there.

Presentations, Photos and Publicity

The studio's work was presented and shared in a unique way as well. Otto taught students how to photograph their models 'in process' to show the generative nature of the task. He also demonstrated how to enhance the realism of their final models by photographing them from a human perspective with real clouds and shadows in the background. Otto's enduring role as the ever-present photographic chronicler of lightweight structural design for the IL seems to begin here in this studio.

This studio clearly fit within an evolving perspective of American architectural education. The studio's purpose was not practice based, it was ideological and innovative. Passonneau called it, 'Creative activity from a search of understanding', and boasted that 'The students became intensely excited [...] Each discovery was particularly his own.'[35] Otto was proud of his teaching experience and regularly mentioned it in his correspondence for the next few years.

Frei Otto with students during a discussion of the results of a form-finding exercise, Washington University (1958)

Evolutions in Teaching: Yale University, UC Berkeley, Harvard and MIT, 1960–1962

In Germany, Otto's practice and research work at the EL began to gain momentum so his teaching opportunities were limited to shorter, more intensive activities. In the beginning months of 1959, Otto was a guest instructor at the Ulm School of Design (Hochschule für Gestaltung Ulm, HfG Ulm). His students explored the potential adaptability of structures, although they did so primarily through drawings and diagrams and not modelling.[36] In 1959, he also served as an assistant to Peter Poelzig at the TU Berlin for a seminar on lightweight structures.

In the autumn of 1960, Otto's next teaching opportunity was at one of the premier learning institutions in the United States, Yale University. Otto co-taught a six-week course, 'Structures: Traditional and Lightweight', with Yale's Professor King-lui Wu.[37] Despite the presence of one of Saarinen and Severud's most famous buildings on campus, the Ingalls Rink (1953–1957), they chose not to start from a case study perspective. Instead Otto and Wu opted for a project-based approach to design an 'Assembly and Exhibition Hall for Chicago'. The designs featured trusses, space frames, a large pneumatic tent and a large flat roof supported by four large tree-like column structures.[38] In a lecture, Otto described how the tree-like minimum path forms were 'making themselves' through the use of inverting hanging chains.[39] This is the first evidence of the tree-like element in Otto's career; it inspired extensive future design and research by others at the IL and became manifest as a signature design element in Otto's work.

In 1962, Otto taught briefly at three other iconic American architectural institutions: University of California, Berkeley; Harvard University; and MIT. With these prestigious appointments, it became clear that Otto's reputation had evolved to be an internationally respected designer, researcher and instructor. The short time commitments at each school also revealed the growing constraints on Otto's time.

In the autumn of 1962, the renowned American architect and educator Charles Moore hired Otto to teach a four-week seminar to graduate architecture students at UC Berkeley. Fourteen students from around the world prepared a final report that included Otto's lecture notes, form-finding models and photographs of a large-scale steel rebar lattice gridshell they had built during the seminar. At the beginning of the course, Otto again relied on case study work. Students mimicked a Gaudí methodology by creating hanging catenary models that evolved from single chains to three-dimensional lattice 'domes'.[40] The model scales increased until the students could extrapolate the geometry of the final lattice shell's slope and form from the model's hanging cables.

A local contractor provided steel reinforcing rods, and students devised a connection system for the joints that would allow movement during completion. The students assembled the shell in a brick courtyard by laying the bars flat on the ground, securing them together in a grid, lifting the structure in place using only human labour and temporary supports, and securing the final locations for the supports. The final double-curved lattice form enclosed an impressively large area of approximately 7.6 × 7.6 metres with a maximum height of 3 metres.

The impact of this work was immediate. The shell was built during the 3rd International Association for Shell and Spatial Structures (IASS) conference in San Francisco, which was attended by an cohort of the most influential shell designers; Otto noted that many conference attendees were 'interested bystanders' to the construction process.[41] The modelling measurement method used in the seminar would be used again for the German Pavilion and the Munich Olympic Stadium.[42] Otto would return to a similar large-scale construction exercise during the construction of a prototype that would become the IL headquarters.[43] The person responsible for integrating *both* these efforts at the IL was a student in this class at UC Berkeley, R. Larry Medlin. In 1964, Medlin joined Otto

From the very beginning, Frei Otto staged photographs of student models in order to give the designs a sense of scale and a realism, Washington University (1958)

Student model with tree-style supports; these forms, derived from hanging chains, were a common element in Otto's work throughout his career, Yale University (1960)

at the EL in Berlin and served as a research associate, instructor and primary model maker at the IL. Medlin left Germany in 1967 for Washington University, where he led the Lightweight Construction Center from 1968 to 1973.[44] Medlin went on to serve as Director for the School of Architecture at the University of Arizona for thirty years. Another student in the class, Edward Allen, became one of the most influential educators in building technology in America. As a professor at MIT, Yale and the University of Oregon, he wrote a dozen books on structural design and material assemblies. He received the Topaz Medallion, the highest educational honour for American architectural educators.

At the conclusion of a four-week course, students constructed a freestanding doubly curved gridshell based on their model prototypes, UC Berkeley (1962)

Before the structure was elevated, students joined the lattice framework and the stiffening core, UC Berkeley (1962)

Diagramming Optimized Structures and the Development of Parametrics

Weeks after completing the course at Berkeley, Otto presented lectures at Harvard and MIT. In his lectures, Otto contemplated 'The Task of an Architect'. He wondered if designers had the right tools to design for humanity. Unlike his previous lectures, he openly discussed more specific technical aspects of this work including reflections about how structural forms could be altered and optimized.

During his time at MIT, Otto's sketchbook provided one of the most elucidative diagrams of this era – a hand-drawn matrix that diagrammed structural parameters and forms. He proposed a visual classification system to help designers understand the parameters of structural behaviour and material utilization.[45] This was a logical evolution of the 'finding forms through modelling' approach that linked parameters with performance. This matrix evolved across the next decade to become a generative system for structural analysis that Otto referenced frequently.[46] This method of comparing structural parameters to forms, stresses and materials served as the basis for what is now known as computational parametric generative modelling of structures.[47]

Practice, Teaching and Limitations of Visiting Teaching Appointments

Otto was at a crossroads in his career as an educator. Although the teaching experiences in the United States were rewarding, Otto did not teach there again. There were many benefits to being an educator abroad. Teaching allowed for an exchange of ideas that helped him promote the widespread use of light-weight structures. The open-ended teaching model in the United States offered him opportunities to experiment, at least indirectly, with physical models and optimized forms. He was able to reach international audiences by sharing images of student work through his publications and presentations. Simply put, being an educator in the United States benefitted Otto – with limits.

More obvious drawbacks became apparent, too. He was away from home, his practice and the experiments of the EL in West Berlin. In a letter to Catalano in 1956, years before his first teaching position, Otto worried about the prospect of missed opportunities in practice: 'If I should go to the United States, I would not want to give up these European possibilities.' He also worried that in America he would have fewer opportunities for 'pure research work, especially on the development of the extreme light constructions'.[48] Although his friends Buckminster Fuller and Félix Candela had teaching appointments dedicated almost primarily to research, Otto knew it was quite unusual for an American instructor to receive such an appointment.

There were also the practical limitations caused by an academic calendar and limited student expertise that he no doubt found frustrating. His research would only progress slowly if he relied on student work in studios. Otto realized that in each new location he would start over from the same point of knowledge and then lead students through a familiar step-by-step process of learning through case study and modelling. As his teaching appointments diminished in duration, this became more problematic. Teaching in the United States did not advance the technical research questions he cared about most and it limited his practice opportunities.

Experimental Ideas for Academic Institutions, 1960–1964

Otto considered teaching opportunities in West Germany, where research appointments were more common. However, after a failed attempt to earn a full-time teaching position at the Technical College of Karlsruhe (Technische Hochschule Karlsruhe), Otto began to feel that he did not fit the expectations of the

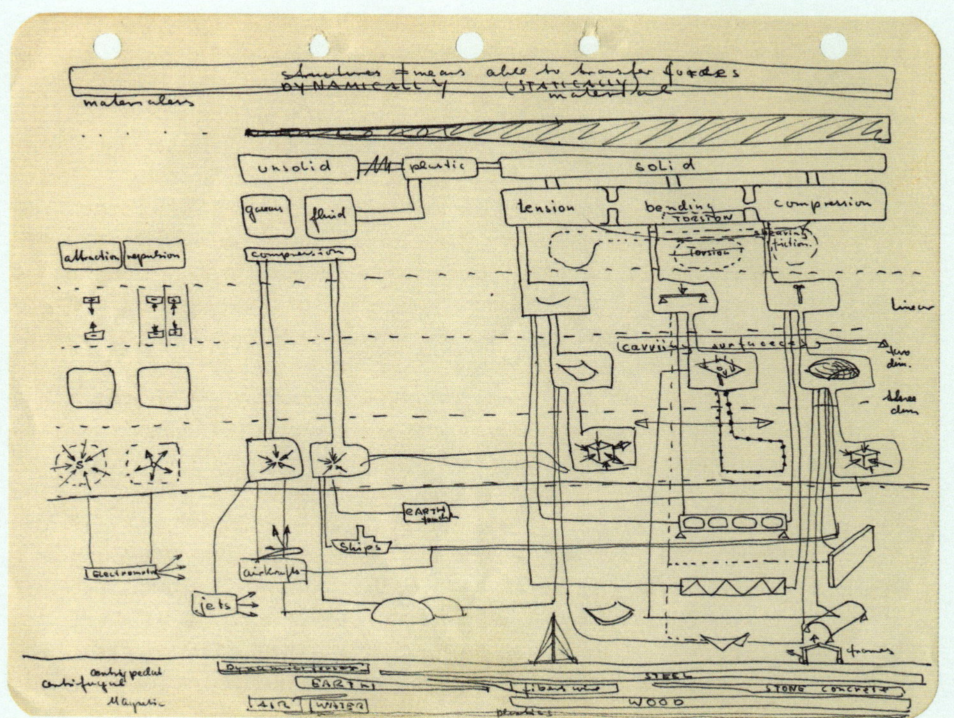

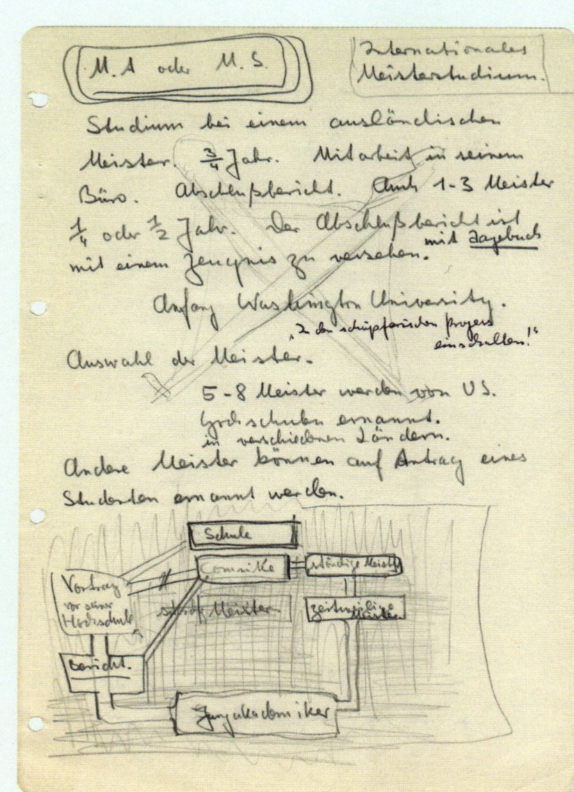

German technical school.[49] He still believed in the ability of vibrant educational institutions to advance larger questions of humanity and design, but did not see any existing opportunities. So Otto proposed one.

While teaching at Yale in 1960, Otto penned an open letter to the Governing Mayor of West Berlin proposing an International Academy in Berlin, 'a place where 3,000–5,000 of the best academics [...] in the world [could] come together to work on previously unachieved goals for a period of time'. He wanted scientists and artists to work together in one place on common global problems. Based on his teaching experiences, he proposed a nontraditional higher-educational institution ('no tests or lectures') that could be staffed by an international cohort of guest lectures and experts from around the world. He lamented that, 'there is currently no place where real international cooperation can take place beyond this'.[50] Although the letter was well-received, nothing advanced.

Otto enjoyed being around students but, by his own admission, was sceptical of the constraints of regular teaching schedules, lectures and assessments. Instead of teaching in a traditional one-way communication, which relied on the primacy of the instructor to have answers that were imparted to students, Otto 'wanted to motivate and interest students in basic research on themes related to lightweight structures, etc.'[51] He wanted to find an academic setting to match these priorities.

Throughout his teaching, Otto had contemplated (and diagrammed) proposals for how educational/research facilities might best be organized. In his sketchbook from 1963, he diagrammed a 'Master Studio' educational research programme. Otto explained, 'My concept intended a pure research institute for top-level research, free of teaching commitments.'[52] In this model, high-profile instructors (Otto called them 'famous people') would select the best students to work with them on their research. Courses would skip, 'normal teaching' in lieu of

Diagram from Frei Otto's sketchbook on structural parameters, forms and forces; the visual classification of the behaviour of structures in a flowchart facilitates optimal solutions for minimizing the utilization of materials (1960)

Frei Otto, notes and diagrams for an international master's course (1960)

work in small workshops with students. The ultimate degree would be a PhD with a research topic selected by the students that 'must be free. Everyone must be allowed to take his own way'.[53] Otto's proposal was a very American approach to education, but he was thinking internationally.

The IL and the Beginning of New Chapters as an Educator, 1964

In 1964, Otto got his wish. Fritz Leonhardt appointed Otto as the Director for the Institute for Lightweight Structures at the Stuttgart Institute of Technology. Immediately upon its founding, Otto sought to create a learning atmosphere based on many of his formative experiences in the United States. His teaching methods, research projects and connections with innovative practices at IL became globally renowned. Although the West German architectural education system was still a few years away from its own pedagogical evolution, Otto fought to maintain the freedom for design exploration he had felt in the United States by encouraging an array of student research topics.

Several former American students joined him at the IL to continue their formative work, and still more would join throughout the following years. He continued to publish updates about his ongoing research through a series of IL publications (nos 1–41, 1969–1995), and he lectured continuously around the world for the remainder of his career. His idealized prospect of opening an international school of academics that studied science and art never materialized quite as he expected. But because Otto was a tremendous educator, this institute became something more.

1 saai, Werkarchiv FO, Studierenden-Skizzenbuch [Student Sketchbooks], 1949–1950.
2 See Conrad Roland, *Frei Otto: Structures*, London 1965.
3 Frei Otto, 'Mies van der Rohe. Bericht einer Amerikafahrt', in: *Neue Bauwelt*, 6/36, 1951, pp. 593 f.; Frei Otto, 'Besuch bei Erich Mendelsohn', in: *Die neue Stadt*, 5/1, 1952, pp. 30–32; Frei Otto, 'Ein Besuch bei Frank Lloyd Wright', in: *Neue Bauwelt*, 7/2, 1952, pp. 24–26.
4 Fred N. Severud, 'Turtles and Walnuts, Morning Glories and Grass', in: *Architectural Forum*, September 1945, pp. 149–162, here p. 149.
5 saai, Werkarchiv FO, letter from Otto to Severud, 20 March 1951.
6 saai, Werkarchiv FO, letter from Severud to Otto, 23 July 1951.
7 Frei Otto, 'Die Raleigh-Arena', in: *Bautechnik*, 28/10, October 1951, pp. 254 f.
8 See Joachim Kleinmanns and Martin Kunz, 'The Path to Lightweight Construction: Frei Otto's Early Work', in: Georg Vrachliotis et al. (eds), *Frei Otto: Thinking by Modeling*, exhib. cat., ZKM | Center for Art and Media Karlsruhe, Leipzig 2017, pp. 31–40.
9 saai, Werkarchiv FO, letter from Otto to Severud, 7 November 1952.
10 saai, Werkarchiv FO, letter from Otto to Severud, 8 July 1954.
11 saai, Werkarchiv FO, letter from Otto to Severud, 8 July 1954.
12 saai, Werkarchiv FO, letter from Severud to Otto, 14 October 1954.
13 Fred N. Severud and Raniero G. Corbelleti, 'Hung Roofs', *Progressive Architecture*, no. 2, March 1956, pp. 99–107, here pp. 104 and 105.
14 saai, Werkarchiv FO, letter from Severud to Otto, 11 May 1956.
15 Frei Otto, 'Lasten werden in die Luft gehängt. Kritisches zur Konstruktion der Kongresshalle in Berlin', *Bauwelt*, 47/42, 1956, p. 1001.
16 See Barbara Miller Lane, 'The Berlin Congress Hall 1955–1957', in: *Perspectives in American History*, no. 1, new series, 1984, pp. 131–185.
17 saai, Werkarchiv FO, letters from Otto to Catalano, 26 August and 6 November 1956.
18 saai, Werkarchiv FO, letter from Otto to Severud, 30 July 1957.
19 saai, Werkarchiv FO, letter from Severud to Otto, 9 August 1957.
20 See Cornelia Escher, 'Model – Experiment – Environment', in *Frei Otto: Thinking by Modeling*, pp. 53–60.
21 See Andrew Saint, *Architect and Engineer: A Study in Sibling Rivalry*, New Haven, CT/London 2007, pp. 469–484.
22 See Greig Crysler, 'Critical Pedagogy and Architectural Education', *Journal of Architectural Education*, 48/4, May 1995, pp. 208–217.
23 See Alexander Caragonne, *The Texas Rangers: Notes from an Architectural Underground*, Cambridge, MA, 1995.
24 See Jill E. Pearlman, *Inventing American Modernism: Joseph Hudnut, Walter Gropius, and the Bauhaus Legacy at Harvard*, Charlottesville and London 2007.
25 'Joesph R. Passonneau, 90', *The Record*, Washington University in St Louis, 30 August 2011, https://source.wustl.edu/2011/08/joseph-r-passonneau-90/ (accessed in June 2024).
26 Joseph Passonneau, 'Nature and the Architect', *Washington University Magazine*, November 1959, pp. 24–29, here p. 26 and p. 27.
27 Frei Otto, 'The Task', lecture presented at Washington University and the University of Illinois Urbana, 1958, reprinted in *Mitteilungen der Entwicklungsstätte für den Leichtbau (EL)*, no. 7, 1961, pp. 2–7, here p. 4.
28 Frei Otto, 'Lightweight Building, A Way to Human Architecture', lecture for fifth year architecture class, Washington University in St Louis, 22 September 1958, saai, Werkarchiv FO, Texte 1952–1957.
29 See Bill Addis, 'Physical Modelling and Form Finding', in: Sigrid Adriaenssens, Philippe Block, Diederik Veenendaal and Chris Williams (eds), *Shell Structures for Architecture: Form Finding and Optimization*, London/New York 2014, pp. 33–45.
30 Frei Otto, *Das hängende Dach: Gestalt und Struktur*, Berlin 1954, p. 158.
31 See Berthold Burkhardt, 'The Institute for Lightweight Structures: University Institute and Spinners' Centre', in: Winfried Nerdinger (ed.), *Frei Otto: Complete Works; Lightweight Construction, Natural Design*, exh. cat. Architekturmuseum der TU München, Basel/Boston/Berlin 2005, pp. 91–100.
32 Passonneau, 'Nature and the Architect', p. 28.
33 John Koch and Frei Otto, 'Measurements on High and Low Point Membrane', in: *Mitteilungen der Entwicklungsstätte für den Leichtbau (EL)*, no. 7, 1961, pp. 35–39.
34 See Ian Liddell, 'Frei Otto and the Development of Gridshells', in: *Case Studies in Structural Engineering*, no. 4, December 2015, pp. 39–49.
35 Passonneau, 'Nature and the Architect', p. 29.
36 Frei Otto, 'Der Gastkurs an der Hochschule für Gestaltung in Ulm 1959', in: *Mitteilungen der Entwicklungsstätte für den Leichtbau (EL)*, no. 6, 1959, p. 48.
37 *Models, Media, and Methods: Frei Otto's Architectural Research*, curated by Georg Vrachliotis, Yale School of Architecture, 20 February–2 May 2020, https://www.architecture.yale.edu/exhibitions/68-models-media-and-methods-frei-ottos-architectural-research (accessed in June 2024).
38 See Roland, *Frei Otto: Structures*.
39 saai, Werkarchiv FO, Frei Otto, 'Minimal Structures', lecture, 1992.
40 'Lightweight Structures', report on student activities, UC Berkeley, May 1963, saai, Werkarchiv FO.
41 'Lightweight Structures'.
42 See Rob Whitehead, 'Evolution of Modeling for Lightweight Structures: Creating the Munich Olympic Stadium Roof (1967–72)', in: *Technology | Architecture + Design*, 6/2, 2022, pp. 212–231.
43 See Joachim Kleinmanns, *Der deutsche Pavillon der Expo 67 in Montreal. Ein Schlüsselwerk deutscher Nachkriegsarchitektur*, Berlin, 2020, pp. 108–113.
44 See Jean Cook, 'Pioneering the Field: The Founding Father of the Fabric Tension Structure Industry', in: *Fabric Architecture*, May/June 1991, reprinted 1 July 2008, https://fabricarchitecturemag.com/2008/07/01/pioneering-the-field-the-founding-father-of-the-fabric-tension-structure-industry/ (accessed in June 2024).
45 saai, Werkarchiv FO, Frei Otto, Atelier-Tagebücher [Studio Diary], 1959–1964.
46 See Philip Drew, *Frei Otto: Form and Structure*, Boulder 1976.
47 See Alexandros Peteinarelis, 'Frei Otto's Contribution – Legacy to Parametric Design and Material Computation', in: Nuno Guimarães, Alexandra Paio, Sancho Oliveira, Filipa Crespo Osório and Maria João Oliveira (eds) *Architecture-In-Play, International Conference July 11th–12th 2016, Conference Proceedings,* Lisbon 2016, pp. 11–23.
48 saai, Werkarchiv FO, letters from Otto to Catalano, August 1956.
49 Kleinmanns and Kunz, 'The Path to Lightweight Construction', p. 36.
50 saai, Werkarchiv FO, Frei Otto, open letter to Willy Brandt, Governing Mayor of West Berlin, 23 October 1960.
51 Burkhardt, 'The Institute for Lightweight Structures: University Institute and Spinners' Centre', p. 97.
52 Burkhardt, p. 97.
53 saai, Werkarchiv FO, letters from Otto to Catalano, August 1956.

Frei Otto in his Warmbronn atelier (c. 1969), photograph by Fritz Dressler

Paths in Interdisciplinary Research and Architectural Exploration

A Conversation with Jan Knippers JK and Achim Menges AM

saai: This monograph is devoted to Frei Otto's understanding of nature, his images of nature and concepts of nature. According to your own past assertions, you both think of yourselves as belonging to this tradition. Certain parallels are partially expected, particularly regarding institutions, owing to your activity at the University of Stuttgart as well as the school's thematic continuity. In concrete terms, how do you see the common themes and parallels?

JK: Perhaps we should begin by saying that, after all, the two of us only came to Stuttgart because of this school, this tradition. In the 1990s, I was studying civil engineering and was a rather unhappy student. At that time, there was still no Internet, and you were not yet confronted with the flood of images we have today. And so, I constantly poked around in the library of the TU Berlin [Technical University of Berlin], looking for something that might interest me. Relatively soon I became aware of Stuttgart, because at that time it was the only centre that went even a little beyond the purely professional issues in engineering. To this day, I still claim to have been the first collaborator of Jörg Schlaich who didn't study under him in Stuttgart. Achim is much younger than I, of course, and can tell a different story, but I believe that the fact that we both landed here in Stuttgart – and not in Braunschweig or Darmstadt or wherever else – has to do with the Frei Otto tradition we are discussing. Unlike in architecture, this collective of conceptually and creatively active innovators, designers, engineers and scholars is a much smaller community than that of architects. These are very small groups in which one person influences the other and has brought them all together. Frei Otto was brought to Stuttgart by Fritz Leonhardt, for example. He was a dyed-in-the-wool Swabian, an engineer hard as nails. All business. But he had a good eye. He saw in Otto that there was something interesting. As Rector of the University of Stuttgart, he put everything in motion in order to attract Otto. The special thing was the act of cooperating across disciplines, which many people don't get. Even at University College London, where I'm currently serving as a guest professor, they're all terrific minds, but *that* is something they simply struggle to achieve.

AM: I feel that there are four angles of reference to Frei Otto's work that are of relevance to us. The overriding point is the idea of interdisciplinary collaboration between architects, engineers and scientists as equals with the understanding that such collaboration can produce genuine gains in knowledge. That is a culture that Frei Otto substantially helped to create at the University of Stuttgart. And I, too, came to Stuttgart because of it. And it was not only a starry-eyed ideal on my part. It also proved to be true.

The second angle is that of lightweight construction [*Leichtbau*]. Today, I would probably no longer call it that, but resource-saving construction [*ressourcenschonendes Bauen*]: building with as little material and as few emissions as possible. That is what makes the whole issue even more timely today. It is simply a matter of keeping our footprint (a term Otto also used to use) on the planet as minimal as possible, in the literal as well as the figurative sense. That is a tradition to which we feel committed as it is probably more relevant and vital today than ever before.

The third angle was born out of lightweight construction, so to speak, namely an interest in nature that reveals wholly different functional and operational principles for structures and architecture. At this point, we need to admit that our approach is certainly different from Otto's, but on a higher level, we share with him the practice of intensive collaboration with biologists and scientists.

The fourth angle that emerges from this tapestry of tradition is of particular interest to me, that is to say, form-finding. This is a method that radically differs from everything that one is taught in classical design theory, as it questions the primacy of geometry. This has truly and profoundly shaped the thinking of students and researchers alike, especially in connection with the digital technologies now available to us. These are the four angles that, to my mind, indicate an evolution at all levels along which our work is closely related to his.

JK: Where I also see similarities is in the objects we build: there is always the requirement that, for one thing, they illuminate and demonstrate a scientifically interesting question, while at the same time, they have an architectonic, aesthetic quality as structures. The Multihalle in Mannheim, for example, even if you don't know the story behind it, is a fascinating structure, just like the roofs of the Olympic Park in Munich. Even if you don't know anything about the form-finding theories and construction developments behind them, their fascination as structures comes from the fact that here something was being tried for the first time. For that reason, they have a certain fresh, experimental quality about them. In our projects, the object, as such, is meant to have an aesthetic quality as well, but also to take a step forward in terms of material systems, construction systems, production processes.

saai: Form-finding, or the logic behind it, is once again being increasingly discussed in relation to new technologies. For Otto, technology was necessary for form-finding – its foundation, to a certain extent – and we have this today, as well, in the so-called digital realm, where there is frequently (at least rhetorically) a technological intention and justification for the form. There is also the question of aesthetics, and one also wants a form to be fascinating aesthetically. We already find that, too, in Otto, as he would not have persisted in his method if he hadn't also found the result beautiful. Precisely this combination of aesthetics or spatial quality and technological urgency or commitment is not always openly communicated as the motivating factor. How is that specifically dealt with in the collaboration between engineers and architects at your school in Stuttgart? How explicitly or implicitly is the form that develops or should develop part of the discussion?

AM: That's an interesting question, and I feel that there actually is a difference. The form-finding methods developed in the 1960s and 1970s, in part by Frei Otto, were concerned as a primary criterion with optimization and thus a best-case scenario. This is reflected in the lightest structure also implicitly being the most beautiful. Digital technologies make it possible to carry out the form-finding process using more criteria, which is now essential. In this way, there is no longer the idealistic or almost dogmatic approach to finding an ideal form. A much more open search has become possible. Owing to a certain notion of form and a tradition

Self-forming wood: Urbach Tower, Remstal Garden Show (2019; above) and the interior of the Wangen Tower, State Garden Show in Wangen im Allgäu (2024; below)

at that time this was impossible because of methodological limitations – at the same time, the form was, in reality, whatever was closer to nature. After all, you don't find in nature the idea that there's an optimal form.

The connection with Otto, however, is by no means only structural; rather, there is also an aesthetic interest, namely that the resulting form always be authentic. Something that does not correspond to any predefined formal idiom but rather develops its own. Discovery of these expressive forms is especially exciting. For our works, this is a journey we are only now undertaking. For the majority of projects realized over the past fifteen years, one can now establish a taxonomy.

JK: I would like to go back to this point about nature, for a moment. I discussed this with Frei Otto, and he thought it altogether absurd that anyone would translate structures from nature into technology. He also rejected the concept of biomimetics and didn't use it. Indeed, he always argued precisely the opposite: he felt that he was the one who could explain to biologists how their biological systems function mechanically. That is to say that he never felt that he had drawn inspiration from biology for his structures and works.

saai: Can we dig a little deeper into that? There are statements by Frei Otto according to which, for him, it was a *knowledge* of nature and not the *use* of nature that was most important. How would you characterize your position on bionics? This appears to be somewhat different from Otto's, after all.

AM: He always spoke of natural constructions, but what he meant was that they *develop* naturally and, with that, he also revealed a reference to – or explanations and insights for – the sciences engaged with animate nature, as Jan has said. And yes, we do that differently. For me, collaboration with biologists and participating in an actual contribution to biological knowledge has always given me a chance to think differently as a designer, in a systematic, scientifically rigorous way: you get to know new operating principles. Constructive principles having to do with the relationship between form, material, structure and environment, or learning processes that simply lie far beyond what we find in the tradition of our own field or in our discipline's traditional frame of reference. For us, biology has actually been a reservoir of such operational and educational principles that we carried over into construction engineering and whose architectural consequences we have investigated. I would like to say, however, that Otto also did so, in part, even though he perhaps didn't think it suited the narrative of his work and formulated it differently, probably also to set himself apart from other contemporary scholars – I think of figures like Werner Nachtigall, for example.

JK: As a structural engineer one has one's own perspective. We have to ensure the structure's integrity and verify it with structural analysis. That leads to the fact that one very quickly begins to think in typologies. One always employs the same structural systems, the same building materials, which are reliable and easy to calculate. By collaborating with biologists we get away from this narrow spectrum of typologies. One example is filament structures. In nature, the filament principle is ubiquitous, a way to achieve very finely graduated structural properties with minimal expenditure of material by way of the fibre orientation and density, in plants, for example, or the exoskeletons of insects. Fibrous structures are virtually unknown in construction engineering, however. Engagement with natural structures has inspired us to take a new look at filaments. We have developed robotic winding procedures for the fabrication of fibrous architectural building components that make a load-adjusted orientation of the filaments possible, as is the case in natural structures. The possible filament orientation is also limited by the requirements of its fabrication and is, for that reason, statically acceptable

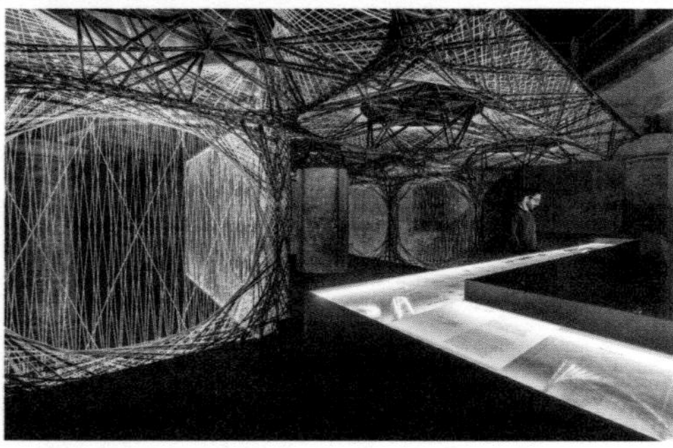

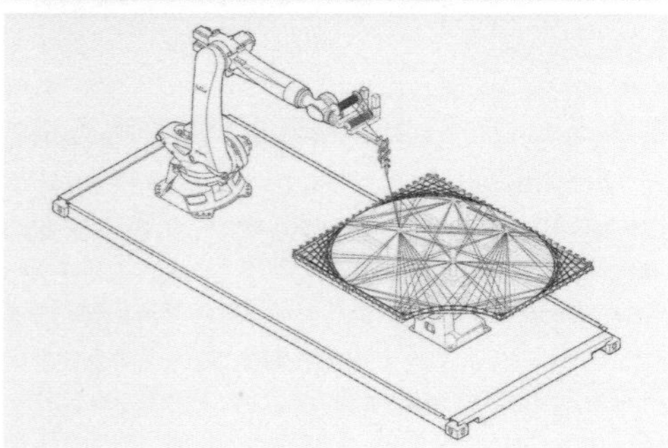

Fibrous architecture: Maison Fibre at the Venice Architecture Biennale (2021), interior of the pavilion and robotic fabrication

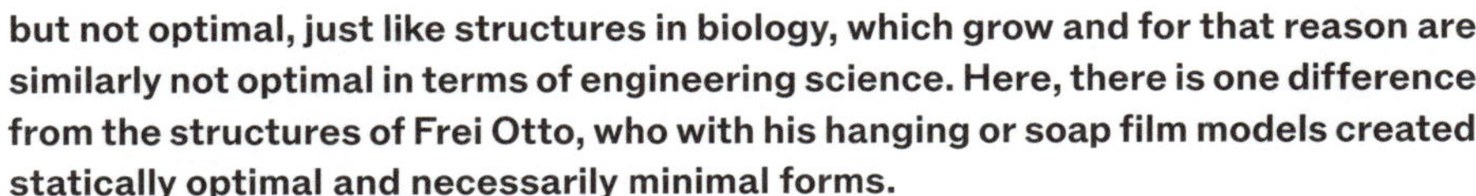

but not optimal, just like structures in biology, which grow and for that reason are similarly not optimal in terms of engineering science. Here, there is one difference from the structures of Frei Otto, who with his hanging or soap film models created statically optimal and necessarily minimal forms.

saai: That brings us to the question of disciplines. As part of a university reform in the late 1960s the Architecture Faculty in Stuttgart was broken up into disciplines more clearly than had been the case before. As an architect Otto had worked much like an engineer, and he was critical of this institutional splintering into various disciplines. Which is perhaps why he tried to do things differently in his own group. In an interview, Peter Hübner felt, altogether approvingly, that Otto's style of form-finding, invention and design through interdisciplinary collaboration benefited architects since – in what he called their arrogance and naivete – they believed they could uproot trees and move mountains. Today how do you view what is architectural, on the one hand, and what is interdisciplinary, on the other hand? Is there still a possibility or even the need to work in a non-disciplinary manner, in the sense that one does not even make these distinctions in the first place?

AM: The 'non-disciplinary' is an expression of architects' belief in their own omnipotence, of being able to do anything and everything. Working in an interdisciplinary way is the precise opposite of this. Since interdisciplinarity only works when each researcher contributes their specific disciplinary competence to an interdisciplinary project. That puts into question the usual hierarchy in architecture, according to

BUGA Fibre Pavilion, German National Garden Show in Heilbronn (2019) and its robotic fabrication

which architecture stands on a higher level and only delegates to specialist engineers or calls upon their consultation, as in consulting engineers. It also questions traditional, institutional barriers. My experience has been that the most exciting projects are those in which each discipline involved attains new insight for themself. If the whole is of interest solely to the designers, then the biologists very soon have no desire to participate further. In plenty of cases, interdisciplinarity fails to work for that very reason. Few researchers would be interested in only doing preliminary legwork or merely performing services. That is the opposite of what we adhere to as a scientific model. For us, it is a model for how we can think of ourselves not only as architects or structural engineers but also, quite generally, as builders of the next generation.

Because it is relatively difficult to implement within previous disciplinary frameworks and organizations, we have come up with a degree course open in terms of discipline that, as a pedagogical model, aims to convey precisely this new form of interdisciplinary collaboration as an important skill – with architecture-related approaches, I would say. To be sure, the course is based in the Architecture Faculty. This integrative and interdisciplinary approach is important, precisely because we see that the methods of our own disciplines have reached their limits or else have greatly taxed or, indeed, overtaxed the limits of the planet.

We are frequently asked what this collaboration with biology is all about, what the point ultimately is. Looking at it quite objectively, it is a fact that we can no longer continue to build the way we have. Thus, every other approach, every investigative step, every alternative path is worth taking, and is therefore justified. There cannot be 'more of the same'. To be sure, there was still a completely different world view four or five years ago than there is today. That we cannot continue as we have has now very definitely shifted into the focus of our discourse. For me, it is also a further justification for fundamental research.

JK: If we are to believe the stories of our older colleagues, Otto was never truly involved in teaching, neither among the architects nor among the engineers. He had his 'club' and a few disciples who possibly took an elective course with him. For us, things are altogether different, as we have a regularly scheduled interdisciplinary course of study. That is already one difference. The second is that in personal conversation with Frei Otto I came to understand that he placed very great value on being seen as an architect. He thought of himself as the person who finds forms – and therefore engineers, for example Ted Happold or Fritz Leonhardt are, to put it crudely, the ones responsible for seeing that it holds up, who say how thick the cable or how wide the lath has to be. Frei Otto never said, I am *everything*. He said, I am the architect who finds the form.

saai: It was this sense of himself that was responsible for much of the conflict over the roof of the Munich Olympic Stadium, for which he understood himself to have been the architect and not a contributing expert or engineer.

JK: It was my personal sense that he particularly resented the business around the roof structure in Munich up to the time of his death. As a young engineer, I attended his farewell lecture at the University of Stuttgart. As I remember, in it he expressed his disappointment that he had contributed many ideas that others in Munich failed to realize as he had wanted and then these ideas were used in subsequent stadium structures for their own economic benefit.

saai: He ultimately claimed that he wanted to understand the whole. He pursued this sense of the whole, from the microscopically small to the cosmically vast. That seems interesting also in view of your approaches, inasmuch as one understands the expansion of the field under Otto not in terms of the number of disciplines involved but rather in this sense of the expansion of scale in design. For you, too, it comes down to processing information out of very small concerns, things that in reality elude the usual focus of architecture. Is there also a methodological parallel here to Otto? Those considered visionaries are frequently associated only with the grand scale.

AM: At the time when Frei Otto was active, visionaries always had an eye on the entire planet. There are legendary stories about the hours-long conversations between Otto and Richard Buckminster Fuller. If a vision failed to have this planetary dimension, it also failed to have the relevance with which to pass as a grand vision. If you were to consider yourself part of the avant-garde of the time, as a visionary, aiming for the very grand was almost a necessity in the work of the 1960s and 1970s. Today, that is perhaps less broadly acceptable.

saai: Frei Otto explored a world that was not at all accessible to ordinary design because it lies beyond what we can perceive with the naked eye or capture with a pencil. But that is precisely where the connection to digital technologies lies.

AM: Here, I'd like to quote the words of Sanford Kwinter, who said that digital technology is not a tool, though it is often thought to be one. Instead, a technological achievement, like the microscope or the telescope, are what provide us with a completely different view of what was always there, though it had not been readily visible to us before. I find it very exciting that there are complex interrelationships or modes of behaviour that can only now, with digital methods, be detected, explored and thus included in one's designs. One example is our research into wooden structural elements that form themselves. It is not as if we have rediscovered wood or that wood is now different or behaves differently than it always has: it shrinks and swells depending on its moisture content. It is just that we can far better understand this specific behaviour thanks to digital technologies. With this information, the material's inherent form-changing process can become a part of form-finding on the architectural and engineering-scientific level. Integrating the interrelationship between the moisture content of the microfibril structures of wood cells and large-scale, self-formed wood building elements opens up new possibilities for design. That leads us to Otto's models. To be sure, not only can we find a suitable form, but we can also steer it using digital technologies. Thus a novel interplay is created between the physical and digital generation of forms.

saai: If we recall Reinhold Martin's theory that material is always a hybrid of nature and culture – and thus never simply only an economic or technical 'resource' – different forms necessarily arise depending on the concept of nature or material. If both concepts have changed historically, it no longer remains the same material – in this case the same wood. Then perhaps 'your' wood is not the same material in its cultural-historical context?

AM: Wood is only one small example, but it's interesting because it questions things that we know from our textbooks, like designing and planning wood construction supposedly appropriate to the material. That would never lead to what we're doing. Even so, the approach to self-forming wooden construction elements is derived directly from the material. It thus supersedes normative typological approaches that prescribe how certain things should be. With respect to material, for example, the Louis Kahn school of thought listens to a brick, and the only thing that brick can say is 'Build with me a preconceived typology.' By contrast, our approach attempts to view the material itself in a new way, to engage with it and develop something original – in true dialogue with the material and not merely questioning it rhetorically.

saai: With regard to the question of materiality, how do you see the role of neural networks in your processes? On the one hand, they allow us to understand certain things for the first time ever, as Achim just described, not necessarily only technologically. Also for example, with respect to aestheticization, they promote the development of a specific look that is then transformed back into the collective expectation held amidst architects: that is to say, the expected style in architecture generated by artificial intelligence (AI). How do you approach these questions? Do you programme, train or feed your own, self-learning AI? Do you worry about a so-called 'black box' development so that at some point you can no longer follow the decision-making and calculation processes of neural networks? Where do you see the boundary between increased cognitive faculties or simulation capabilities and the point at which you can no longer retrace anything?

Wooden shells: BUGA Wood Pavilion at the German National Garden Show in Heilbronn (2019; above) and the ICD/ITKE Research Pavilion at the University of Stuttgart (2015/16; below)

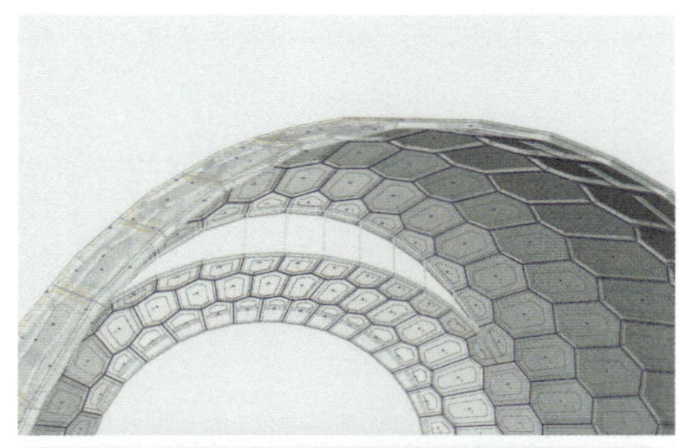

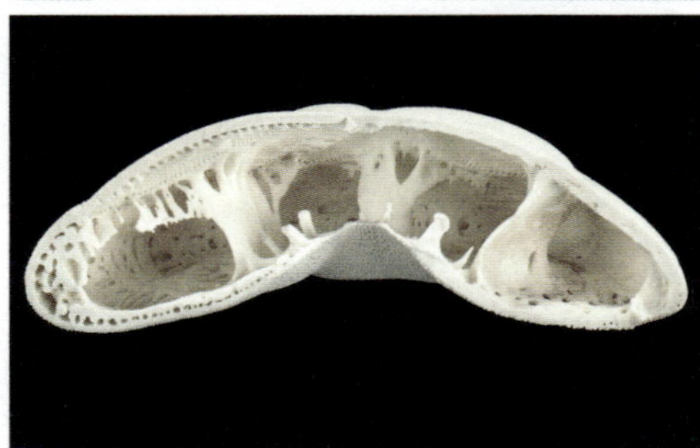

AM: Aside from AI image generators, with which the fascination will probably soon fade (after each AI summer ultimately comes an AI autumn), I feel that data-based approaches that then result in AI-driven methods are very, very promising. And that is not only for understanding the complex phenomena we are investigating but also for integrating those phenomena that elude classical analytical methods. This can definitely be a real stimulus in our field. If we come back to the example of self-forming wood, up to now we have determined that with analytical methods. We did not, however, develop these ourselves; they were developed by our cooperating partners at the ETH Zurich, and we then integrated them into our design methods. We thus began with these classical analytical methods that require a huge amount of input parameters and then provide a very precise result. But truly, one can better capture material behaviour, which is a bit different each time because every piece of wood is a little different, by way of data-based approaches. We're now beginning to use AI methods for this, which is very, very exciting, as it can be incorporated into the design process much more readily. I also don't believe that fundamentally there is a scenario of data-driven versus analytical methods. The former is more something that can play a role in the exploratory design process, whereas one still needs very precise analytical methods when it's a matter of verifying a design reliably. To that extent, I feel that AI has great value in the exploratory step, while the analytical step remains necessary, at least when you want to build something in reality within current institutional and legal frameworks.

Altogether I see artificial intelligence as a genuine asset. We currently find ourselves in a very exciting moment, one in which we first have to discover when these methods lead to a true increase in knowledge and when they are really only the continuation or amplification of what was already there. The way they're employed in the creative process at the moment is more the latter. Most basically, we need to develop 'grey box' models, which let designers take part in the process. And we need to consider and dispel the corresponding tendentious assumptions and biases. But, of course, that is the case with many methods, not only AI.

JK: Artificial intelligence can offer an important contribution in the shift towards bio-based building materials. One of the main reasons for the near ubiquitous use of concrete and steel is due in large part to the fact that we can easily and reliably predict and calculate their material behaviour. Once we make the switch to renewable, bio-based materials, we face a much greater variability, including many defects. It does not matter whether it is natural stone, wood or biofibres, there are variances in their mechanical qualities of several hundred percent.

In such a process, AI could provide a meaningful contribution, as a first step, if the mechanical qualities were narrowed down using digital images and their comparison with material tests were stored in databases. There is an exciting trajectory at this junction between artificial intelligence and biogenic materials, where we can try to tame the natural variability and heterogeneity of the material a little in order to make it tangible, understandable and usable from an engineering point of view. As a second step, we could give these materials their own voice in the design process. We will get there only with design methods that can precisely integrate this variability and heterogeneity. But that is the long-term vision by which we can use AI to discard the ballast that industrialization, with its norming, standardization and homogeneity, has brought along with it. I've not yet seen any convincing attempts to use AI in the development of support structures and load-bearing systems themselves. But that will also come, sooner or later.

saai: Speaking of heterogeneity and adaptation, Frei Otto interpreted adaptability and growth not only as formal analogies from or to nature, but also as direct reactions to vital processes. For example, the adaptable house or city responds to social activities and processes within

livMatS Biomimetic Shell, Freiburg (2023), construction drawing

Sand dollar, a biological model for the form of the segmented timber shells

society. In your work, is there a level at which comparable social implications are found?

AM: I would place this facet of Frei Otto's work in the 1960s and 1970s, at a time when it was still altogether possible to offer such analogies and, indeed, to criticize the prevailing architecture. There's a social component in every facet of our work, as well, but it turns out to be more modest than in the world of the grand visionaries. Today it is still difficult to maintain that a house can grow with society the way a tree grows in nature.

But it is really very important to say that the methods we have developed or even the architecture – the material and construction systems – produced with them, as well as the fabrication and construction processes, are never conceived as a form of technology-reliant automatization or even as differentiation from the relevant social dimensions and human processes, but are rather conceived as a new step forward. If I look at the design methods that we have developed, they permit a new form of interaction between humans and machines. They no longer strive for the deterministic best case provided by the machine, though oddly enough, it is still frequently read that way. Instead, it's an open process of negotiation that you can engage in only because you have a digital co-pilot, which helps to find a solution, but not just by itself. I feel that these negotiation processes are profoundly social. They take place just as much in the production process as in the conceptualization of the material and structural systems – and ultimately in the way these building structures can reorient the relationship between architecture and society. That is less obviously social than was the case of the visions expressed in Frei Otto's day. But, in any case, it is a genuine interest for both of us.

JK: It is very important to us to show that computer-based planning or digital production does not lead to either repetitive panel system buildings like those of the 1960s or 1970s or else some high gloss façade as found today in the Middle East or in China. We can contribute to a diverse and attractive built environment. That is a very important aspect and includes the social component. We are often accused of being robot fetishists (or as Gerd de Bruyn formulated it, 'techno-fascists' – though he said it with a wry smile). In the end, it's a matter of quality, of a built environment worth living in.

saai: The social question is part and parcel of the aesthetic openness. Frei Otto was obviously very open, as one sees from the eco-houses [*Ökohäuser*] in Berlin of the 1980s, for example, which turned out to be anything but elegant. He accepted the fact that in the course of a do-it-yourself approach and transformation process the result may be very far from the elegant forms he otherwise sought. Is such openness, even the acceptance of a non-elegant state conceivable for you?

AM: Absolutely, elegance is never a precondition. There are many aspects we research in which the results are completely open, so there's never been a desire for a pre-defined or even 'slick' aesthetic. If you look at our structures first-hand, you immediately see that we have taken new paths on a material level, and the materials and spaces reflect that. The aesthetics are thus not the predefined goal but rather the consequence of our exploratory process.

It is also very important that we include socio-cultural and socio-economic aspects in our projects, as we do in our teaching and research. We feel that the seeming opposition between culture and ecology, and therefore cultural and ecological concerns, is outdated. Socio-cultural aspects are always (for us, but otherwise probably for a long time) intrinsically intertwined with socio-economic and ecological aspects. That is an extremely exciting process of negotiation that the younger generation no longer thinks of as a conflict. Our research can contribute to this discourse.

saai: Otto remarked that he was glad not to have belonged to the first, traditionalist Stuttgart School because he would not have been able to free himself from it formally or officially. He later criticized the way in which the school was split up into disciplines in the 1960s. How do you stand on the various positions in the historical development of the Stuttgart School given the fact that with your teaching and research you yourselves have created a sphere of influence?

AM: What is special about the University of Stuttgart is that it definitely provides a very pluralistic field that accords equal value to diverse tendencies. One important thing that sets us apart from other architecture faculties is that here dissertations and theses may be written across all disciplines with every different orientation or emphasis. That is by no means a given, and at most institutions it is still impossible or only permitted with substantial hurdles. To me, precisely this coexistence of the most varied approaches is one of the notable features of the current Stuttgart School, beyond lightweight construction. This is more of a kind of implicit branding. The variety is a defining characteristic. It even goes beyond the individual faculties. It is an experiential form of the overriding interdisciplinary collaboration.

JK: I am a classical teacher of structural engineering, to be sure, and from some of my colleagues at other universities, I see how they live an isolated, wallflower existence. That has never been the case here. Not from day one. There has always been dialogue on an equal footing between every discipline. From the beginning, I have worked on degree dissertations and design projects. This has not only been tolerated but expressly encouraged. Such cooperation within the faculty and across the departments is truly something that defines Stuttgart. For me, that is the Stuttgart School. The culture of cooperation makes Stuttgart something special – and that has always had something to do with the individuals. The older ones influence those to come.

saai: Do you have the impression that the way research funding works in Germany today inhibits or hinders such cooperation? Such funding tends to promote prioritization, as you do in Stuttgart, after all, which then reinforces itself.

JK: Just now I am on the Grants Committee for Collaborative Research Centres (SFB/CRC) of the German Research Foundation (DFG). It is clear to see that interdisciplinary, exploratory and discursively oriented projects have a harder time in this system. But not because they aren't desirable. Rather, it is because projects that are narrower in scope, for which clear criteria can be applied in their formal assessment, are easier to evaluate. In the end, you have fifty applications, all of which are very good, but for financial reasons, you can support only twenty-five of them – in such a highly competitive situation in which projects from the most varied academic disciplines are in direct competition with each other, interdisciplinary projects frequently draw the short straw. That pains me to my very core.

AM: Even so, it is one of Germany's truly great achievements that we still have a relatively independent, hundred percent publicly supported system for research funding. You can complain that only one percent of the DFG's budget goes to architecture, but it's also true that the DFG distributes its grant monies according to the number of applications submitted. That means that where there's considerable interest, there's also considerable support. And where there's little interest, there's little support. To this day, I fail to understand why our disciplines in particular were able to operate at universities for fifty years forgotten by research, or perhaps even elevated above research, although to my thinking tremendous insights – including personal ones for every individual – could have been achieved through research activity. It is also a question of a culture of participation. Every architect considers it a matter of course that he or she sit on competition juries. But when it's a matter of serving on an expert committee of the DFG, instead of helping to shape the realm of research, most say that's not something for me. Yet, it's a privilege to be able and to be permitted to conduct research. But with the generational change across universities, we will see that the problems facing the next generation of architects will require different mechanisms, different approaches, and there will eventually also be greater enthusiasm for research.

saai: One last question: Many students from abroad apply for scholarships in order to join you in Stuttgart. This international visibility could have to do with your question of what research in architecture can be today. Is that something that sets you apart on the world stage? How do you both explain why your emphases and approaches have made you an international magnet?

AM: The school's tradition may sound like a localized phenomenon, but it isn't. Perhaps it would be just as interesting for you to ask why we are not more attractive in Germany, because conversely it is unfortunately the case that we don't get a large number of applications from German students. I think that has something to do with the differences in the structures of educational systems abroad, some of which are much more open than ours. Interestingly, we have a great many applications from English-speaking countries, which previously never gave a thought to look towards Germany. I feel that our approach, engaging with students in truly open-ended research is an attraction, that students from abroad are interested in being part of this exploratory process. Yet, this is precisely what makes us less interesting to many students here in Germany. They already have a clearer notion of what they want to specialize in because they have already been institutionally shunted into one discipline or other by the time they start a master's course. For us, in any case, the influx from abroad is welcome; being able to work with select, highly involved, motivated students is nothing short of a real privilege, because it is self-accelerating phenomenon: if you have super engaged, super motivated students, you naturally have outstanding results that then attract still more motivated students.

One final word regarding the critical appraisal of Frei Otto: I am delighted to see that there will be a new book about him, as he continues to be a great inspiration and his work, perhaps precisely because of its variety and incongruity, is absolutely fascinating. First as a student and then also as a teacher, I had the privilege of hearing him in person at the Architectural Association in London, where his works were far better known than they had been in Germany when I was still studying. Frei Otto had so many trailblazing ideas and game-changing approaches that are now relevant more than ever. Only one example: a gridshell made of wood is an extremely good load-bearing structure and incredibly resource-efficient. Nonetheless, only a handful were built. Sadly, this also shows that the quality of a concept is not necessarily directly proportional to its later success in building practice – which also says a great deal about the conservative forces in the building sector. Even Frei Otto did not escape unscathed. At his eighty-fifth birthday celebration at the University of Stuttgart, I was altogether amazed to discover how a man who, to my youthful perception, had accomplished so much could be so openly disillusioned at the end of his life.

JK: It was really rather tragic, as he was truly disappointed. When I was still a relatively young professor, I invited Otto to lecture and naively booked the small auditorium. Never in my life have I seen such a packed auditorium – and I certainly never will again. He was so touched that the next generation of university colleagues would come to hear him that he had tears in his eyes. Really, he had fallen out in one way or another with many people, although he was such a friendly person. But, somehow, he did not see or appreciate much outside his own work. I hope that won't be the case with us.

saai: Many thanks for speaking with us.

This conversation took place on 30 May 2024 and was conducted for saai by Joaquín Medina Warmburg and Anna-Maria Meister.

Jan Knippers (born in 1962) is Professor at the University of Stuttgart, where he heads the Institute of Building Structures and Structural Design (Institut für Tragkonstruktionen und Konstruktives Entwerfen, ITKE). Among his main interests as a structural engineer are adaptable architecture, bionics, new materials and efficient load-bearing structures in the realm of construction. Between 2014 and 2019, Knippers was the Speaker for the Collaborative Research Centre of the German Research Foundation (DFG) TRR 141 'Biological Design and Integrative Structures' at the Universities of Stuttgart, Tübingen and Freiburg. Since 2019, he is the Deputy Speaker for the German Research Foundation's Cluster of Excellence 2120 'Integrative Computational Design and Construction for Architecture' (IntCDC). He directs the firm Jan Knippers Ingenieure in Stuttgart.

Achim Menges (born in 1975) studied architecture in Darmstadt and London. At the University of Stuttgart he directs the Institute for Computational Design and Construction (ICD), where biomimetic approaches are pursued in teaching and research. He became known internationally through his practical investigation of performative material and building systems in full-scale prototypes and experimental structures developed in collaboration with Jan Knippers. Menges is the Speaker for the Cluster of Excellence 2120 'Integrative Computational Design and Construction for Architecture' (IntCDC).

Together, Jan Knippers and Achim Menges are co-directors of the international, interdisciplinary research-oriented master's programme ITECH – Integrative Technologies and Architectural Design Research at the University of Stuttgart

Further Reading

Jan Knippers, Ulrich Schmid and Thomas Speck (eds), *Biomimetics for Architecture: Learning from Nature*, Basel 2019.

Achim Menges and Jan Knippers, *Architecture, Research, Building: ICD/ITKE 2010/20*, Basel 2021.

Growing Architecture

A Conversation with Ferdinand Ludwig FL

saai: You have contributed extensively to the development of Baubotanik – living architecture – both practically and theoretically, devoting your doctoral work at the University of Stuttgart to the innovative concept. In the milieu of Frei Otto, as well, figures such as Wolf Hilbertz and Rudolf Doernach have conducted research in the area of architecture consisting of or utilizing living organisms. What exactly does this involve?

FL: We define Baubotanik as architecture composed with and composed of living trees, in which the tree forms an integral component of the architectural structure. The tree may contribute by carrying loads, by acting as a stiffener, by shaping spaces or else by influencing the microclimate or the ecological equilibrium. For this, we tend to use the term 'environmental design' [*Umweltgestaltung*] rather than architecture, since we do not design buildings in the conventional sense. Baubotanik takes up many things that are actually quite old – the tradition of so-called *Tanzlinden* in Germany [literally 'dance linden', linden trees with platforms in their branches used by villagers for dancing during local festivities], living bridges in India – always however in order to respond to contemporary problems and current needs. When I began my studies in Stuttgart in 2000, Frei Otto had already left the university. At the same time, broader reflections on his work had not yet really begun. At that time, our studies essentially bypassed Frei Otto's contribution. These ideas were, however, discussed regularly, for example in the 1987 issue of *Daidalos* entitled 'Baum und Architektur' [Tree and Architecture],[1] which I encountered as a young architecture student, and through which I became aware of Arthur Wiechula's work with growing houses made of living trees.[2] That must have been around 2001 or 2002, or thereabouts. That gave rise to many things.

saai: With regard to form-finding, are Frei Otto's approaches at odds with Baubotanik, as you understand it? And how does all of this look in non-European contexts?

FL: Indeed, a number of approaches, including the guiding and the shaping and fixing of natural forms, would seem to contradict Frei Otto's ideas about form-finding. In our book, *Growing Architecture*,[3] we discuss two historical tendencies. The first is, in fact, exemplified by the *Tanzlinde*, which functions in formal and spatial terms. Here, it is a question of the geometrical reshaping of nature by humans, also of the projection onto nature of a kind of divine geometry, for example through the symbolism of the twelve branches. This involved the marked modification or even reinterpretation of growth patterns, an attempt to attain an ideal form desired by God. Also spoken of in this connection was a 'beautification of the tree' through the introduction of stringently horizontal branches and branches

that grew radially outward, branches which came as close as possible to an ideal form. Such a perfected geometry contradicts Frei Otto's natural-physical solutions that optimize the distribution of forces. His approach is, however, detectable in the second historical tendency, the one we are invoking with the term Baubotanik, namely the living root bridges of the Khasi people of India, which were completely unknown in Germany until around fifteen years ago. These follow an almost functionalist approach – organic architecture in the sense of a useful form generated through the guiding and knotting of the aerial roots of rubber trees: here, it's a question of crossing the river and getting from point A to point B, and the tree serves as a co-actor that makes this possible. In this case, there are absolutely no blueprints defining the form, not a single drawing. It's purely a question of performance: How do we guide the forces, how do we create a pathway? This results in structures that correspond very closely to Frei Otto's principle of the transfer of forces, coupled with the physiological requirements of the tree.

saai: Are such approaches free from preconceived aesthetic ideas?

FL: The will to shape forms is already inherent. With regard to the living bridges we investigated, they have been viewed in a way that is too black and white. We catalogued the bridges, generating 3D models of a few of them with the help of photogrammetry and conducted numerous interviews with village elders, who are often responsible for the bridges. Based on these findings, we developed a planning approach that updates the process of negotiation with the tree, translating it into a digitally guided design process. We utilized this approach for the first time with the Arbor Kitchen project. Thirty-two plane trees were planted to form an elliptical layout and then shaped, first to form a diagonal wall structure, and then the main branches were guided towards the centre to create an imagined roof ridge. After ten years of growth, we 3D scanned the resulting structure and gave them to our students, who used a parametric process to design a roof for the structure. The growth process was used, in the process, as the primary principle of formal development: the shape of the roof follows the now further developed growth of the tree – which was never truly 'natural', having been co-designed by humans. In our modern world of technological construction, the complex geometry of the roof could only be designed and built using digital tools, while the Khasi construct their bridges intuitively, based on traditional knowledge and practices, something that is possible only because they themselves are so closely bound up with the ecosystem in which they live.

saai: Also of relevance in this context, it would seem, is Frei Otto's intense interest in growing structures in connection with the social principle of adaptability. Does a comparable concept of participation play a role in your work as well?

FL: We are intensely preoccupied with this issue. We are, however, faced with the problem that we still have no occupants. Of course, other people are involved in our projects, and we have come to realize that the projects only develop well in the long run when there are 'troubleshooters', which is to say, an individual who takes up the project personally and informs us when something goes awry, when something dies and so forth. It has also been our experience that, in some instances, the need for consistency and the necessity for expert knowledge, which means the professional care of tree growth, is sometimes difficult to reconcile with participation as it's currently conceived. Implementing participation for raised beds is straightforward enough: if the plants aren't watered for a year and they die off, you can simply plant something new next year. But when a tree is cut incorrectly once, or doesn't receive water, or is fertilized incorrectly, it's ruined. Here, you need to find a different form of user interaction. Certainly, the timeline of most participatory projects is much shorter, is clocked a lot faster,

Ferdinand Ludwig, Oliver Storz and Cornelius Hackenbracht, Baubotanik Footbridge in Wald-Ruhestetten on Lake Constance (2005)

Living root bridge of the Khasi in Wah Thyllong, India

than the growth of a tree. In our fast-paced times, it's far from easy to establish long-term interaction.

saai: The factor of 'time as a building material' plays a substantial role as well in the long range and comparatively slow processes of adaptation and transformation of urban structures. How do the approaches of Baubotanik relate to the morphological processes and structures of the city?

FL: We have developed three different approaches to designing with time. The first is a purely gardening approach, which involves planting a sapling and developing it into a specific structure over a period of decades through horticultural manipulation. The second is a constructive approach, where I purchase the tree as living building material in a certain dimension, which is to say, I pay a tree nursery for the necessary time. To this end, we just concluded a research project involving tree façades, in which we planted a minimalist Baubotanik. With trees very close to the façade of a social housing project that already had heights of 8 to 9 metres from the start. The third approach to incorporating time, which we call plant addition, involves the formation of a structure that incorporates young trees, which are allowed to grow into one another. Emerging in the course of time is a kind of collective organism. The green volume of the mature tree, however, is present from day one. That sums up the various parameters with which we play. And depending upon which category, which strategy is used, you of course have a very different kind of impact on the development of a city or an architectural project. It is then a question of exploring a fruitful relationship between tree growth and urban growth, between slow and rapid – whereby, from the perspective of Baubotanik, the city often grows more quickly than the trees.

saai: You can plant a tree, but not a forest: before a large number of trees can become a 'forest', numerous additional participants are necessary, from microbiota to animals to fungi. Actually, things are no different with a city. Here, as well, there are a multitude of participants (whether or not they possess 'agency') that transform a multiplicity of buildings into a complex system, a 'city'. The city cannot simply be 'built'. Do you have the sense that a growing awareness of the role of the microbiome, for example, has been helpful in the reception of your approaches? I mean a recognition that the ground is not simply a homogenous mass of soil, that the forest is more than an accumulation of trees, the city perhaps more than a large number of buildings?

FL: There is increasingly more discussion today about the question of whether the 'soil' in its totality is perhaps also a life form, which you can't simply transport here or there like building material, but that instead relocating the soil amounts to a kind of transplantation since it's part of a larger system. This growth of systems thinking helps us in our planning as well, where thinking in terms of other cycles and forms of dependency is very important. But, at the same time, we continually shift between systemic, 'posthuman' and functionalist-anthropocentric ways of thinking. In the end, it's always an act of compromise. In many cases, for example, we plant trees primarily to provide shade, hence as an 'ecosystem service' for people, and only then do we consider which type of tree to choose, for example one that provides sustenance for birds or insects – but if a given tree species triggers allergies in people, then we would just as soon find an alternative.

saai: What impact do these acts of planting and these amenities have on the relationship between public and private spaces in the city?

FL: Oftentimes, older trees that play a structural role in the city are found in open public spaces and are, therefore, decoupled from architecture. And it is this

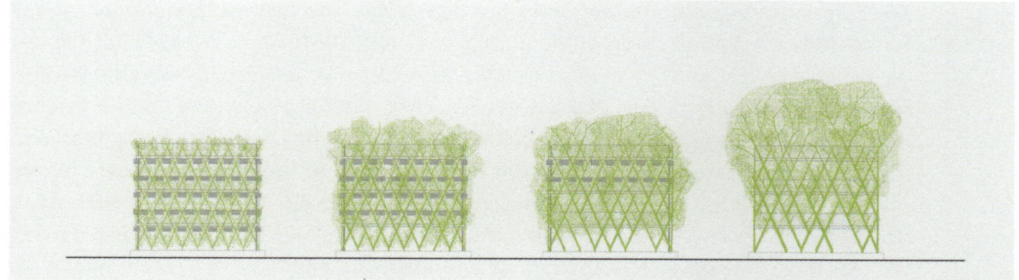

permanent green structure of the city that is preserved even when the architecture has been replaced three times. When we conceive of buildings and trees in an integrated way, something new happens: the tree becomes interwoven with the built city and its temporality. Imagine the interior of a building being replaced, while the living shell remains in place. Or the building disappearing to make way for a green open space. In either case, new constellations emerge. What happens if we conceive black figure-ground planning diagrams and green planning diagrams together rather than alongside one another? Here, we are still in the early stages. Our contribution to the House of the Future in Berlin was conceived in exactly this way, but the jury decided it was not really a building and therefore couldn't possibly win.

saai: Frei Otto conceptualized the triad nature–human–technology. After fifty years, these three points of the triangle, both the concept of nature as well as that of the human subject and of technology, have been reconceived. At least they have lost their unambiguous meaning and stability. Is it still possible or desirable today to engage in research and practice within this triangle, or do we need a completely different frame of reference?

FL: In relation to this triangle, we try to perceive humanity as a part of nature and not in opposition to it. Approaches such as regenerative design, where we situate our work, presuppose a co-evolution between ecosystem and humanity.

Office for Living Architecture (OLA), Plane Tree Cube in Nagold (2012), developmental stages (above) and the potential state of the interior 20–30 years after planting (below)

We can no longer situate humanity outside of the ecosystem. We simply regard humanity as a species with cultural baggage. But we have to realize that we are an integral component of a world that we have altered so dramatically that we can hardly speak any longer of Nature per se. That has long been the case – in landscape architecture, it's regarded as common sense. At times, however, it seems incredible that pristine, unspoiled nature might no longer exist. Where can we find it? If we search for it in the Amazon, we soon realize it's actually a manmade or 'cultural' forest, as the research has shown.[4] Seen from this angle, the only way we can have Nature is to conceive of humanity as a part of it. Which means, in other words, that one axis of the triangle has dwindled away. For those of us who work in the field of Baubotanik, living architecture is a part of nature. We also work in the direction of multispecies design, designing for nonhuman lifeforms. This means incorporating not just human beings, but also that which is otherwise designated as nature in this triangular relationship. We speak of 'co-designing' together with the tree – in the recognition that no one has asked the tree whether it wants to participate or not.

saai: In a very similar way, Frei Otto spoke often in later publications and interviews about designing for and with nature – or of humanity as a part of nature, and of designing for other species, something that was conceptualized in the 1970s as an eco-utopia. How is the relationship between subject and object, nature and technology interpreted in Baubotanik?

FL: Here, I'd like to begin by calling attention to the research project ECOLOPES – ECOlogical building enveLOPES – in which I am a participant.[5] The idea is to design the building shells for plants, animals, microbiota and people on an equal footing. That is an exciting concept, in which we are investing a great deal of technological research. On the conceptual level, however, caution is advised, since when we more closely examine many of the concepts used here, we find that they have been conceived from the outset in an anthropocentric way. This is especially obvious with ecosystem services: where it's a question of providing services, the human being is necessarily the service provider or receiver, which is conceptually anthropocentric. The same is true for the concept of nature-based solutions; the question arises: What or who is the intended beneficiary of the solution, if not conceived by and for humans? We need to escape from these contradictory terms, which at least pretend to be open, to be multispecies or posthuman. Strictly speaking, often, there is nothing posthuman about these ideas: clearly, they continue to harbour a completely human-centred functionalism.

saai: The comprehensive demands of technological approaches that are shaped by natural processes, like those of Frei Otto or Buckminster Fuller, involve the problem of the large scale. In contrast to Fuller's global concepts of a universal form, Otto spoke of a 'multiform', whereby, in the interaction with nature, each solution is different from the next. What is the largest scale on which your group has operated? Or is there a medium scale at which you feel that action is most possible?

FL: In reality, our activities are relatively local and small-scale. In the context of our research projects, however, we are involved on a larger scale. In our department, for example, we have created architectural models of the living bridges of the Khasi. To begin with, these are object-orientated representations on scales ranging between 1:10 and 1:50. Through our research, at the same time, we seek to contribute to the preservation of the culture responsible for this living architecture, which is acutely difficult as its existence is dependent to an extreme degree on developments occurring on far larger scales, such as deforestation, changes in land-use, population growth and global climate change. At the same time, our research projects zoom far into plant life, collaborating with partners from the field of botany to investigate structures and processes on a cellular level, which are for example, important in trying to understand the intertwining of branches, trunks and roots. It's not always easy to comprehend or correctly interpret such multiscale contexts. In my view, one of Frei Otto's great strengths was his feel for the right order of scale. With him, the decimal point was always right, so to speak – whether it was a question of the internal pressure of a cell, the statics of a roof or of a global phenomenon. This allowed him, if you will, to correctly calibrate statements by his interdisciplinary research partners. In my teaching, a priority is also to convey this approach. By attempting, for example, to visualize the statistic of some eight billion people, you place the entire world population in a metric grid; in this way, if everyone could hold hands, the entire world population would fit inside of a square measuring 90 × 90 kilometres, which is to say a square that reaches from Munich to Augsburg. That doesn't seem very large. But as soon as you calculate the agricultural surface necessary to sustain all these people, you exceed the imagination of most...

saai: For Otto's holistic approach, quantifiability was an important demand, mediating between technical efficiency and natural-scientific principles. He claimed that building would become as important for biology as biology would be for building. In this context, he invoked the structures constructed by animals or natural processes of growth. Comparatively seldom, however, did he problematize the natural characteristics of building materials, the way, for example, mycelium bricks are being investigated and tested currently.

FL: When Frei Otto spoke of natural constructions, I believe he was referring less to biology than to the physics of nature, strictly speaking. For him, a soap film was a natural form in the sense of physics. His collaborations with biologists were mainly concerned with structural and formal analogies that were translated in a highly intelligent way to architectural structures, and which broke down the physical principles behind them. You can criticize that approach while, nevertheless, recognizing its enormous importance, since physics applies to everything. Through such analogies, you can arrive at new architectural structures, forms and functions, even new production processes. At the IL, however, there was an intensive preoccupation with actually 'living' architecture taking place for an extended period of time. And during the period when Werner Sobek still headed the IL/ILEK, there was a folder of slides with images of *Tanzlinden*, presumably assembled by Rainer Graefe.[6] In all likelihood, Graefe conducted his historical research independently as part of the collaborative research centre in which he participated.

Ferdinand Ludwig, Wilfrid Middelton, Qiguan Shu, Cornelius Hackenbracht and project team, Arbor Kitchen (outdoor kitchen) in Wald-Ruhestetten (planted in 2012, roofing up to 2022)

Office for Living Architecture (OLA), Plane Tree Cube in Nagold (2012), detail of one growth point (2021) and the exterior view (2019)

You can't assume that Frei Otto's core interests encompassed everything. As I mentioned, I feel his primary interest was in the physics of nature and *not* in the biology of nature. That is also evident in his examination of biological cells. He was not concerned, for example, with DNA as a biological code, but instead, he investigated the subdivision of the cell as a 'pneumatic' bisection. This approach is very consistent with a biomimetic approach such as the one Frei Otto pursued, in principal. However, when it is a question of the direct use of life processes, an examination of biology, for example with regard to metabolic processes, is required. In Baubotanik, this means primarily photosynthesis. And since we know how inefficient photosynthesis is – only approximately three percent of annual sunlight is stored in a tree as wood – we speak in Baubotanik of the biological limits of growth. This determines how much wood biomass can accrue each year and how much can survive on a given surface area. This mass is astonishingly minimal – it's estimated to be around 0.045 cubic metres per square metre of surface area. And this brings us back, full circle, to Frei Otto, who designed the Multihalle in Mannheim with Carlfried Mutschler in 1974, which uses approximately this quantity of wood mass. The paradox here is not just that the inefficiency of photosynthesis necessitates that trees use the arduously generated biomass in a highly efficient way, it also necessitates that the principles of lightweight construction be followed in the field of Baubotanik. Here, we find a complicated situation in which, once again, decimal places and scale play a role – which, in turn, points at the way Frei Otto brought together conceptual work and quantification.

saai: One gets the impression that in such a contentious field, we need to liberate ourselves more fully from universal answers. Instead, it seems that multiple solutions for subsegments on various scales make more sense in order to produce a more heterogeneous set of answers.

FL: It's an extremely difficult balancing act. We need a plurality of approaches to finding solutions. And these must be able to sort themselves into the big picture containing a wide range of options. You mustn't believe you'll be capable of solving every problem by using your own little approach. Instead, you need to have enough self-confidence and humility to pursue your own approach while recognizing that it's only one of 500,000 contributions that are moving in the right direction. We can only arrive at a solution if the other 499,999 continue their work as well. In my view, that's where the difficulty lies.

saai: At the start of our conversation, you framed Baubotanik within an overarching field of environmental design. As early as fifty years ago, this concept showed great promise in the context of interdisciplinary problem-solving. How do the various disciplines come together in your projects?

FL: During my studies, I barely came into contact with the disciplines around landscape architecture, which I represent today in my research and teaching. For decades, landscape architecture had to satisfy itself with a niche function: with the ancillary design of surrounding spaces that had to be dealt with after an architectural project reached completion. Only in the last twenty years did the idea really gain momentum in Germany (though earlier elsewhere, in the Netherlands, for example) according to which landscape planning had to precede urban planning. There is enough literature on how urban planning develops from the spatial features of the landscape, its bodies of water, topography and so forth, and not causally from a grid conceived by humans. If we begin to conceive of cities in this way, and then derive the architecture on that basis, the approaches advocated by Frei Otto will again become relevant. They correspond to this way of thinking. All too often, you find yourself added to a project almost as an afterthought: the building is finished, and it now requires some landscaping, something green or a few trees. Which doesn't really work. Each green element, each tree has its own needs, roots and so forth. At the same time, it alters the façade, through the growth of moss or else through the incidence of light. Planning needs to be carried out in an integrated way, with regard to the hydrologic balance as well. Otherwise, ultimately, you will need additional resources for watering or fertilization, for example.

saai: In relation to Baubotanik, how does such an integration of knowledge take place in concrete terms?

FL: Quite often, we work together with botanists or with plant biomechanics, as well as currently with ecologists, but also structural engineers. Working as professors in our department are landscape ecologists, structural engineers, architects, landscape architects, all the way to computer scientists. We are very interdisciplinary in our orientation and try to really live that. When it comes to building on existing structures, for example, this means that beyond a collaboration between architects and engineers with regard to the supporting structure and the building technology, we also take into account ecology and water infrastructure, even involving soil specialists and soil researchers. This basic idea of sitting around the table together from the earliest stages is definitely a legacy of Frei Otto.

This conversation took place in Munich on 16 April 2024 and was conducted for saai by Joaquín Medina Warmburg and Anna-Maria Meister.

Ferdinand Ludwig (born in 1980) holds the chair for Green Technologies in Landscape Architecture at the Technical University of Munich (TU Munich). He studied architecture at the University of Stuttgart, where he earned a doctorate in the field of Baubotanik, a fundamental approach to engineering with living plants. Together with Daniel Schönle and Jakob Rauscher, he leads the Office for Living Architecture (OLA) in Stuttgart.

Further Reading

Ferdinand Ludwig, *Botanische Grundlagen der Baubotanik und deren Anwendung im Entwurf*, doctoral thesis, Universität Stuttgart 2012.

Ferdinand Ludwig and Daniel Schönle, *Growing Architecture: How to Design and Build with Trees*, Basel 2023.

1 See 'Baum und Architektur' in: *Daidalos*, no. 23, 1987.

2 Arthur Wiechula, *Wachsende Häuser aus lebenden Bäumen entstehend*, Berlin 1926, reprinted Cottbus 1995; Arthur Wiechula, *Lebende Holzhäuser unter Mitwirkung der Natur*, Leipzig 1927, reprinted Cottbus 1995.

3 Ferdinand Ludwig and Daniel Schönle, *Wachsende Architektur. Einführung in die Baubotanik*, Basel 2023, published in English as *Growing Architecture: How to Design and Build with Trees*, Basel 2023.

4 See Charles R. Clement et al., 'The Domestication of Amazonia Before European Conquest', in: *Proceedings of the Royal Society B: Biological Sciences*, 282/1812, 7 August 2015, doi.org/10.1098/rspb.2015.0813.

5 See Wolfgang Weisser et al., 'Creating Ecologically Sound Buildings by Integrating Ecology, Architecture and Computational Design', in: *People and Nature*, 5/1, 2023, pp. 4–20.

6 The Institute for Lightweight Structures (Institut für leichte Flächentragwerke, IL) at the University of Stuttgart was founded by Frei Otto in 1964, and he continued to chair in until 1991. The structural engineer Werner Sobek was appointed head of the IL in 2001 which he expanded to become the Institute for Lightweight Structures and Conceptual Design (Institut für Leichtbau Entwerfen und Konstruieren, ILEK). As a research associate at the IL, Rainer Graefe took part in the two DFG collaborative research centers SFB/CRC 64 'Weitgespannte Flächentragwerke' (Widespan Surface Structures; 1971–1985) and SFB/CRC 230 'Natürliche Konstruktionen – Leichtbau in Architektur und Natur' (Natural Structures – Lightweight Construction in Architecture and Nature; 1984–1995), where he led the subproject 'Geschichte des Konstruierens' (History of Structural Design). See Rainer Graefe, *Bauten aus lebenden Bäumen. Geleitete Tanz- und Gerichtslinden*, Aachen/Berlin 2014.

Frei Otto taking photographs on his terrace in Warmbronn (1971)

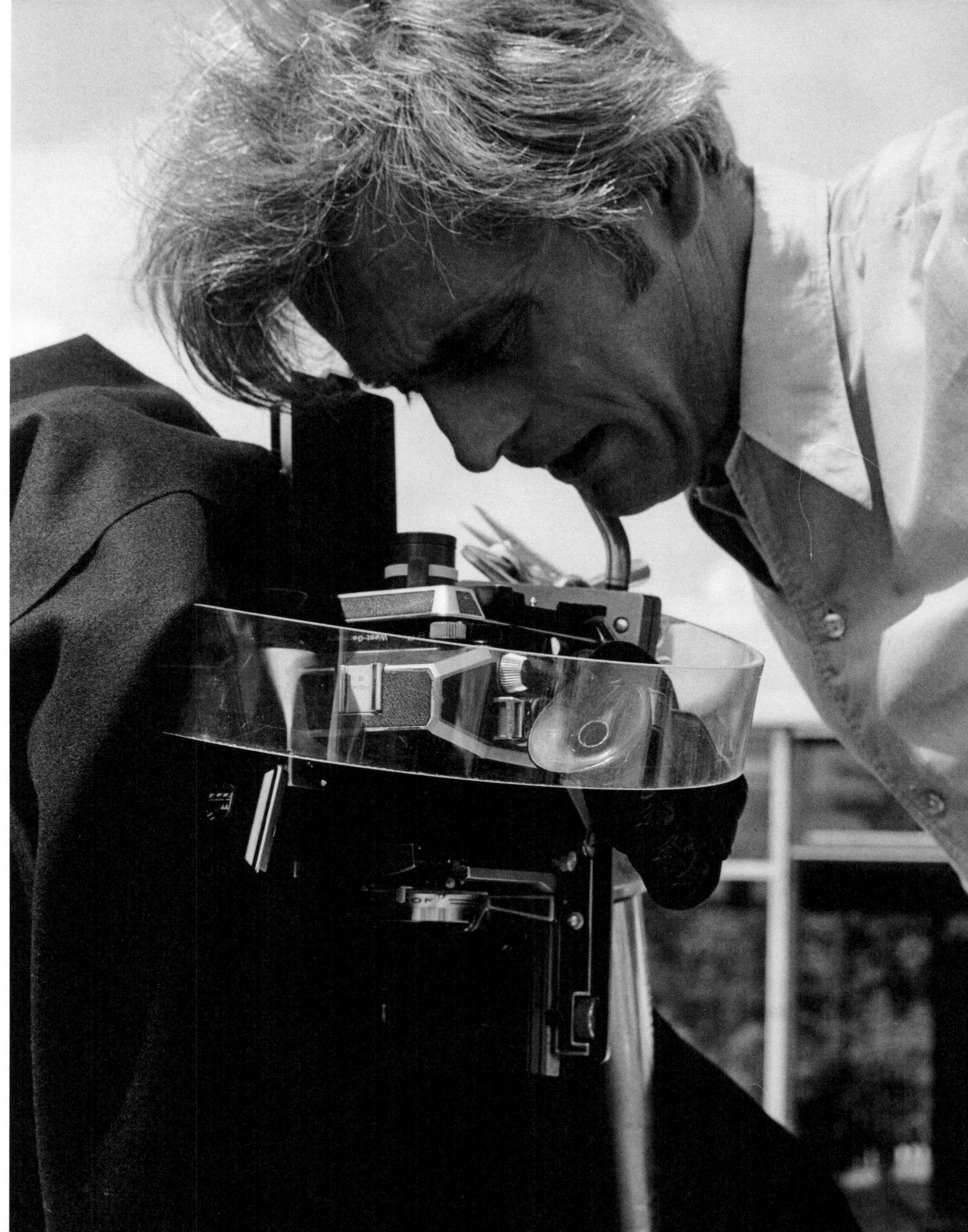

Biography

1925 Frei Otto is born on 31 May in Siegmar outside Chemnitz (Saxony). His father, the sculptor Paul Otto, is a member of the Deutscher Werkbund. Frei grows up between Chemnitz and Berlin, where he attends the Schadow Secondary School in Berlin-Zehlendorf. As an adolescent, he completes an apprenticeship as a stonemason during school holidays and learns hang gliding.

1943 Completes his Abitur (school leaving exam) in Berlin and begins studying architecture at the city's Technische Hochschule (technical college).

1943–1945 Military service as an aeroplane pilot in a fighter squadron.

1945–1947 Prisoner of war in France near Chartres, where he is active as a camp architect.

1948–1952 Resumes studies in architecture at the Technical University of Berlin (Technische Universität Berlin, TU Berlin). Receives a scholarship from the German Academic Scholarship Foundation.

1950/51 During a study trip through the USA, studies political and social sciences and city planning at the University of Virginia in Charlottesville. During this trip, thanks to the mediation of Walter Gropius, he meets a series of expatriate European architects, among them Ludwig Mies van der Rohe, Erich Mendelsohn, Richard Neutra and Eero Saarinen, as well as the American doyen Frank Lloyd Wright.

1952 After receiving his Diplom degree, works as a freelance architect with an office in Berlin-Zehlendorf.

1953/54 Writes his doctoral thesis, *Das hängende Dach* (The Hanging Roof) and receives a Doctor of Engineering from the TU Berlin. In the course of this research, he comes into contact with the Stuttgart structural engineer and professor Fritz Leonhardt. Also initiated during this period is his long-time collaboration with the tent-making concern Stromeyer & Co. in Konstanz.

1958 Founds the Institute for the Development of Lightweight Construction (Entwicklungsstätte für den Leichtbau, EL), for which he erects an experimental building in Berlin-Zehlendorf. Publication of the first issues of *Mitteilungen der Entwicklungs-stätte für den Leichtbau*. Becomes a member of the French architecture group GEAM (Groupe d'Études d'Architecture Mobile) and teaches as a guest professor at Washington University in St Louis, Missouri, and as a guest lecturer at the Universidad Nacional Autónoma de México in Mexico City.

1959 Construction in Berlin-Zehlendorf of the studio building of the EL, designed to test the principles of lightweight construction. Guest lecturer at the Ulm School of Design (Hochschule für Gestaltung Ulm, HfG Ulm).

1960 Realizes (until 1963) the Protestant Church in Berlin-Zehlendorf together with Ewald Bubner. Guest professor at Yale University in New Haven, Connecticut.

1961 While working as an assistant to Peter Poelzig – Hans Poelzig's son – at the Institute for Hospital Building of the TU Berlin, Frei Otto leads seminars on lightweight construction. As part of the Studium Generale, attends lectures by the biologist Johann-Gerhard Helmcke, a Professor of Biology and Anthro-pology, and the two co-found the research group 'Biology and Building'.

1962 Lecturer at the TU Berlin, where he leads a seminar on minimal structures. Guest professorships at the University of California, Berkeley, and the Massachusetts Institute of Technology and Harvard University in Cambridge, Massachusetts. He also leads a seminar at the Universidad del Zulia in Maracaibo, Venezuela.

1964 Appointed head of the newly established Institute for Light-weight Structures (Institut für leichte Flächentragwerke, IL) at the Stuttgart Institute of Technology (Technische Hochschule Stuttgart, TH Stuttgart) on the initiative of Fritz Leonhardt.

1965/66 Named an Honorary Professor at the TH Stuttgart. Research contract awarded to the IL for the German Pavilion at Expo 67 in Montreal, for which a prototype is erected in Stuttgart-Vaihingen. The structure is later upgraded for use as the seat of the IL.

1966 Frei Otto begins planning and constructing (until 1971) his residence and atelier in Warmbronn near Stuttgart. Decisive participation by Rob Krier, then Otto's associate.

1967 Realization of the German Pavilion at Expo 67 in Montreal as a large tent conceived together with the architect Rolf Gutbrod. The prototype erected in Stuttgart-Vaihingen is preserved as a research station for the IL.

1969 Founding member of the Collaborative Research Centre (CRC) 64 'Widespan Surface Structures' of the German Research Foundation (DFG). Establishes a studio in Warmbronn with Ewald Bubner (known, beginning in 1986, as the Atelier Frei Otto Warmbronn).

1970 Serves as an advisor to the 'roof planning group' responsible for realizing the roof construction of the sports facilities for the Summer Olympic Games in Munich in 1972 based on a design by Behnisch & Partner. Becomes a member of the Akademie der Künste (Academy of Arts) in West Berlin.

1971 Solo exhibition of his work at the Museum of Modern Art in New York. Feasibility study 'City in the Arctic', in collaboration with the offices of Kenzo Tange and Ove Arup & Partners.

1973 Awarded an Honorary Doctorate by Washington University in St Louis.

1974 Awarded the Thomas Jefferson Medal in Architecture.

1975 For the German National Garden Show (Bundesgartenschau) in Mannheim, construction of the Multihalle according to designs by Carlfried Mutschler, based on a wooden gridshell concept developed primarily by Frei Otto.

1976 Appointed Full Professor at the University of Stuttgart.

1977 Appointed Honorary Professor at the Universidad Nacional Federico Villarreal in Lima, Peru.

1980 Awarded an Honorary Doctorate by the University of Bath, England. Jointly with Rolf Gutbrod, receives the Aga Khan Award for Architecture for the Conference Centre in Mecca, Saudi Arabia. Wins competition for the Diplomatic Club in Riyadh, Saudi Arabia, realized until 1986 in collaboration with the structural engineer Edmund 'Ted' Happold and the architectural office Omrania.

1980–1991 As part of the International Building Exhibition in West Berlin (IBA), planned for 1987, produces designs for adaptable eco-houses at Askanischer Platz in Kreuzberg, ultimately realized in a modified form in Berlin-Tiergarten beginning in 1988.

1981 The travelling exhibition *Natural Structures* for the Institut für Auslandsbeziehungen in Stuttgart is shown worldwide at Goethe Institutes.

1982 Becomes Honorary Member of the Royal Institute of British Architects (RIBA) in London.

1984 Launch of the CRC 230 'Natural Structures – Lightweight Construction in Architecture and Nature', funded by the German Research Foundation, under the aegis of Frei Otto at the IL and the University of Tübingen (until 1995).

1991 Retires from teaching and from directing the IL at the University of Stuttgart.

1992 In conjunction with receiving the Prize of the Deutscher Werkbund in Bavaria, co-curates the exhibition *Finding Form* together with Bodo Rasch at the Villa Stuck in Munich.

1998 Together with the architectural office Omrania (Riyadh) and the engineering office Buro Happold (London), receives the Aga Khan Award for Architecture for the headquarters of the Diplomatic Club in Riyadh.

2005 The Architekturmuseum der TU München organizes the exhibition *Frei Otto: Lightweight Construction, Natural Design* at the Pinakothek der Moderne in Munich, devoted to Otto's lifework and curated by Winfried Nerdinger. Awarded the Royal Gold Medal of the Royal Institute of British Architects (RIBA).

2006 Awarded the Praemium Imperiale for Architecture.

2010 The saai | Southwest German Archive for Architecture and Civil Engineering at the Karlsruhe Institute of Technology (KIT) becomes the home of the creative estate and the work archive from Frei Otto's studio in Warmbronn, including more than four hundred models.

2015 Frei Otto dies on 9 March in Leonberg-Warmbronn. Shortly before his death, he learns he will be receiving the Pritzker Architecture Prize, which is awarded posthumously.

Selected Literature

1954 Frei Otto, *Das hängende Dach. Gestalt und Struktur*, doctoral thesis, Berlin 1954; facsimile reprint, Stuttgart/Dresden 1990.

1956 Frei Otto, 'Die Stadt von morgen und das Einfamilienhaus', in: *Baukunst und Werkform*, no. 12, 1956, pp. 642–652.

1958 *Mitteilungen der Entwicklungsstätte für den Leichtbau*, nos 1–9, Berlin 1958–1963.

1959 *Anpassungsfähig bauen/Adaptable Building/L'Architecture adaptable, Mitteilungen der Entwicklungsstätte für den Leichtbau*, no. 6, Berlin, June 1959.

1962 Frei Otto (ed.), *Zugbeanspruchte Konstruktionen. Gestalt, Struktur und Berechnung von Bauten aus Seilen, Netzen und Membranen*, vol. 1: 'Pneumatische Konstruktionen' (Frei Otto), 'Berechnung von Membranen' (Rudolf Trostel), 'Zugverankerung im Baugrund' (Frei Otto), Frankfurt a. M./Berlin 1962. Published in English as *Tensile Structures: Design, Structure, and Calculation of Buildings of Cables, Nets, and Membranes*, vol. 1: 'Pneumatic Structures' (Frei Otto), 'Calculation of Membranes' (Rudolf Trostel), 'Tension Anchoring in the Foundations' (Frei Otto), Cambridge, MA, 1967 (also translated into Hungarian and Russian).

1965 Conrad Roland, *Frei Otto – Spannweiten. Ideen und Versuche zum Leichtbau. Ein Werkstattbericht*. Berlin/Frankfurt a. M./Vienna 1965. Published in English as *Frei Otto: Structures*, London 1972.

1966 Frei Otto (ed.), *Zugbeanspruchte Konstruktionen. Gestalt, Struktur und Berechnung von Bauten aus Seilen, Netzen und Membranen*, vol. 2: 'Grundbegriffe und Übersicht der zugbeanspruchten Konstruktionen' (Frei Otto), 'Berechnung von Seilen, Seilnetzen und Seilwerken' (Friedrich-Karl Schleyer), Berlin 1966. Published in English as *Tensile Structures: Design, Structure, and Calculation of Buildings of Cables, Nets, and Membranes*, vol. 2: 'Basic Concepts and Survey of Tensile Structures' (Frei Otto), 'Analysis of Cables, Cable Nets, and Cable Structures' (Friedrich-Karl Schleyer), Cambridge, MA, 1969.

1969 *IL – Mitteilungen des Instituts für leichte Flächentragwerke*, nos 1–41, Universität Stuttgart 1969–1995.

1971 *IL 3 – Biologie und Bauen 1: Das Individuum und sein Milieu. Über die kritische Situation in der wachsenden Sozietät. Tierbauten, Städtebau und biologische Erkenntnis*, Stuttgart 1971 (a bilingual publication as *Biology and Building 1*).

1972 Ludwig Glaeser, *The Work of Frei Otto*, exh. cat. Museum of Modern Art, New York 1972.
Mitteilungen des SFB 64 'Weitgespannte Flächentragwerke', nos 1–79, Universität Stuttgart 1972–1985.

1973 *IL 6 – Biologie und Bauen 3. Spinnennetze, Konstruktion der Knochen. Biophysikalisches Generalmodell. 3-dimensionale Anaglyphenbilder. Photogrammetrische Vermessung dünner Seifenhäute*, Stuttgart 1973 (a bilingual publication as *Biology and Building 3*).

1975 *IL 14 – Anpassungsfähig Bauen*, Stuttgart 1975 (a bilingual publication as *Adaptable Architecture*).

1976 Philip Drew, *Frei Otto: Form and Structure*, Boulder/London 1976. Translated into German as *Frei Otto. Form und Konstruktion*, Stuttgart 1976.

1981 *IL 27 – Natürlich Bauen,* Stuttgart 1981 (a bilingual publication as *Natural Building*).

1982 Frei Otto et al., *Natürliche Konstruktionen. Formen und Konstruktionen in Natur und Technik und Prozesse ihrer Entstehung*, Stuttgart 1982.

1984 Berthold Burkhardt (ed.), *Frei Otto. Schriften und Reden, 1951–1983*, Braunschweig/Wiesbaden 1984.
Konzepte des SFB 230, Universität Stuttgart and Universität Tübingen, nos 1–50, Stuttgart 1984–1995.

1985 Frei Otto, 'Tragende Lebewesen', in: *Konzepte des SFB 230*, no. 9, Stuttgart 1985.
Frei Otto with Hermann Kendel (eds), *Wohn-Be-Reiche im Garten, IBA Berlin 1987. Vorbereitende Studie für das Bauvorhaben 'Ökohaus' Berlin*, Warmbronn 1985.
IL 28 – Diatomeen 1. Schalen in Natur und Technik. Morphogenetische Analyse und Merkmalssynthese in Diatomeen-Schalen von J.-G. Helmcke. Theoretische und experimentelle Grundlagen. Prozesse der Formentstehung. Schalenmorphogenese, Stuttgart 1985 (a bilingual publication as *Diatoms 1: Shells in Nature and Technics*).

1988 *Mitteilungen des SFB 230 'Natürliche Konstruktionen – Leichtbau in Architektur und Natur'*, nos 1–9, Stuttgart 1988–1994.
Frei Otto, *Gestaltwerdung. Zur Formentstehung in Natur, Technik und Baukunst* (*arcus, Architektur und Naturwissenschaft*, no. 4), Cologne 1988.

1990 'Radiolarien. Schalen in Natur und Technik. Die Radiolarien im stereoskopischen Bild von J.-G. Helmcke. Prozesse der Formbildung von K. Bach', in: *IL 33 – Mitteilungen des Instituts für leichte Flächentragwerke*, Stuttgart 1990 (a bilingual publication as 'Radiolaria: Shells in Nature and Technics').

1994 *IL 37 – Alte Baumeister. Was könnten die alten Baumeister erfunden haben?*, Stuttgart 1994 (a bilingual publication as *Ancient Architects*).

1995 Frei Otto with Bodo Rasch, *Gestalt finden. Auf dem Weg zu einer Baukunst des Minimalen*, exh. cat. on the occasion of the 1992 Deutscher Werkbund Bayern Prize, Stuttgart-Fellbach 1995. Published in English as *Finding Form: Towards an Architecture of the Minimal,* Stuttgart-Fellbach 1995.
IL 35 – Pneu und Knochen. Das Konstruktionsprinzip Pneu in der lebenden Natur. Weiche Pneus, feste Pneus, Schalentiere, Knochen, Stuttgart 1995 (a bilingual publication as *Pneu and Bone*).

1996 Frei Otto, *Architektur Natur* (Warmbronner Schriften 7, Christian-Wagner-Gesellschaft), Warmbronn 1996.
Klaus Teichmann and Joachim Wilke (eds), *Prozess und Form 'Natürlicher Konstruktionen': Der Sonderforschungsbereich 230*, Berlin 1996.

1997 Frei Otto, 'Grundlagen einer Baukunst von morgen', in: *Der Architekt*, Oktober 1997, pp. 589 f.

2005 Winfried Nerdinger et al. (eds), *Frei Otto. Das Gesamtwerk. Leicht bauen, natürlich gestalten*, exh. cat. Architekturmuseum der TU München, Basel/Boston/Berlin 2005. Published in English as *Frei Otto: Complete Works; Lightweight Construction, Natural Design*, Basel/Boston/Berlin 2005).

2008 *Frei Otto: Conversación con Juan María Songel*, Barcelona 2008.

2013 Eda Schaur (ed.), *Konstruktion und Gestaltung. Neue Formwelten für Architektur,* Innsbruck 2013.
José Luis Moro (ed.), *Frei Otto zum 85sten*, Festschrift zum Symposium anlässlich seines 85. Geburtstags am 26. Oktober 2010 [commemorative publication for the symposium held on the occasion of his 85th birthday on 26 October 2010], Universität Stuttgart, Institut für Entwerfen und Konstruieren, Stuttgart 2013.

2015 Irene Meissner and Eberhard Möller (eds), *Frei Otto: forschen, bauen, inspirieren/A Life of Research, Construction, and Inspiration*, Munich 2015.
Rudolf Finsterwalder (ed.), *Form Follows Nature. Eine Geschichte der Natur als Modell für Formfindung in Ingenieurbau, Architektur und Kunst. Mit einem Vorwort von Kristin Feireiss und einem unveröffentlichten Interview mit Frei Otto/A History of Nature as Model for Design in Engineering, Architecture and Art: With a Preface by Kristin Feireiss and an Unpublished Interview with Frei Otto*, Basel 2015.

2017 Georg Vrachliotis et al. (eds), *Frei Otto. Denken in Modellen*, exh. cat. ZKM | Center for Art and Media Karlsruhe, Leipzig 2017. Published in English as *Frei Otto: Thinking by Modeling*, Leipzig 2017.
Georg Vrachliotis, *Frei Otto, Carlfried Mutschler: Multihalle*, Leipzig 2017.

2020 Joachim Kleinmanns, *Der deutsche Pavillon der Expo 67 in Montreal. Ein Schlüsselwerk deutscher Nachkriegsarchitektur*, Berlin 2020.

Authors

Mechthild Ebert (born 1988 in Halle an der Saale, Germany) studied architecture at the Bauhaus-Universität Weimar and the Universidade Federal de Minas Gerais in Belo Horizonte, Brazil. She has been a research associate at the saai since 2020, where she co-curated the exhibition *Building for an Open Society* (Stuttgart, 2022), among others. Previously she was responsible for the Hans Hollein Archive at the Az W and MAK, Vienna. At the Architekturzentrum Wien, she curated the exhibition *Hans Hollein Unpacked: The Haas-Haus* (2019). The focus of her research is on the role of the architecture archive in producing and perpetuating narratives of architectural history, and how the latter can be called into question.

Daniela Fabricius (born 1976 in New York, USA) is an architectural historian and theorist. She is an Assistant Professor at the Weitzman School of Design of the University of Pennsylvania in Philadelphia and holds a PhD in Architectural History and Theory from Princeton University. She is the author of *The Ethics of Calculation: Architecture and Rationalism in Postwar Germany*, which will be published by the University of Minnesota Press in 2025. She is also the author and editor of a forthcoming book on the feminist architectural theorist Jennifer Bloomer, called *A Minor Architecture: The Work of Jennifer Bloomer.*

Szilvia Gellai (born 1980 in Gyoma, Hungary) is a postdoctoral fellow at the Institut für Germanistik at the Universität Wien, Vienna, where she researches and teaches along the interface between literary, media and cultural studies. She earned her doctorate from KIT with her thesis *Netzwerkpoetiken in der Gegenwartsliteratur* (2018), on the poetics of networking in contemporary literature. In 2021, she was a fellow with the LOEWE interdisciplinary research project 'Architectures of Order'. Recent publications include the essay *Glass Scenographies: Notes on Spaces of One's Own* (2023) and articles related to her habilitation project 'Bauformen der Transparenz. Lebensversuche unter Glas' (Architectural forms of transparency: experiments in living under glass) in the magazines *Kritische Berichte*, *Technikgeschichte* and *Figurationen* (2020/21).

Sean Keller (born 1970 in Pittsburgh, USA) is an Associate Professor and Associate Dean at the IIT College of Architecture in Chicago. As a historian and critic, he focuses on the relationship of architecture and technology after 1945. He is the author of *Automatic Architecture: Motivating Form After Modernism* (2017). His next book (co-authored) analyses the architecture, art and landscape of the 1972 Olympics in Munich, and is forthcoming from Yale University Press. He is currently a member of the School of Historical Studies at the Institute for Advanced Study in Princeton.

Joachim Kleinmanns (born 1957 in Brühl near Cologne, Germany) is a freelance researcher based in Detmold. He studied architectural and art history and German literary history, earning a doctorate in 1985. He subsequently became active in the field of built heritage conservation and historical building research. In 1994, he moved to KIT as head of the documentation centre of the CRC 315 'Preservation of Historically Significant Structures', with a lectureship in the preservation of historic buildings, and worked at the saai from 2006 to 2020. He has curated exhibitions on architectural and cultural history and has authored and edited numerous publications on architectural research, building preservation and the conservation of monuments, as well as on twentieth-century architecture, including studies on Fritz Leonhardt, Rolf Gutbrod and Frei Otto.

Martin Kunz (born 1977 in Ludwigshafen am Rhein, Germany) is a research associate at the saai at KIT, where he studied architecture with a focus on urban planning. The primary focus of his research is on twentieth-century architectural history, particularly the work of figures such as Frei Otto, Günter Behnisch, Egon Eiermann, Hans Herkommer and Otto Ernst Schweizer, whose archives are housed at the saai.

Joaquín Medina Warmburg (born 1970 in Cádiz, Spain) is a professor of architectural and building history at KIT and is part of the directorship of the saai. He studied architecture at the ETSA Sevilla and at the RWTH Aachen, where he earned a doctorate in 2003. He subsequently worked around Europe and the Americas, and headed the Walter Gropius Chair of the German Academic Exchange Service (DAAD) at the Universidad Torcuato Di Tella in Buenos Aires, Argentina, from 2011 to 2015. One focus of his research is the interface between architecture and environmental history in the context of the internationalization processes of modernism. His publications explore the history of modern architecture in Germany, Spain and Latin America, as well as individual protagonists of pre- and post-war Modernism.

Irene Meissner (born 1961 in Kassel, Germany) has worked at the Architekturmuseum of the TU Munich since 2001. She studied architecture at the TH Darmstadt, earning a doctorate from the TU Munich with a thesis on Sep Ruf. Her research focus is on German architecture in the twentieth century. She has co-curated numerous exhibitions, including *Exemplarisch. Konstruktion und Raum in der Architektur des 20. Jahrhunderts* (2002); *Frei Otto: Lightweight Construction, Natural Design* (2005) and *The Olympic City of Munich* (2022). Since 2023, she has headed the archive of the Architekturmuseum and is responsible for its scholarly analysis and reappraisal for the public.

Anna-Maria Meister (born 1977 in Regensburg, Germany) heads the research group 'Coded Objects' in the Lise Meitner Excellence Program of the Max Planck Society at the Kunsthistorisches Institut in Florenz (KHI), Florence, and is a professor of architectural theory and co-director of the saai at KIT. She is an architect with a PhD from Princeton University, a Master of Science from Columbia University and a Diplom degree from the TU Munich. The focus of her research is on processes of design and the design of processes, as well as the materiality of knowledge systems and their construction. Most recently, she was a co-editor of *Radical Pedagogies* (2022) and of the interdisciplinary publications *Entangled Temporalities* (2023) and *Are You a Model?* (2024).

Walter Scheiffele (born 1946 in Eggenfelden, Germany) studied design and design theory in Munich, Ulm and Braunschweig. He earned a doctorate from the Universität Bremen with a thesis on 'Wilhelm Wagenfeld und die moderne Glasindustrie' (1994), on Wilhelm Wagenfeld and the modern glass industry. He was a guest professor for design theory and history at UdK Berlin, the Kunsthochschule Berlin-Weißensee and the National Hangzhou Art College, is a member of the foundation boards of the Karl-Mey-Stiftung at the Deutsches Technikmuseum Berlin and the Stiftung Industrie- und Alltagskultur. His exhibitions and publications on cultural and design history include *bauhaus junkers sozialdemokratie* (2003), *Das Leichte Haus* (2016) and *Karl Mey und Wilhelm Wagenfeld* (2016). He has authored research works on the history of design in East Germany, among them *Ostmoderne – Westmoderne* (2019) and *Karl Clauss Dietel* (2021) with Steffen Schuhmann.

Jos Tomlow (born 1951 in Roermond, Netherlands) is an architect and historian of structural engineering. He studied architecture at the TU Delft, where he cofounded the Gaudí Research Group in 1976. In 1982, he participated in the reconstruction of Gaudí's hanging model for the Church of Colònia Güell at the Institute for Lightweight Structures (IL) at the Universität Stuttgart, earning a doctorate on the subject under Frei Otto and Jürgen Joedicke. Between 1988 and 1995, he was active with the CRC 230 'Natural Structures – Lightweight Building in Architecture and Nature', and was a professor of the fundamentals of design and built heritage conservation at the Hochschule Zittau/Görlitz from 1995 to 2017. He recently authored studies on Frei Otto's participation in the creation of the roofs of the Olympic Park in Munich and on Otto's residence and studio in Warmbronn.

Georg Vrachliotis (born 1977 in Berlin, Germany) is a Professor of Theory of Architecture and Digital Culture at TU Delft. He earned his doctorate from ETH Zurich and served from 2016 as the Dean of the Faculty of Architecture at KIT, where he also held a Professorship in Architectural Theory and directed the saai | Archive for Architecture and Civil Engineering. He has co-curated exhibitions on Frei Otto, including *Sleeping Beauty: Reinventing Frei Otto's Multihalle* (Venice Architecture Biennale, 2018), *Frei Otto: Thinking by Modeling* at ZKM (Karlsruhe, 2016) and *Models, Media, and Methods: Frei Otto's Architectural Research* (Yale School of Architecture, 2020).

Christiane Weber (born 1973 in Göppingen, Germany) heads the Institute of Architectural History at the Universität Stuttgart. Before that, she was a professor for the history of structural engineering at the Universität Innsbruck. She studied architecture in Karlsruhe and Paris, as well as art history at the TU Karlsruhe and Université de Strasbourg. In 2010, she earned her doctorate from the TU Braunschweig, and her habilitation from the Universität Innsbruck in 2019. Her research focuses on the development of structural engineering in architecture, civil engineering and urban planning in the age of industrialization up until the post-war era. She researches and publishes on technical educational systems, on the legacy of the architectural culture in border regions and on structural engineering in pre- and post-war Modernism.

Rob Whitehead (born 1970 in Oklahoma City, USA) is an Associate Professor of Architecture and Associate Dean at Iowa State University's College of Design. Trained as an architect at Iowa State University and the University of Texas at Austin, his work focusses on structural design and pedagogy for architects, including historical approaches to experimental structural forms and design methods. He is the author of *Structures by Design: Thinking, Making, Breaking* (2019) and a co-author of *Design-Tech: Building Science for Architects* (2025). In 2023, he was elevated as a member of the American Institute of Architects College of Fellows (FAIA) for his contributions to education and architectural practice.

Image Credits

t top, b bottom, r right, l left, c center

From the saai | Archiv für Architektur und Ingenieurbau am Karlsruher Institut für Technologie

Werkarchiv Frei Otto: 6/7, 8/9, 10/11, 12/13, 14/15, 16/17, 18/19, 20/21, 22/23, 26, 27, 28, 29, 30, 31, 32, 33, 34, 38/39, 50, 54, 55, 56, 57, 58, 59, 60/61, 65, 66, 67, 70, 71, 72, 73, 74, 75, 76, 77, 79, 81, 82, 83, 84, 88, 89, 90, 92 l, 102, 104, 110 tr, 110 b, 111, 113, 114/115, 118, 119 b, 131 t, 132, 133, 138/139, 141, 143, 145, 147, 148 b, 151 b, 152, 153 t, 154, 156 t, 161 b, 164, 168, 169, 170, 171, 172, 173, 176, 177, 180/181, 184, 185, 186 b, 187, 188/189, 190, 191, 192, 193, 207, 210, 211, 215, 216, 218, 219, 220, 221, 223, 226/227 (F. Dressler), 248, 249, 254/255, Front Cover
Werkarchiv Behnisch & Partner: 24/25, 120/121 (C. Kandzia), 122, 123, 124, 125
Werkarchiv Rolf Gutbrod: 108 t, 112
Werkarchiv Carlfried Mutschler & Partner: 130, 131 b, 134 (R. Häusser), 135 t (R. Häusser), 135 b, 136 (R. Häusser), 137 (R. Häusser),
B. Seeland, C. Engel: 1, 92 r, 110 tl, 119 t, 178, 179, 186 t

Architekturmuseum der TU München: 146 t (beh-14-1), 148 t
Archive Berthold Burkhardt: 108 b, 146 b, 256
Archive Karin Gutbrod: 109
Bildarchiv der Bayerischen Staatsbibliothek, Fotoarchiv Max Prugger: 126/127 (L98-22)
Bill Dutfield: 162 t
Evangelisches Landeskirchliches Archiv in Berlin: 64 (ELAB 3/1419)
HfG Archiv, Museum Ulm: 205
ICD/ITKE, Universität Stuttgart: 229, 230, 231, 234, 235
ILEK Archiv: 195, 196, 198, 199, 200, 201
ingenhoven associates: Back Cover
Ferdinando Iannone: 245 b
Ferdinand Ludwig: 241 b
Joaquín Medina Warmburg: 101
Cira Moro: 241 t
Office for Living Architecture: 243, 245 t
Private Collection Wilhelm Delbeck: 140
Kristina Pujkilovic: 244
Yves Klein Archive, Paris: 97 t

From Publications

Das hängende Dach, 1954: 94 (p. 117), 95 t (p. 117), 95 c (p. 117), 142 (cover)
Das wachsende Haus, 1932: 97 b (p. 149), 45 (cover)
Der Raum als Membran, 1926: 98 (cover)
Deutsche Bauzeitung, 1960: 96 b (p. 88)
Die Auflösung der Städte, 1920: 44 l (p. 12)
Die Form, August 1927: 41 t (p. 249; pp. 242/243)
Die Pflanze als Erfinder, 1920: 42 t (cover)
Die wachsende Siedlung nach biologischen Gesetzen, 1932: 44 r (p. 23)
Engineering, no. 62, 1896: 99 (p. 481)
Entretiens sur l'architecture, vol. II, 1872: 100 r (p. 284)
Frei Otto: Complete Works; Lightweight Construction, Natural Design, 2005: 144 (p. 365)
Gestalt finden, 1995: 159 (pp. 34, 35, 38, 39)
Landhäuser von Hermann Muthesius, 1912: 100 l (p. 152)
Mitteilungen der Entwicklungsstädte für den Leichtbau, no. 6, 1959: 47 t (cover)
Mitteilungen des Instituts für leichte Flächentragwerke, no. 6, 1973: 197 (cover)
Mitteilungen des Instituts für leichte Flächentragwerke, no. 8, 1975: 153 b (p. 208), 155 t (p. 287), 155 b (p. 297)
Mitteilungen des Instituts für leichte Flächentragwerke, no. 13, 1978: 156 b (p. 81)
Mitteilungen des Instituts für leichte Flächentragwerke, no. 18, 1988: 151 t (p. 330)
Natürliche Konstruktionen, 1982: 47 bl (p. 85), 47 br (p. 104)
On Growth and Form, 1917 (1942): 161 t (p. 978)
Umwelt und Innenwelt der Tiere, 1921: 43 (p. 63)
Wie bauen? Bau und Einrichtung der Werkbundsiedlung am Weißenhof in Stuttgart 1927, 1927: 42 b (p. 158)
Wegweisung der Technik, 1929: 41 b (pp. 61/62)
Von der Bebauung der Erde, 1949: 46 (p. 21, p. 23)
Wohn-Be-Reiche im Garten der IBA Berlin, 1987: 87 (cover, pp. 28, 30, 47)
'Wohnhäuser, von der Sonne beheizt', in: *Neue Bauwelt*, no. 24, 1949: 95 b (p. 375)
Yves Klein/Werner Ruhnau. Dokumentation der Zusammenarbeit in den Jahren 1957–1960, 1976: 96 t (p. 45)

Every effort has been made to identify and credit copyright holders and secure permission. Despite extensive investigation, it was not always possible to do so. Justified claims will be compensated within the scope of customary agreements.

Colophon

Frei Otto
1925–2015
Building with Nature

Edited by
Joaquín Medina Warmburg and
Anna-Maria Meister
with Mechthild Ebert and Martin Kunz

Front Cover: The German Pavilion at Expo 67 in Montreal (1967)
Page 1: Study for '58° North', Canada (1981), model
Page 256: Frei Otto on the gridshell of the German Pavilion at Expo 67 in Montreal (1966)
Back Cover: Frei Otto at a meeting in the offices of Ingenhoven Architects (2004)

Munich · London · New York 2025
A member of Penguin Random House Verlagsgruppe GmbH
Neumarkter Strasse 28 · 81673 Munich

produktsicherheit@penguinrandomhouse.de
(The above information is also mandatory information according to GPSR)

A CIP catalogue record for this book is available from the British Library.
A Library of Congress Control Number is available.

Editorial Direction Prestel: Markus Eisen
Copy-Editing: José Enrique Macián y Fijałkowski
Design and Layout: Torsten Köchlin
Production Management: Cilly Klotz
Translation (German to English):
Ian Pepper (Preface, Ebert, Scheiffele, Vrachliotis, Conversation with Ludwig, Captions, Appendix) and Russell Stockman (Ebert, Gellai, Kleinmanns, Kunz, Medina-Warmburg, Meissner, Meister, Tomlow, Weber, Conversation with Knippers and Menges)
Separations: LUDWIG: media gmbh, Zell am See
Printing and Binding: Livonia Print, Riga
Typeface: ABC ROM
Paper: Munken Print White, 115 g/m²

Penguin Random House Verlagsgruppe
FSC® N001967

Printed in Latvia

ISBN 978-3-7913-7750-6 (English edition)
ISBN 978-3-7913-7749-0 (German edition)

www.prestel.com

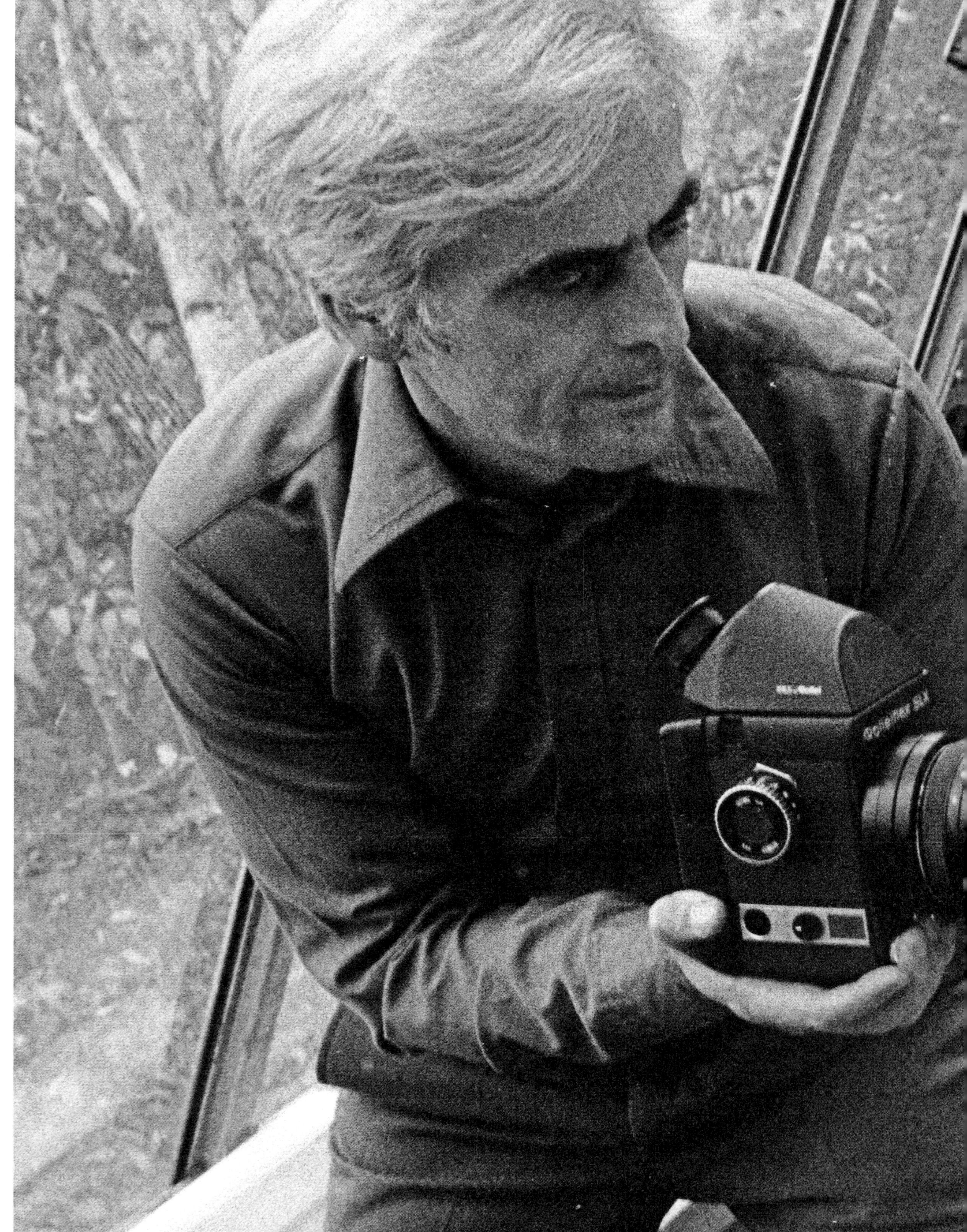

Frei Otto photographing a model in his Warmbronn atelier (1978)